Teen Titans

LIFE AND DEATH

TEEN TITANS: LIFE AND DEATH

Published by DC Comics.
Cover and compilation copyright
© 2006 DC Comics.
All Rights Reserved.

Originally published in single magazine
form in TEEN TITANS 29-33,
TEEN TITANS ANNUAL 1,
ROBIN 146-147, INFINITE CRISIS 5-6.
Copyright © 2005, 2006 DC Comics.
All Rights Reserved.

DC Comics,
1700 Broadway, New York, NY 10019
A Warner Bros. Entertainment Company
Printed in Canada. First Printing.
ISBN: 1-4012-0978-5
ISBN 13: 978-1-4012-0978-0
Cover illustration by Tony S. Daniel and Kevin Conrad.
Cover color by Jeromy Cox.
Back cover illustration by Jerome Moore.
Back cover color by Richard & Tanya Horie.
Logo designed by Terry Marks.

Teen Titans

LIFE AND DEATH

Geoff Johns	Marlo Alquiza	Jeromy Cox
Bill Willingham	Richard Bonk	Tanya & Richard Horie
Bill Williams	Sean Parsons	Guy Major
Marv Wolfman	Nelson	Rod Reis
Writers	Lary Stucker	Colorists
	Andy Owens	
Tony S. Daniel	Oclair Albert	Phil Balsman
Todd Nauck	Mariah Benes	Comicraft
Scott McDaniel	Alex Lei	Rob Leigh
Ed Benes	Drew Geraci	Nick J. Napolitano
Dale Eaglesham	Wayne Faucher	Letterers
Tom Grindberg	Art Thibert	
Elton Ramalho	Norm Rapmund	
Phil Jimenez	Andy Lanning	
Pencillers	Jerry Ordway	
	Ivan Reis	
	Inkers	

WHAT DO TEENAGED SUPERHEROES DO ON THE WEEKENDS? THEY HANG WITH THE TEEN TITANS!

CYBORG: VICTOR STONE. HALF MAN. HALF MACHINE.

ROBIN: TIM DRAKE. BATMAN'S DETECTIVE PROTÉGÉ.

BEAST BOY: GARFIELD LOGAN. ANIMAL SHAPE-SHIFTER.

RAVEN: EMPATHIC DAUGHTER OF THE DEMON TRIGON.

WONDER GIRL: CASSIE SANDSMARK. BLESSED WITH THE POWERS OF THE GODS.

KID FLASH: BART ALLEN. THE LATEST SUPER SPEEDSTER FOLLOWING THE LEGACY OF THE FLASH.

SPEEDY: MIA DEARDEN. ARCHER SIDEKICK TO GREEN ARROW.

SUPERBOY: CONNER KENT. CLONED FROM THE WORLD'S GREATEST HERO, SUPERMAN, AND THE WORLD'S GREATEST VILLAIN, LEX LUTHOR.

WHAT DO TEEN TITANS RESERVE MEMBERS DO WHEN CALLED ON FOR HELP? THEY JOIN THE FIGHT!

NIGHTWING: DICK GRAYSON. FORMER ROBIN AND BATMAN'S DETECTIVE PROTÉGÉ.

FLASH: WALLY WEST. FORMER KID FLASH AND THE SECOND SUPER SPEEDSTER TO FOLLOW THE LEGACY OF THE FLASH.

STARFIRE: PRINCESS KORIAND'R. CONVERTS SOLAR ENERGY INTO STARBOLTS.

HERALD: MAL DUNCAN. WIELDER OF THE GABRIEL'S HORN, WHICH OPENS THE DOOR TO LIMBO.

BUMBLEBEE: KAREN BEECHER-DUNCAN. CREATOR OF THE CYBERNETIC BUMBLEBEE COSTUME.

RED STAR: LEONID KOVAR. ABILITY TO BURST INTO AND CONTROL FLAME.

BABY WILDEBEEST: IN MOMENTS OF TENSION, TRANSFORMS TO A FULL-GROWN RAGING WILDEBEEST.

PANTHA: SUBJECT X-24. CATLIKE REFLEXES AND AGILITY, PLUS RAZOR-SHARP CLAWS.

MIRAGE: MIRIAM DELGADO. ILLUSION CASTER WITH UNKNOWN PSIONIC ABILITIES.

TERRA: TARA MARKOV. CONTROLS GRAVITY AND EARTH.

RISK: CODY DRISCOLL. DAREDEVIL WITH FIVE TIMES THE SPEED, STRENGTH AND STAMINA OF A NORMAL HUMAN.

ARGENT: TONI MONETTI. MANIPULATES PLASMA BURSTS.

JOTO: ISAIAH CROCKETT. MASTER OF HEAT MANIPULATION.

JOKER'S DAUGHTER: DUELA DENT. PRANKSTER DAUGHTER OF AN UNKNOWN SUPER-VILLAIN WHO CAN KEEP A SECRET.

FLAMEBIRD: BETTE KANE. ATHLETIC ROBIN-GROUPIE WHO DOES THE BEST SHE CAN.

BUSHIDO: RYUKO ORSONO. MARTIAL ARTS AND WEAPONS EXPERT CONTINUING HIS FAMILY'S LEGACY.

WHAT DO THE TEEN TITANS WHO'VE RECENTLY RETURNED FROM THE DEAD DO? THEY COME BACK TO HARASS OR SEEK HELP FROM THE TITANS.

RED HOOD: JASON TODD. FORMER ROBIN AND BATMAN'S DETECTIVE PROTÉGÉ.

TROIA: DONNA TROY. BEING OF INFINITE POSSIBILITIES.

WHAT DO THE TITANS WHO'VE DIED IN THE LINE OF DUTY DO? THEY REST IN PEACE, UNTIL NOW...

OMEN: LILITH CLAY. TELEPATH.

AQUAGIRL: TULA. GIRL OF ATLANTIS.

KOLE: KOLE WEATHERS. WEAVER OF CRYSTAL.

PHANTASM: DANNY CHASE. EMBODIMENT OF THE THOUSAND SOULS OF AZARATH.

HAWK & DOVE: HANK & DON HALL. CHAMPIONS OF CHAOS & ORDER.

WHAT DO FREAKS WHO WANT TO PROTECT THE WORLD DO? THEY JOIN THE DOOM PATROL!

CHIEF: NILES CAULDER. SCIENTIFIC GENIUS.

ROBOTMAN: CLIFF STEELE. HUMAN BRAIN IN A ROBOT BODY.

NEGATIVE MAN: LARRY TRAINOR. SHARES A BODY WITH A NEGATIVE ENERGY BEING.

ELASTI-GIRL: RITA FARR. ABILITY TO GROW, SHRINK AND STRETCH.

NUDGE: MI-SUN. TEENAGED TELEPATH.

GRUNT: FOUR-ARMED GORILLA.

WHAT DO TEENAGED HEROES DO AFTER SPENDING YEARS IN LIMBO? THEY GO MAD AND TRY TO CHANGE THE UNIVERSE!

SUPERBOY-PRIME: KAL-EL. LAST SURVIVOR OF THE PLANET KRYPTON IN THE DIMENSION EARTH-PRIME, MANIPULATED INTO BELIEVING HE CAN HELP RESTORE HIS PLANET.

ALEXANDER LUTHOR: SON OF LEX LUTHOR OF EARTH-3. MAD ARCHITECT OF THE INFINITE CRISIS IS TRYING TO CREATE A PERFECT EARTH, DESTROYING THOSE HE DEEMS UNWORTHY.

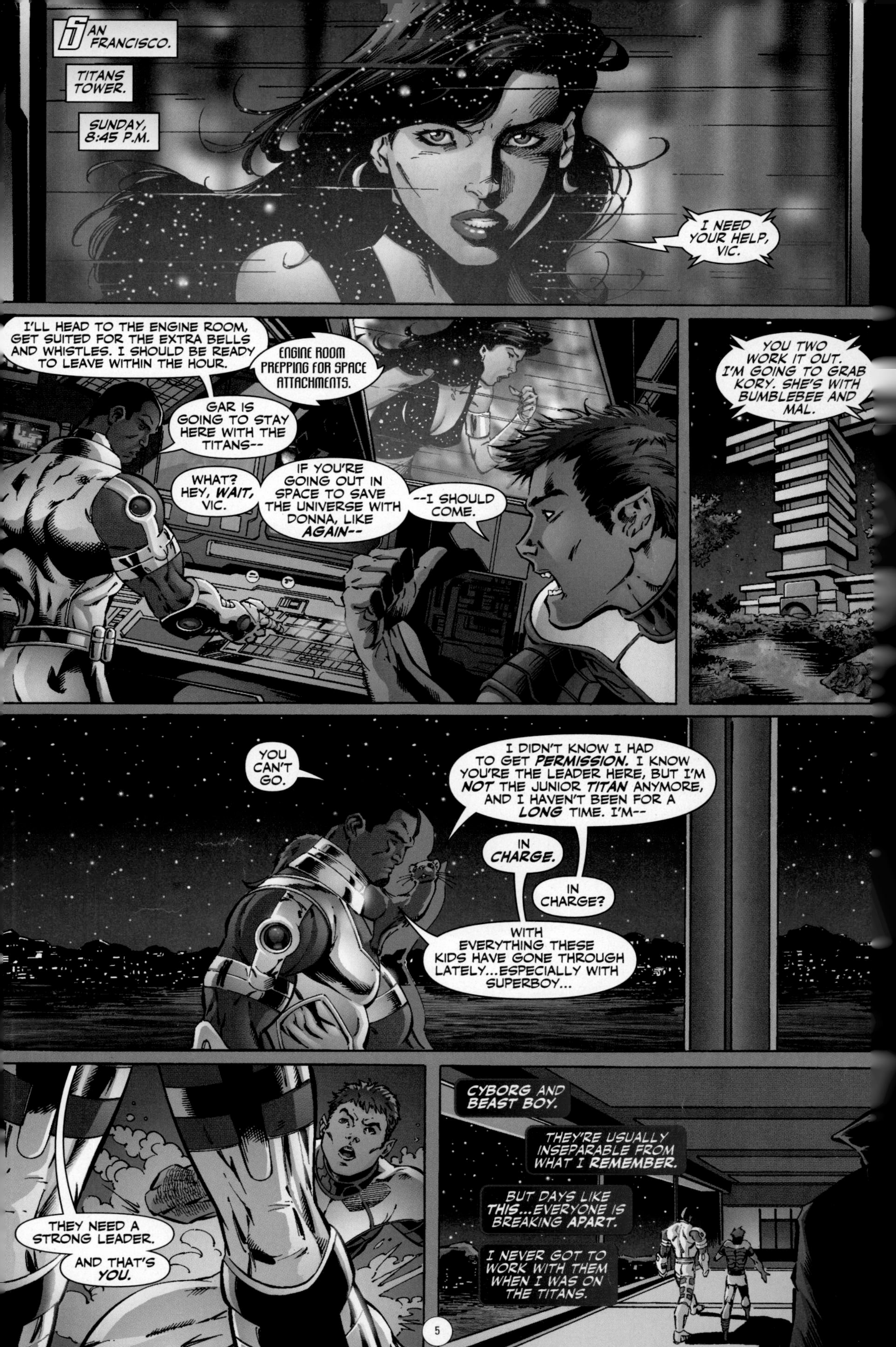
SAN FRANCISCO.
TITANS TOWER.
SUNDAY, 8:45 P.M.
I NEED YOUR HELP, VIC.
I'LL HEAD TO THE ENGINE ROOM, GET SUITED FOR THE EXTRA BELLS AND WHISTLES. I SHOULD BE READY TO LEAVE WITHIN THE HOUR.
ENGINE ROOM PREPPING FOR SPACE ATTACHMENTS.
GAR IS GOING TO STAY HERE WITH THE TITANS--
WHAT? HEY, WAIT, VIC.
IF YOU'RE GOING OUT IN SPACE TO SAVE THE UNIVERSE WITH DONNA, LIKE AGAIN--
--I SHOULD COME.
YOU TWO WORK IT OUT. I'M GOING TO GRAB KORY. SHE'S WITH BUMBLEBEE AND MAL.
YOU CAN'T GO.
I DIDN'T KNOW I HAD TO GET PERMISSION. I KNOW YOU'RE THE LEADER HERE, BUT I'M NOT THE JUNIOR TITAN ANYMORE, AND I HAVEN'T BEEN FOR A LONG TIME. I'M--
IN CHARGE.
IN CHARGE?
WITH EVERYTHING THESE KIDS HAVE GONE THROUGH LATELY...ESPECIALLY WITH SUPERBOY...
THEY NEED A STRONG LEADER.
AND THAT'S YOU.
CYBORG AND BEAST BOY.
THEY'RE USUALLY INSEPARABLE FROM WHAT I REMEMBER.
BUT DAYS LIKE THIS...EVERYONE IS BREAKING APART.
I NEVER GOT TO WORK WITH THEM WHEN I WAS ON THE TITANS.

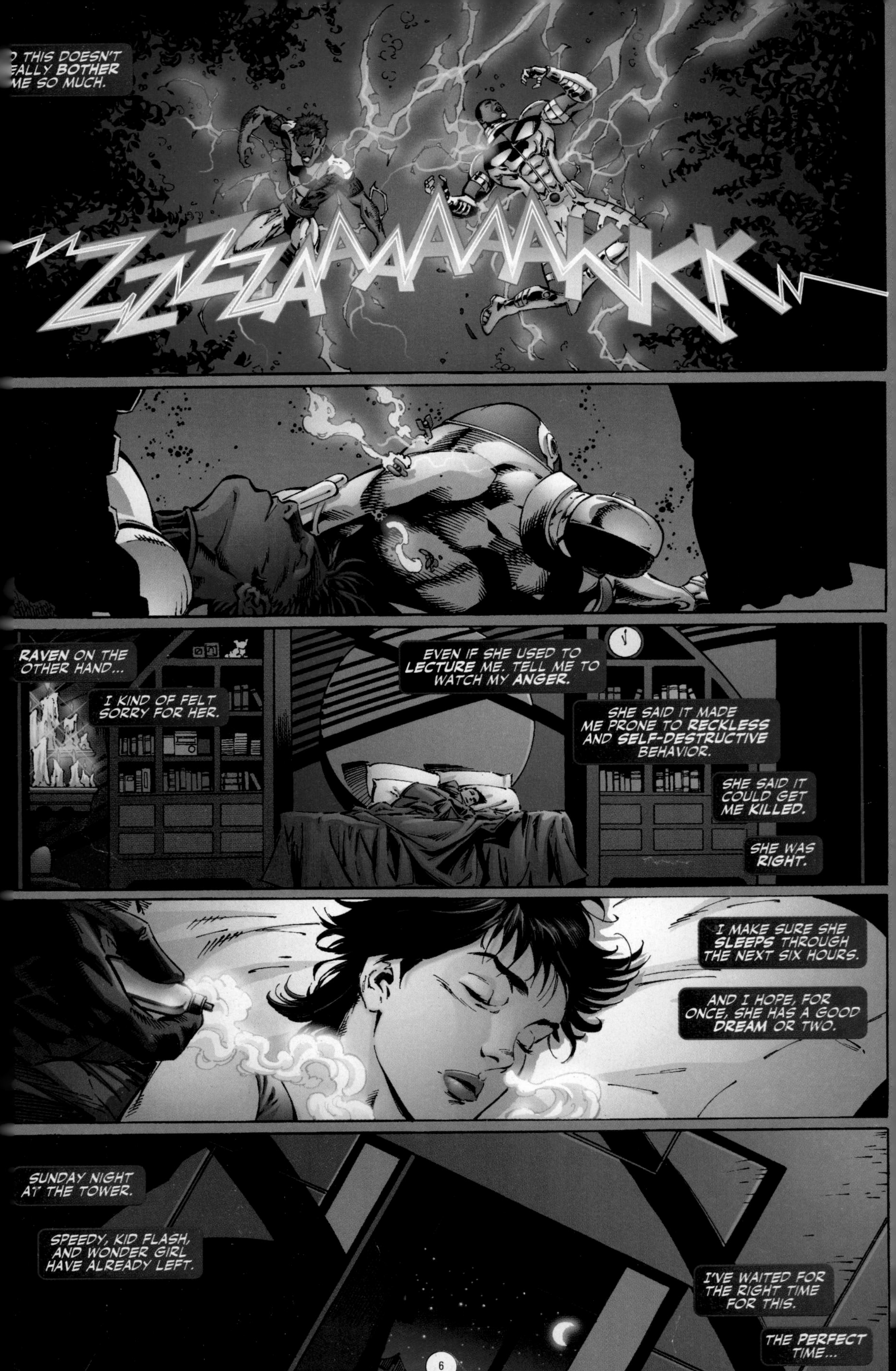

SO THIS DOESN'T REALLY BOTHER ME SO MUCH.
ZZZAAAAAAKKK
RAVEN ON THE OTHER HAND...
I KIND OF FELT SORRY FOR HER.
EVEN IF SHE USED TO LECTURE ME. TELL ME TO WATCH MY ANGER.
SHE SAID IT MADE ME PRONE TO RECKLESS AND SELF-DESTRUCTIVE BEHAVIOR.
SHE SAID IT COULD GET ME KILLED.
SHE WAS RIGHT.
I MAKE SURE SHE SLEEPS THROUGH THE NEXT SIX HOURS.
AND I HOPE, FOR ONCE, SHE HAS A GOOD DREAM OR TWO.
SUNDAY NIGHT AT THE TOWER.
SPEEDY, KID FLASH, AND WONDER GIRL HAVE ALREADY LEFT.
I'VE WAITED FOR THE RIGHT TIME FOR THIS.
THE PERFECT TIME...

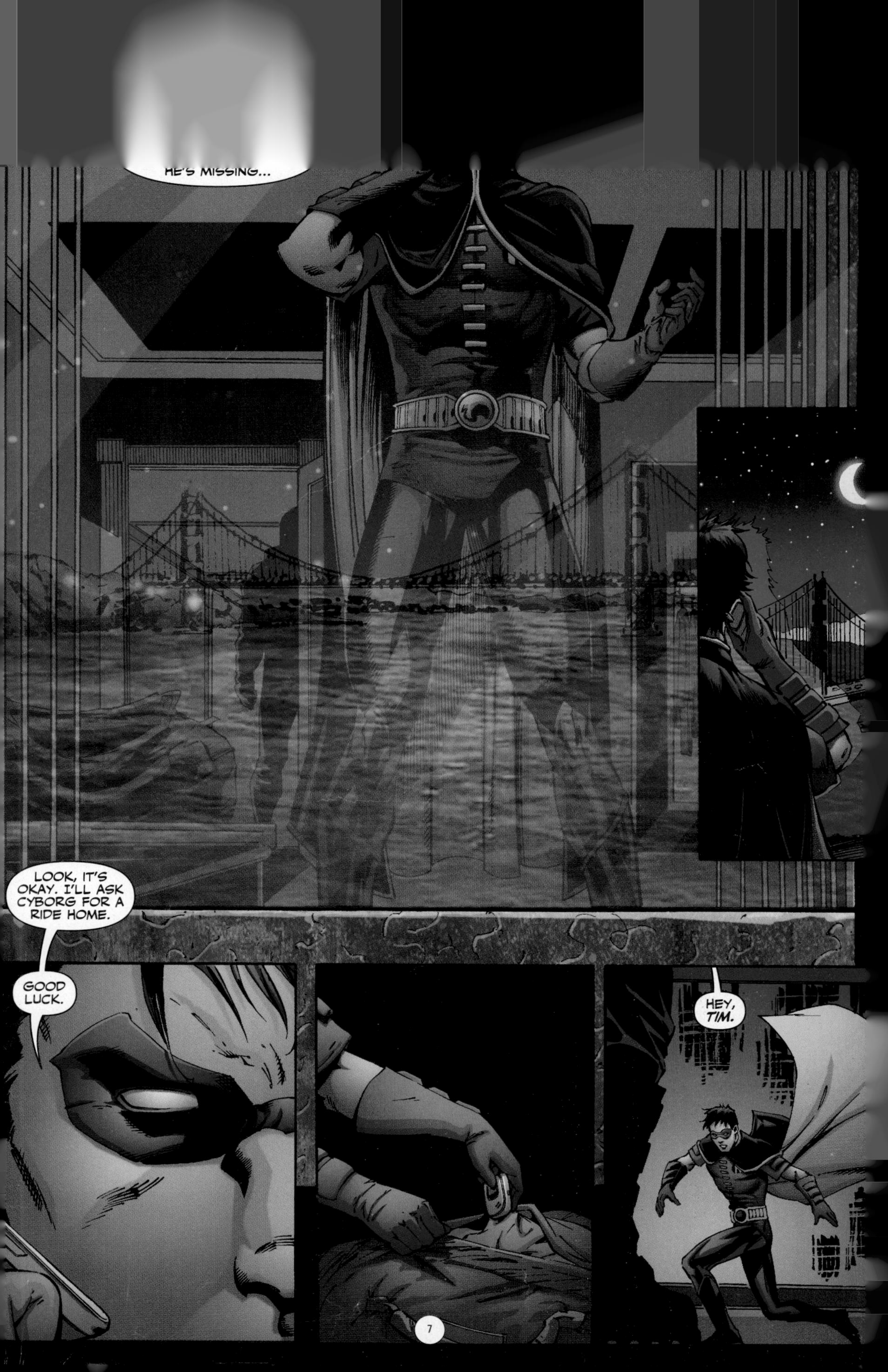
HE'S MISSING...
LOOK, IT'S OKAY. I'LL ASK CYBORG FOR A RIDE HOME.
GOOD LUCK.
HEY, TIM.

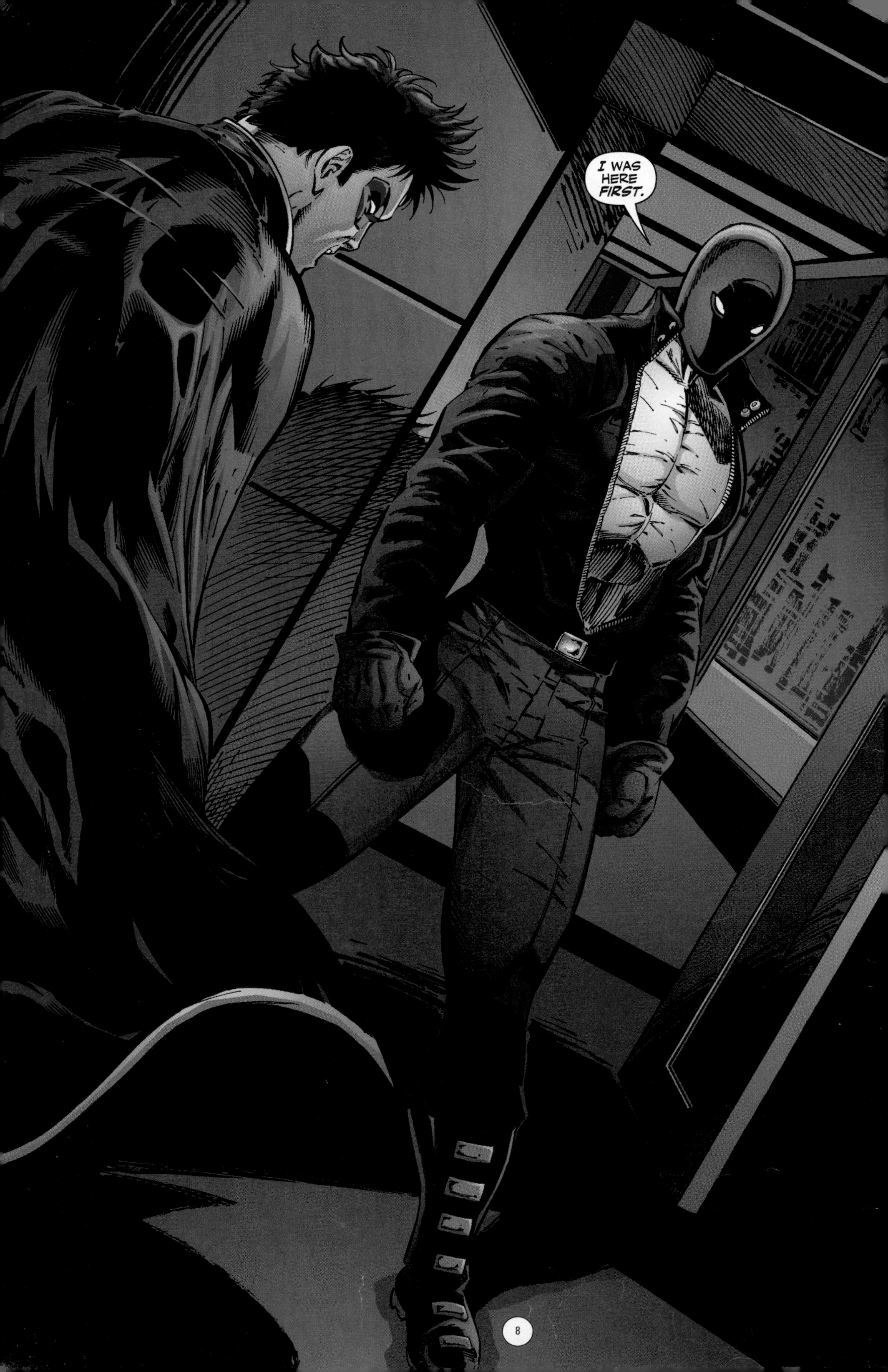
I WAS HERE FIRST.

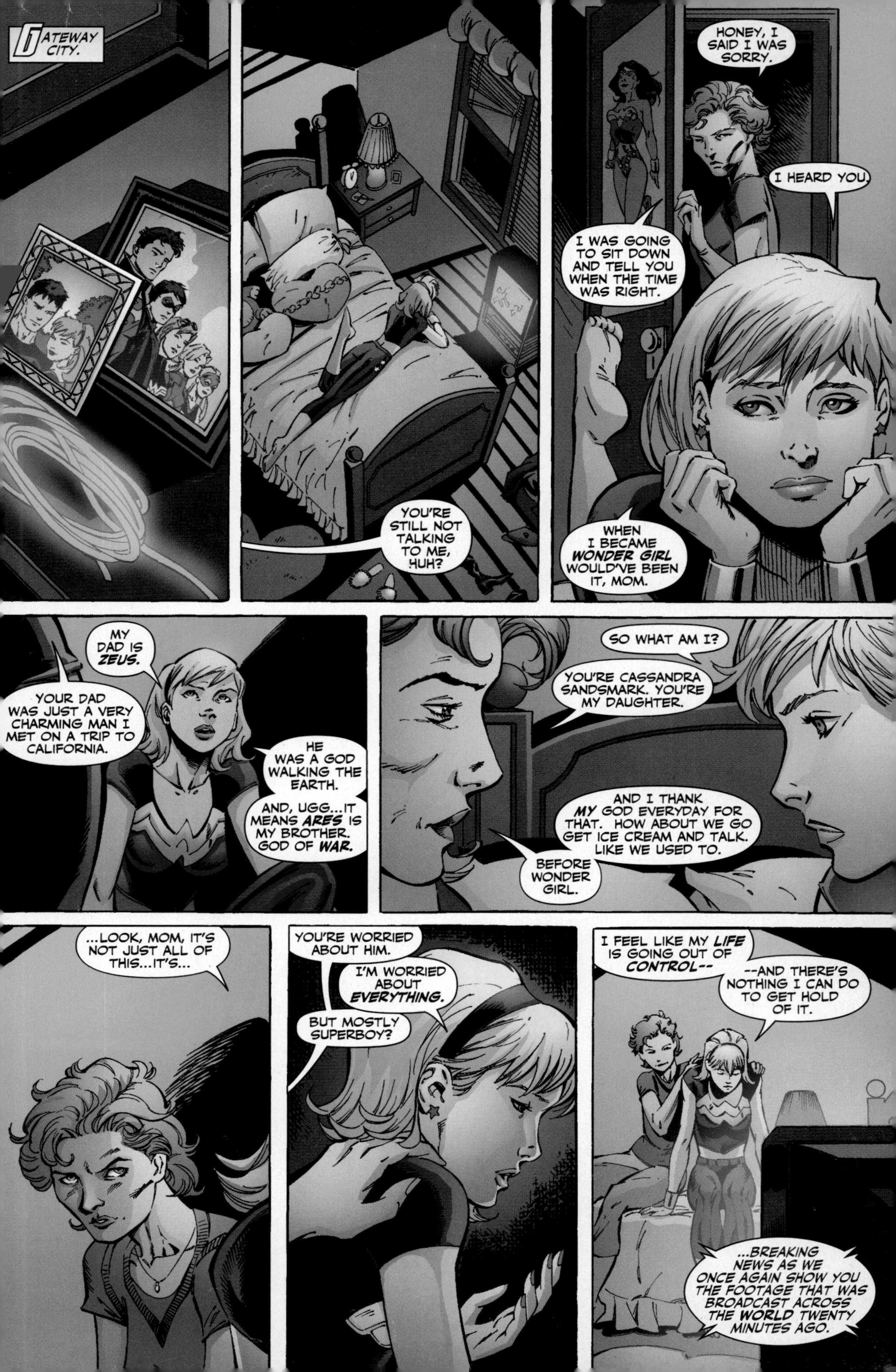
GATEWAY CITY.
YOU'RE STILL NOT TALKING TO ME, HUH?
HONEY, I SAID I WAS SORRY.
I HEARD YOU.
I WAS GOING TO SIT DOWN AND TELL YOU WHEN THE TIME WAS RIGHT.
WHEN I BECAME WONDER GIRL WOULD'VE BEEN IT, MOM.
MY DAD IS ZEUS.
YOUR DAD WAS JUST A VERY CHARMING MAN I MET ON A TRIP TO CALIFORNIA.
HE WAS A GOD WALKING THE EARTH.
AND, UGG...IT MEANS ARES IS MY BROTHER. GOD OF WAR.
SO WHAT AM I?
YOU'RE CASSANDRA SANDSMARK. YOU'RE MY DAUGHTER.
AND I THANK MY GOD EVERYDAY FOR THAT. HOW ABOUT WE GO GET ICE CREAM AND TALK. LIKE WE USED TO.
BEFORE WONDER GIRL.
...LOOK, MOM, IT'S NOT JUST ALL OF THIS...IT'S...
YOU'RE WORRIED ABOUT HIM.
I'M WORRIED ABOUT EVERYTHING.
BUT MOSTLY SUPERBOY?
I FEEL LIKE MY LIFE IS GOING OUT OF CONTROL--
--AND THERE'S NOTHING I CAN DO TO GET HOLD OF IT.
...BREAKING NEWS AS WE ONCE AGAIN SHOW YOU THE FOOTAGE THAT WAS BROADCAST ACROSS THE WORLD TWENTY MINUTES AGO.

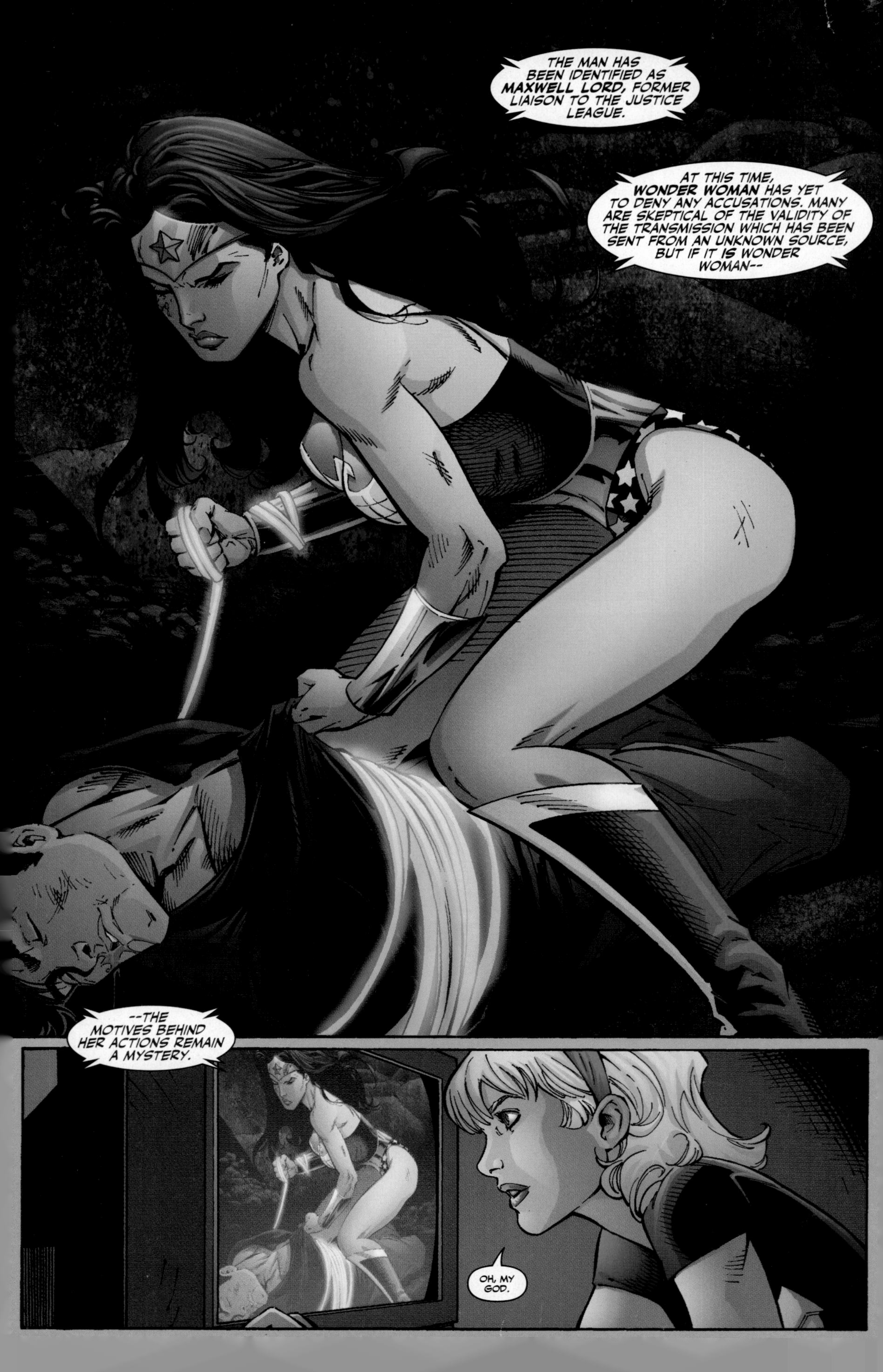
THE MAN HAS BEEN IDENTIFIED AS MAXWELL LORD, FORMER LIAISON TO THE JUSTICE LEAGUE.
AT THIS TIME, WONDER WOMAN HAS YET TO DENY ANY ACCUSATIONS. MANY ARE SKEPTICAL OF THE VALIDITY OF THE TRANSMISSION WHICH HAS BEEN SENT FROM AN UNKNOWN SOURCE, BUT IF IT IS WONDER WOMAN--
--THE MOTIVES BEHIND HER ACTIONS REMAIN A MYSTERY.
OH, MY GOD.

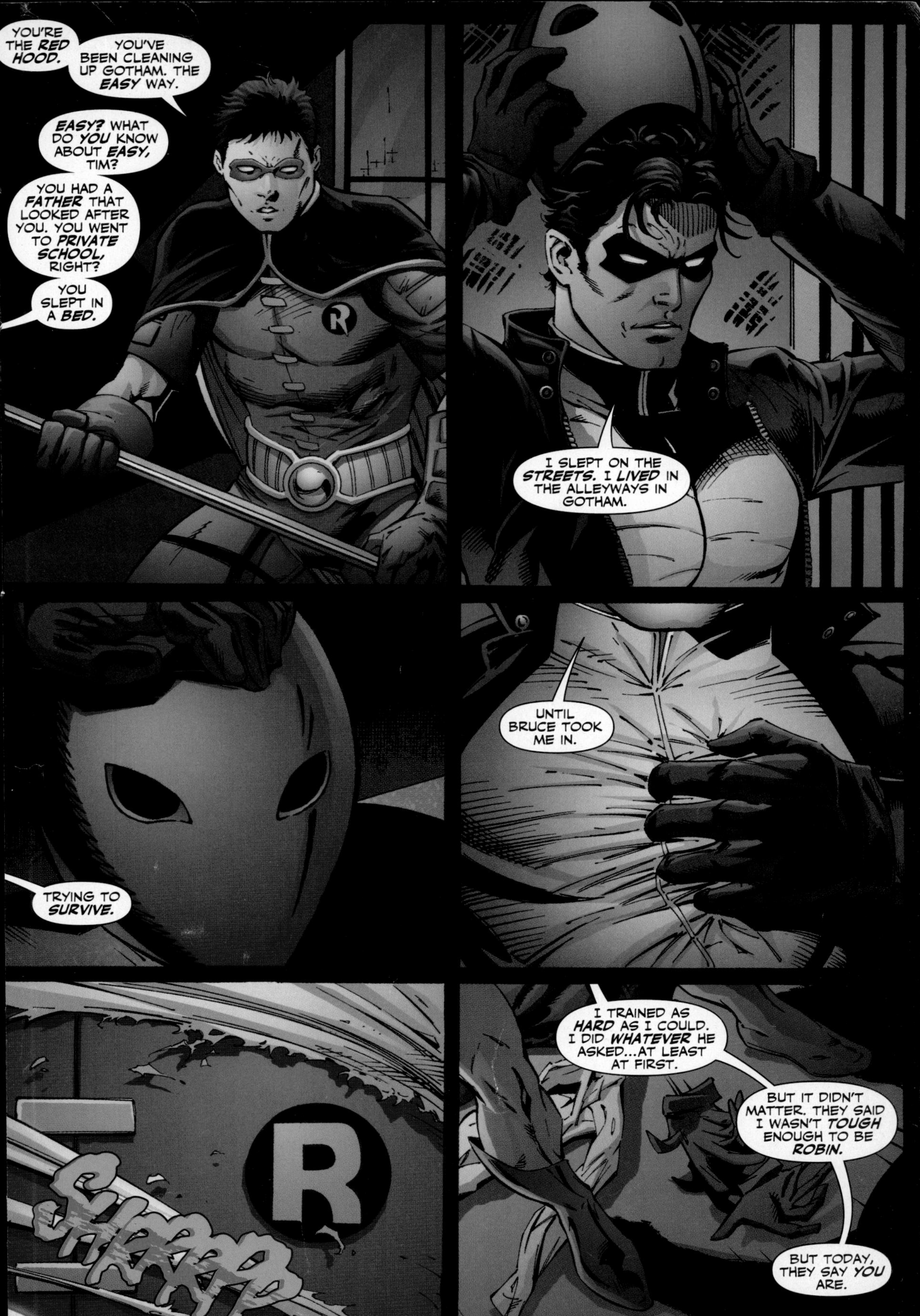

YOU'RE THE RED HOOD.
YOU'VE BEEN CLEANING UP GOTHAM. THE EASY WAY.
EASY? WHAT DO YOU KNOW ABOUT EASY, TIM?
YOU HAD A FATHER THAT LOOKED AFTER YOU. YOU WENT TO PRIVATE SCHOOL, RIGHT?
YOU SLEPT IN A BED.
I SLEPT ON THE STREETS. I LIVED IN THE ALLEYWAYS IN GOTHAM.
TRYING TO SURVIVE.
UNTIL BRUCE TOOK ME IN.
SHRRRP
I TRAINED AS HARD AS I COULD. I DID WHATEVER HE ASKED...AT LEAST AT FIRST.
BUT IT DIDN'T MATTER. THEY SAID I WASN'T TOUGH ENOUGH TO BE ROBIN.
BUT TODAY, THEY SAY YOU ARE.

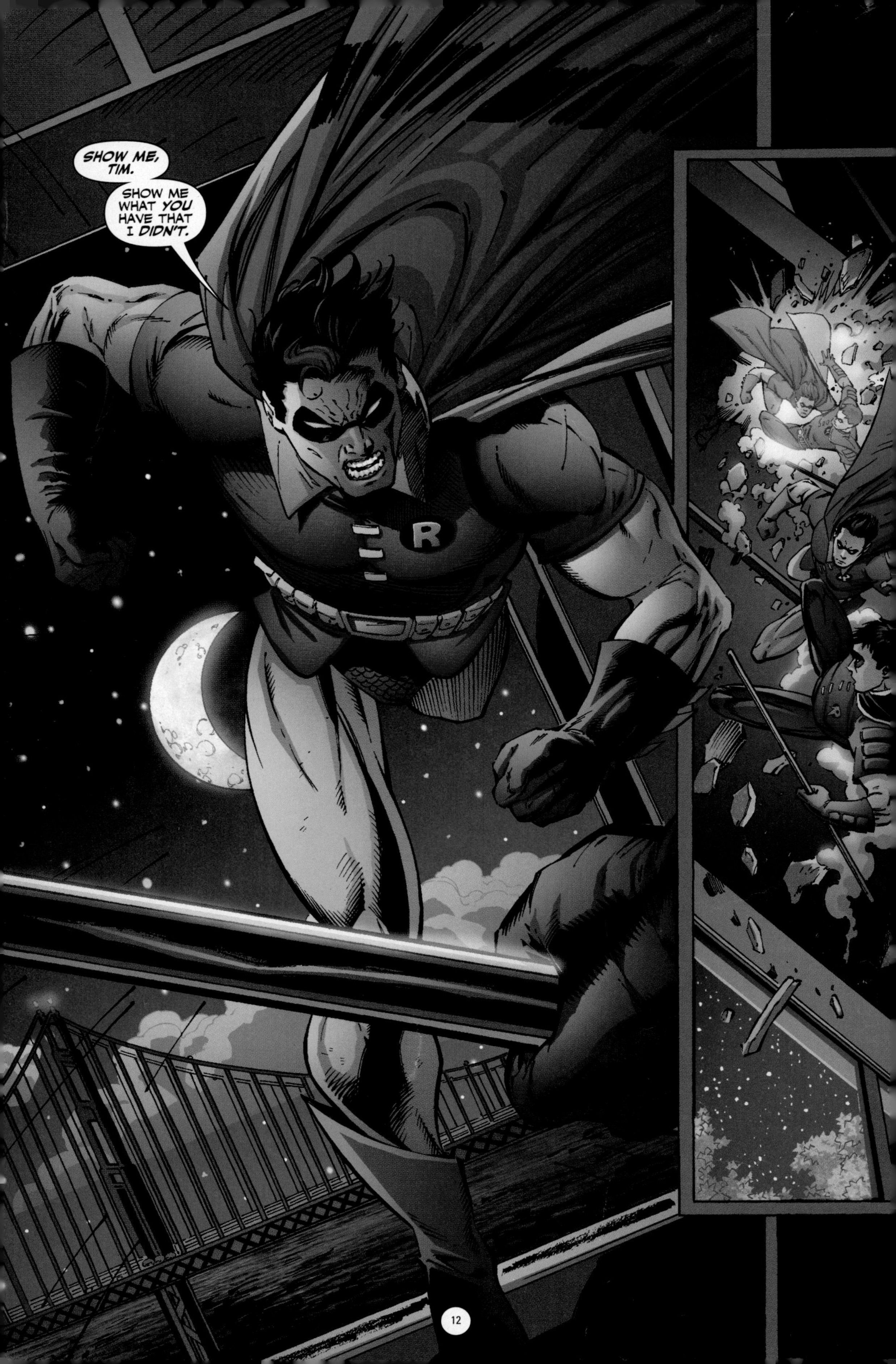
SHOW ME, TIM.
SHOW ME WHAT YOU HAVE THAT I DIDN'T.

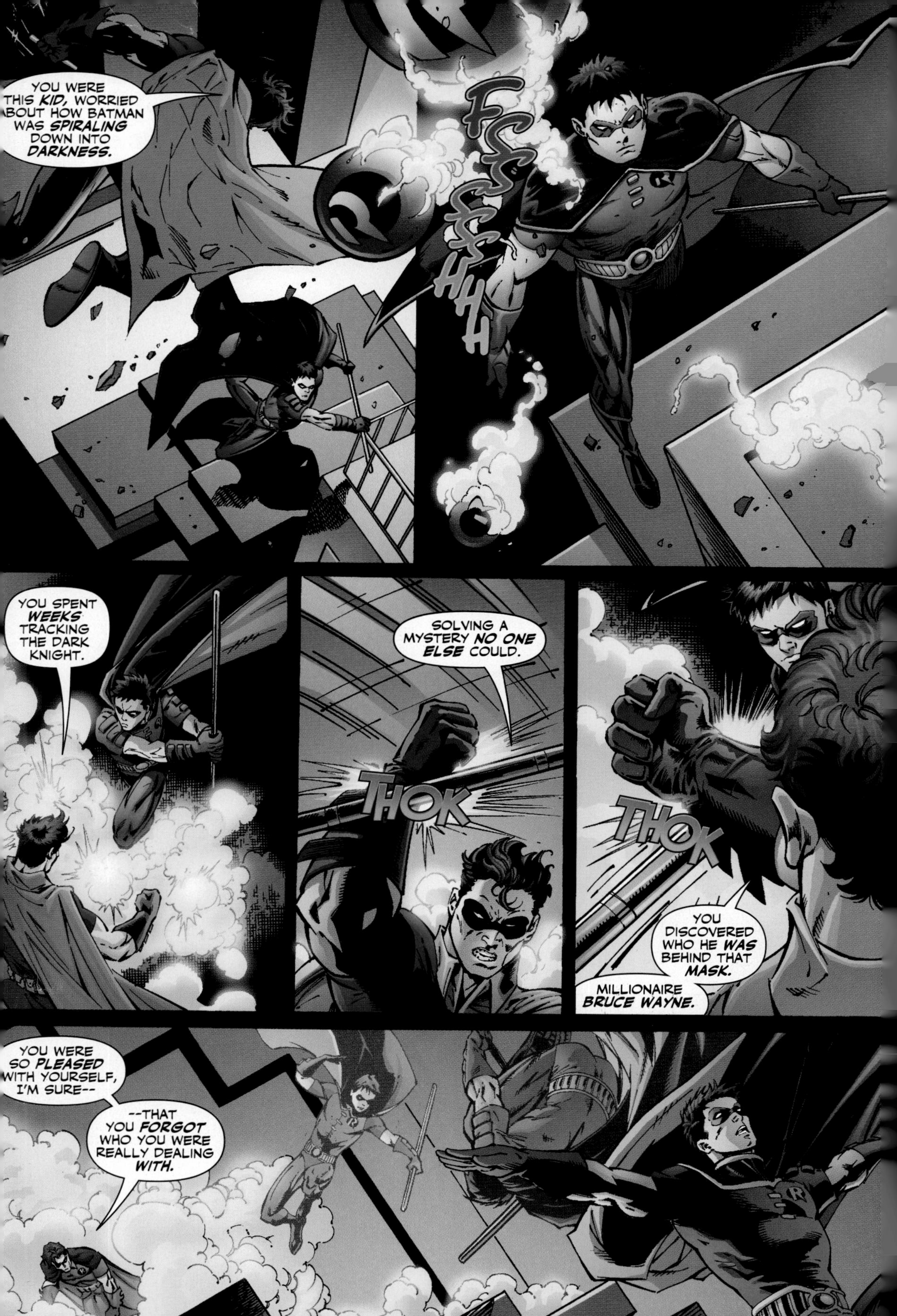

YOU WERE THIS KID, WORRIED ABOUT HOW BATMAN WAS SPIRALING DOWN INTO DARKNESS.
FSSSSHHHH
YOU SPENT WEEKS TRACKING THE DARK KNIGHT.
SOLVING A MYSTERY NO ONE ELSE COULD.
THOK
THOK
YOU DISCOVERED WHO HE WAS BEHIND THAT MASK.
MILLIONAIRE BRUCE WAYNE.
YOU WERE SO PLEASED WITH YOURSELF, I'M SURE--
--THAT YOU FORGOT WHO YOU WERE REALLY DEALING WITH.

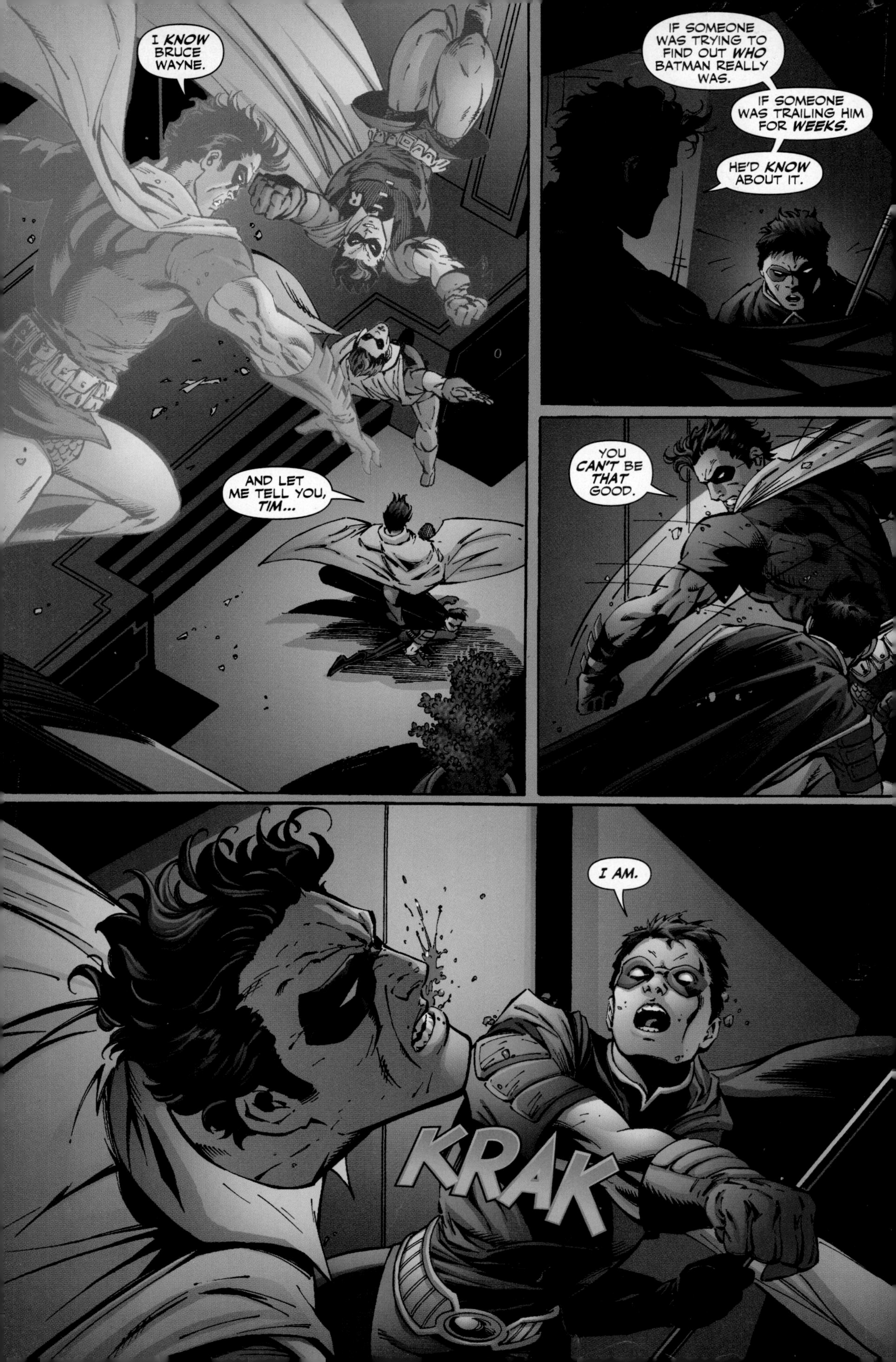
I KNOW BRUCE WAYNE.
AND LET ME TELL YOU, TIM...
IF SOMEONE WAS TRYING TO FIND OUT WHO BATMAN REALLY WAS.
IF SOMEONE WAS TRAILING HIM FOR WEEKS.
HE'D KNOW ABOUT IT.
YOU CAN'T BE THAT GOOD.
I AM.
KRAK

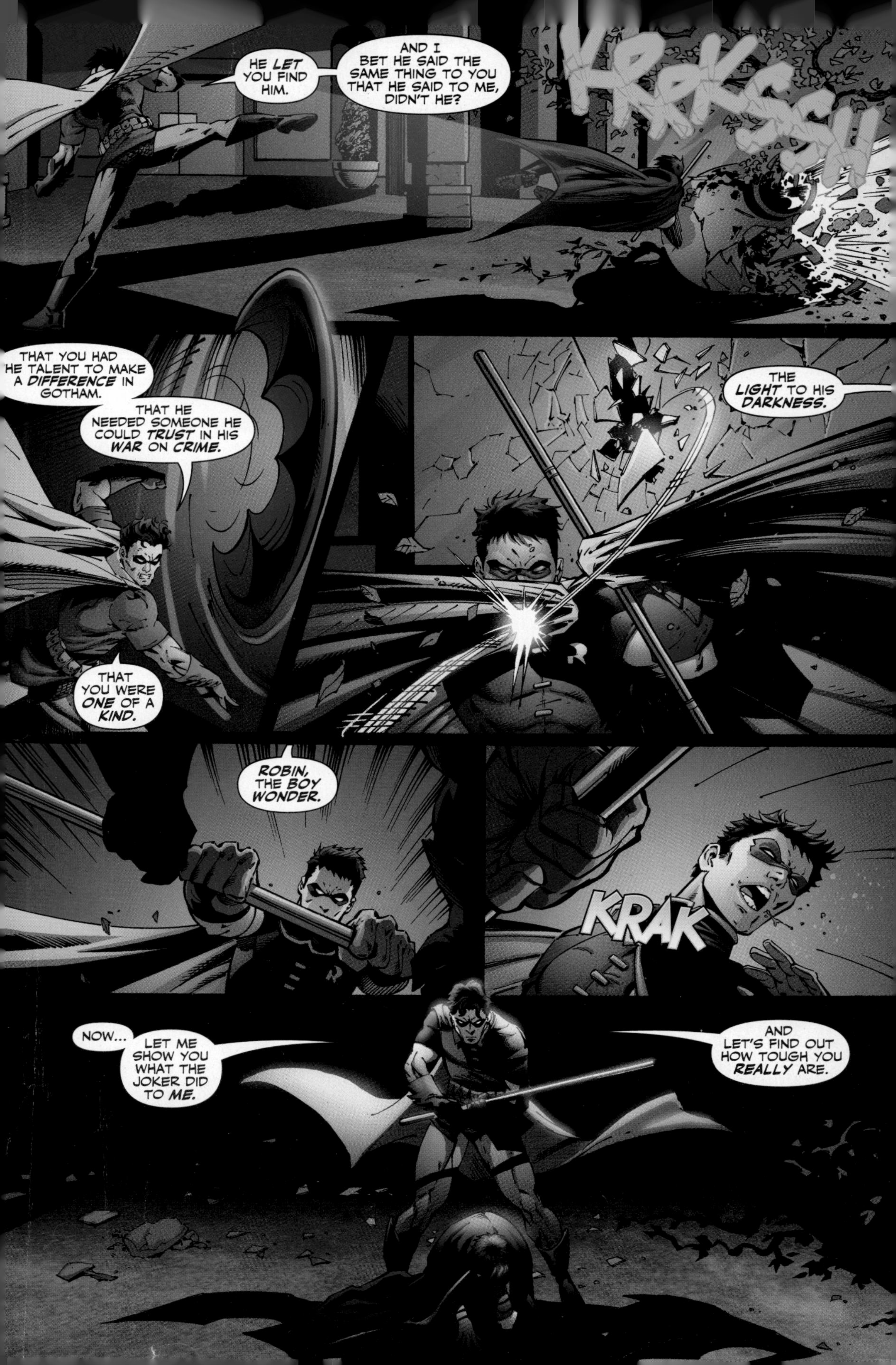

HE LET YOU FIND HIM.
AND I BET HE SAID THE SAME THING TO YOU THAT HE SAID TO ME, DIDN'T HE?
KRRKSSH
THAT YOU HAD HE TALENT TO MAKE A DIFFERENCE IN GOTHAM.
THAT HE NEEDED SOMEONE HE COULD TRUST IN HIS WAR ON CRIME.
THAT YOU WERE ONE OF A KIND.
THE LIGHT TO HIS DARKNESS.
ROBIN, THE BOY WONDER.
KRAK
NOW...
LET ME SHOW YOU WHAT THE JOKER DID TO ME.
AND LET'S FIND OUT HOW TOUGH YOU REALLY ARE.

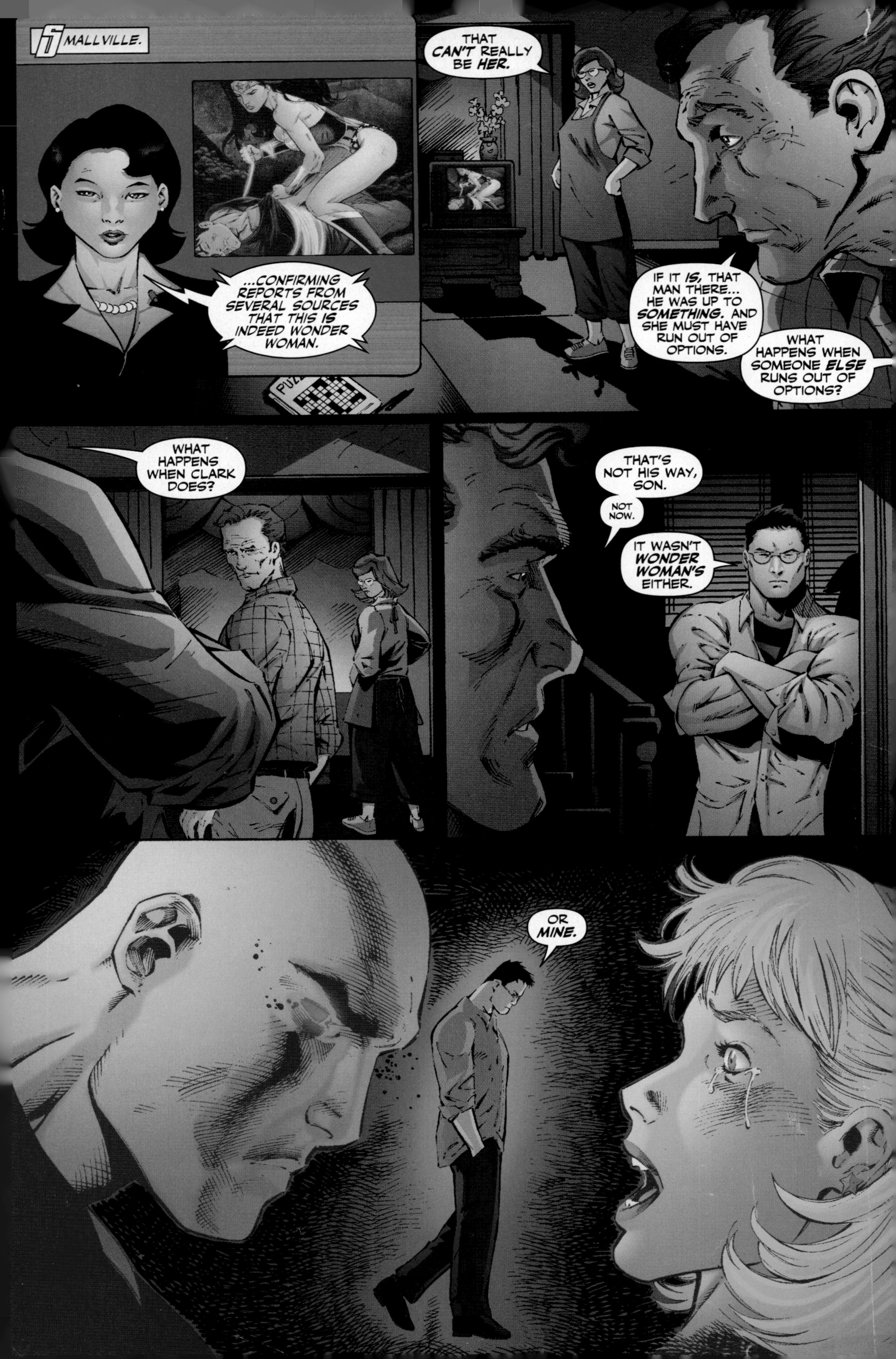
SMALLVILLE.
...CONFIRMING REPORTS FROM SEVERAL SOURCES THAT THIS IS INDEED WONDER WOMAN.
THAT CAN'T REALLY BE HER.
IF IT IS, THAT MAN THERE... HE WAS UP TO SOMETHING. AND SHE MUST HAVE RUN OUT OF OPTIONS.
WHAT HAPPENS WHEN SOMEONE ELSE RUNS OUT OF OPTIONS?
WHAT HAPPENS WHEN CLARK DOES?
THAT'S NOT HIS WAY, SON.
NOT NOW.
IT WASN'T WONDER WOMAN'S EITHER.
OR MINE.

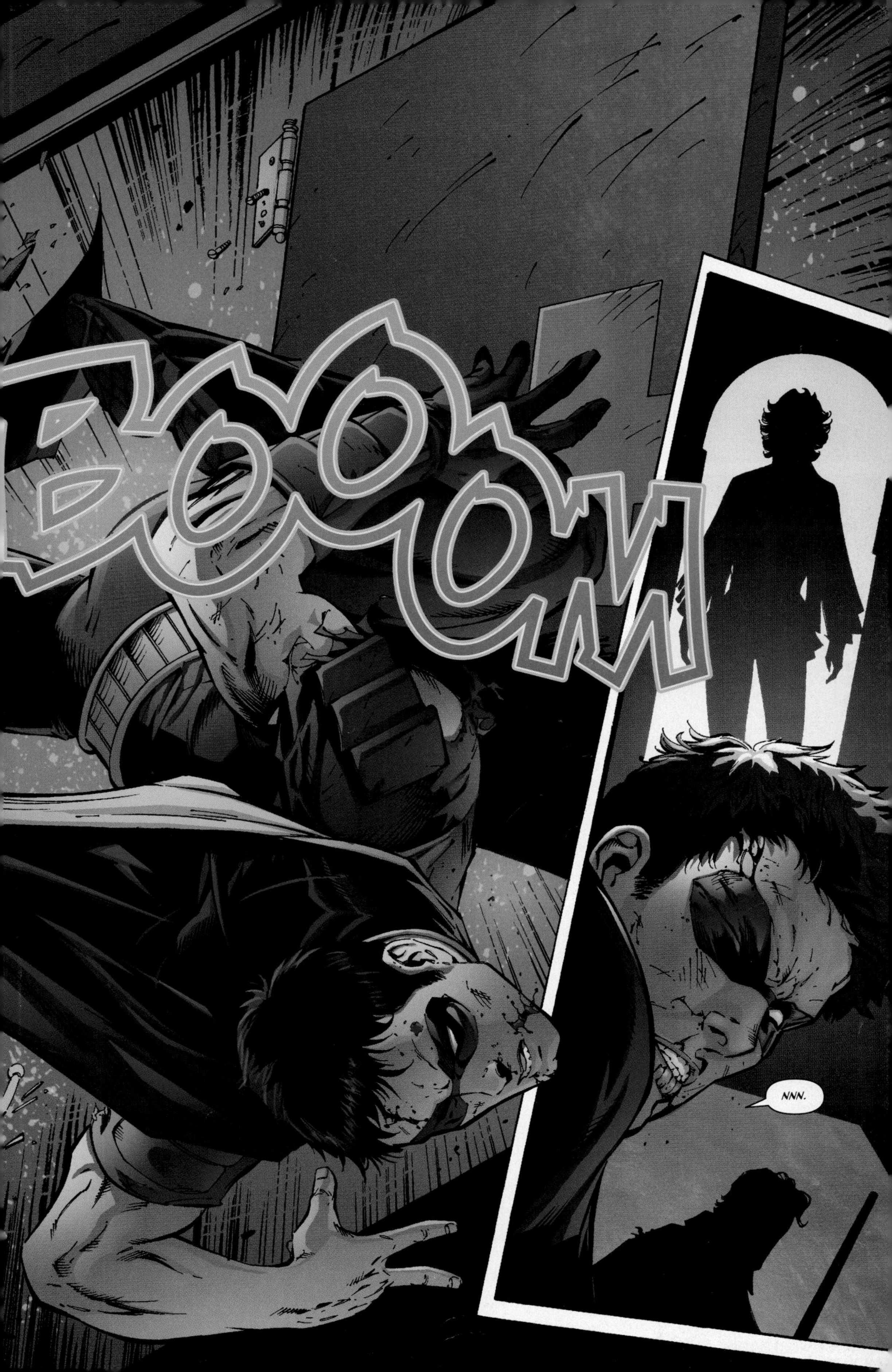
BOOOM
NNN.

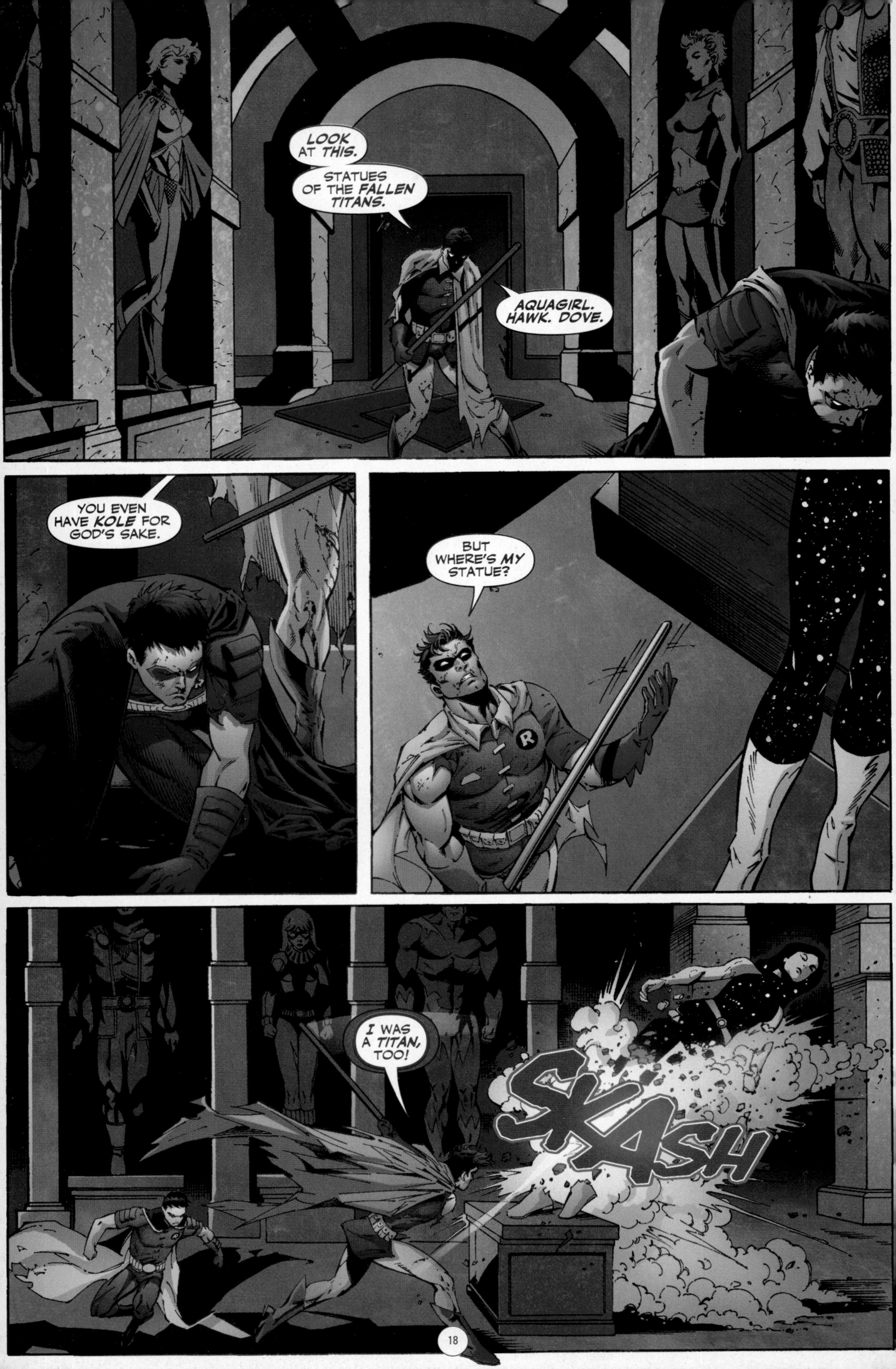
LOOK AT THIS.
STATUES OF THE FALLEN TITANS.
AQUAGIRL. HAWK. DOVE.
YOU EVEN HAVE KOLE FOR GOD'S SAKE.
BUT WHERE'S MY STATUE?
I WAS A TITAN, TOO!
SKASH

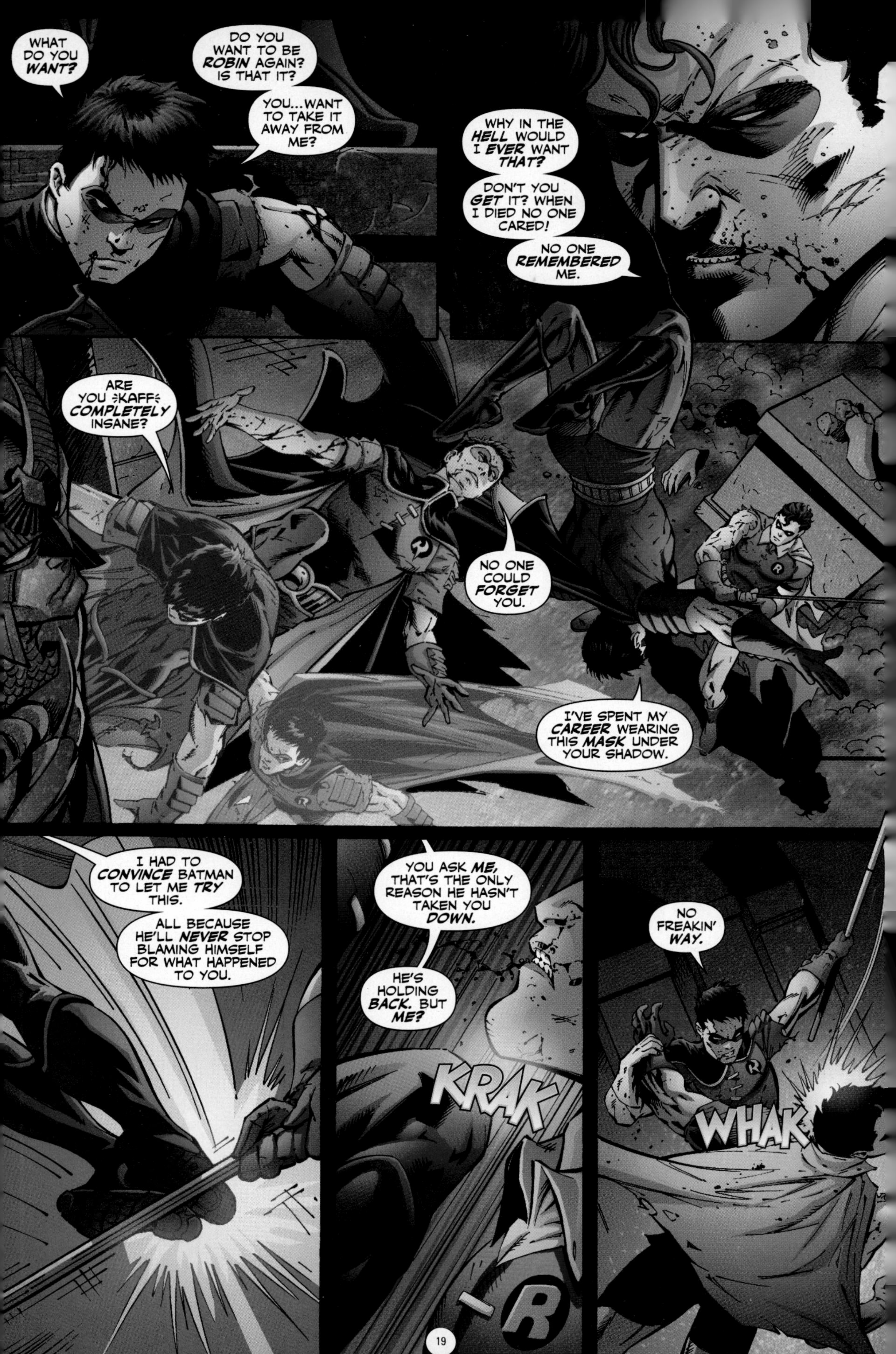
WHAT DO YOU WANT?
DO YOU WANT TO BE ROBIN AGAIN? IS THAT IT?
YOU...WANT TO TAKE IT AWAY FROM ME?
WHY IN THE HELL WOULD I EVER WANT THAT?
DON'T YOU GET IT? WHEN I DIED NO ONE CARED!
NO ONE REMEMBERED ME.
ARE YOU ⁑KAFF⁑ COMPLETELY INSANE?
NO ONE COULD FORGET YOU.
I'VE SPENT MY CAREER WEARING THIS MASK UNDER YOUR SHADOW.
I HAD TO CONVINCE BATMAN TO LET ME TRY THIS.
ALL BECAUSE HE'LL NEVER STOP BLAMING HIMSELF FOR WHAT HAPPENED TO YOU.
YOU ASK ME, THAT'S THE ONLY REASON HE HASN'T TAKEN YOU DOWN.
HE'S HOLDING BACK. BUT ME?
KRAK
NO FREAKIN' WAY.
WHAK

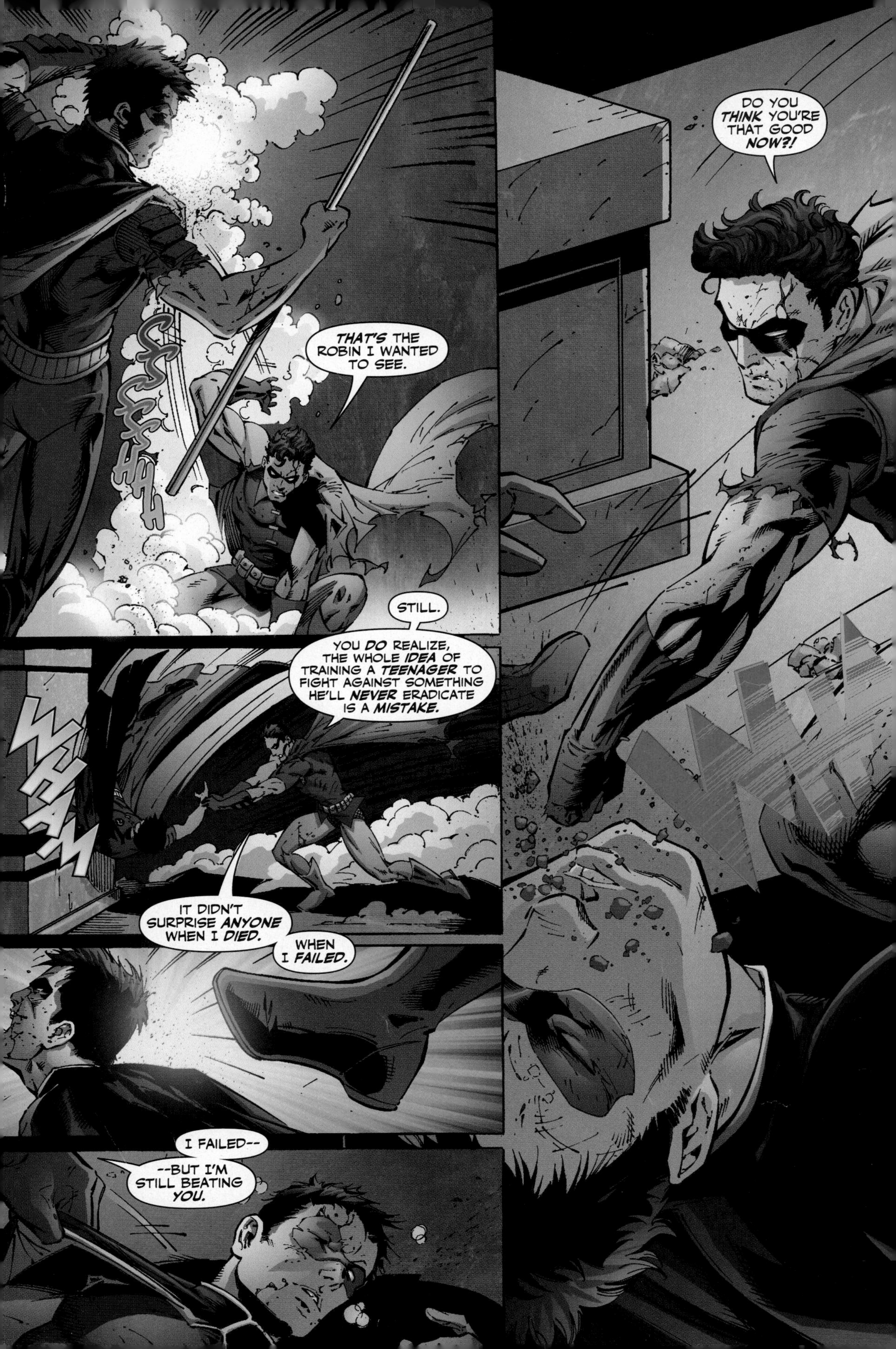

CHSHHH
THAT'S THE ROBIN I WANTED TO SEE.
DO YOU THINK YOU'RE THAT GOOD NOW?!
STILL.
YOU DO REALIZE, THE WHOLE IDEA OF TRAINING A TEENAGER TO FIGHT AGAINST SOMETHING HE'LL NEVER ERADICATE IS A MISTAKE.
WHAM
IT DIDN'T SURPRISE ANYONE WHEN I DIED.
WHEN I FAILED.
I FAILED--
--BUT I'M STILL BEATING YOU.

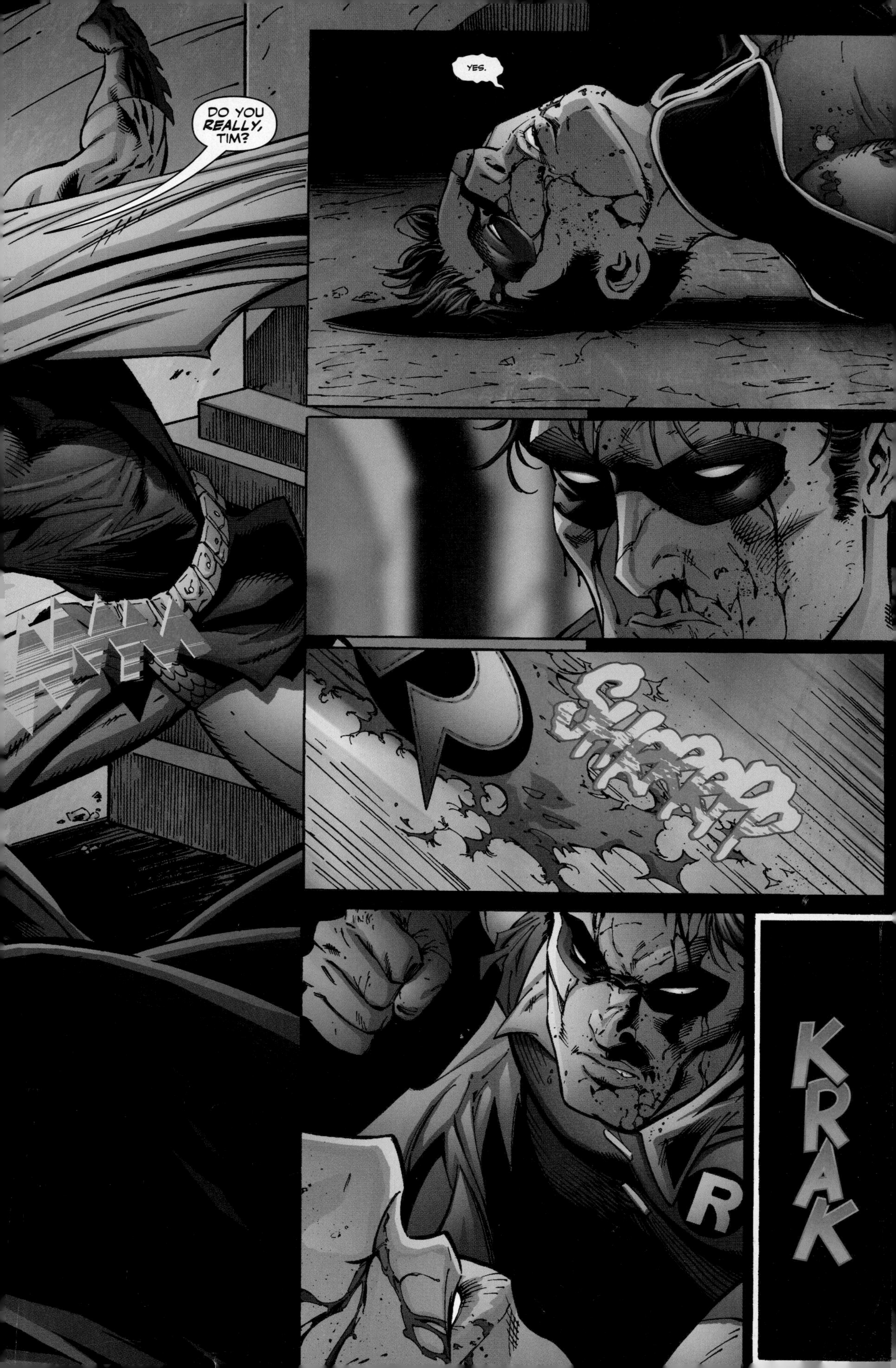

DO YOU *REALLY,* TIM?
YES.
KRAK

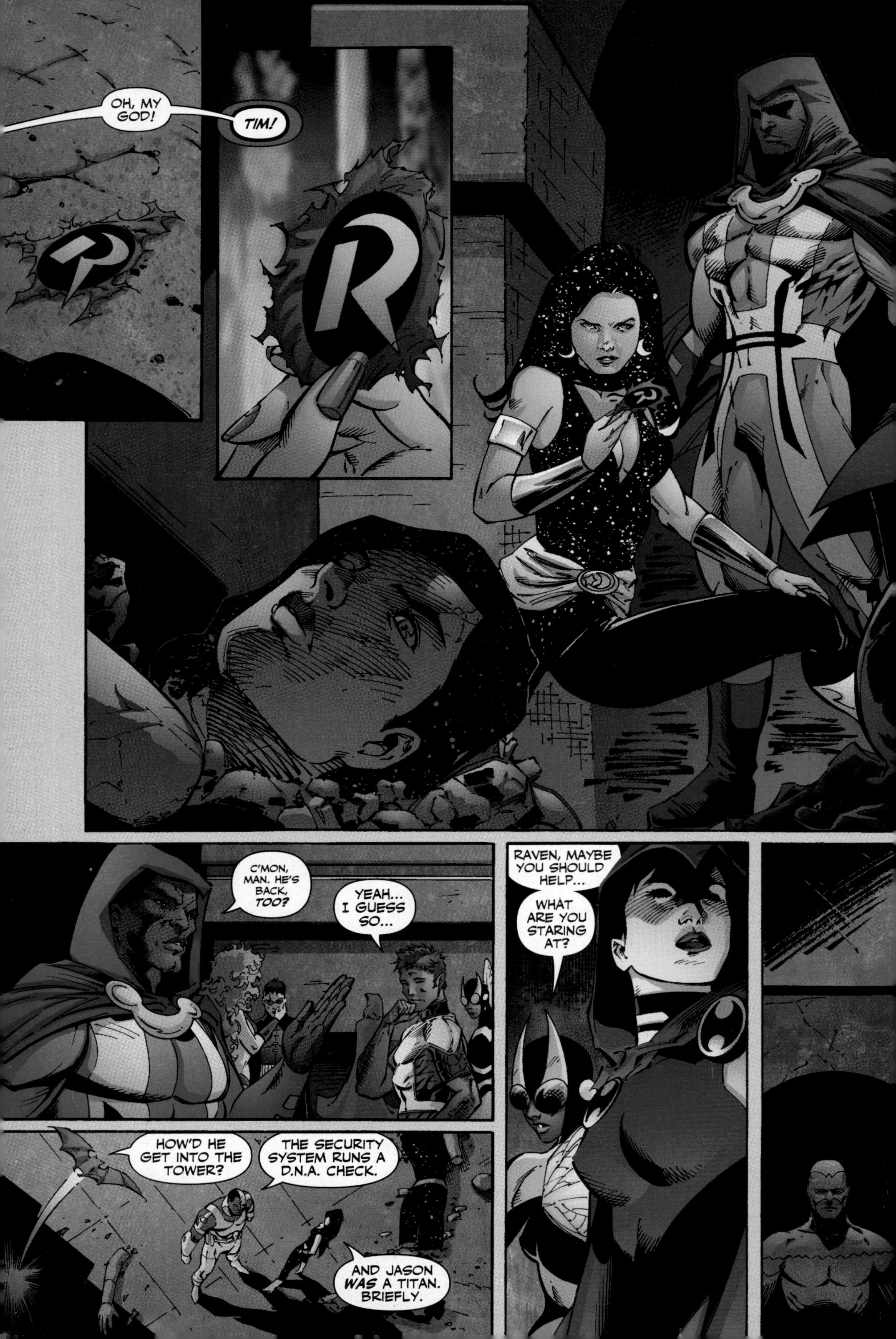
OH, MY GOD!
TIM!
C'MON, MAN. HE'S BACK, TOO?
YEAH... I GUESS SO...
HOW'D HE GET INTO THE TOWER?
THE SECURITY SYSTEM RUNS A D.N.A. CHECK.
AND JASON WAS A TITAN. BRIEFLY.
RAVEN, MAYBE YOU SHOULD HELP...
WHAT ARE YOU STARING AT?

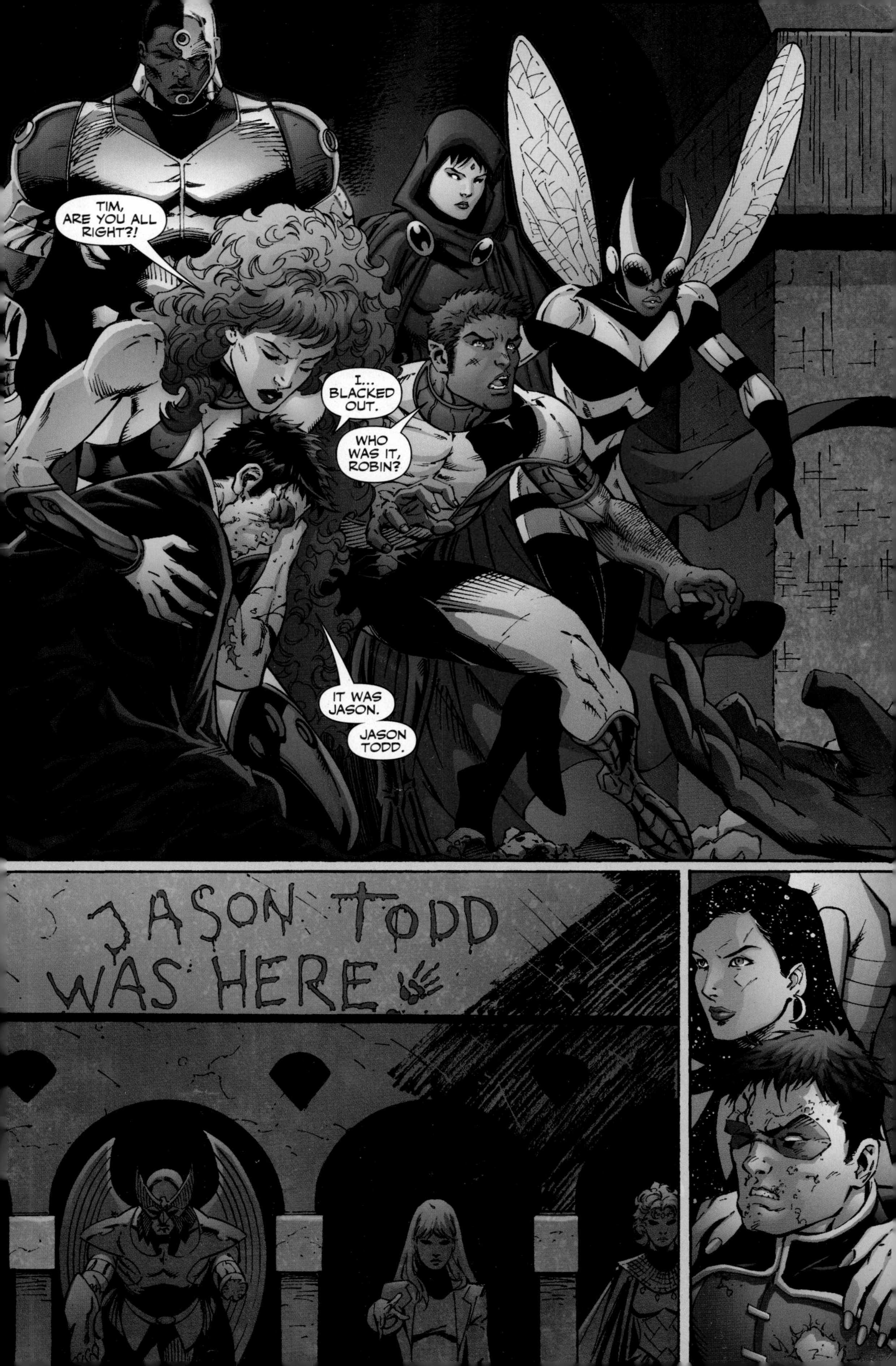
TIM, ARE YOU ALL RIGHT?!
I... BLACKED OUT.
WHO WAS IT, ROBIN?
IT WAS JASON.
JASON TODD.
JASON TODD WAS HERE

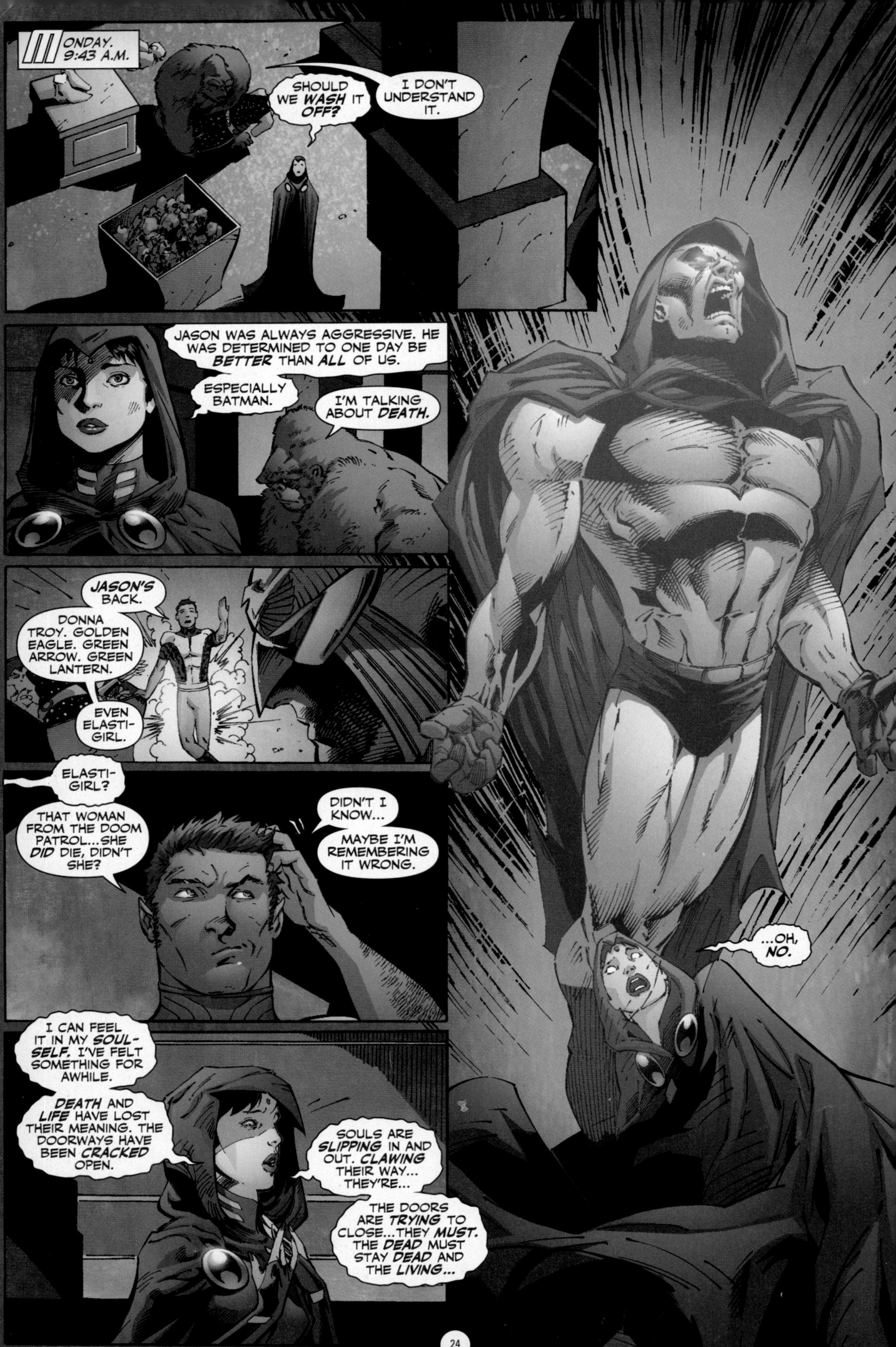
MONDAY. 9:43 A.M.
SHOULD WE WASH IT OFF?
I DON'T UNDERSTAND IT.
JASON WAS ALWAYS AGGRESSIVE. HE WAS DETERMINED TO ONE DAY BE BETTER THAN ALL OF US.
ESPECIALLY BATMAN.
I'M TALKING ABOUT DEATH.
JASON'S BACK.
DONNA TROY. GOLDEN EAGLE. GREEN ARROW. GREEN LANTERN.
EVEN ELASTI-GIRL.
ELASTI-GIRL?
THAT WOMAN FROM THE DOOM PATROL...SHE DID DIE, DIDN'T SHE?
DIDN'T I KNOW...
MAYBE I'M REMEMBERING IT WRONG.
I CAN FEEL IT IN MY SOUL-SELF. I'VE FELT SOMETHING FOR AWHILE.
DEATH AND LIFE HAVE LOST THEIR MEANING. THE DOORWAYS HAVE BEEN CRACKED OPEN.
SOULS ARE SLIPPING IN AND OUT. CLAWING THEIR WAY... THEY'RE...
THE DOORS ARE TRYING TO CLOSE...THEY MUST. THE DEAD MUST STAY DEAD AND THE LIVING...
...OH, NO.

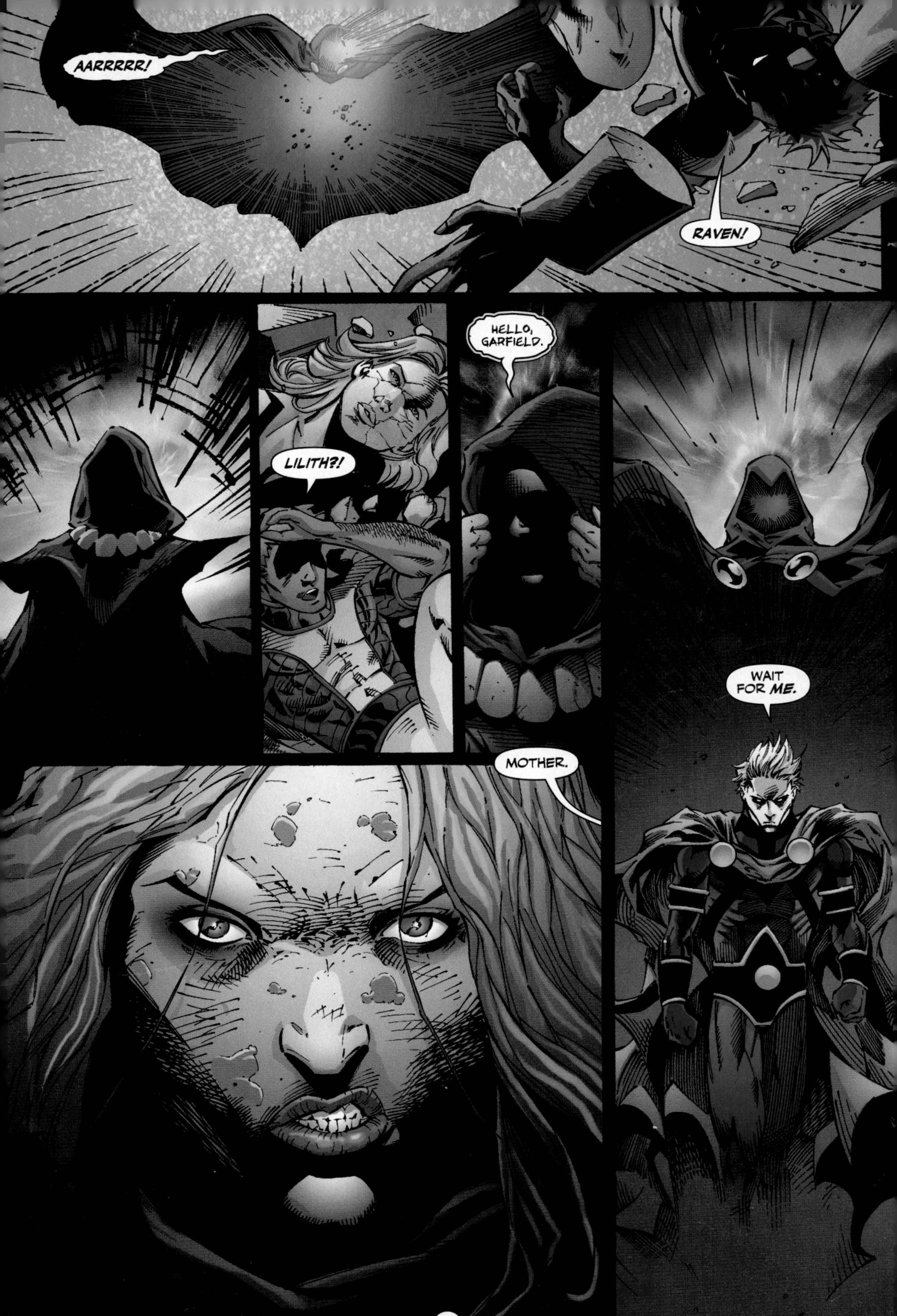
AARRRRR!
RAVEN!
LILITH?!
HELLO, GARFIELD.
WAIT FOR ME.
MOTHER.

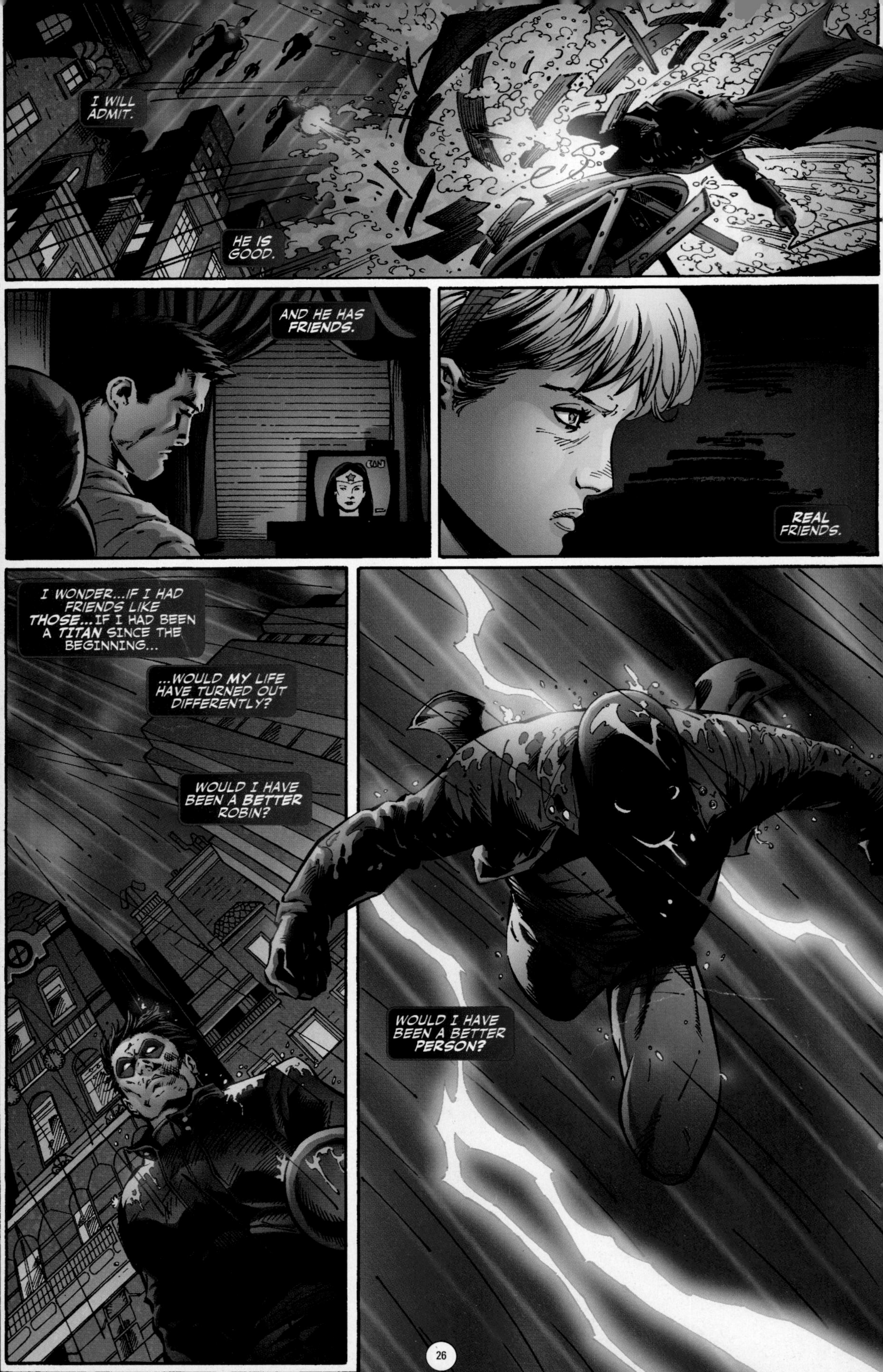

I WILL ADMIT.
HE IS GOOD.
AND HE HAS FRIENDS.
REAL FRIENDS.
I WONDER...IF I HAD FRIENDS LIKE THOSE...IF I HAD BEEN A TITAN SINCE THE BEGINNING...
...WOULD MY LIFE HAVE TURNED OUT DIFFERENTLY?
WOULD I HAVE BEEN A BETTER ROBIN?
WOULD I HAVE BEEN A BETTER PERSON?

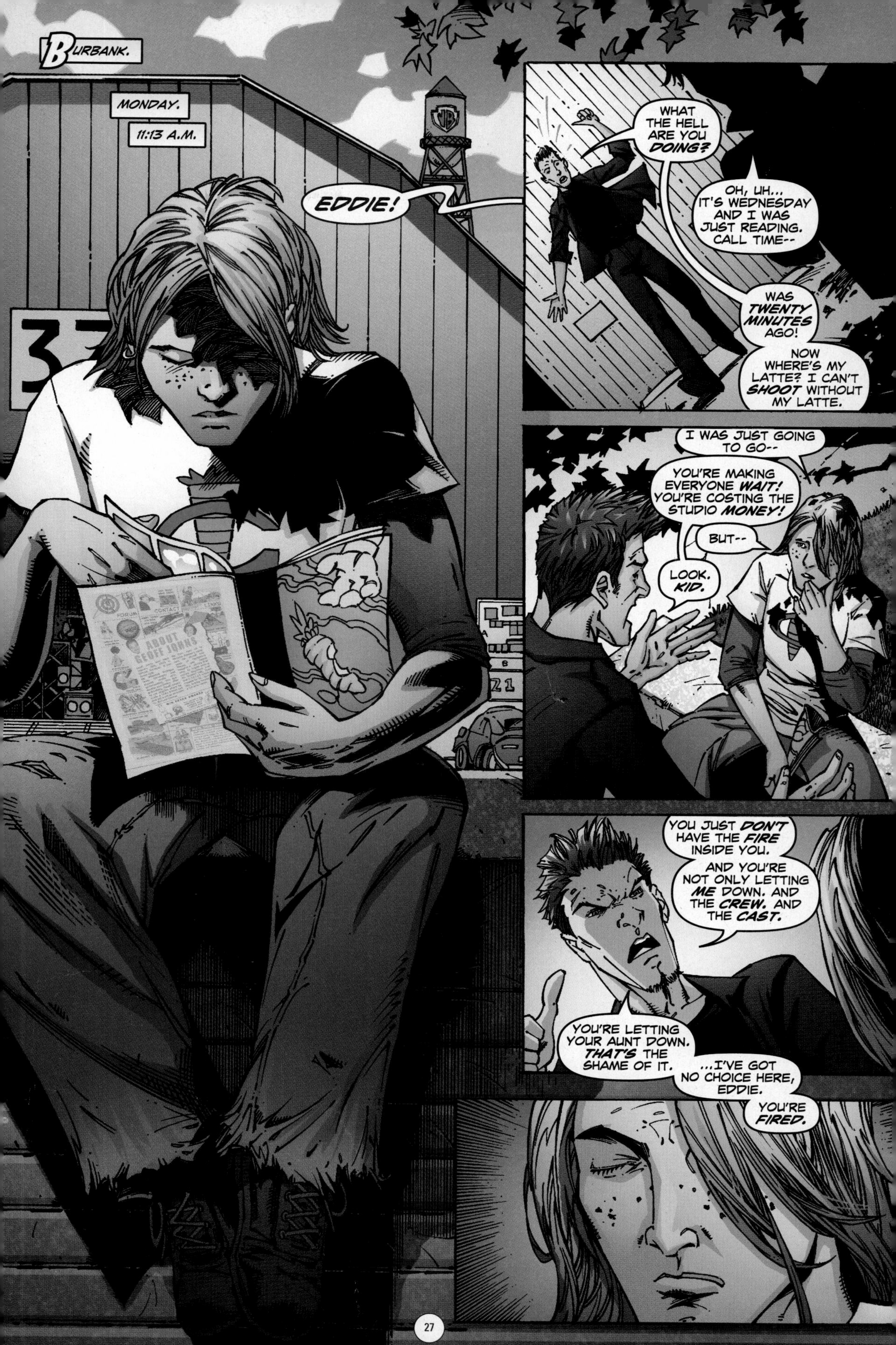
BURBANK.
MONDAY.
11:13 A.M.
EDDIE!
WHAT THE HELL ARE YOU DOING?
OH, UH... IT'S WEDNESDAY AND I WAS JUST READING. CALL TIME--
WAS TWENTY MINUTES AGO!
NOW WHERE'S MY LATTE? I CAN'T SHOOT WITHOUT MY LATTE.
I WAS JUST GOING TO GO--
YOU'RE MAKING EVERYONE WAIT! YOU'RE COSTING THE STUDIO MONEY!
BUT--
LOOK. KID.
YOU JUST DON'T HAVE THE FIRE INSIDE YOU.
AND YOU'RE NOT ONLY LETTING ME DOWN. AND THE CREW. AND THE CAST.
YOU'RE LETTING YOUR AUNT DOWN. THAT'S THE SHAME OF IT.
...I'VE GOT NO CHOICE HERE, EDDIE.
YOU'RE FIRED.

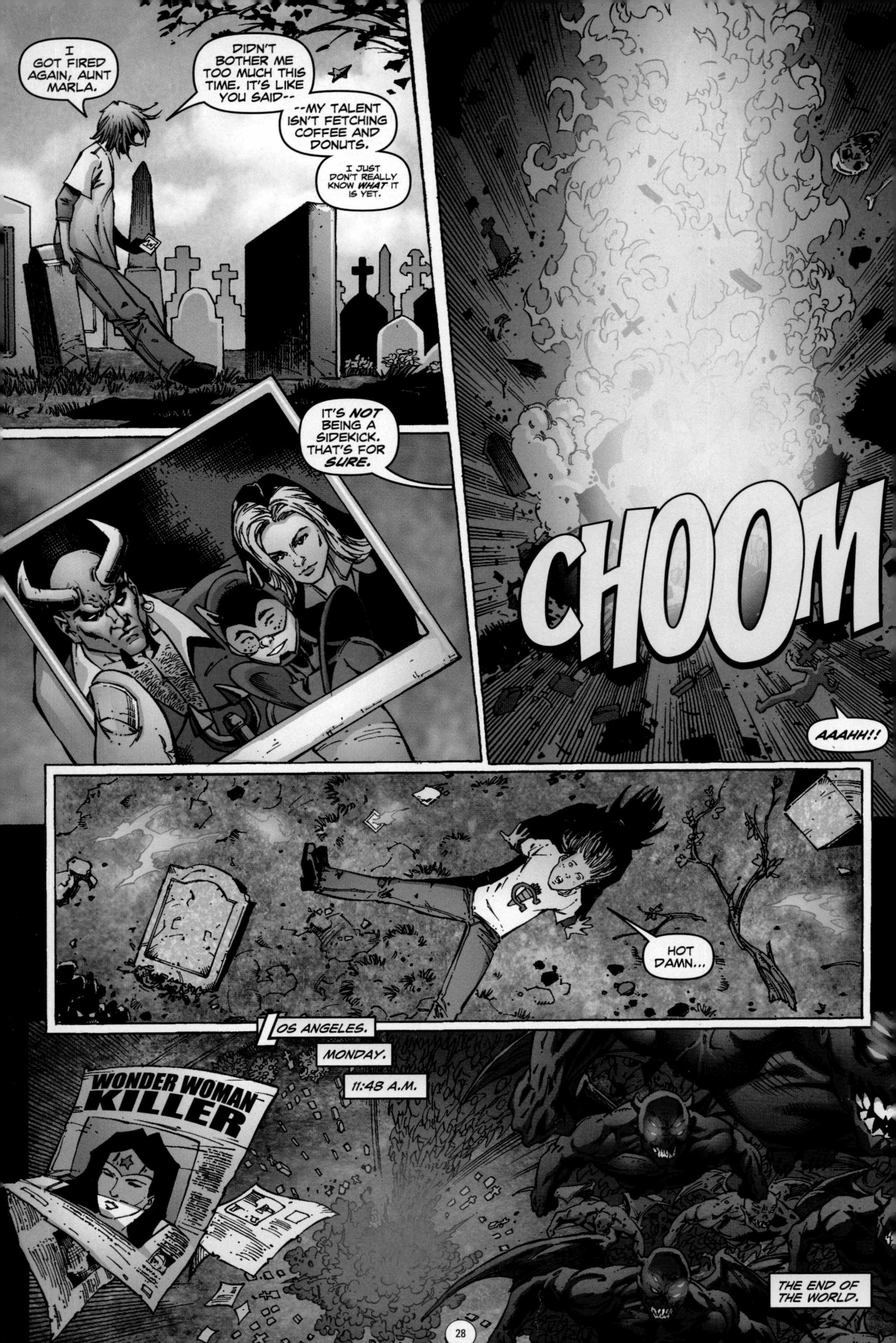
I GOT FIRED AGAIN, AUNT MARLA.
DIDN'T BOTHER ME TOO MUCH THIS TIME. IT'S LIKE YOU SAID--
--MY TALENT ISN'T FETCHING COFFEE AND DONUTS.
I JUST DON'T REALLY KNOW *WHAT* IT IS YET.
IT'S *NOT* BEING A SIDEKICK. THAT'S FOR *SURE*.
CHOOM
AAAHH!!
HOT DAMN...
LOS ANGELES.
MONDAY.
11:48 A.M.
WONDER WOMAN KILLER
THE END OF THE WORLD.

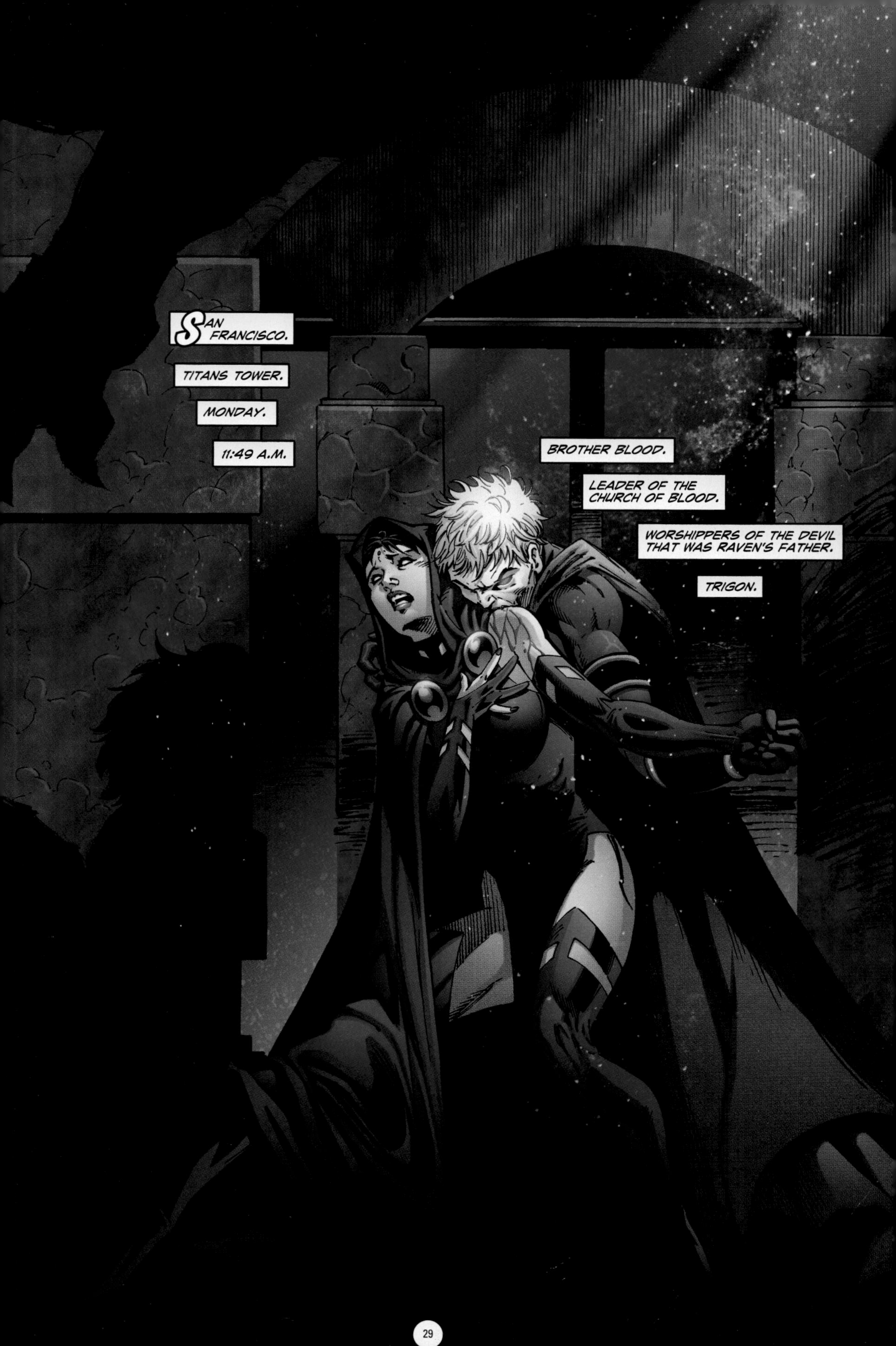
SAN FRANCISCO.
TITANS TOWER.
MONDAY.
11:49 A.M.
BROTHER BLOOD.
LEADER OF THE CHURCH OF BLOOD.
WORSHIPPERS OF THE DEVIL THAT WAS RAVEN'S FATHER.
TRIGON.

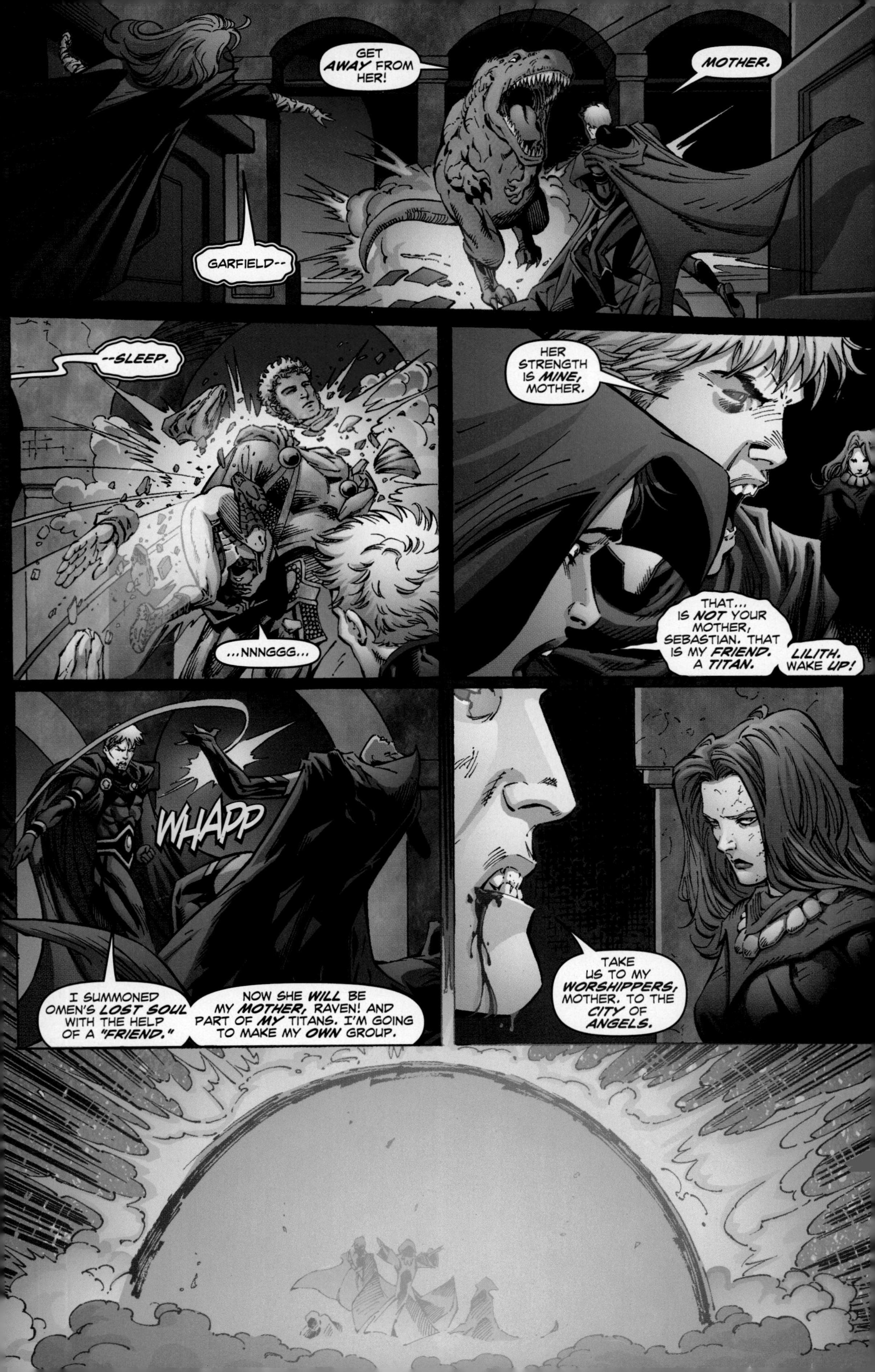

GET AWAY FROM HER!
MOTHER.
GARFIELD--
--SLEEP.
...NNNGGG...
HER STRENGTH IS MINE, MOTHER.
THAT... IS NOT YOUR MOTHER, SEBASTIAN. THAT IS MY FRIEND. A TITAN.
LILITH. WAKE UP!
WHAPP
I SUMMONED OMEN'S LOST SOUL WITH THE HELP OF A "FRIEND."
NOW SHE WILL BE MY MOTHER, RAVEN! AND PART OF MY TITANS. I'M GOING TO MAKE MY OWN GROUP.
TAKE US TO MY WORSHIPPERS, MOTHER. TO THE CITY OF ANGELS.

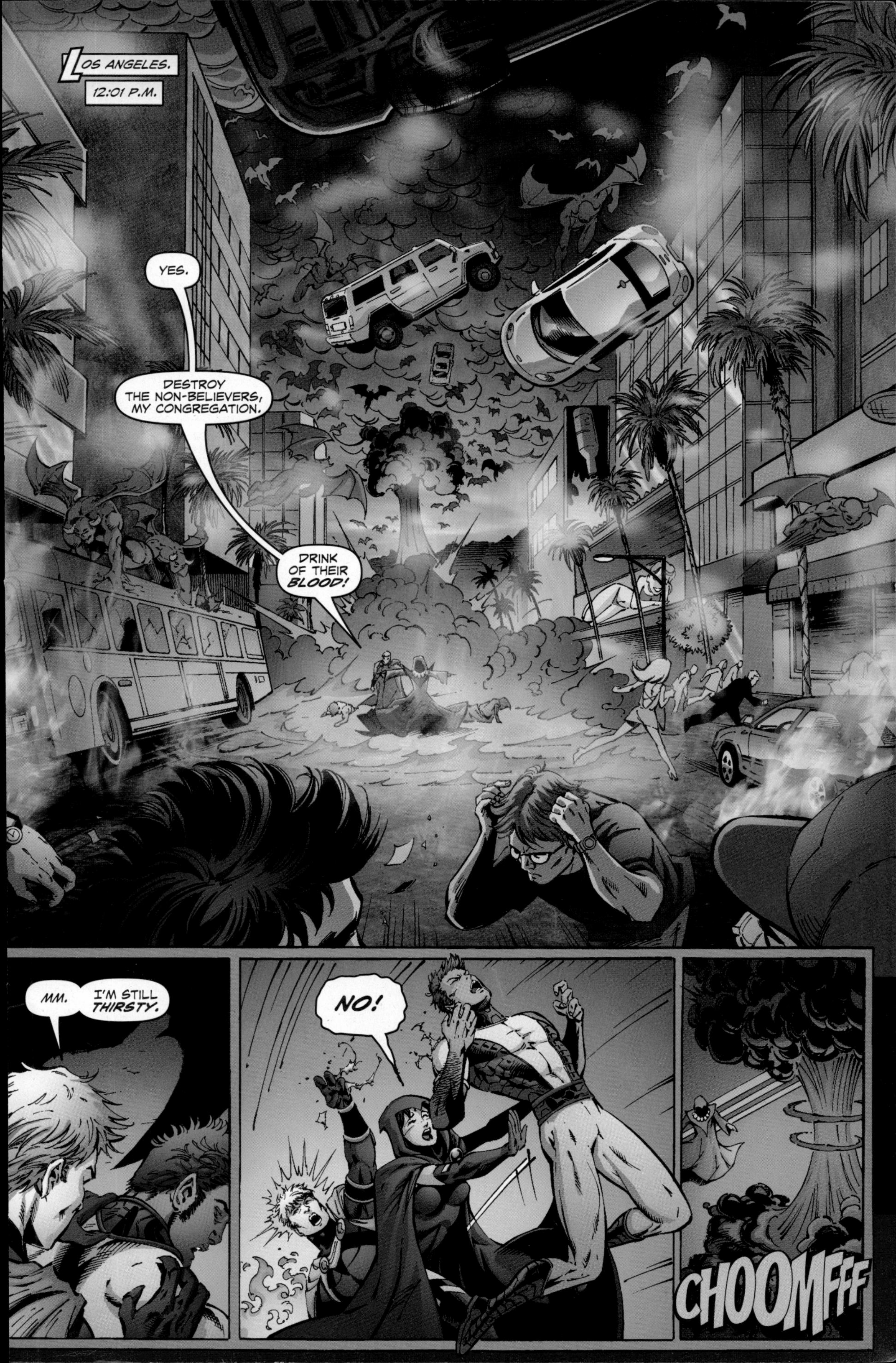
LOS ANGELES.
12:01 P.M.
YES.
DESTROY THE NON-BELIEVERS, MY CONGREGATION.
DRINK OF THEIR BLOOD!
MM.
I'M STILL THIRSTY.
NO!
CHOOMFFF

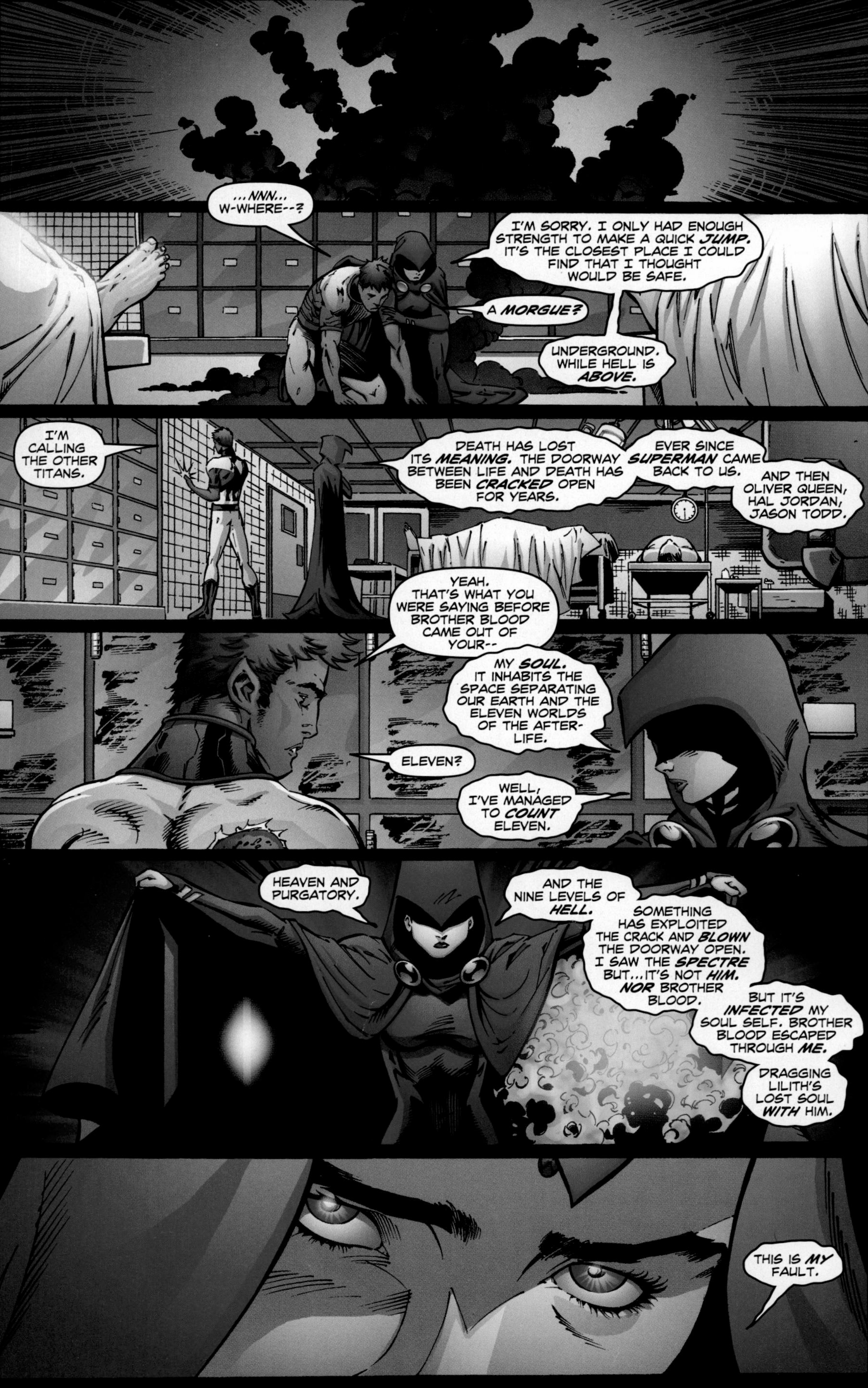
...NNN... W-WHERE--?
I'M SORRY. I ONLY HAD ENOUGH STRENGTH TO MAKE A QUICK JUMP. IT'S THE CLOSEST PLACE I COULD FIND THAT I THOUGHT WOULD BE SAFE.
A MORGUE?
UNDERGROUND. WHILE HELL IS ABOVE.
I'M CALLING THE OTHER TITANS.
DEATH HAS LOST ITS MEANING. THE DOORWAY BETWEEN LIFE AND DEATH HAS BEEN CRACKED OPEN FOR YEARS.
EVER SINCE SUPERMAN CAME BACK TO US.
AND THEN OLIVER QUEEN, HAL JORDAN, JASON TODD.
YEAH. THAT'S WHAT YOU WERE SAYING BEFORE BROTHER BLOOD CAME OUT OF YOUR--
MY SOUL. IT INHABITS THE SPACE SEPARATING OUR EARTH AND THE ELEVEN WORLDS OF THE AFTER-LIFE.
ELEVEN?
WELL, I'VE MANAGED TO COUNT ELEVEN.
HEAVEN AND PURGATORY.
AND THE NINE LEVELS OF HELL.
SOMETHING HAS EXPLOITED THE CRACK AND BLOWN THE DOORWAY OPEN. I SAW THE SPECTRE BUT...IT'S NOT HIM. NOR BROTHER BLOOD.
BUT IT'S INFECTED MY SOUL SELF. BROTHER BLOOD ESCAPED THROUGH ME.
DRAGGING LILITH'S LOST SOUL WITH HIM.
THIS IS MY FAULT.

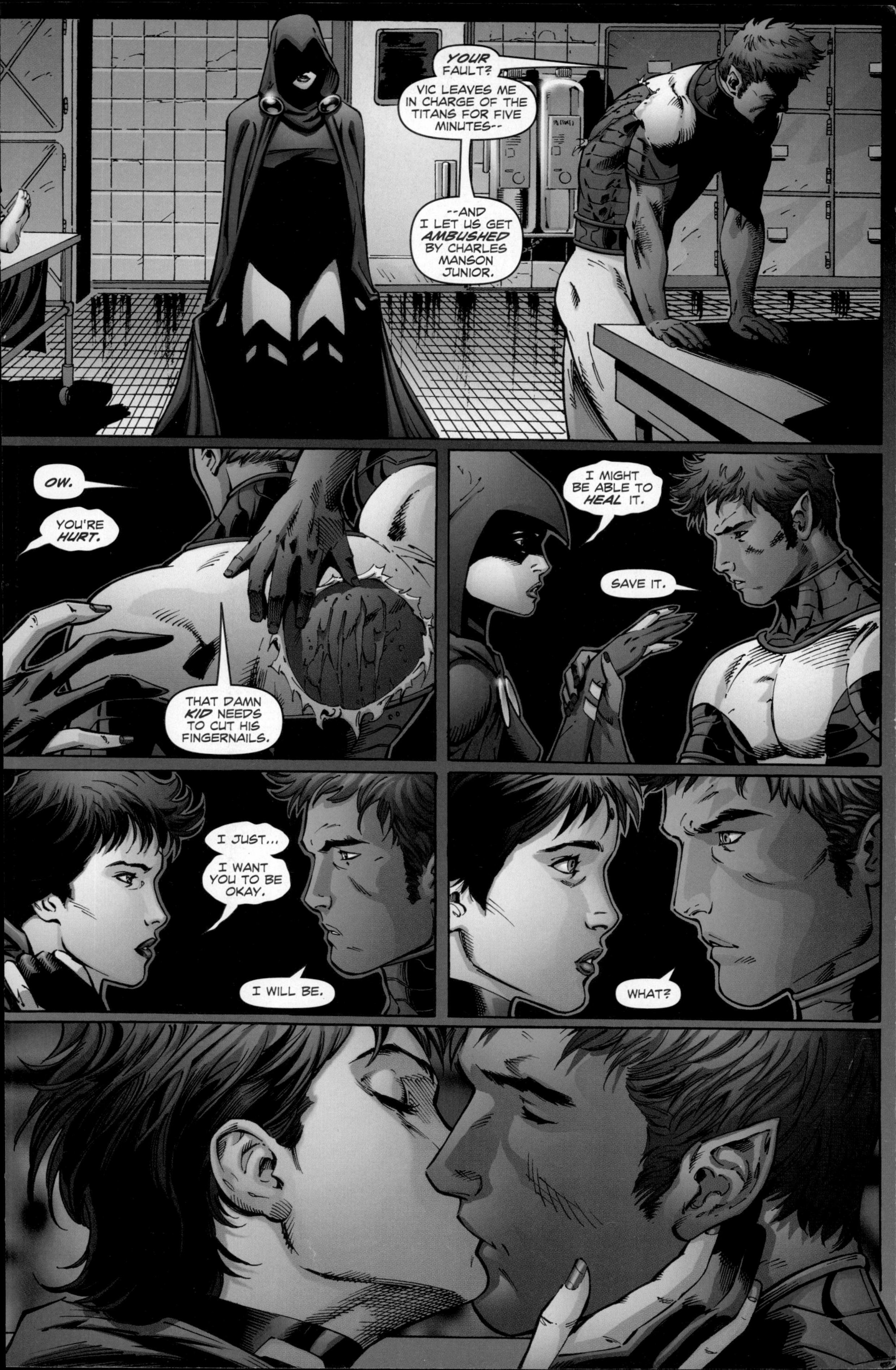
YOUR FAULT?
VIC LEAVES ME IN CHARGE OF THE TITANS FOR FIVE MINUTES--
--AND I LET US GET AMBUSHED BY CHARLES MANSON JUNIOR.
OW.
YOU'RE HURT.
THAT DAMN KID NEEDS TO CUT HIS FINGERNAILS.
I MIGHT BE ABLE TO HEAL IT.
SAVE IT.
I JUST...
I WANT YOU TO BE OKAY.
I WILL BE.
WHAT?

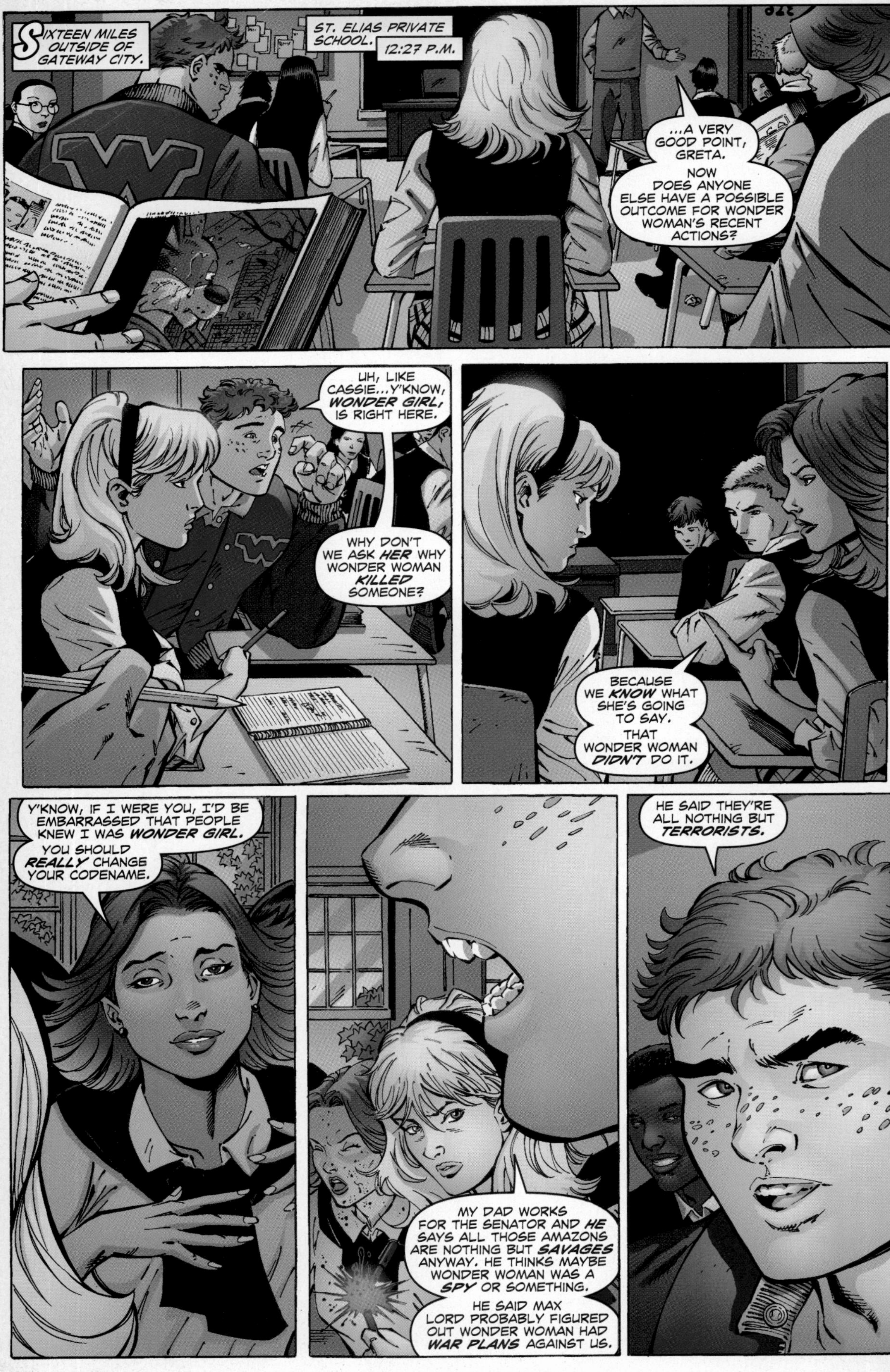
SIXTEEN MILES OUTSIDE OF GATEWAY CITY.
ST. ELIAS PRIVATE SCHOOL.
12:27 P.M.
...A VERY GOOD POINT, GRETA.
NOW DOES ANYONE ELSE HAVE A POSSIBLE OUTCOME FOR WONDER WOMAN'S RECENT ACTIONS?
UH, LIKE CASSIE...Y'KNOW, WONDER GIRL, IS RIGHT HERE.
WHY DON'T WE ASK HER WHY WONDER WOMAN KILLED SOMEONE?
BECAUSE WE KNOW WHAT SHE'S GOING TO SAY.
THAT WONDER WOMAN DIDN'T DO IT.
Y'KNOW, IF I WERE YOU, I'D BE EMBARRASSED THAT PEOPLE KNEW I WAS WONDER GIRL.
YOU SHOULD REALLY CHANGE YOUR CODENAME.
MY DAD WORKS FOR THE SENATOR AND HE SAYS ALL THOSE AMAZONS ARE NOTHING BUT SAVAGES ANYWAY. HE THINKS MAYBE WONDER WOMAN WAS A SPY OR SOMETHING.
HE SAID MAX LORD PROBABLY FIGURED OUT WONDER WOMAN HAD WAR PLANS AGAINST US.
HE SAID THEY'RE ALL NOTHING BUT TERRORISTS.

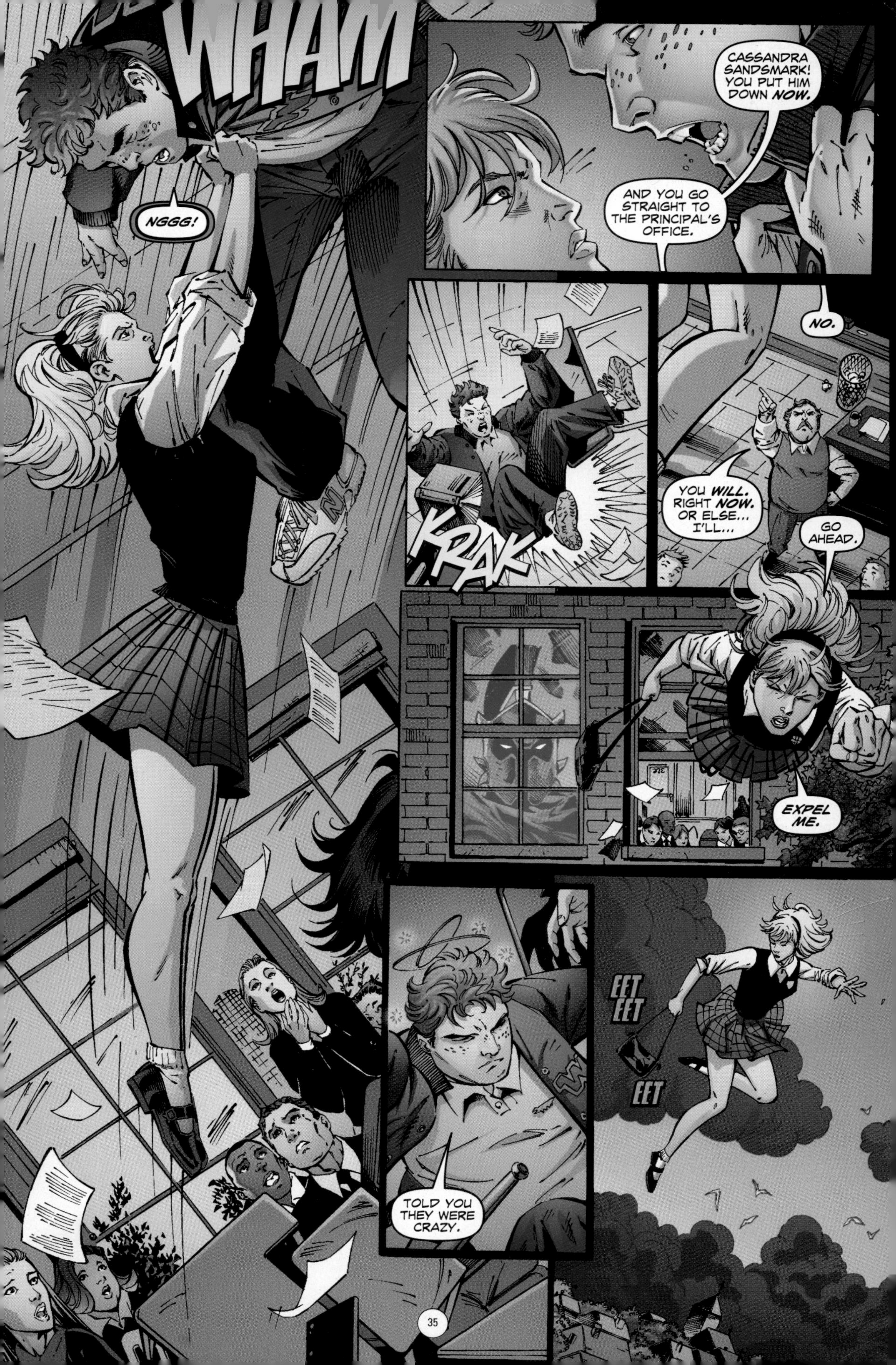
WHAM
NGGG!
CASSANDRA SANDSMARK! YOU PUT HIM DOWN NOW.
AND YOU GO STRAIGHT TO THE PRINCIPAL'S OFFICE.
NO.
KRAK
YOU WILL. RIGHT NOW. OR ELSE... I'LL...
GO AHEAD.
EXPEL ME.
EET EET
EET
TOLD YOU THEY WERE CRAZY.

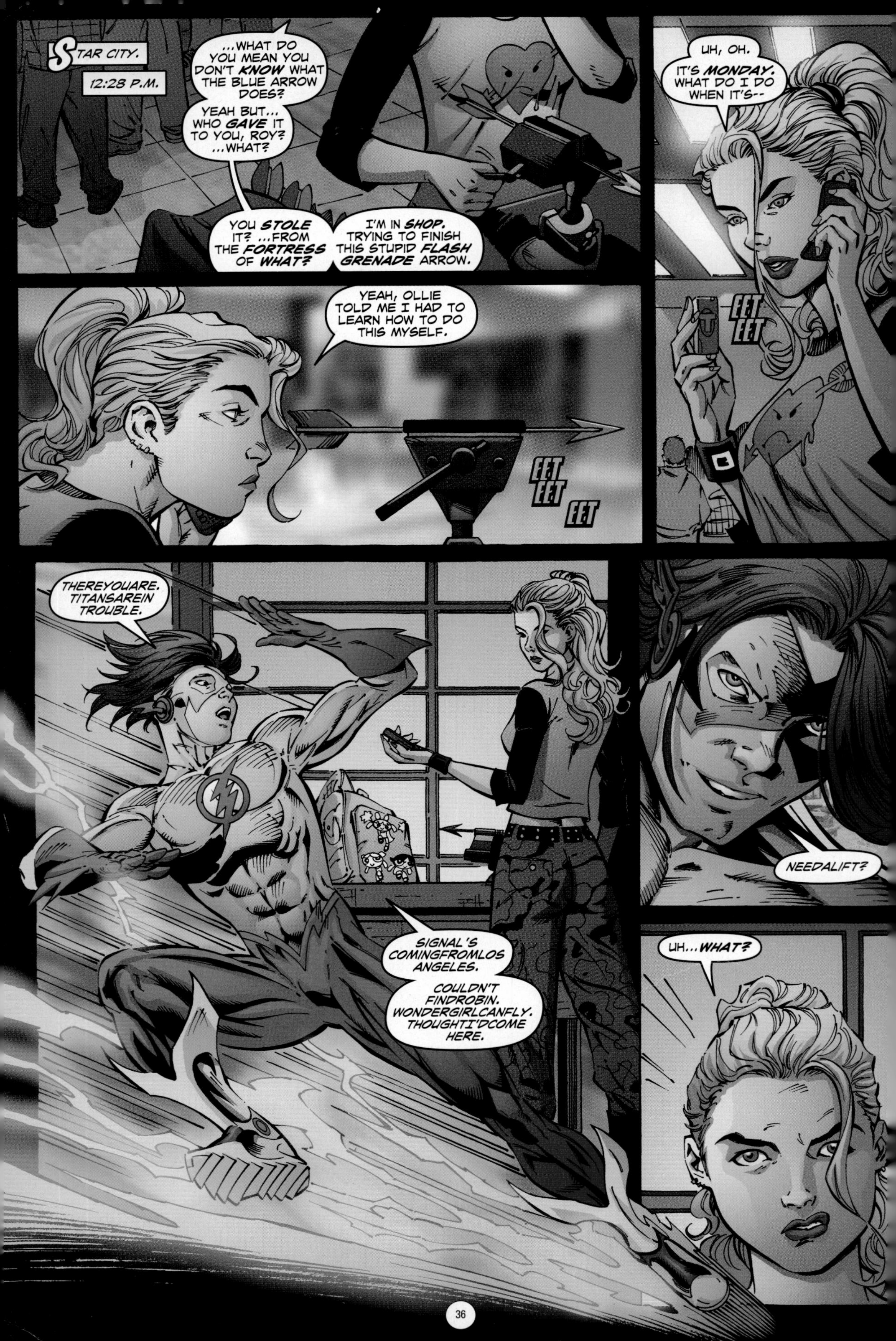
STAR CITY.
12:28 P.M.
...WHAT DO YOU MEAN YOU DON'T KNOW WHAT THE BLUE ARROW DOES?
YEAH BUT... WHO GAVE IT TO YOU, ROY? ...WHAT?
YOU STOLE IT? ...FROM THE FORTRESS OF WHAT?
I'M IN SHOP. TRYING TO FINISH THIS STUPID FLASH GRENADE ARROW.
UH, OH.
IT'S MONDAY. WHAT DO I DO WHEN IT'S--
YEAH, OLLIE TOLD ME I HAD TO LEARN HOW TO DO THIS MYSELF.
EET EET
EET EET EET
THEREYOUARE. TITANSAREIN TROUBLE.
SIGNAL'S COMINGFROMLOS ANGELES.
COULDN'T FINDROBIN. WONDERGIRLCANFLY. THOUGHTI'DCOME HERE.
NEEDALIFT?
UH...WHAT?

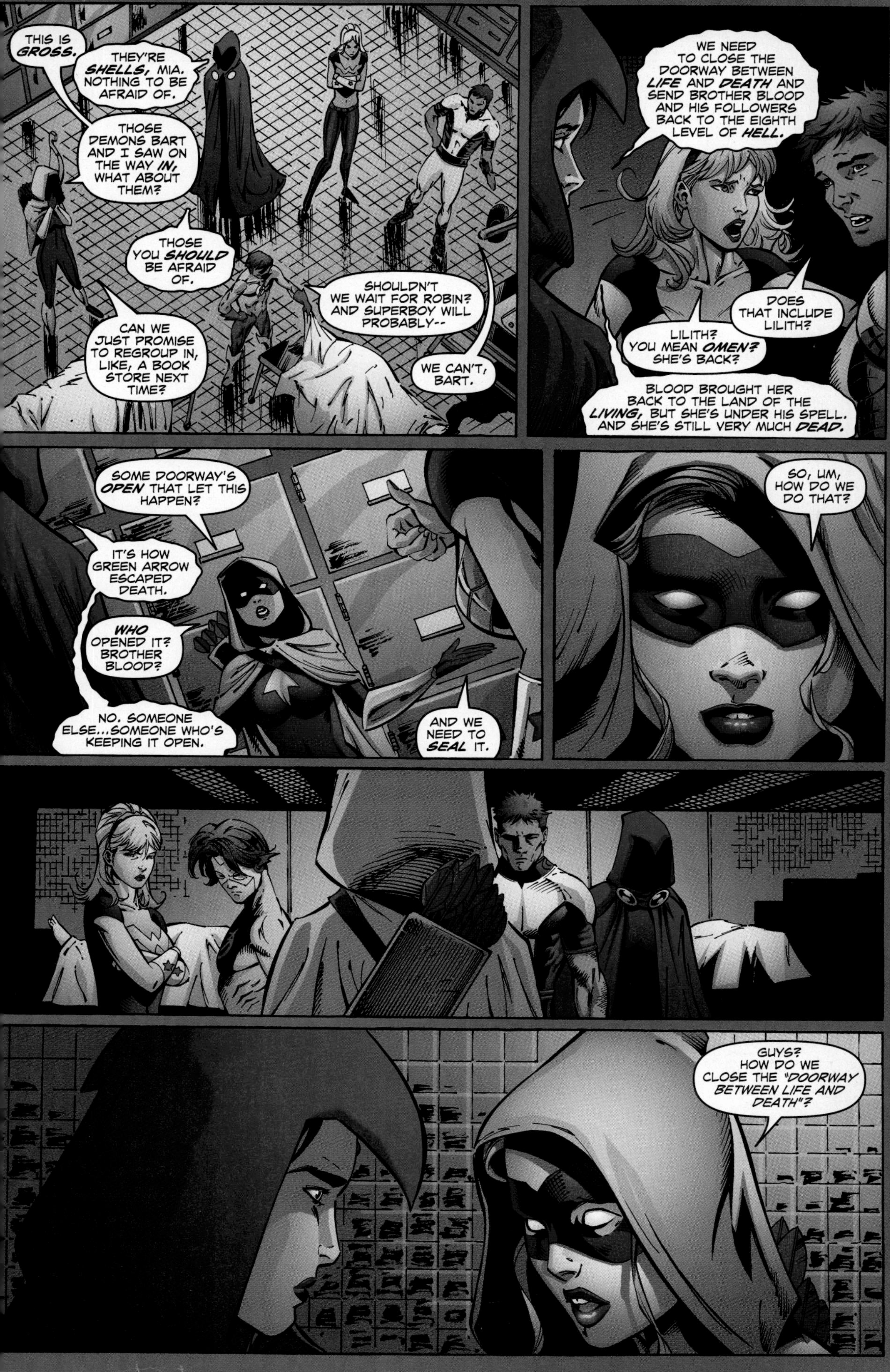
THIS IS GROSS.
THEY'RE SHELLS, MIA. NOTHING TO BE AFRAID OF.
THOSE DEMONS BART AND I SAW ON THE WAY IN, WHAT ABOUT THEM?
THOSE YOU SHOULD BE AFRAID OF.
CAN WE JUST PROMISE TO REGROUP IN, LIKE, A BOOK STORE NEXT TIME?
SHOULDN'T WE WAIT FOR ROBIN? AND SUPERBOY WILL PROBABLY--
WE CAN'T, BART.
WE NEED TO CLOSE THE DOORWAY BETWEEN LIFE AND DEATH AND SEND BROTHER BLOOD AND HIS FOLLOWERS BACK TO THE EIGHTH LEVEL OF HELL.
DOES THAT INCLUDE LILITH?
LILITH? YOU MEAN OMEN? SHE'S BACK?
BLOOD BROUGHT HER BACK TO THE LAND OF THE LIVING, BUT SHE'S UNDER HIS SPELL. AND SHE'S STILL VERY MUCH DEAD.
SOME DOORWAY'S OPEN THAT LET THIS HAPPEN?
IT'S HOW GREEN ARROW ESCAPED DEATH.
WHO OPENED IT? BROTHER BLOOD?
NO. SOMEONE ELSE...SOMEONE WHO'S KEEPING IT OPEN.
AND WE NEED TO SEAL IT.
SO, UM, HOW DO WE DO THAT?
GUYS? HOW DO WE CLOSE THE "DOORWAY BETWEEN LIFE AND DEATH"?

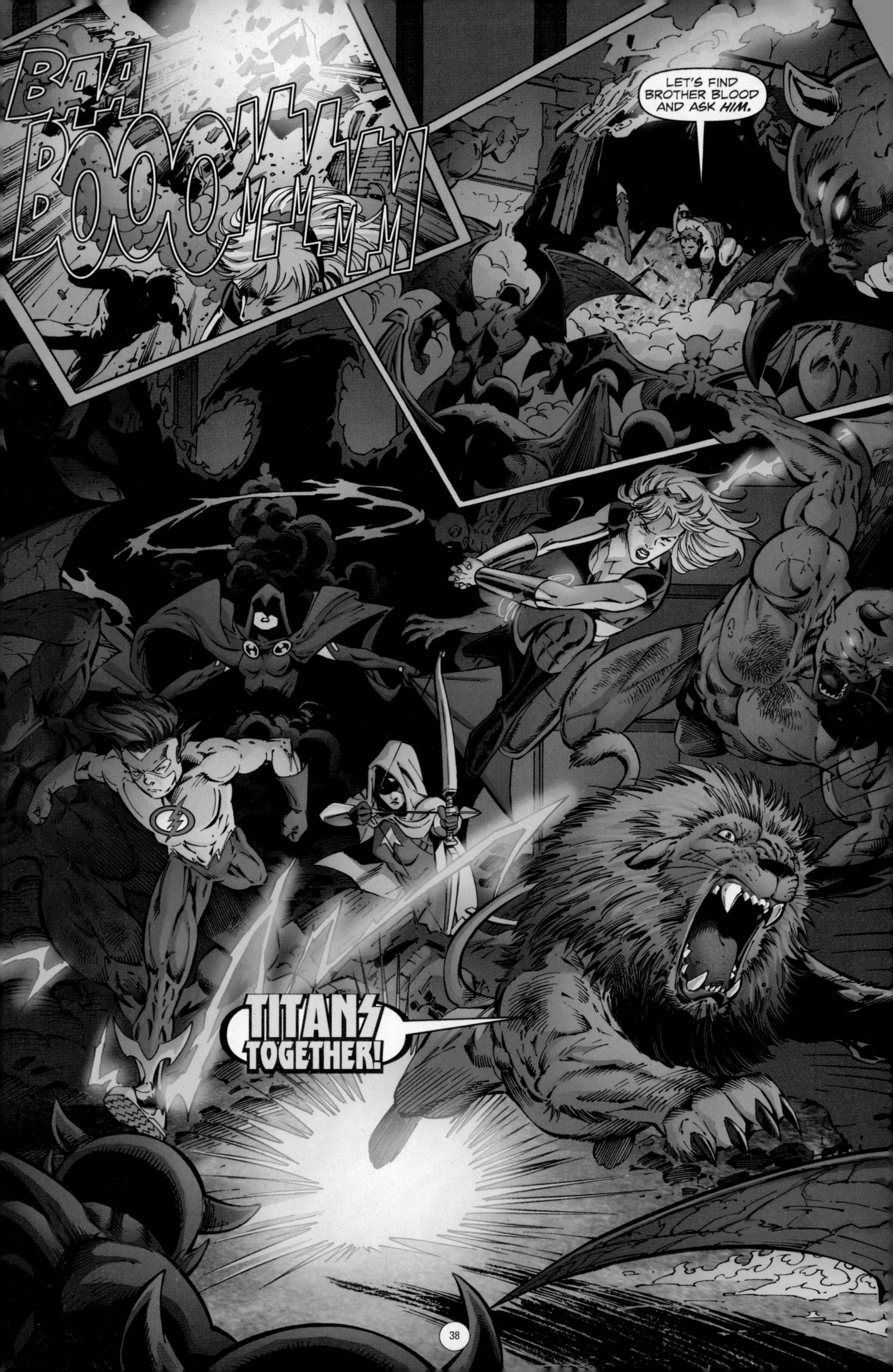
BRA BOOOOOMMMMMM
LET'S FIND BROTHER BLOOD AND ASK *HIM*.
TITANS TOGETHER!

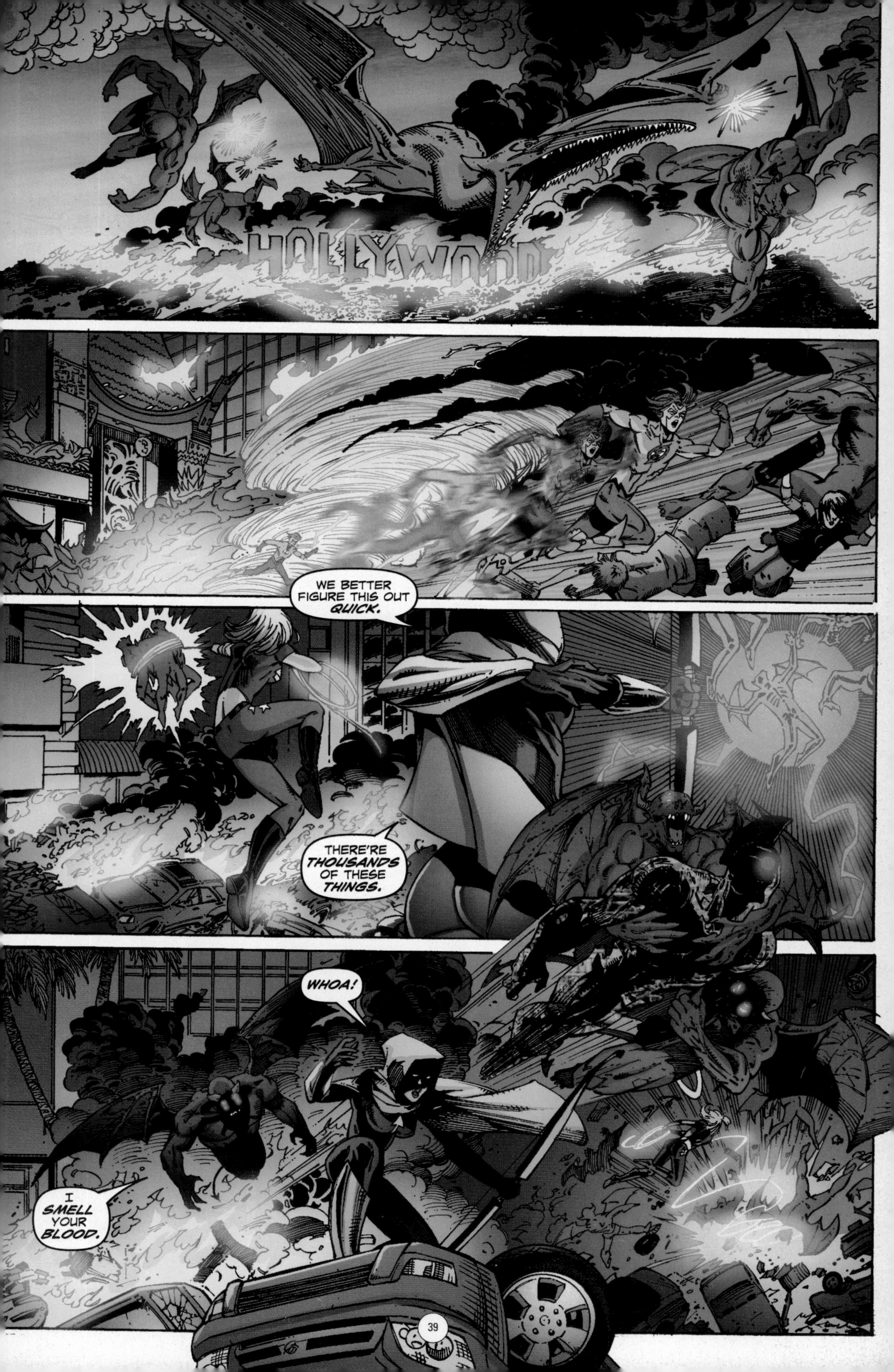
HOLLYWOOD
WE BETTER FIGURE THIS OUT QUICK.
THERE'RE THOUSANDS OF THESE THINGS.
WHOA!
I SMELL YOUR BLOOD.

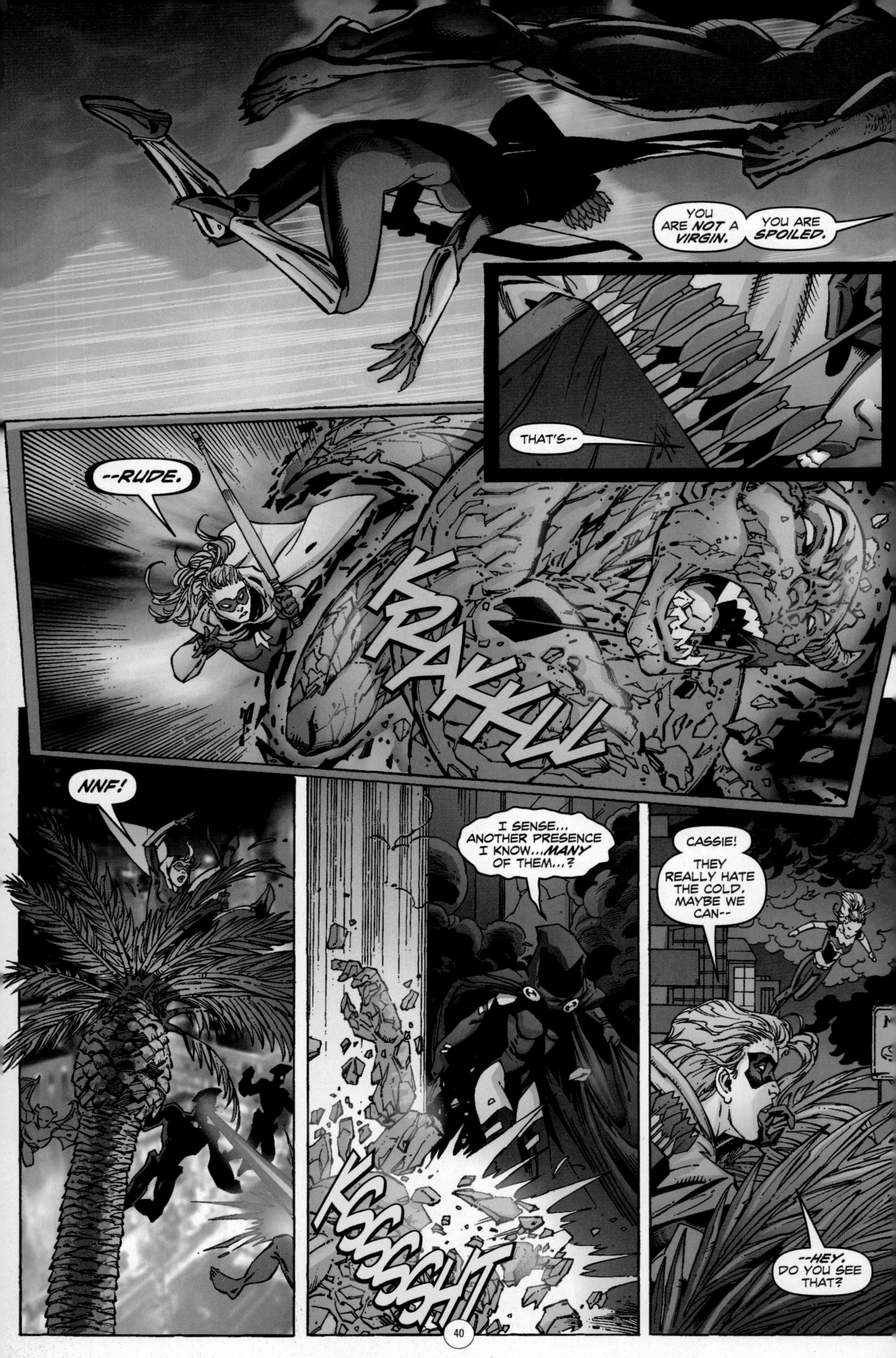

YOU ARE NOT A VIRGIN.
YOU ARE SPOILED.
THAT'S--
--RUDE.
KRAKKLL
NNF!
I SENSE... ANOTHER PRESENCE I KNOW...MANY OF THEM...?
KSSSSCHT
CASSIE!
THEY REALLY HATE THE COLD. MAYBE WE CAN--
--HEY. DO YOU SEE THAT?

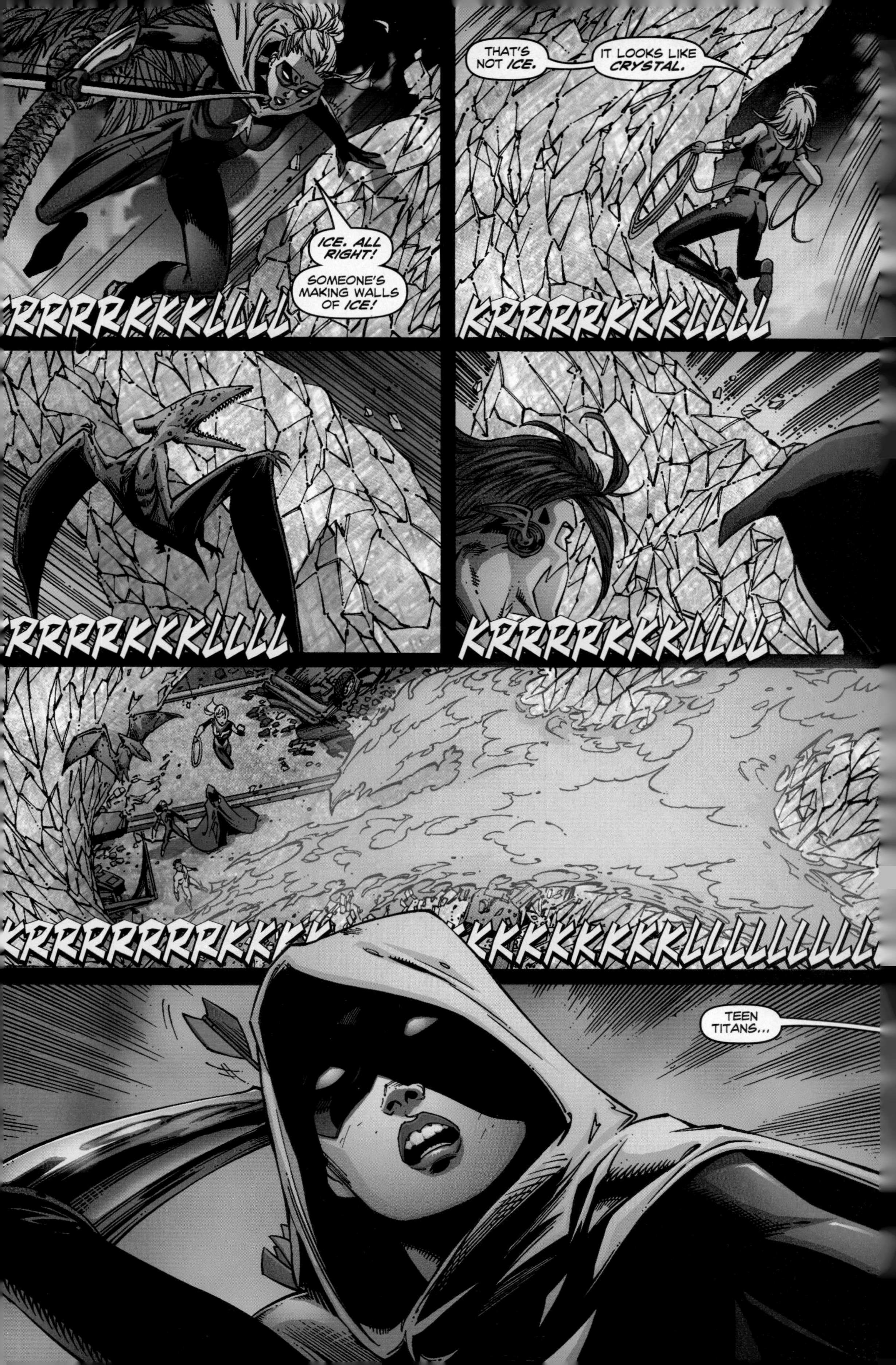
ICE. ALL RIGHT!
SOMEONE'S MAKING WALLS OF ICE!
KRRRRKKKLLLL
THAT'S NOT ICE.
IT LOOKS LIKE CRYSTAL.
KRRRRKKKLLLL
KRRRRKKKLLLL
KRRRRKKKLLLL
KRRRRRRRRKKK
KKKKKKKKRLLLLLLLLL
TEEN TITANS...

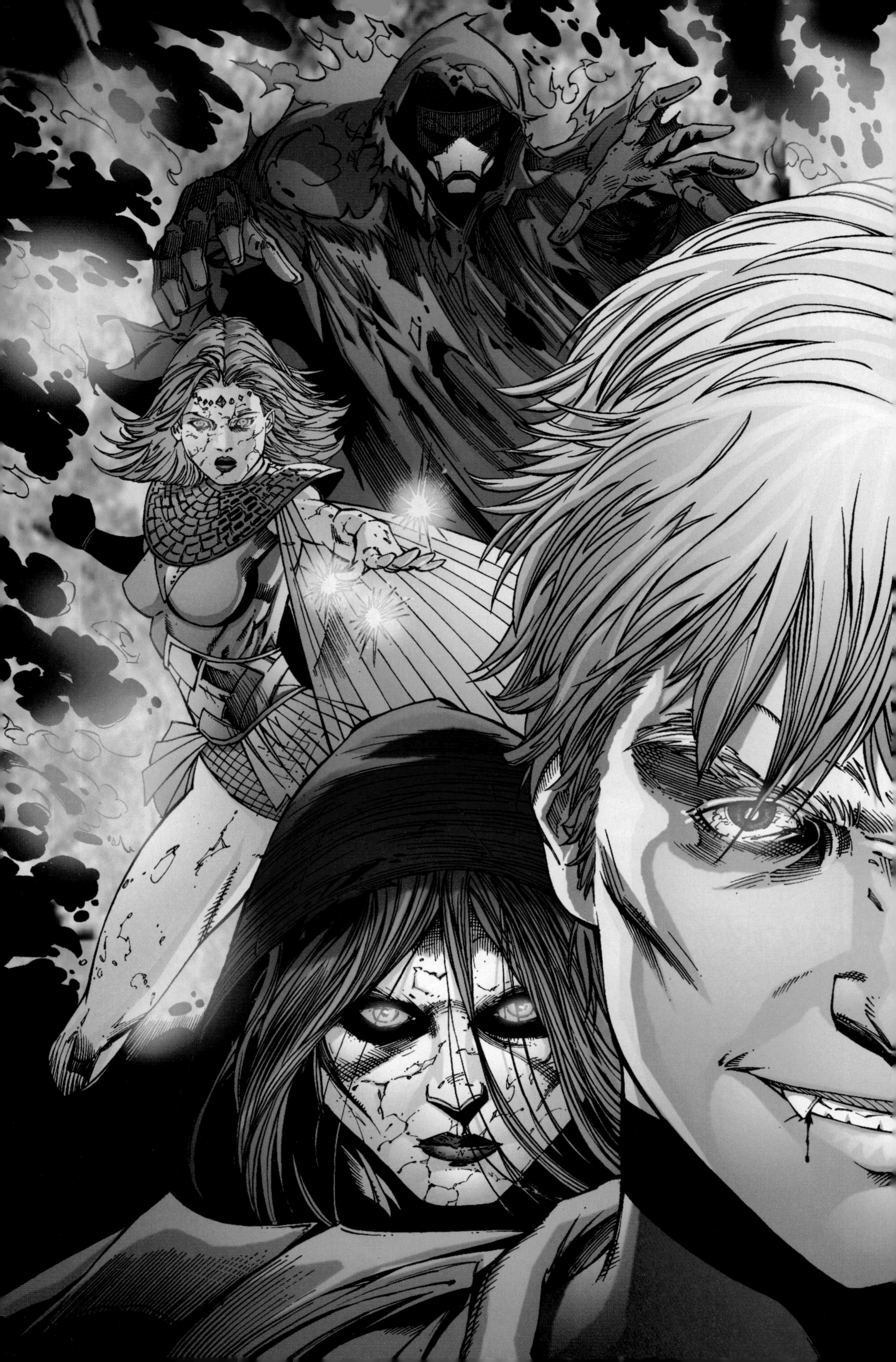

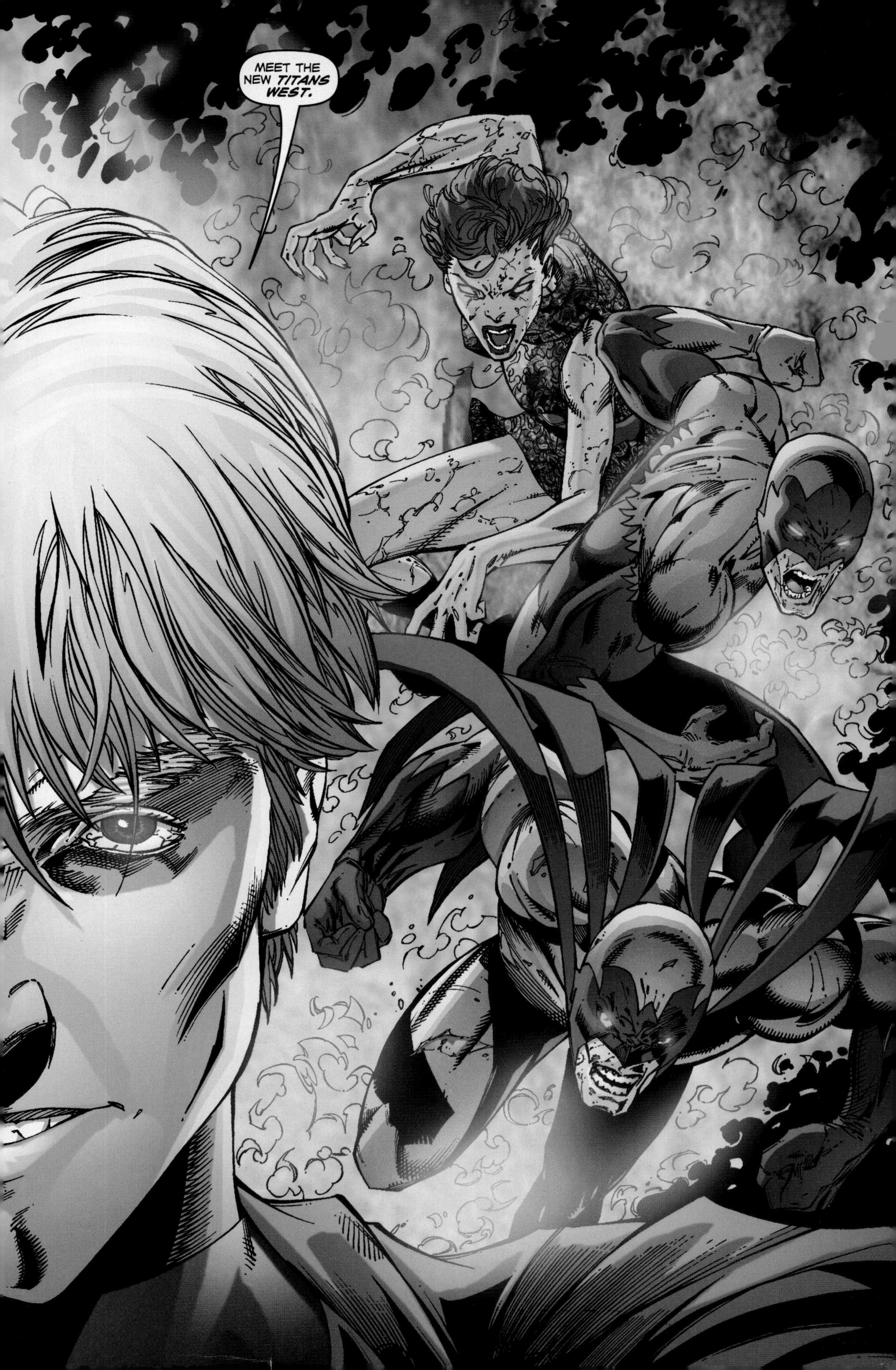
MEET THE NEW TITANS WEST.

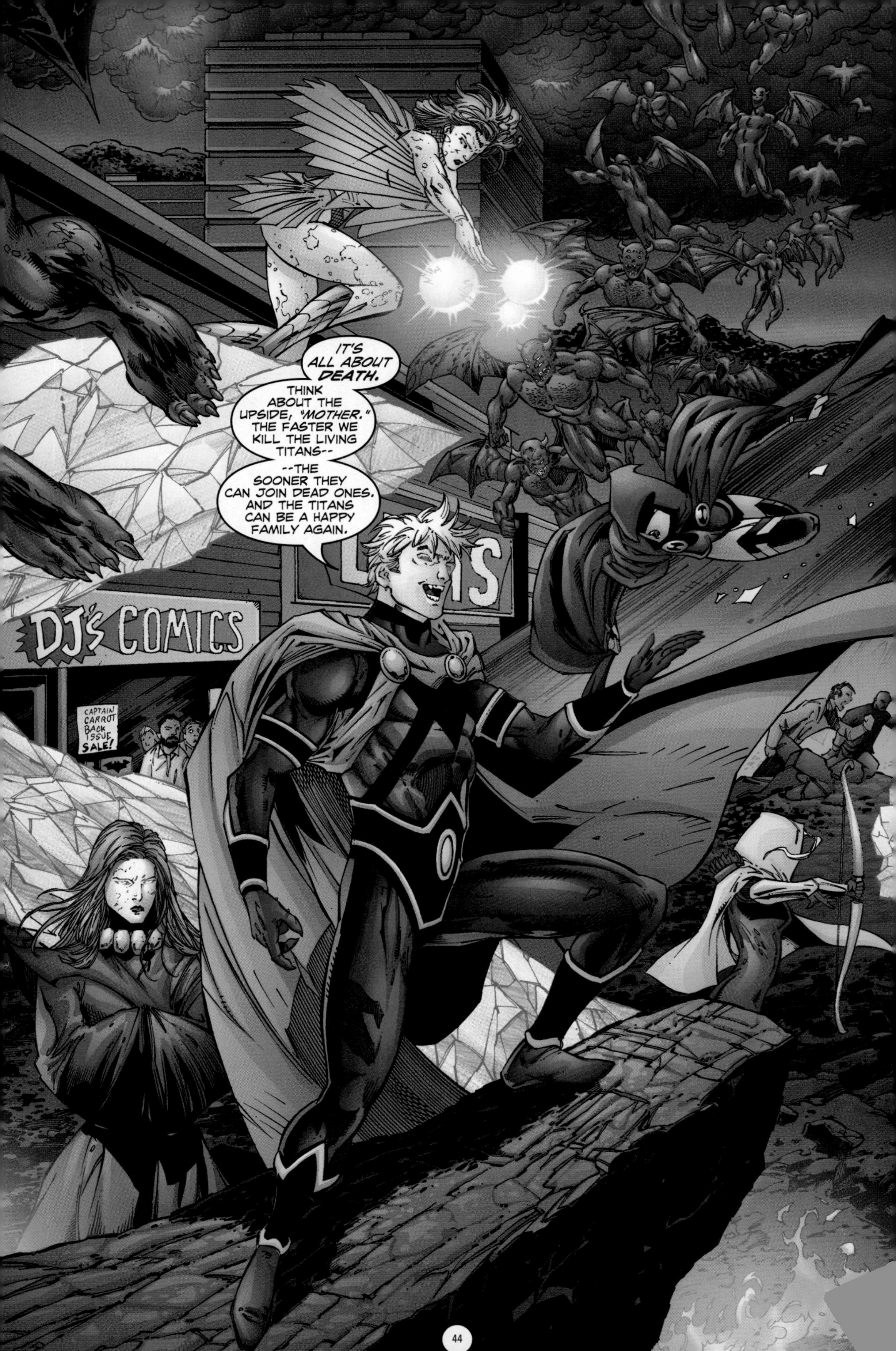
IT'S ALL ABOUT DEATH.
THINK ABOUT THE UPSIDE, "MOTHER." THE FASTER WE KILL THE LIVING TITANS--
--THE SOONER THEY CAN JOIN DEAD ONES. AND THE TITANS CAN BE A HAPPY FAMILY AGAIN.
DJ's COMICS
CAPTAIN CARROT BACK ISSUE SALE!

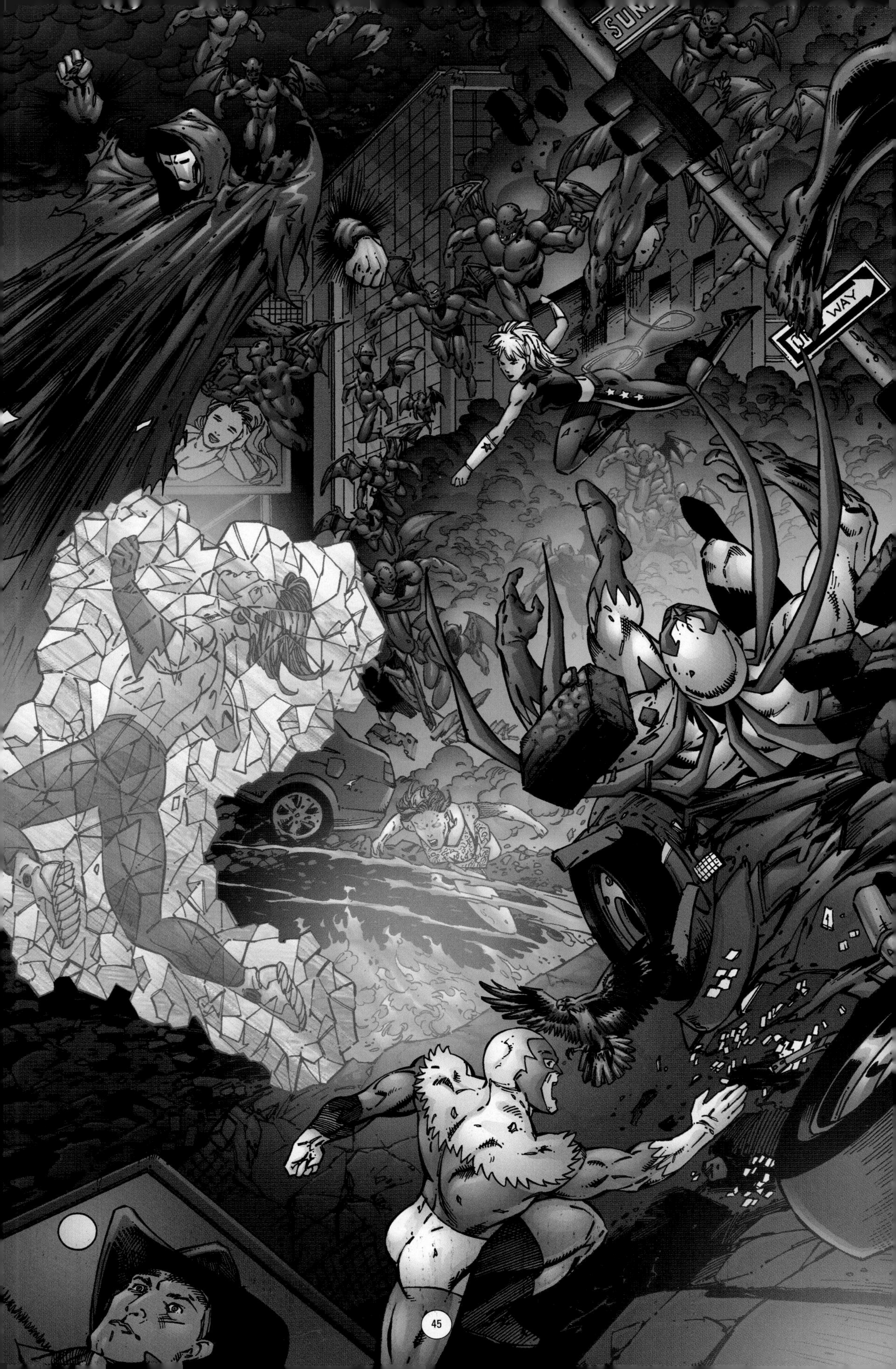
WAY

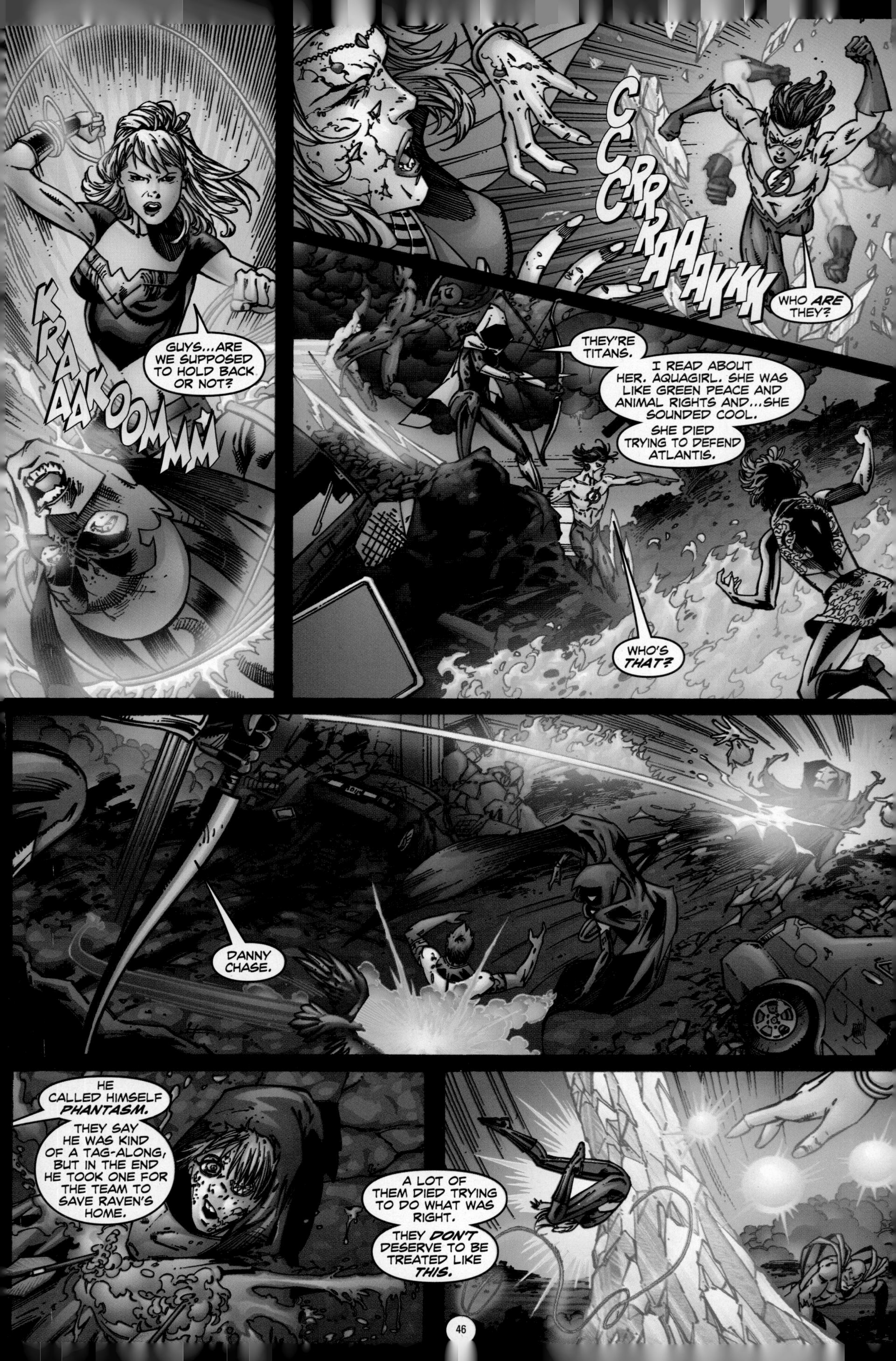
CCCRRRAAAAKKKK
WHO ARE THEY?
KRAAAKOOMMM
GUYS...ARE WE SUPPOSED TO HOLD BACK OR NOT?
THEY'RE TITANS.
I READ ABOUT HER. AQUAGIRL. SHE WAS LIKE GREEN PEACE AND ANIMAL RIGHTS AND...SHE SOUNDED COOL.
SHE DIED TRYING TO DEFEND ATLANTIS.
WHO'S THAT?
DANNY CHASE.
HE CALLED HIMSELF PHANTASM.
THEY SAY HE WAS KIND OF A TAG-ALONG, BUT IN THE END HE TOOK ONE FOR THE TEAM TO SAVE RAVEN'S HOME.
A LOT OF THEM DIED TRYING TO DO WHAT WAS RIGHT.
THEY DON'T DESERVE TO BE TREATED LIKE THIS.

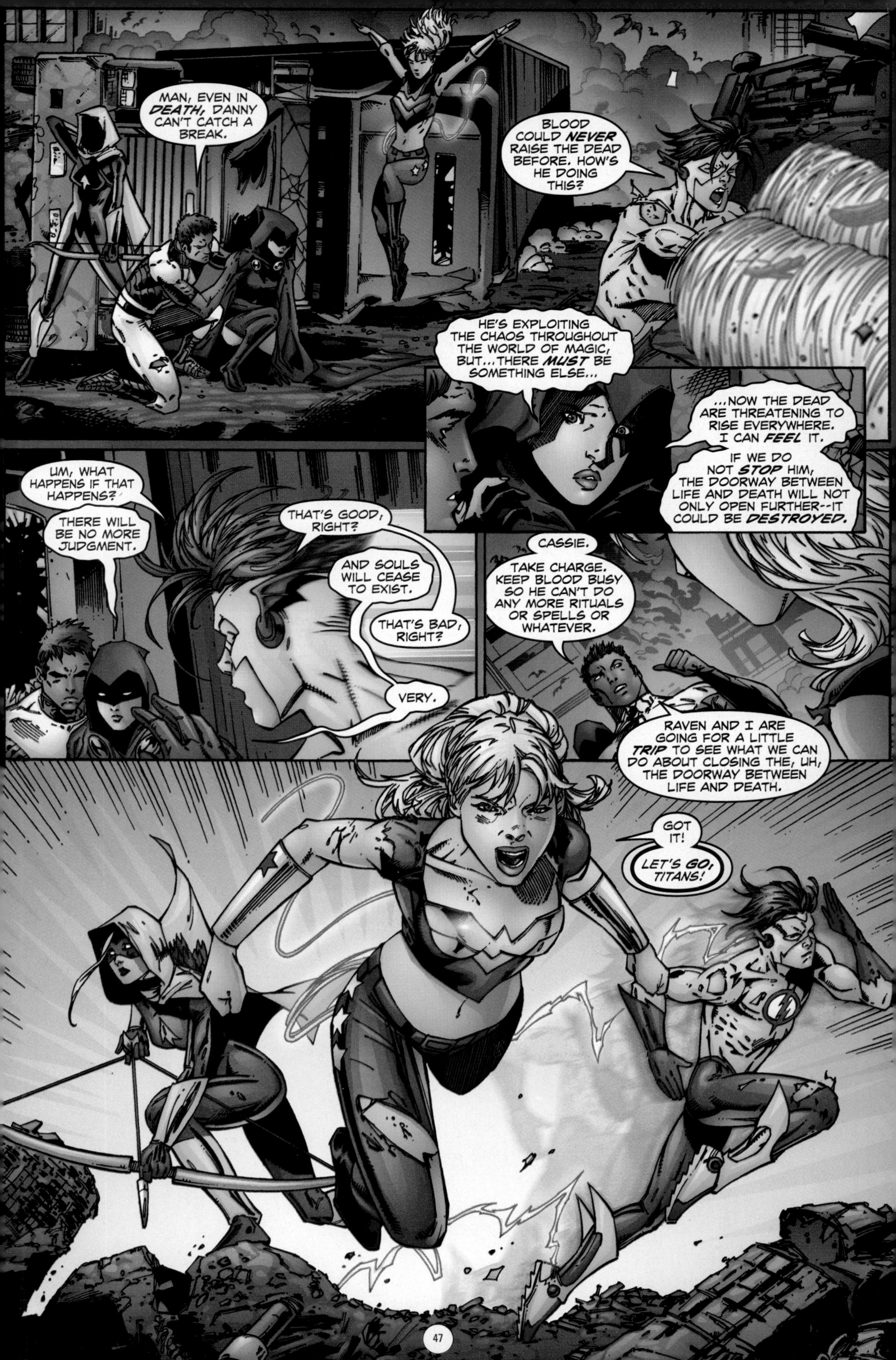

MAN, EVEN IN DEATH, DANNY CAN'T CATCH A BREAK.
BLOOD COULD NEVER RAISE THE DEAD BEFORE. HOW'S HE DOING THIS?
HE'S EXPLOITING THE CHAOS THROUGHOUT THE WORLD OF MAGIC, BUT...THERE MUST BE SOMETHING ELSE...
...NOW THE DEAD ARE THREATENING TO RISE EVERYWHERE. I CAN FEEL IT.
IF WE DO NOT STOP HIM, THE DOORWAY BETWEEN LIFE AND DEATH WILL NOT ONLY OPEN FURTHER--IT COULD BE DESTROYED.
UM, WHAT HAPPENS IF THAT HAPPENS?
THERE WILL BE NO MORE JUDGMENT.
THAT'S GOOD, RIGHT?
AND SOULS WILL CEASE TO EXIST.
THAT'S BAD, RIGHT?
VERY.
CASSIE.
TAKE CHARGE. KEEP BLOOD BUSY SO HE CAN'T DO ANY MORE RITUALS OR SPELLS OR WHATEVER.
RAVEN AND I ARE GOING FOR A LITTLE TRIP TO SEE WHAT WE CAN DO ABOUT CLOSING THE, UH, THE DOORWAY BETWEEN LIFE AND DEATH.
GOT IT!
LET'S GO, TITANS!

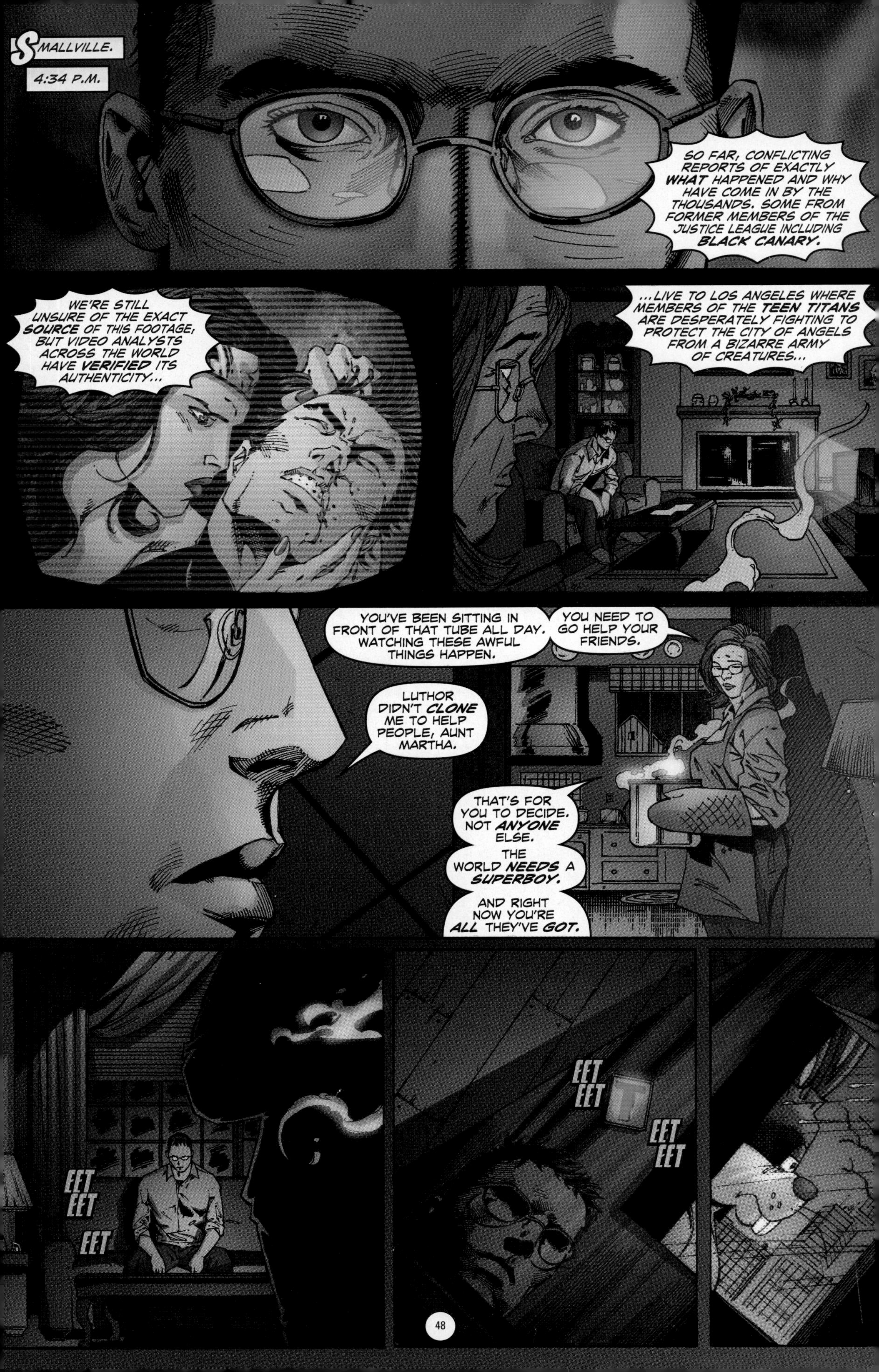
SMALLVILLE.
4:34 P.M.
SO FAR, CONFLICTING REPORTS OF EXACTLY WHAT HAPPENED AND WHY HAVE COME IN BY THE THOUSANDS. SOME FROM FORMER MEMBERS OF THE JUSTICE LEAGUE INCLUDING BLACK CANARY.
WE'RE STILL UNSURE OF THE EXACT SOURCE OF THIS FOOTAGE; BUT VIDEO ANALYSTS ACROSS THE WORLD HAVE VERIFIED ITS AUTHENTICITY...
...LIVE TO LOS ANGELES WHERE MEMBERS OF THE TEEN TITANS ARE DESPERATELY FIGHTING TO PROTECT THE CITY OF ANGELS FROM A BIZARRE ARMY OF CREATURES...
YOU'VE BEEN SITTING IN FRONT OF THAT TUBE ALL DAY. WATCHING THESE AWFUL THINGS HAPPEN.
YOU NEED TO GO HELP YOUR FRIENDS.
LUTHOR DIDN'T CLONE ME TO HELP PEOPLE, AUNT MARTHA.
THAT'S FOR YOU TO DECIDE. NOT ANYONE ELSE.
THE WORLD NEEDS A SUPERBOY.
AND RIGHT NOW YOU'RE ALL THEY'VE GOT.
EET EET
EET
EET EET
EET EET

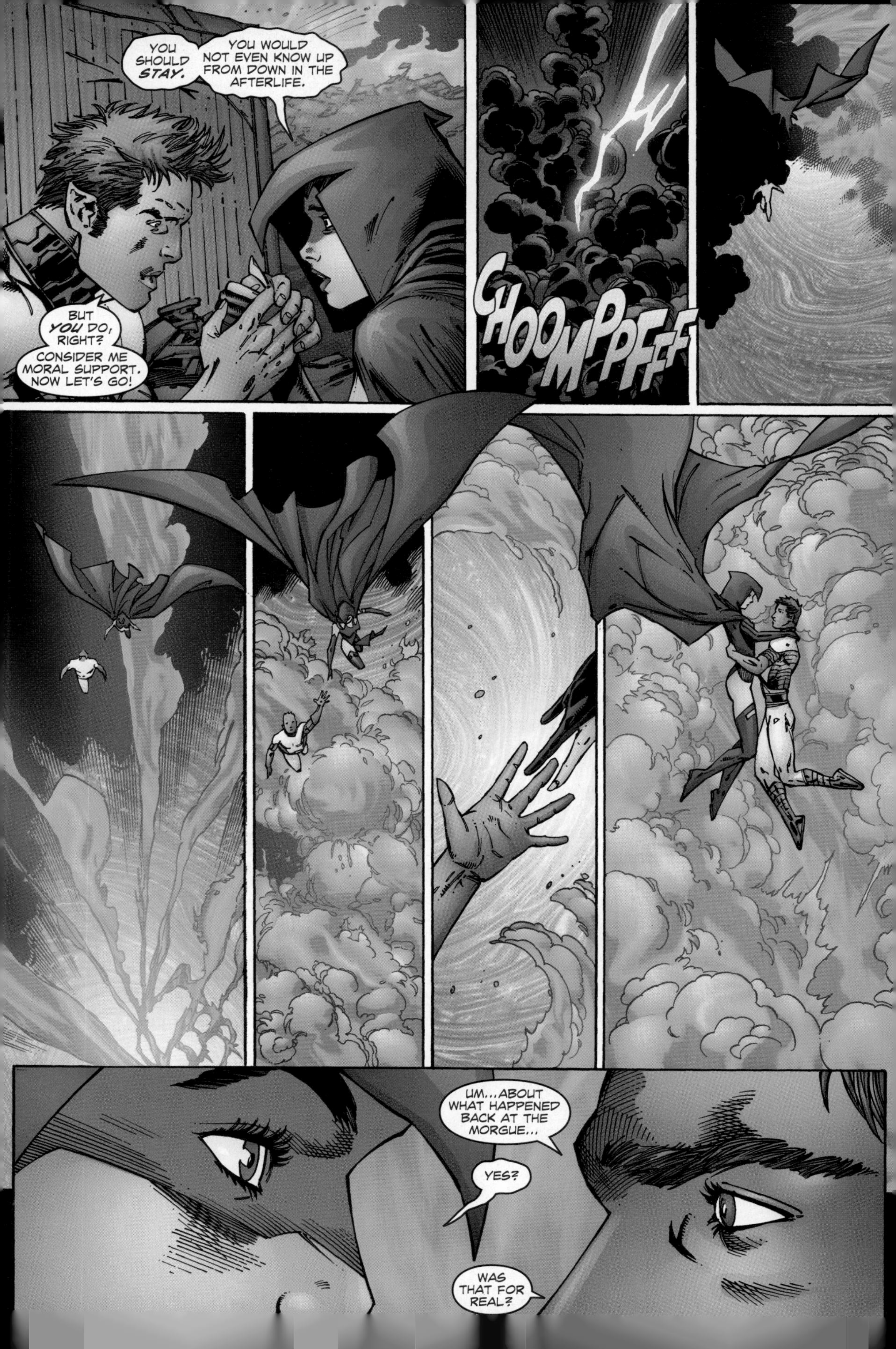
YOU SHOULD STAY.
YOU WOULD NOT EVEN KNOW UP FROM DOWN IN THE AFTERLIFE.
BUT YOU DO, RIGHT? CONSIDER ME MORAL SUPPORT. NOW LET'S GO!
CHOOMPPFFF
UM...ABOUT WHAT HAPPENED BACK AT THE MORGUE...
YES?
WAS THAT FOR REAL?

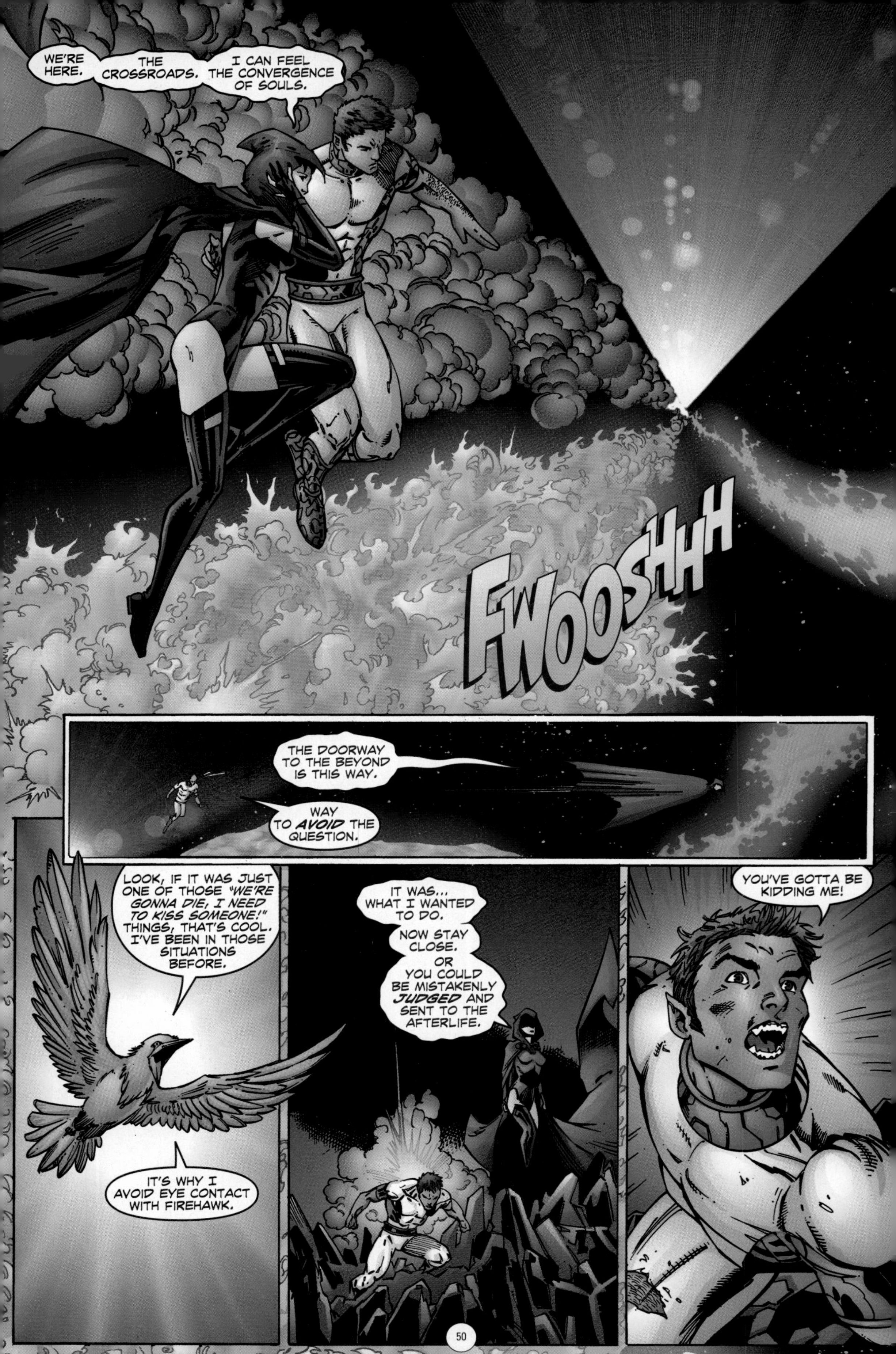
WE'RE HERE.
THE CROSSROADS.
I CAN FEEL THE CONVERGENCE OF SOULS.
FWOOSHHH
THE DOORWAY TO THE BEYOND IS THIS WAY.
WAY TO *AVOID* THE QUESTION.
LOOK, IF IT WAS JUST ONE OF THOSE *"WE'RE GONNA DIE, I NEED TO KISS SOMEONE!"* THINGS, THAT'S COOL. I'VE BEEN IN THOSE SITUATIONS BEFORE.
IT'S WHY I AVOID EYE CONTACT WITH FIREHAWK.
IT WAS... WHAT I WANTED TO DO.
NOW STAY CLOSE.
OR YOU COULD BE MISTAKENLY *JUDGED* AND SENT TO THE AFTERLIFE.
YOU'VE GOTTA BE KIDDING ME!

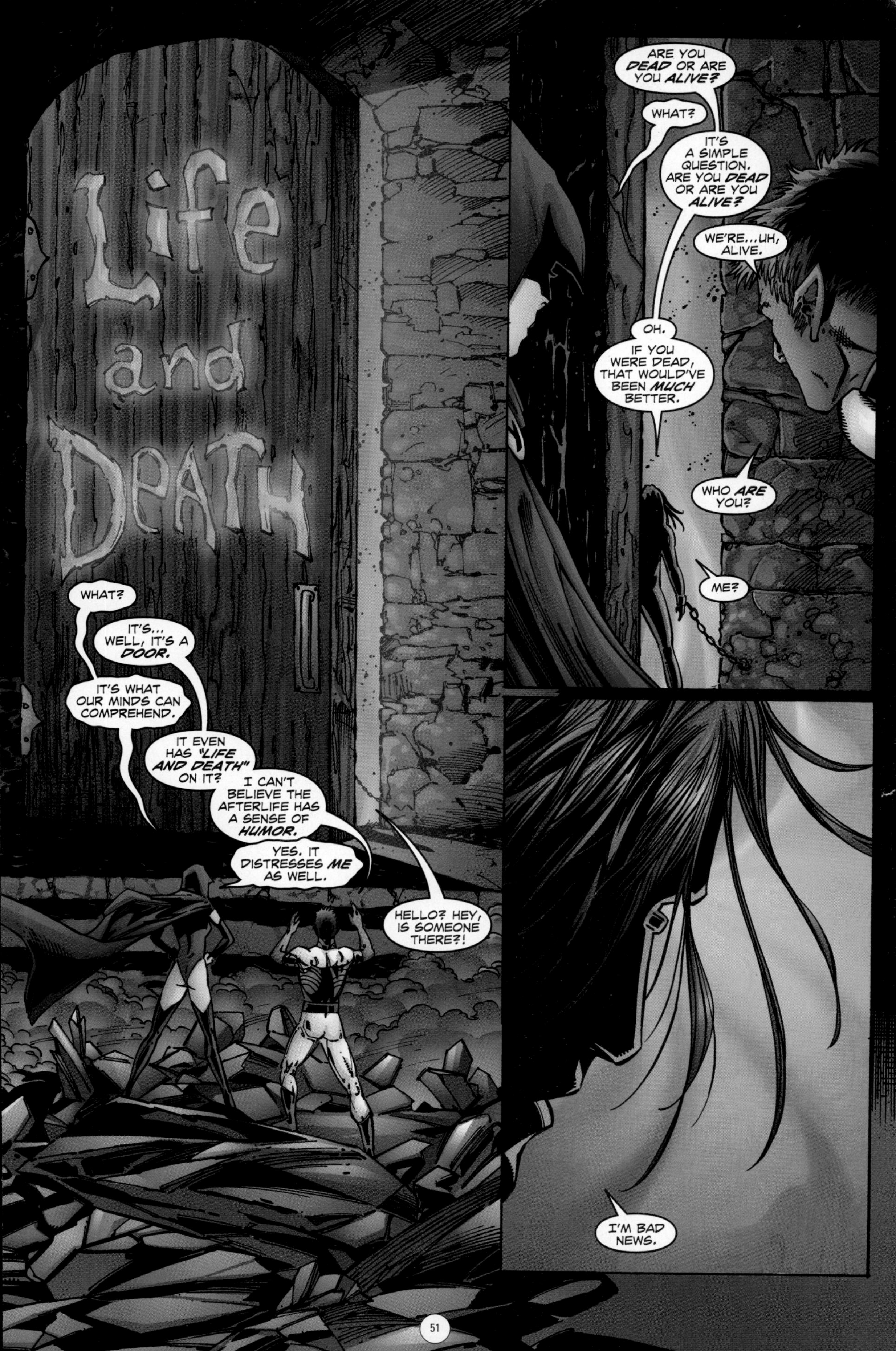
Life and DEATH
WHAT?
IT'S... WELL, IT'S A DOOR.
IT'S WHAT OUR MINDS CAN COMPREHEND.
IT EVEN HAS "LIFE AND DEATH" ON IT?
I CAN'T BELIEVE THE AFTERLIFE HAS A SENSE OF HUMOR.
YES. IT DISTRESSES ME AS WELL.
HELLO? HEY, IS SOMEONE THERE?!
ARE YOU DEAD OR ARE YOU ALIVE?
WHAT?
IT'S A SIMPLE QUESTION. ARE YOU DEAD OR ARE YOU ALIVE?
WE'RE...UH, ALIVE.
OH.
IF YOU WERE DEAD, THAT WOULD'VE BEEN MUCH BETTER.
WHO ARE YOU?
ME?
I'M BAD NEWS.

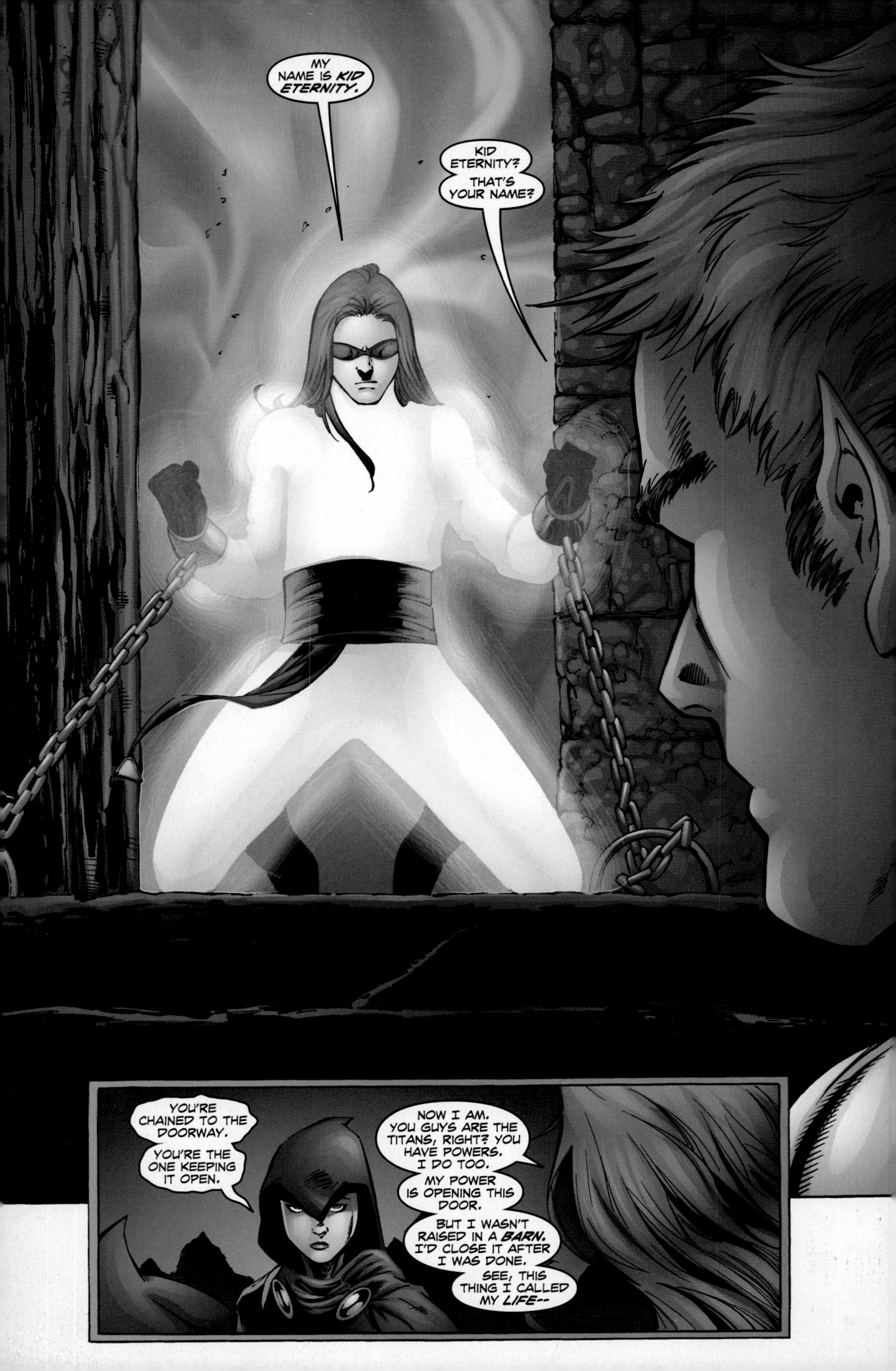

MY NAME IS *KID ETERNITY.*
KID ETERNITY? THAT'S YOUR NAME?
YOU'RE CHAINED TO THE DOORWAY.
YOU'RE THE ONE KEEPING IT OPEN.
NOW I AM. YOU GUYS ARE THE TITANS, RIGHT? YOU HAVE POWERS. I DO TOO.
MY POWER IS OPENING THIS DOOR.
BUT I WASN'T RAISED IN A *BARN.* I'D CLOSE IT AFTER I WAS DONE.
SEE, THIS THING I CALLED MY *LIFE--*

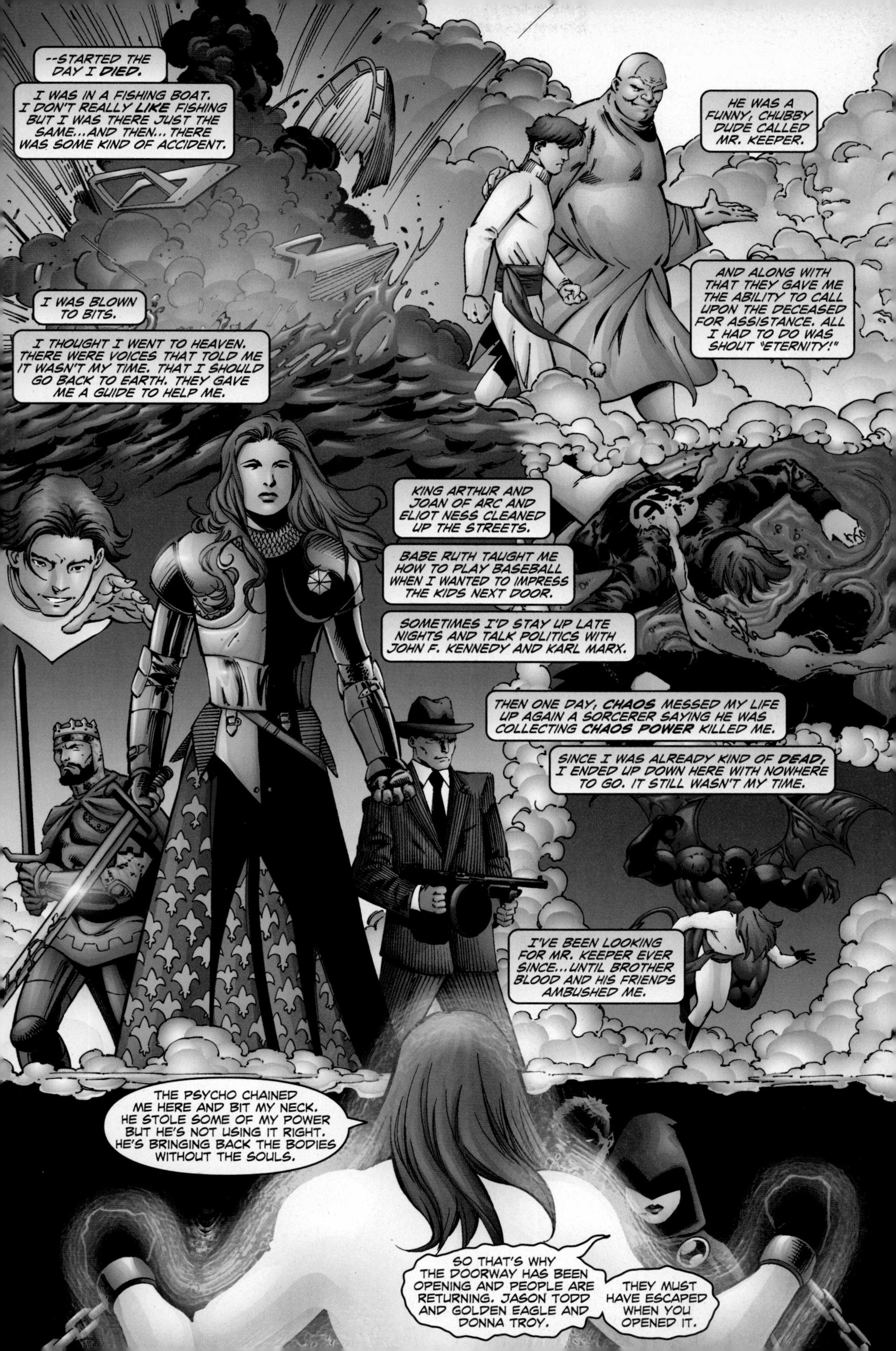

--STARTED THE DAY I DIED.
I WAS IN A FISHING BOAT. I DON'T REALLY LIKE FISHING BUT I WAS THERE JUST THE SAME...AND THEN...THERE WAS SOME KIND OF ACCIDENT.
HE WAS A FUNNY, CHUBBY DUDE CALLED MR. KEEPER.
I WAS BLOWN TO BITS.
I THOUGHT I WENT TO HEAVEN. THERE WERE VOICES THAT TOLD ME IT WASN'T MY TIME. THAT I SHOULD GO BACK TO EARTH. THEY GAVE ME A GUIDE TO HELP ME.
AND ALONG WITH THAT THEY GAVE ME THE ABILITY TO CALL UPON THE DECEASED FOR ASSISTANCE. ALL I HAD TO DO WAS SHOUT "ETERNITY!"
KING ARTHUR AND JOAN OF ARC AND ELIOT NESS CLEANED UP THE STREETS.
BABE RUTH TAUGHT ME HOW TO PLAY BASEBALL WHEN I WANTED TO IMPRESS THE KIDS NEXT DOOR.
SOMETIMES I'D STAY UP LATE NIGHTS AND TALK POLITICS WITH JOHN F. KENNEDY AND KARL MARX.
THEN ONE DAY, CHAOS MESSED MY LIFE UP AGAIN A SORCERER SAYING HE WAS COLLECTING CHAOS POWER KILLED ME.
SINCE I WAS ALREADY KIND OF DEAD, I ENDED UP DOWN HERE WITH NOWHERE TO GO. IT STILL WASN'T MY TIME.
I'VE BEEN LOOKING FOR MR. KEEPER EVER SINCE...UNTIL BROTHER BLOOD AND HIS FRIENDS AMBUSHED ME.
THE PSYCHO CHAINED ME HERE AND BIT MY NECK. HE STOLE SOME OF MY POWER BUT HE'S NOT USING IT RIGHT. HE'S BRINGING BACK THE BODIES WITHOUT THE SOULS.
SO THAT'S WHY THE DOORWAY HAS BEEN OPENING AND PEOPLE ARE RETURNING. JASON TODD AND GOLDEN EAGLE AND DONNA TROY.
THEY MUST HAVE ESCAPED WHEN YOU OPENED IT.

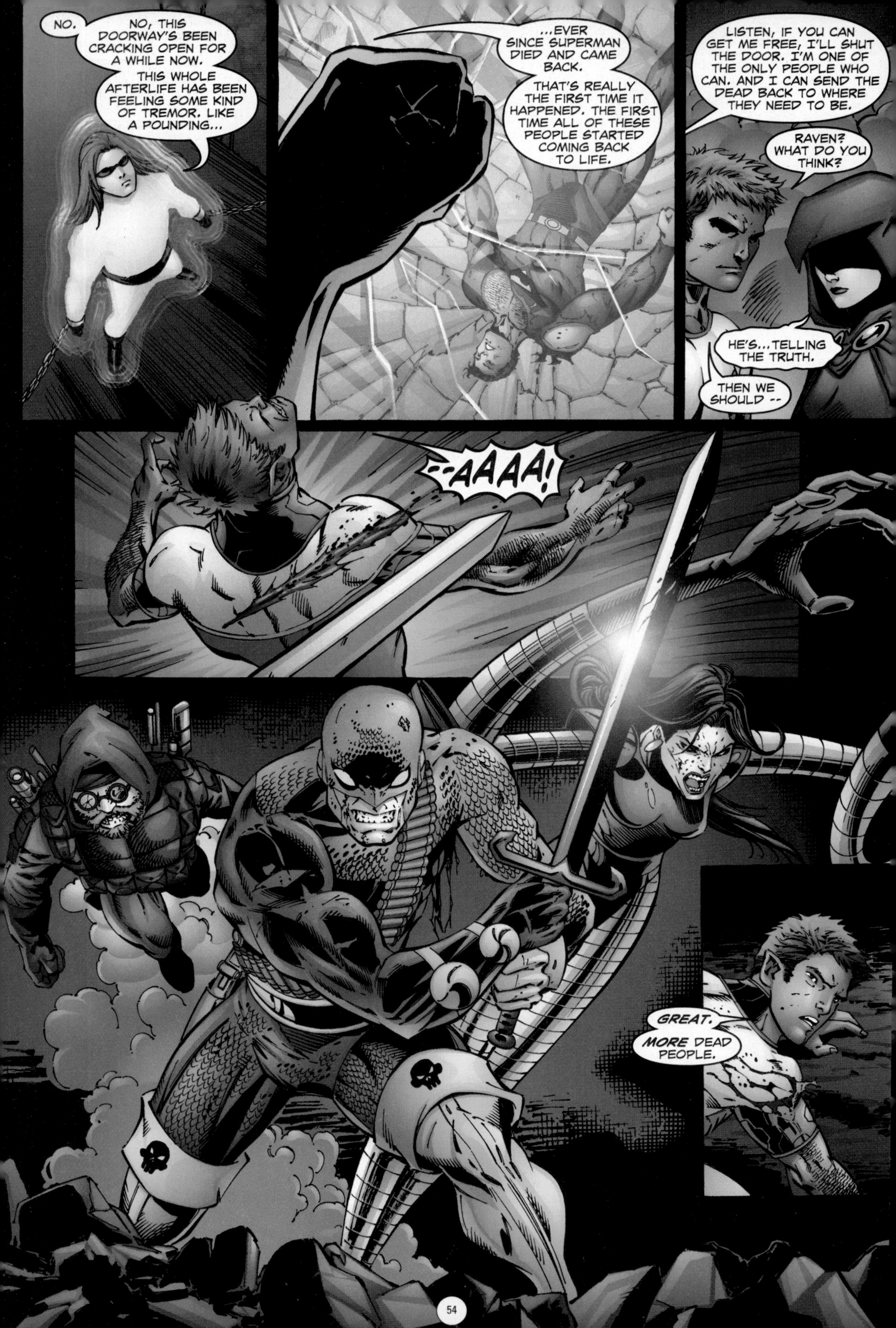
NO.
NO, THIS DOORWAY'S BEEN CRACKING OPEN FOR A WHILE NOW.
THIS WHOLE AFTERLIFE HAS BEEN FEELING SOME KIND OF TREMOR. LIKE A POUNDING...
...EVER SINCE SUPERMAN DIED AND CAME BACK.
THAT'S REALLY THE FIRST TIME IT HAPPENED. THE FIRST TIME ALL OF THESE PEOPLE STARTED COMING BACK TO LIFE.
LISTEN, IF YOU CAN GET ME FREE, I'LL SHUT THE DOOR. I'M ONE OF THE ONLY PEOPLE WHO CAN. AND I CAN SEND THE DEAD BACK TO WHERE THEY NEED TO BE.
RAVEN? WHAT DO YOU THINK?
HE'S...TELLING THE TRUTH.
THEN WE SHOULD --
--AAAA!
GREAT.
MORE DEAD PEOPLE.

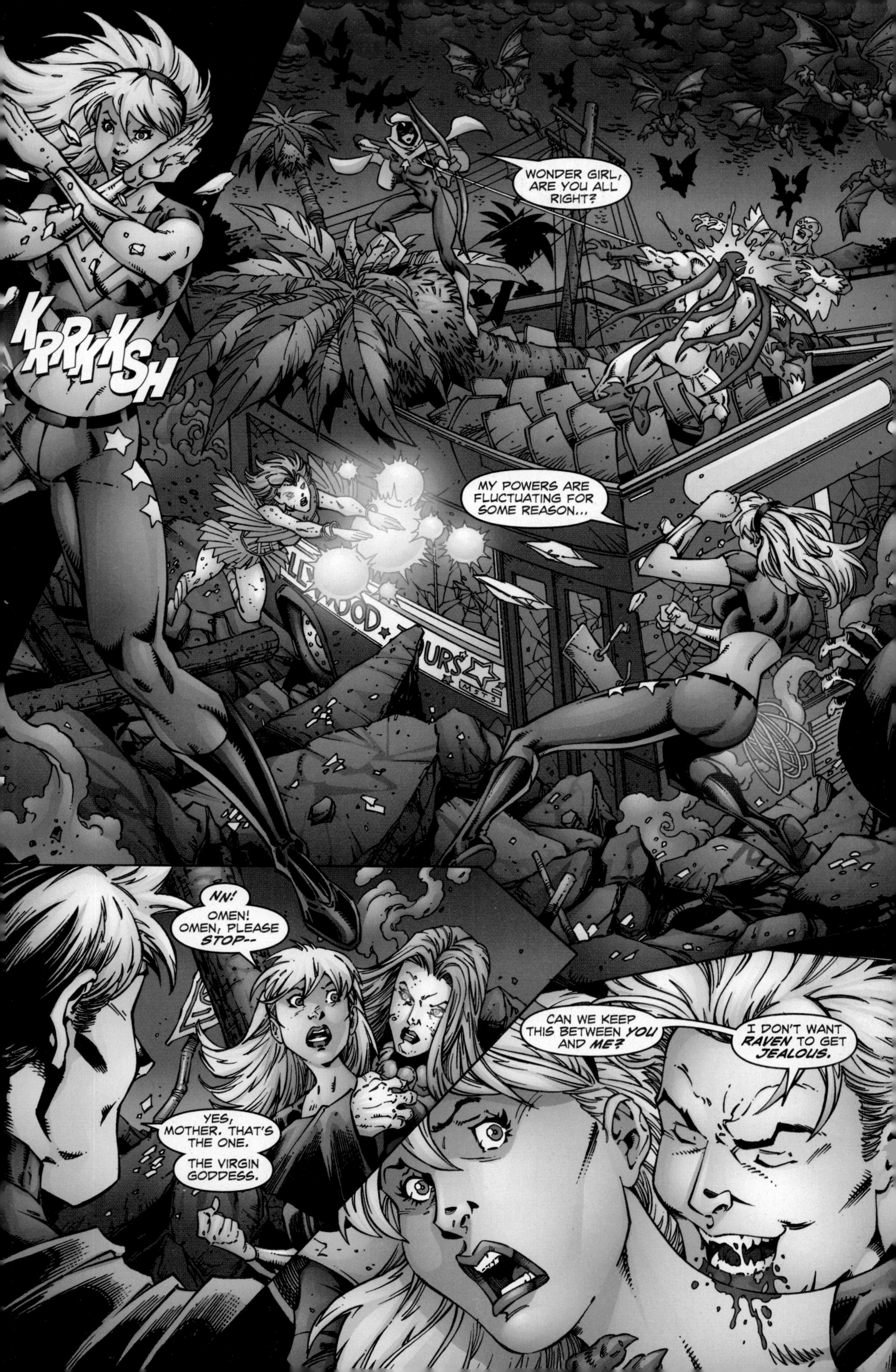
WONDER GIRL, ARE YOU ALL RIGHT?
KRRKKSH
MY POWERS ARE FLUCTUATING FOR SOME REASON...
NN!
OMEN! OMEN, PLEASE STOP--
YES, MOTHER. THAT'S THE ONE.
THE VIRGIN GODDESS.
CAN WE KEEP THIS BETWEEN YOU AND ME?
I DON'T WANT RAVEN TO GET JEALOUS.

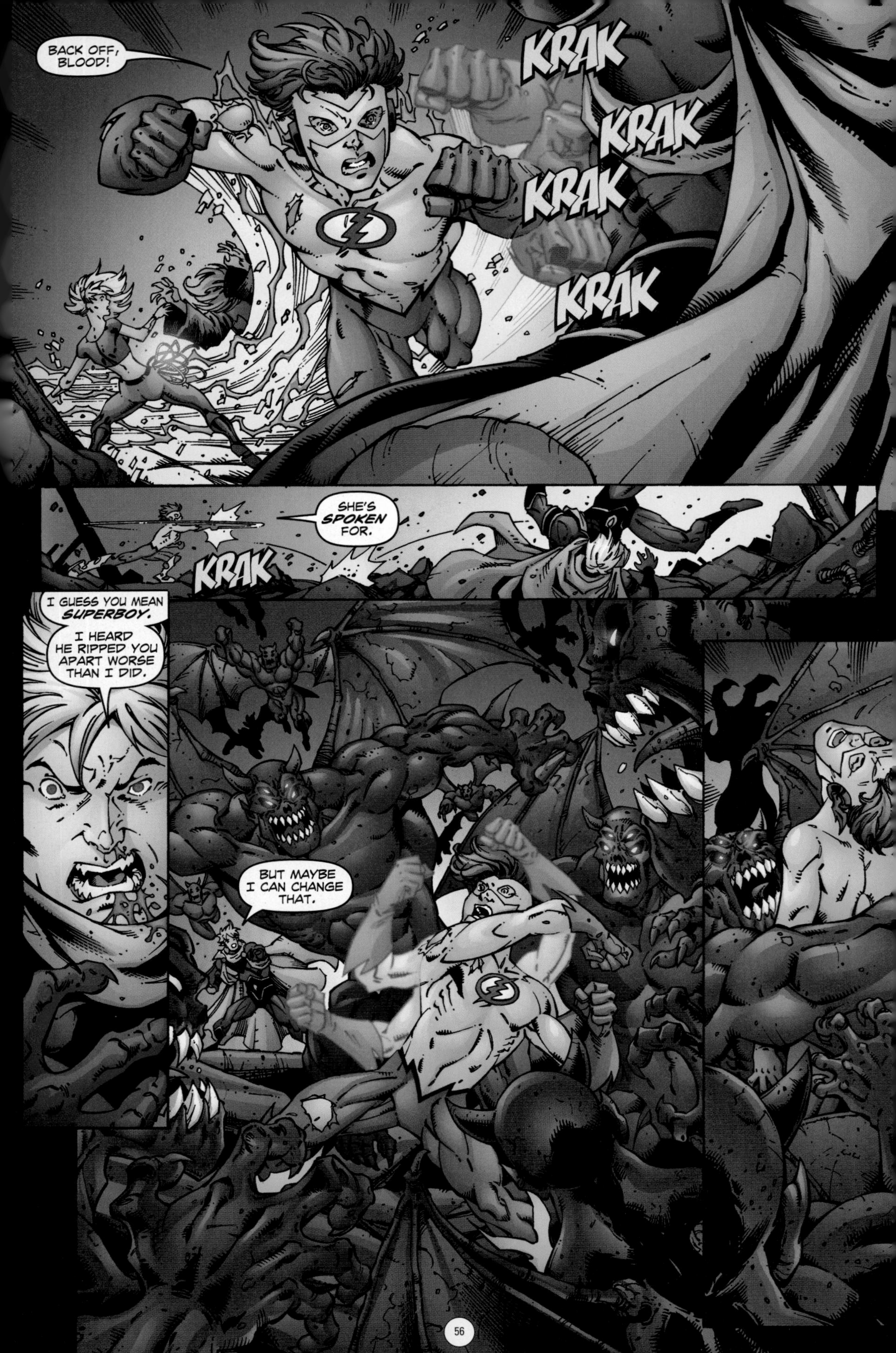
BACK OFF, BLOOD!
KRAK
KRAK
KRAK
KRAK
SHE'S SPOKEN FOR.
KRAK
I GUESS YOU MEAN SUPERBOY.
I HEARD HE RIPPED YOU APART WORSE THAN I DID.
BUT MAYBE I CAN CHANGE THAT.

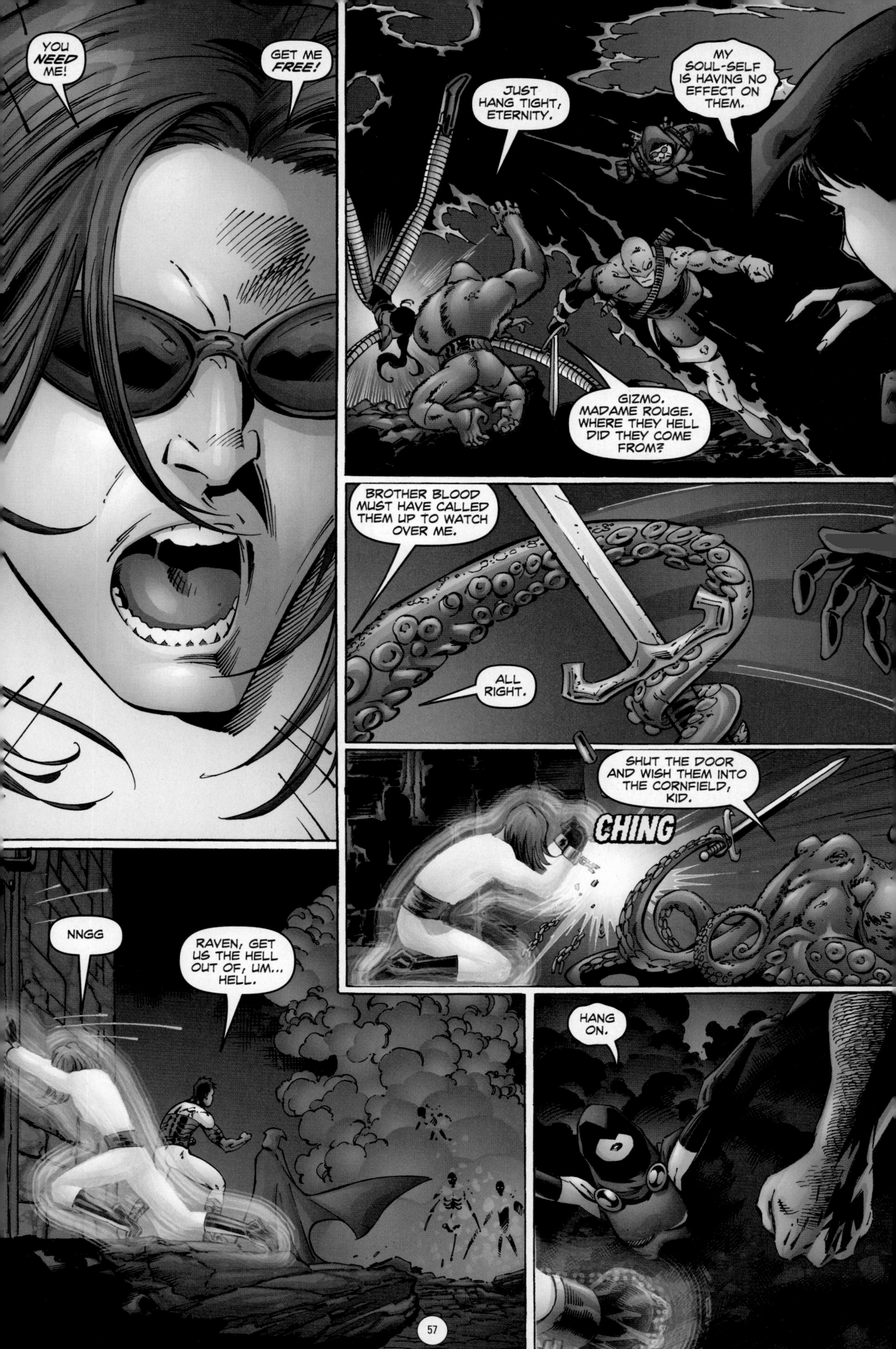

YOU NEED ME!
GET ME FREE!
JUST HANG TIGHT, ETERNITY.
MY SOUL-SELF IS HAVING NO EFFECT ON THEM.
GIZMO. MADAME ROUGE. WHERE THEY HELL DID THEY COME FROM?
BROTHER BLOOD MUST HAVE CALLED THEM UP TO WATCH OVER ME.
ALL RIGHT.
SHUT THE DOOR AND WISH THEM INTO THE CORNFIELD, KID.
CHING
NNGG
RAVEN, GET US THE HELL OUT OF, UM... HELL.
HANG ON.

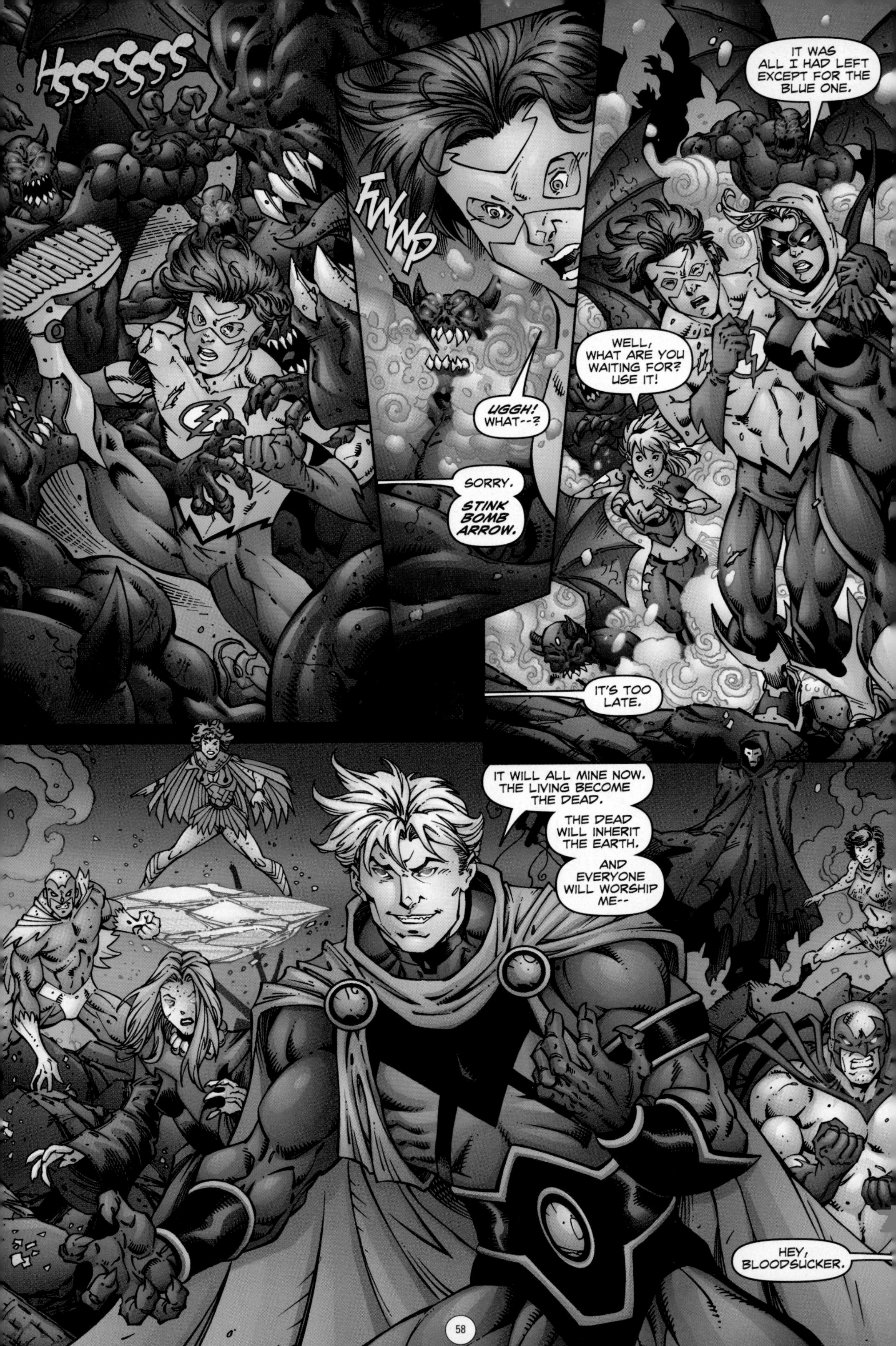
HSSSSSSS
FWWP
UGGH! WHAT--?
SORRY. STINK BOMB ARROW.
IT WAS ALL I HAD LEFT EXCEPT FOR THE BLUE ONE.
WELL, WHAT ARE YOU WAITING FOR? USE IT!
IT'S TOO LATE.
IT WILL ALL MINE NOW. THE LIVING BECOME THE DEAD.
THE DEAD WILL INHERIT THE EARTH.
AND EVERYONE WILL WORSHIP ME--
HEY, BLOODSUCKER.

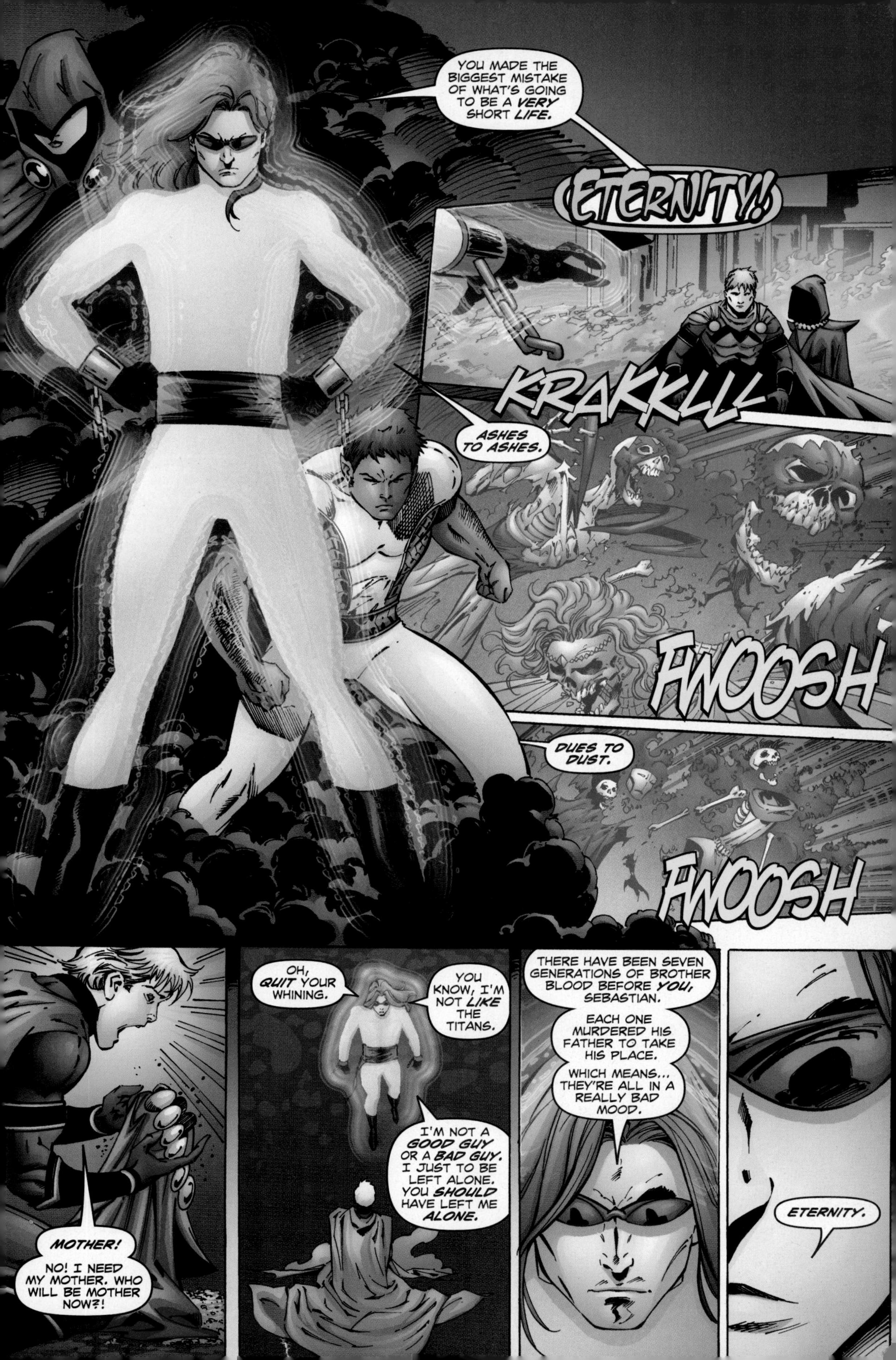
YOU MADE THE BIGGEST MISTAKE OF WHAT'S GOING TO BE A *VERY* SHORT *LIFE*.
ETERNITY!
KRAKKLL
ASHES TO ASHES.
FWOOSH
DUES TO DUST.
FWOOSH
MOTHER!
NO! I NEED MY MOTHER. WHO WILL BE MOTHER NOW?!
OH, *QUIT* YOUR WHINING.
YOU KNOW, I'M NOT *LIKE* THE TITANS.
I'M NOT A *GOOD GUY* OR A *BAD GUY*. I JUST TO BE LEFT ALONE. YOU *SHOULD* HAVE LEFT ME *ALONE*.
THERE HAVE BEEN SEVEN GENERATIONS OF BROTHER BLOOD BEFORE *YOU*, SEBASTIAN.
EACH ONE MURDERED HIS FATHER TO TAKE HIS PLACE.
WHICH MEANS... THEY'RE ALL IN A REALLY BAD MOOD.
ETERNITY.

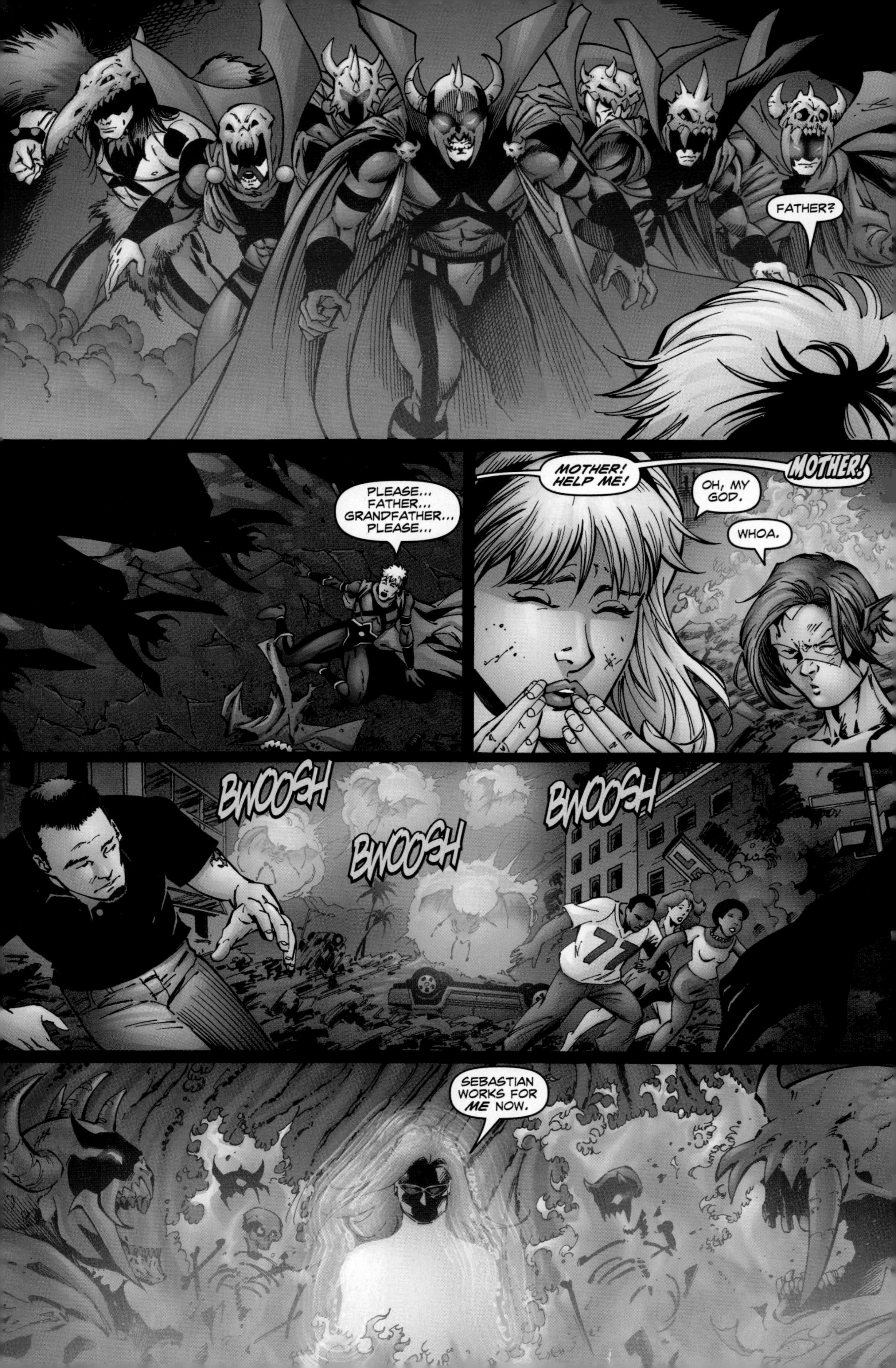
FATHER?
PLEASE... FATHER... GRANDFATHER... PLEASE...
MOTHER! HELP ME!
MOTHER!
OH, MY GOD.
WHOA.
BWOOSH
BWOOSH
BWOOSH
SEBASTIAN WORKS FOR ME NOW.

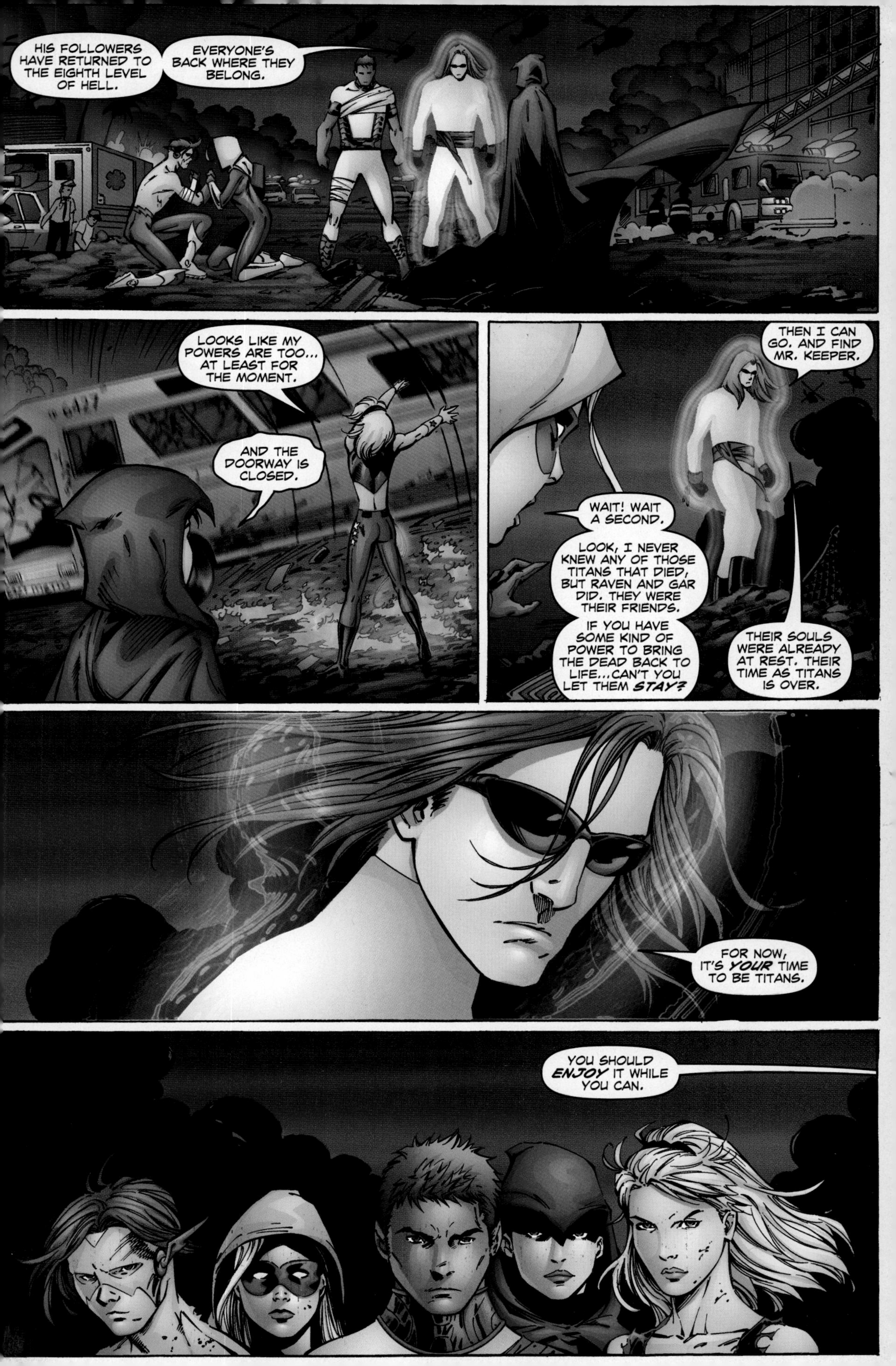
HIS FOLLOWERS HAVE RETURNED TO THE EIGHTH LEVEL OF HELL.
EVERYONE'S BACK WHERE THEY BELONG.
LOOKS LIKE MY POWERS ARE TOO... AT LEAST FOR THE MOMENT.
AND THE DOORWAY IS CLOSED.
THEN I CAN GO. AND FIND MR. KEEPER.
WAIT! WAIT A SECOND.
LOOK, I NEVER KNEW ANY OF THOSE TITANS THAT DIED, BUT RAVEN AND GAR DID. THEY WERE THEIR FRIENDS.
IF YOU HAVE SOME KIND OF POWER TO BRING THE DEAD BACK TO LIFE...CAN'T YOU LET THEM STAY?
THEIR SOULS WERE ALREADY AT REST. THEIR TIME AS TITANS IS OVER.
FOR NOW, IT'S YOUR TIME TO BE TITANS.
YOU SHOULD ENJOY IT WHILE YOU CAN.

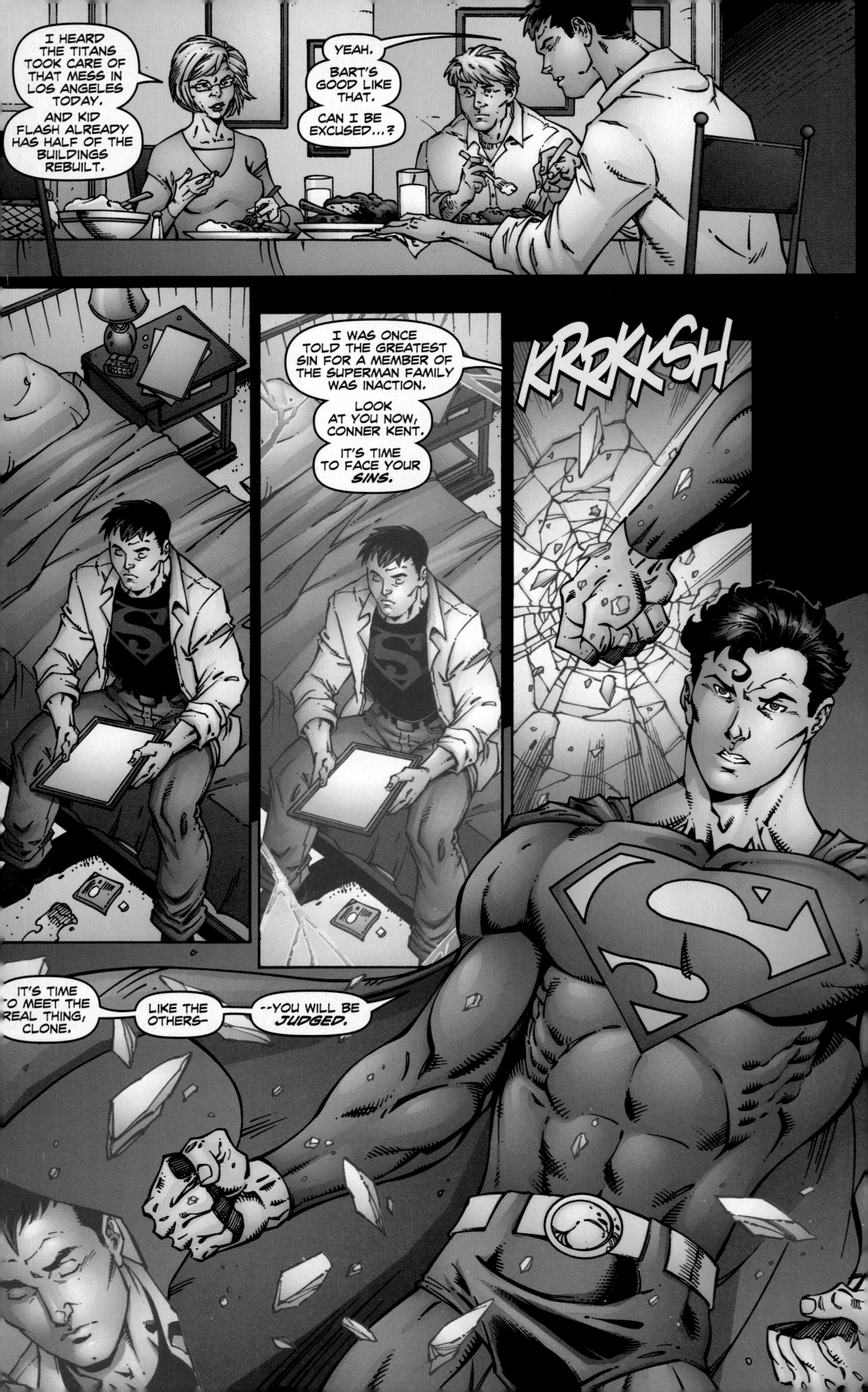

I HEARD THE TITANS TOOK CARE OF THAT MESS IN LOS ANGELES TODAY.
AND KID FLASH ALREADY HAS HALF OF THE BUILDINGS REBUILT.
YEAH.
BART'S GOOD LIKE THAT.
CAN I BE EXCUSED...?
I WAS ONCE TOLD THE GREATEST SIN FOR A MEMBER OF THE SUPERMAN FAMILY WAS INACTION.
LOOK AT YOU NOW, CONNER KENT.
IT'S TIME TO FACE YOUR *SINS.*
KRKKSH
IT'S TIME TO MEET THE REAL THING, CLONE.
LIKE THE OTHERS-
--YOU WILL BE *JUDGED.*

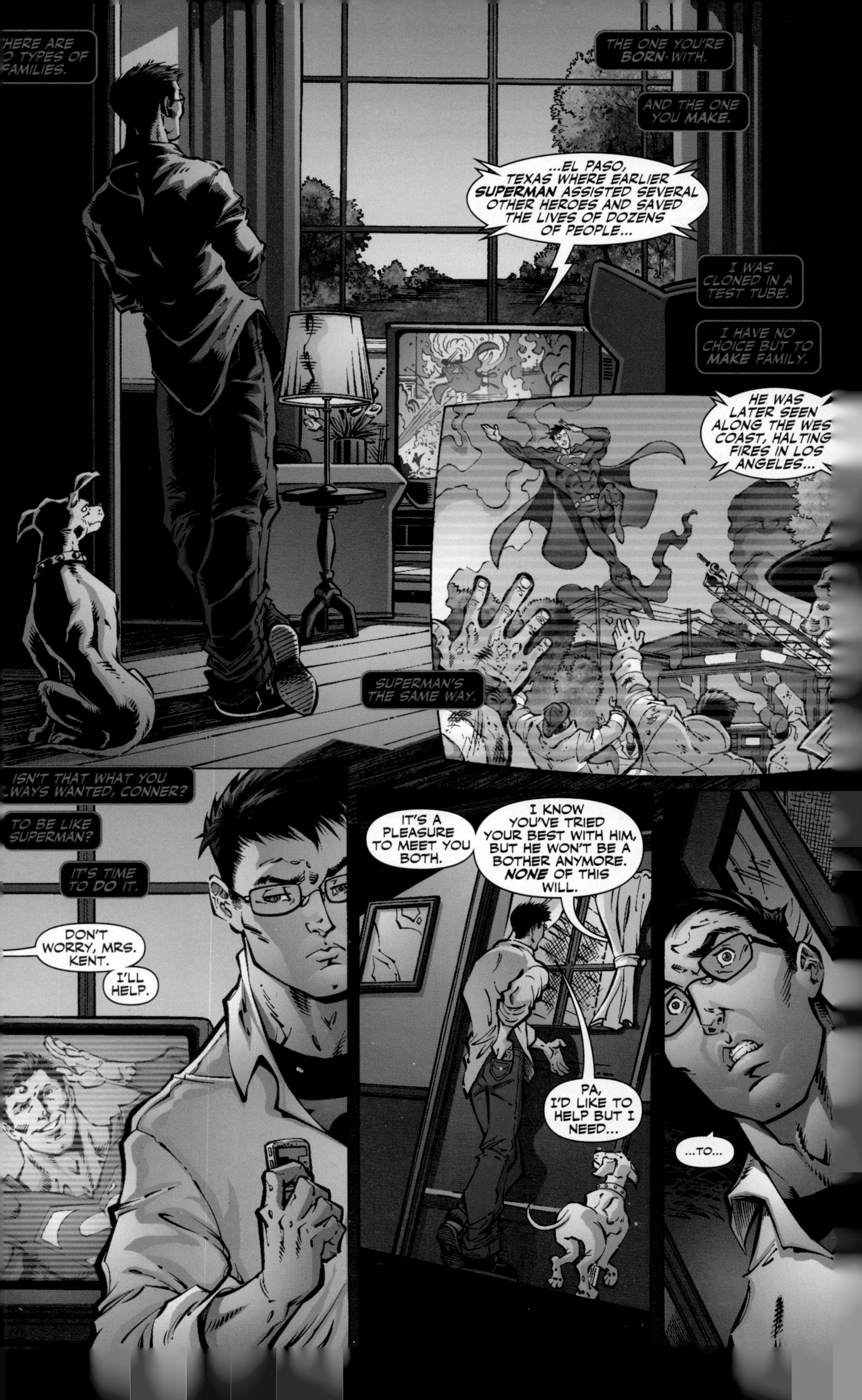

HERE ARE
O TYPES OF
FAMILIES.
THE ONE YOU'RE BORN WITH.
AND THE ONE YOU MAKE.
...EL PASO, TEXAS WHERE EARLIER SUPERMAN ASSISTED SEVERAL OTHER HEROES AND SAVED THE LIVES OF DOZENS OF PEOPLE...
I WAS CLONED IN A TEST TUBE.
I HAVE NO CHOICE BUT TO MAKE FAMILY.
HE WAS LATER SEEN ALONG THE WES COAST, HALTING FIRES IN LOS ANGELES...
SUPERMAN'S THE SAME WAY.
ISN'T THAT WHAT YOU
LWAYS WANTED, CONNER?
TO BE LIKE SUPERMAN?
IT'S TIME TO DO IT.
DON'T WORRY, MRS. KENT.
I'LL HELP.
IT'S A PLEASURE TO MEET YOU BOTH.
I KNOW YOU'VE TRIED YOUR BEST WITH HIM, BUT HE WON'T BE A BOTHER ANYMORE. NONE OF THIS WILL.
PA, I'D LIKE TO HELP BUT I NEED...
...TO...

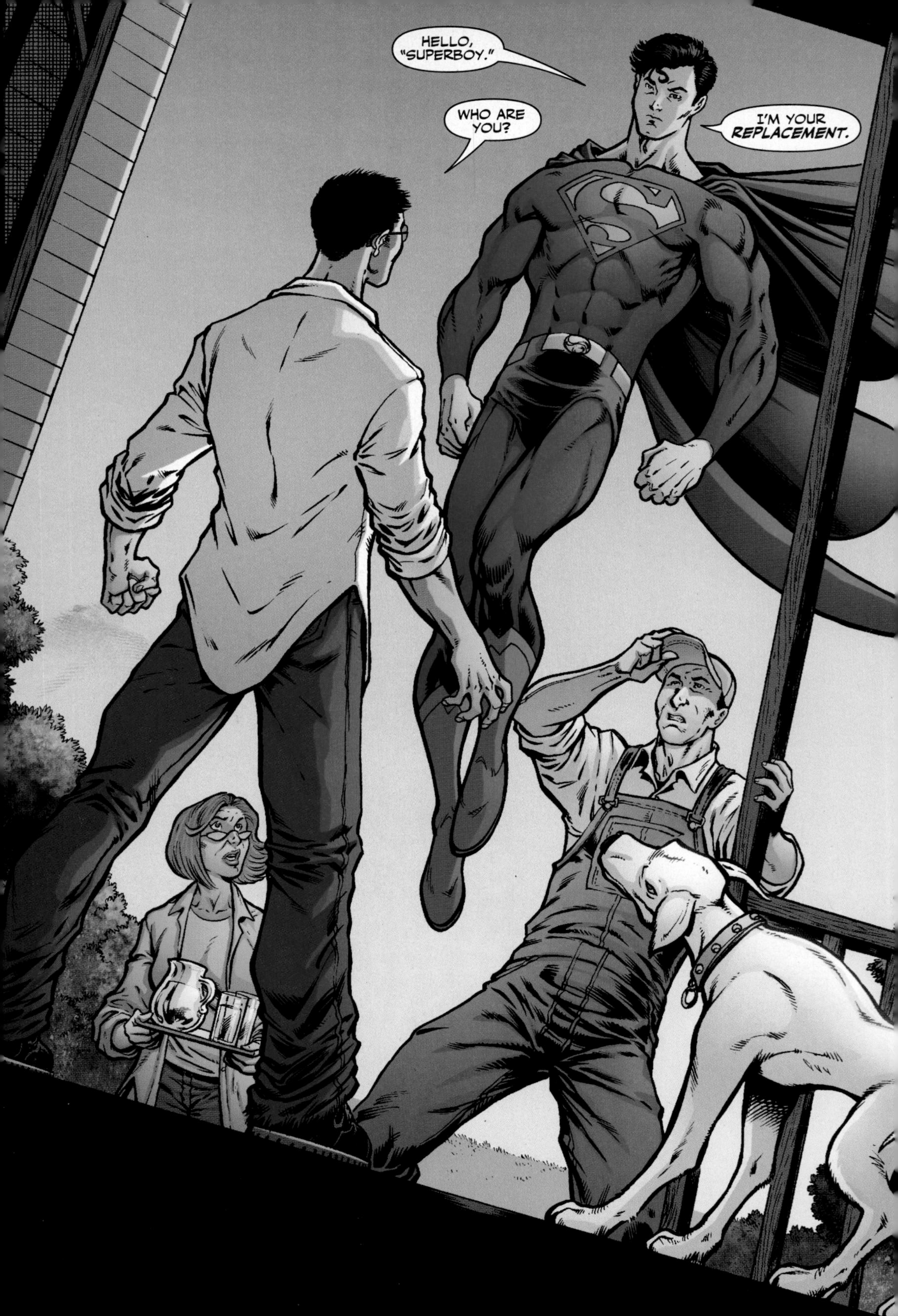
HELLO, "SUPERBOY."
WHO ARE YOU?
I'M YOUR *REPLACEMENT.*

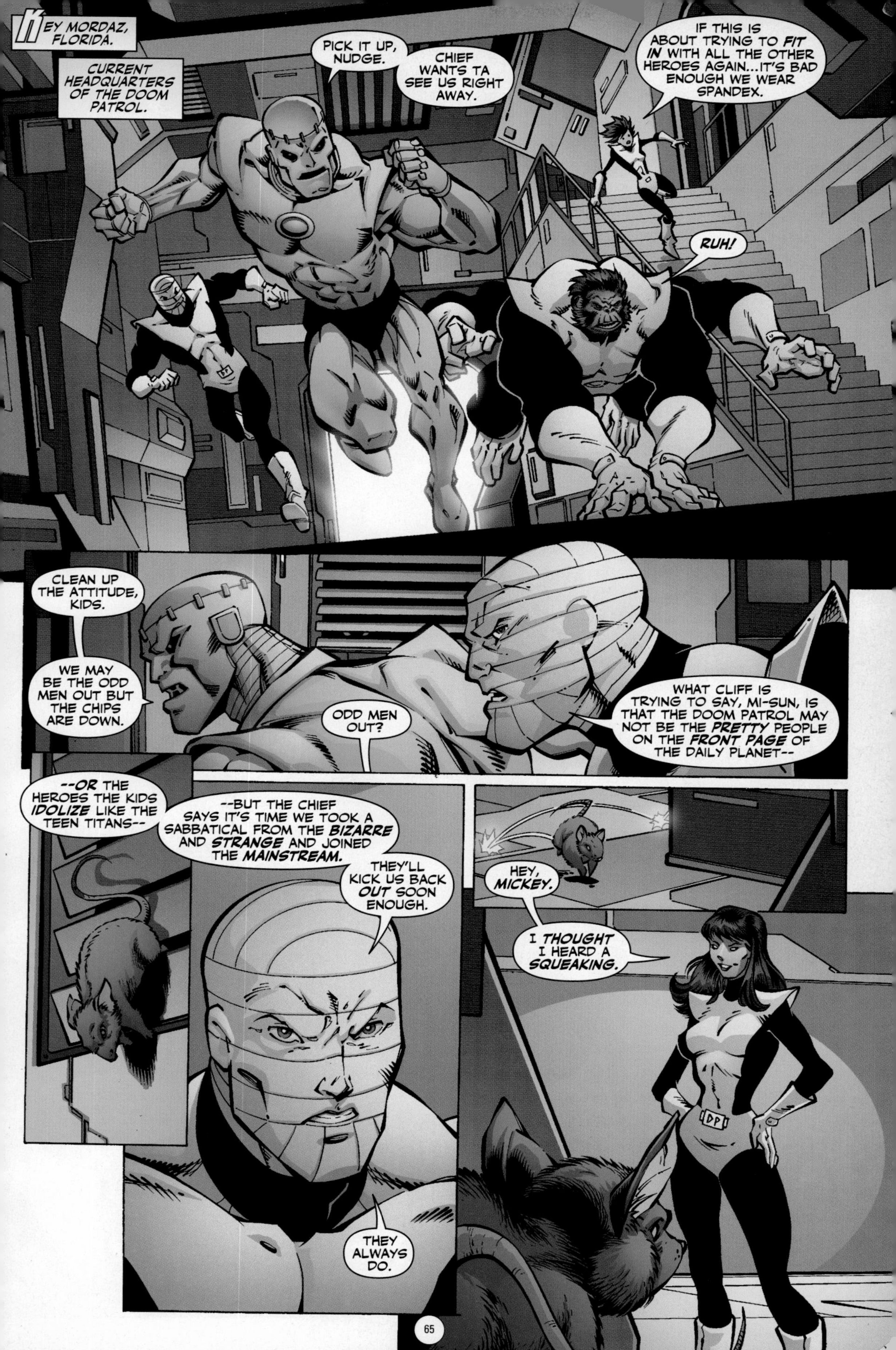
KEY MORDAZ, FLORIDA.
CURRENT HEADQUARTERS OF THE DOOM PATROL.
PICK IT UP, NUDGE.
CHIEF WANTS TA SEE US RIGHT AWAY.
IF THIS IS ABOUT TRYING TO FIT IN WITH ALL THE OTHER HEROES AGAIN...IT'S BAD ENOUGH WE WEAR SPANDEX.
RUH!
CLEAN UP THE ATTITUDE, KIDS.
WE MAY BE THE ODD MEN OUT BUT THE CHIPS ARE DOWN.
ODD MEN OUT?
WHAT CLIFF IS TRYING TO SAY, MI-SUN, IS THAT THE DOOM PATROL MAY NOT BE THE PRETTY PEOPLE ON THE FRONT PAGE OF THE DAILY PLANET--
--OR THE HEROES THE KIDS IDOLIZE LIKE THE TEEN TITANS--
--BUT THE CHIEF SAYS IT'S TIME WE TOOK A SABBATICAL FROM THE BIZARRE AND STRANGE AND JOINED THE MAINSTREAM.
THEY'LL KICK US BACK OUT SOON ENOUGH.
THEY ALWAYS DO.
HEY, MICKEY.
I THOUGHT I HEARD A SQUEAKING.

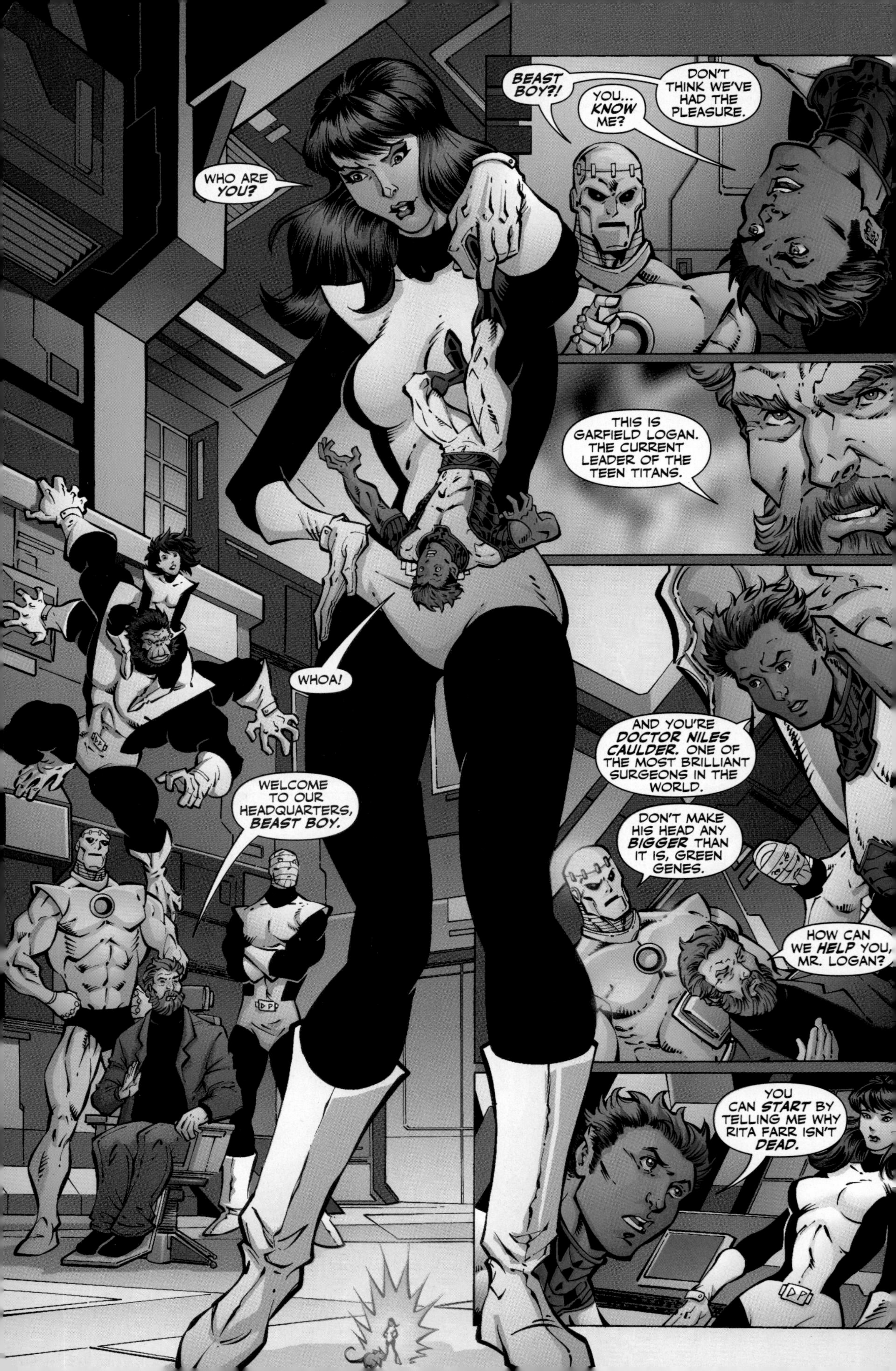
WHO ARE YOU?
BEAST BOY?!
YOU... KNOW ME?
DON'T THINK WE'VE HAD THE PLEASURE.
THIS IS GARFIELD LOGAN. THE CURRENT LEADER OF THE TEEN TITANS.
WHOA!
WELCOME TO OUR HEADQUARTERS, BEAST BOY.
AND YOU'RE DOCTOR NILES CAULDER. ONE OF THE MOST BRILLIANT SURGEONS IN THE WORLD.
DON'T MAKE HIS HEAD ANY BIGGER THAN IT IS, GREEN GENES.
HOW CAN WE HELP YOU, MR. LOGAN?
YOU CAN START BY TELLING ME WHY RITA FARR ISN'T DEAD.

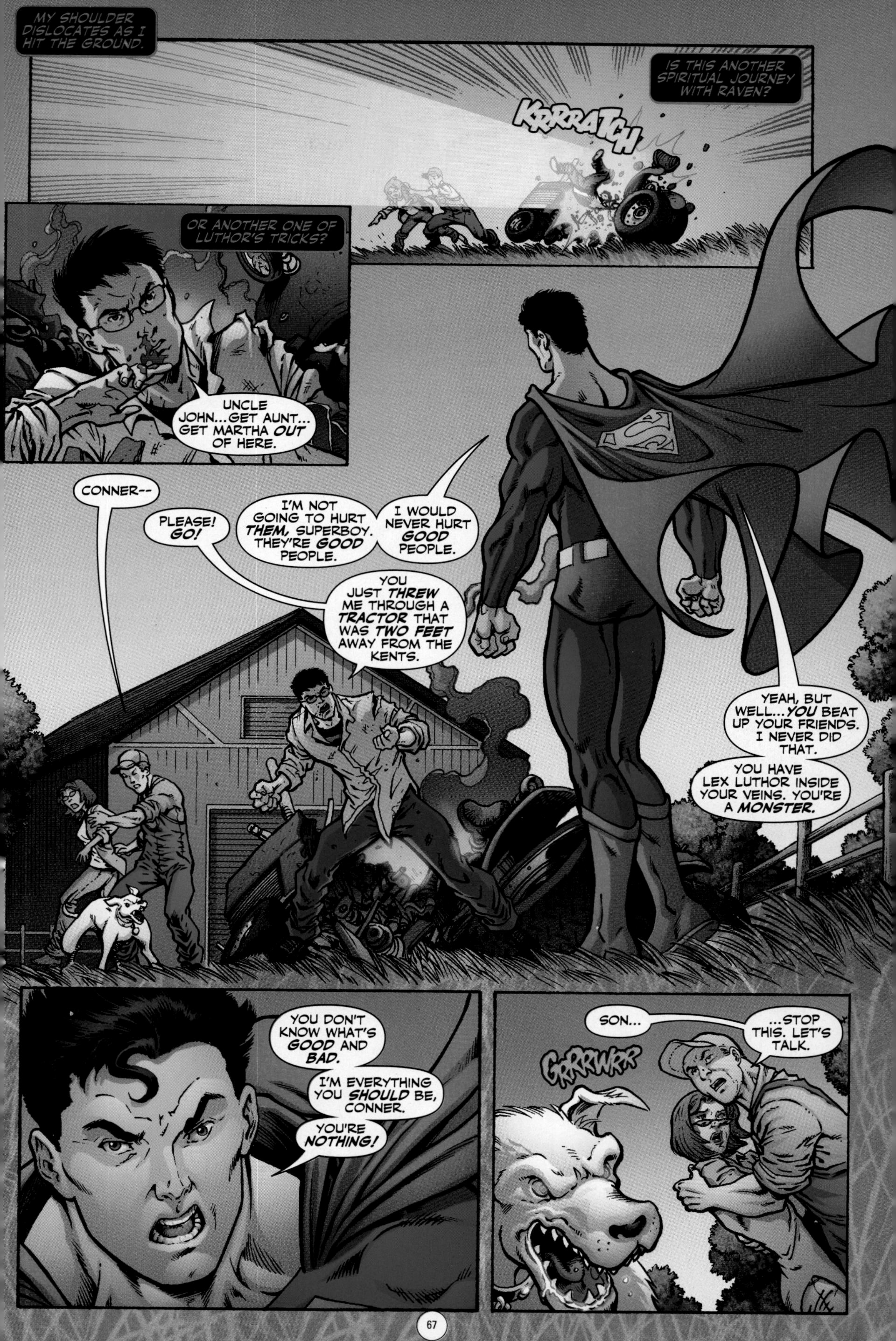

MY SHOULDER DISLOCATES AS I HIT THE GROUND.
IS THIS ANOTHER SPIRITUAL JOURNEY WITH RAVEN?
KRRRATCH
OR ANOTHER ONE OF LUTHOR'S TRICKS?
UNCLE JOHN...GET AUNT... GET MARTHA OUT OF HERE.
CONNER--
PLEASE! GO!
I'M NOT GOING TO HURT THEM, SUPERBOY. THEY'RE GOOD PEOPLE.
I WOULD NEVER HURT GOOD PEOPLE.
YOU JUST THREW ME THROUGH A TRACTOR THAT WAS TWO FEET AWAY FROM THE KENTS.
YEAH, BUT WELL...YOU BEAT UP YOUR FRIENDS. I NEVER DID THAT.
YOU HAVE LEX LUTHOR INSIDE YOUR VEINS. YOU'RE A MONSTER.
YOU DON'T KNOW WHAT'S GOOD AND BAD.
I'M EVERYTHING YOU SHOULD BE, CONNER.
YOU'RE NOTHING!
SON...
...STOP THIS. LET'S TALK.
GRRRWRR

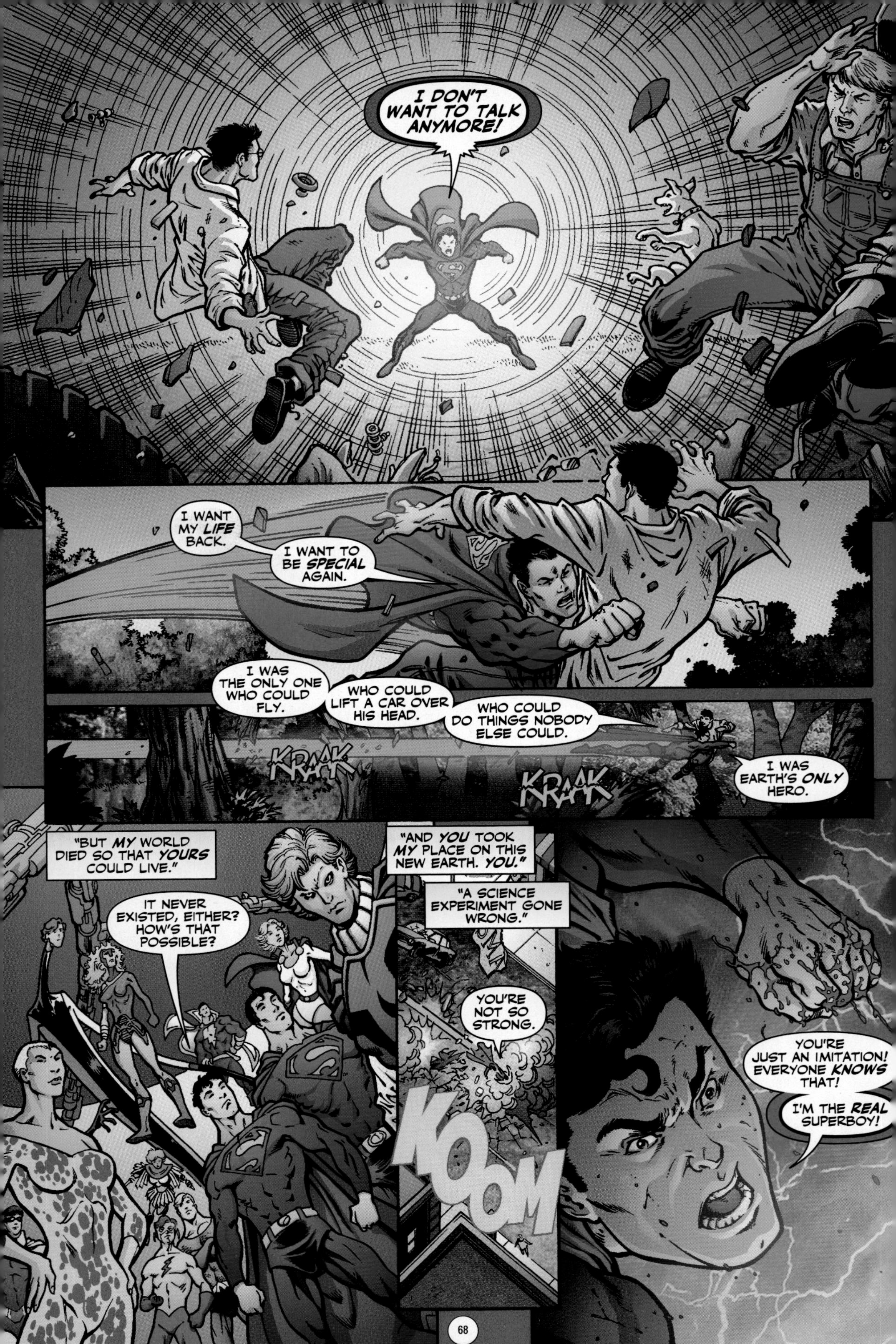
I DON'T WANT TO TALK ANYMORE!
I WANT MY LIFE BACK.
I WANT TO BE SPECIAL AGAIN.
I WAS THE ONLY ONE WHO COULD FLY.
WHO COULD LIFT A CAR OVER HIS HEAD.
WHO COULD DO THINGS NOBODY ELSE COULD.
KRAAK
KRAAK
I WAS EARTH'S ONLY HERO.
"BUT MY WORLD DIED SO THAT YOURS COULD LIVE."
IT NEVER EXISTED, EITHER? HOW'S THAT POSSIBLE?
"AND YOU TOOK MY PLACE ON THIS NEW EARTH. YOU."
"A SCIENCE EXPERIMENT GONE WRONG."
YOU'RE NOT SO STRONG.
KOOM
YOU'RE JUST AN IMITATION! EVERYONE KNOWS THAT!
I'M THE REAL SUPERBOY!

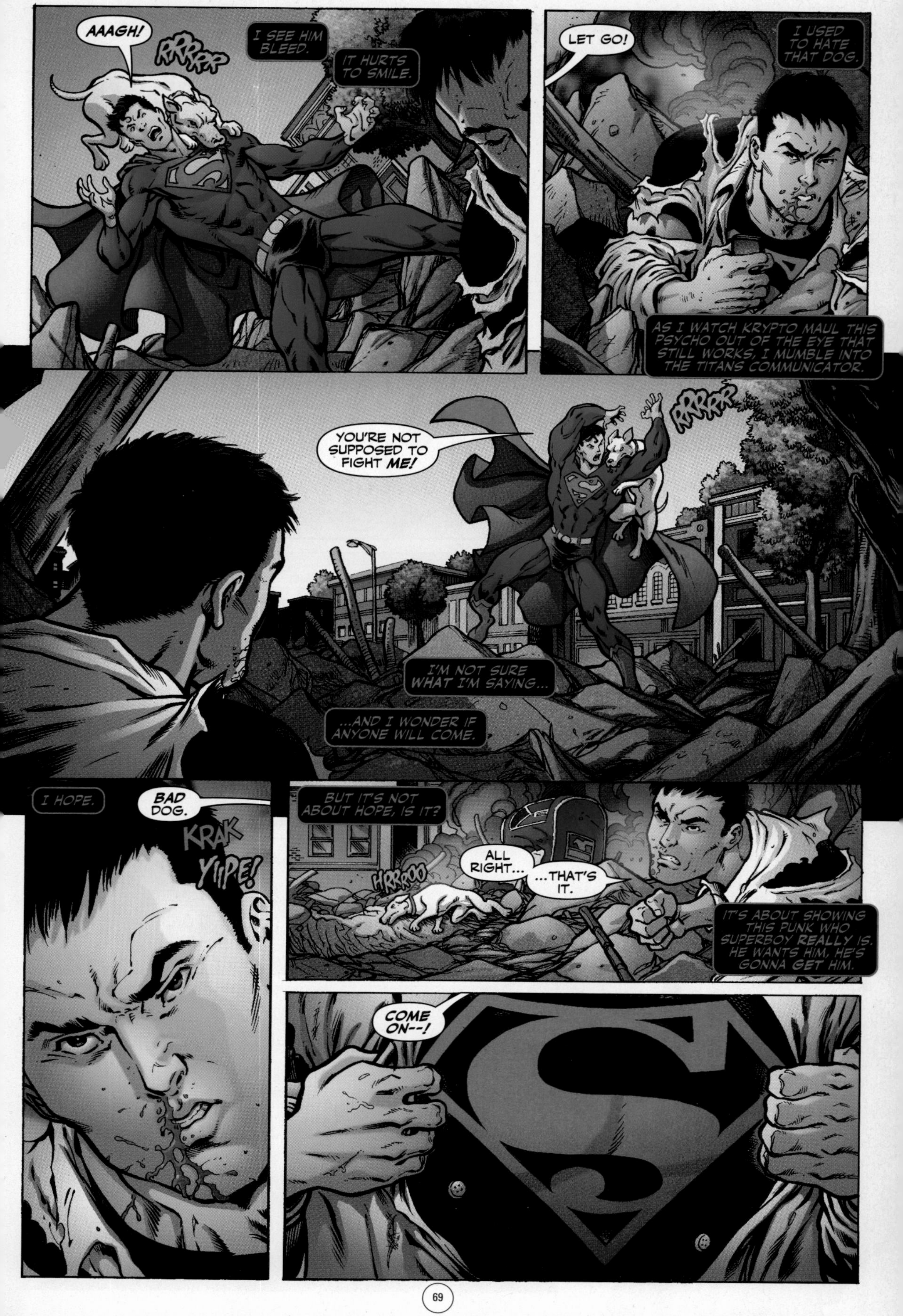
AAAGH!
RRRRR
I SEE HIM BLEED.
IT HURTS TO SMILE.
LET GO!
I USED TO HATE THAT DOG.
AS I WATCH KRYPTO MAUL THIS PSYCHO OUT OF THE EYE THAT STILL WORKS, I MUMBLE INTO THE TITANS COMMUNICATOR.
YOU'RE NOT SUPPOSED TO FIGHT ME!
RRRRR
I'M NOT SURE WHAT I'M SAYING...
...AND I WONDER IF ANYONE WILL COME.
I HOPE.
BAD DOG.
KRAK
YIPE!
BUT IT'S NOT ABOUT HOPE, IS IT?
HRRROO
ALL RIGHT...
...THAT'S IT.
IT'S ABOUT SHOWING THIS PUNK WHO SUPERBOY REALLY IS. HE WANTS HIM, HE'S GONNA GET HIM.
COME ON--!

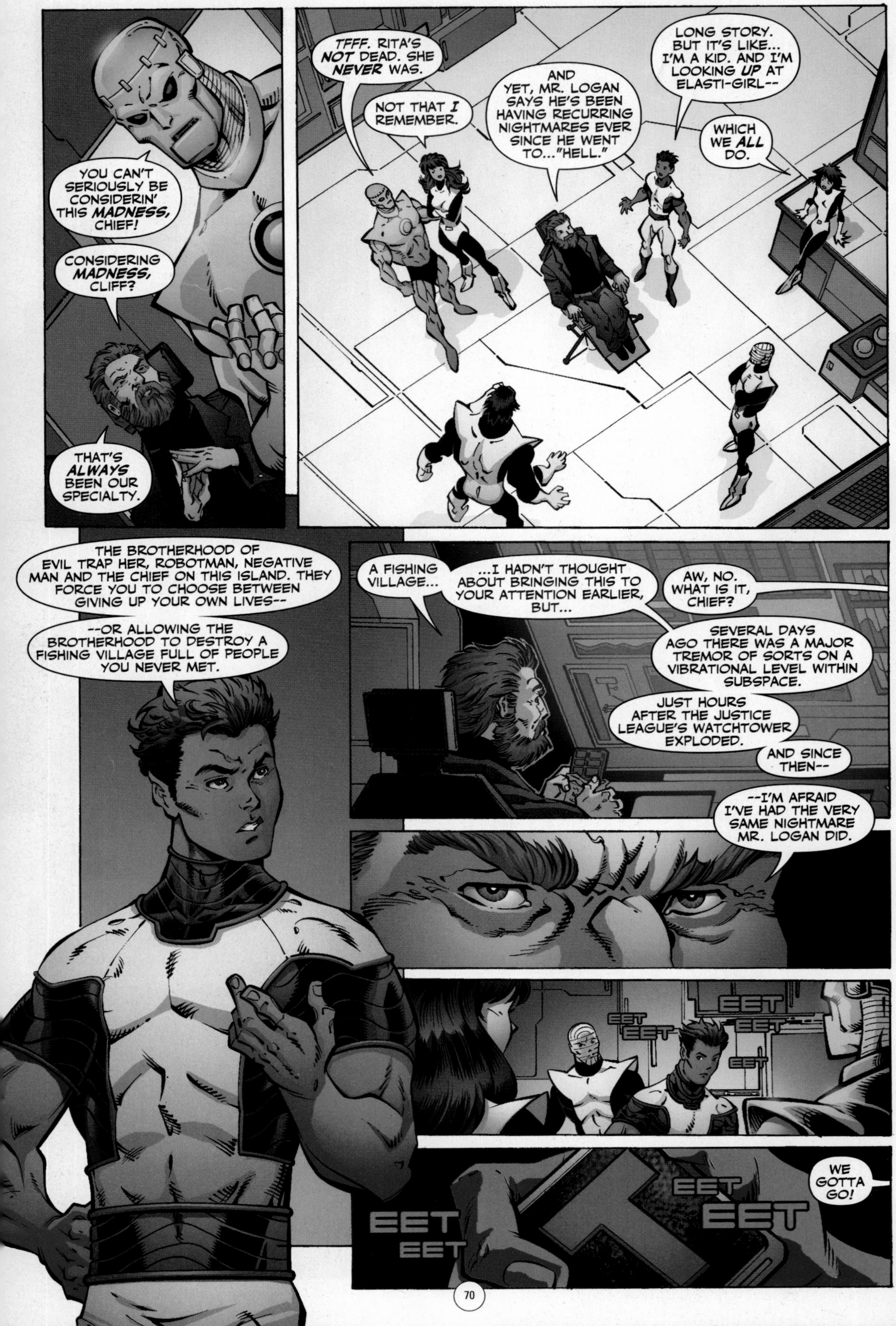
YOU CAN'T SERIOUSLY BE CONSIDERIN' THIS MADNESS, CHIEF!
CONSIDERING MADNESS, CLIFF?
THAT'S ALWAYS BEEN OUR SPECIALTY.
TFFF. RITA'S NOT DEAD. SHE NEVER WAS.
NOT THAT I REMEMBER.
AND YET, MR. LOGAN SAYS HE'S BEEN HAVING RECURRING NIGHTMARES EVER SINCE HE WENT TO..."HELL."
LONG STORY. BUT IT'S LIKE... I'M A KID. AND I'M LOOKING UP AT ELASTI-GIRL--
WHICH WE ALL DO.
THE BROTHERHOOD OF EVIL TRAP HER, ROBOTMAN, NEGATIVE MAN AND THE CHIEF ON THIS ISLAND. THEY FORCE YOU TO CHOOSE BETWEEN GIVING UP YOUR OWN LIVES--
--OR ALLOWING THE BROTHERHOOD TO DESTROY A FISHING VILLAGE FULL OF PEOPLE YOU NEVER MET.
A FISHING VILLAGE...
...I HADN'T THOUGHT ABOUT BRINGING THIS TO YOUR ATTENTION EARLIER, BUT...
AW, NO. WHAT IS IT, CHIEF?
SEVERAL DAYS AGO THERE WAS A MAJOR TREMOR OF SORTS ON A VIBRATIONAL LEVEL WITHIN SUBSPACE.
JUST HOURS AFTER THE JUSTICE LEAGUE'S WATCHTOWER EXPLODED.
AND SINCE THEN--
--I'M AFRAID I'VE HAD THE VERY SAME NIGHTMARE MR. LOGAN DID.
EET EET EET EET EET EET
EET EET EET EET
WE GOTTA GO!

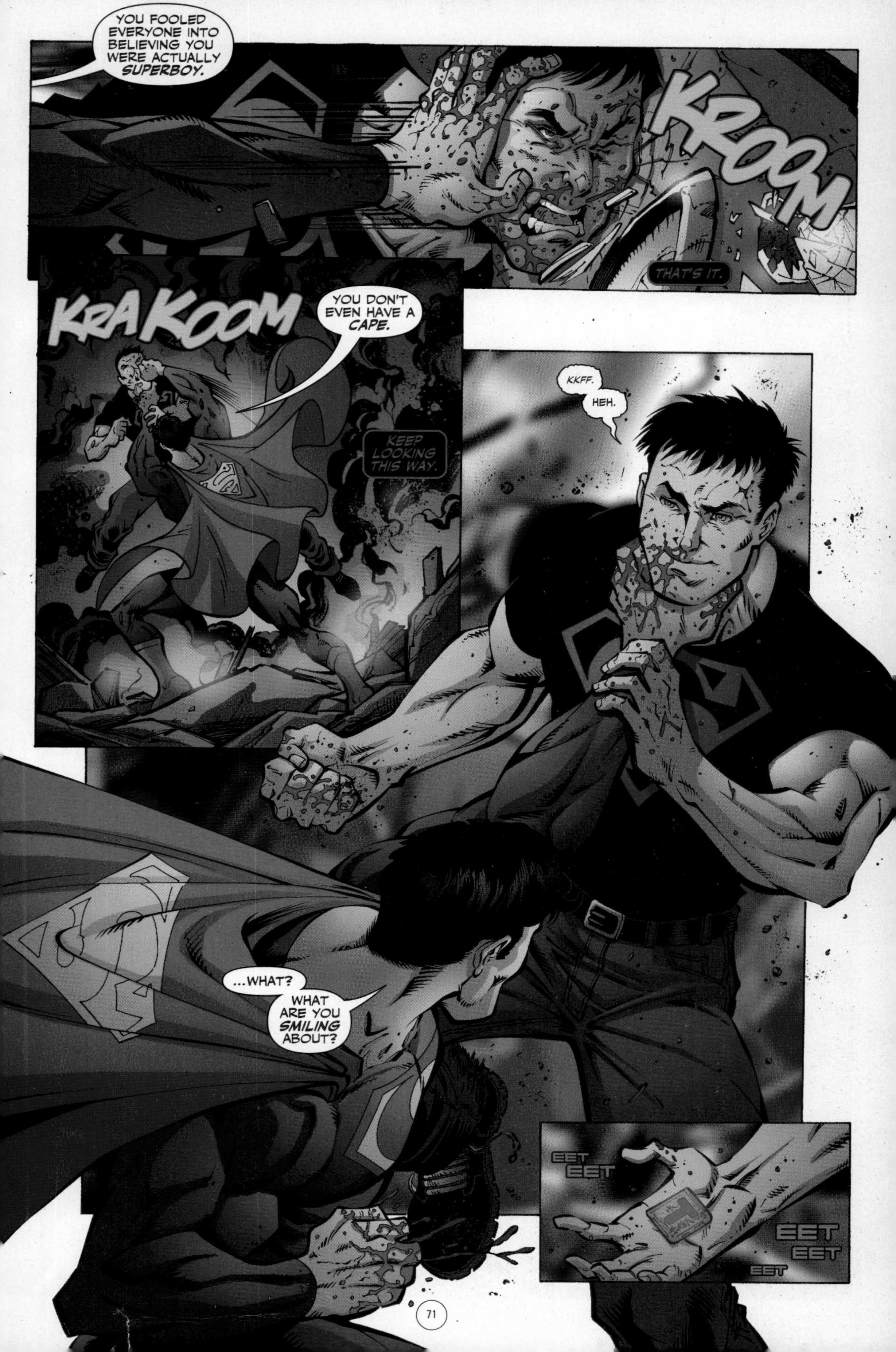

YOU FOOLED EVERYONE INTO BELIEVING YOU WERE ACTUALLY *SUPERBOY.*
KROOM
THAT'S IT.
KRA KOOM
YOU DON'T EVEN HAVE A *CAPE.*
KEEP LOOKING THIS WAY.
KKFF.
HEH.
...WHAT?
WHAT ARE YOU *SMILING* ABOUT?
EET
EET
EET
EET
EET

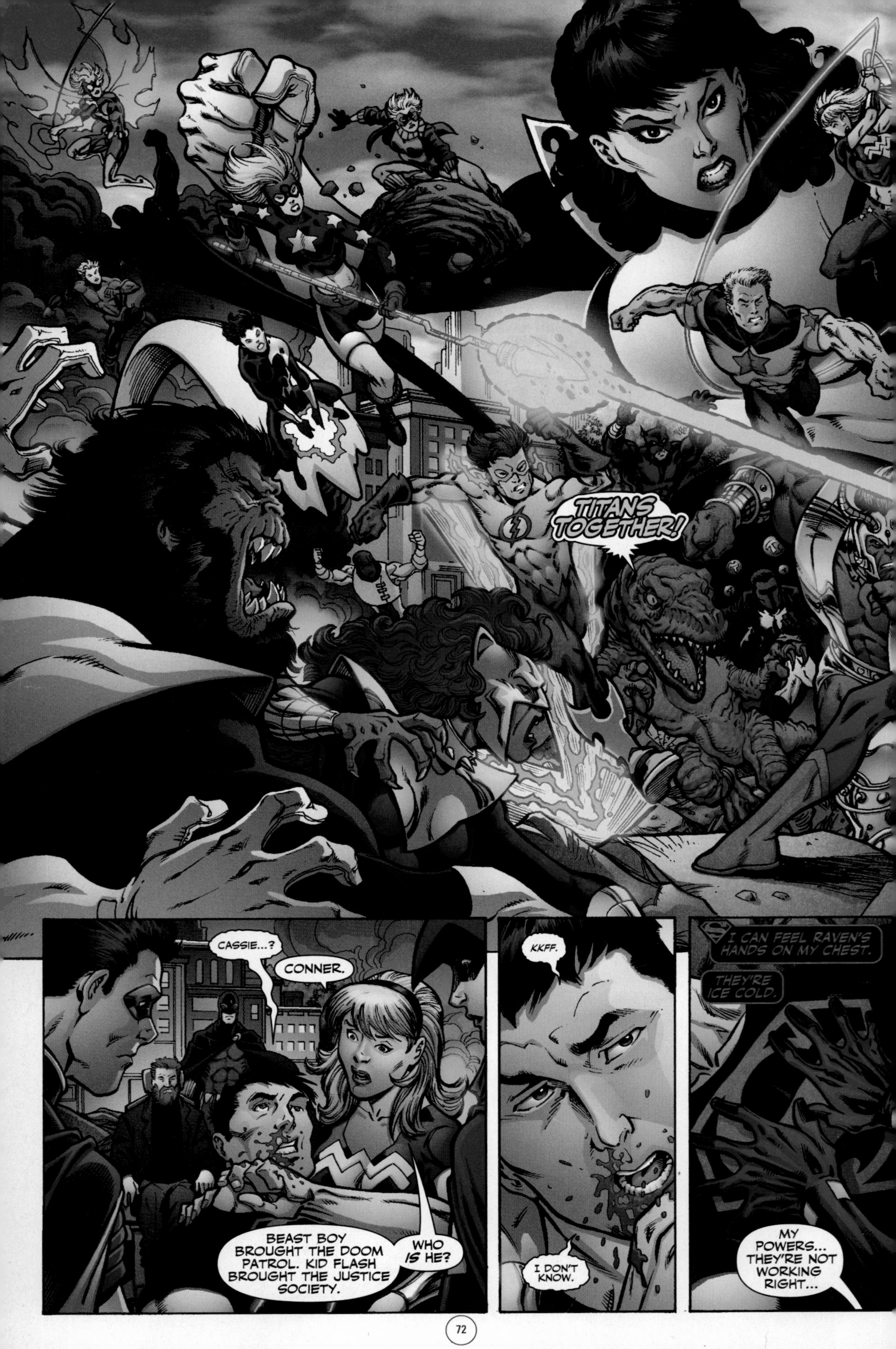
TITANS TOGETHER!
CASSIE...?
CONNER.
BEAST BOY BROUGHT THE DOOM PATROL. KID FLASH BROUGHT THE JUSTICE SOCIETY.
WHO IS HE?
KKFF.
I DON'T KNOW.
I CAN FEEL RAVEN'S HANDS ON MY CHEST.
THEY'RE ICE COLD.
MY POWERS... THEY'RE NOT WORKING RIGHT...

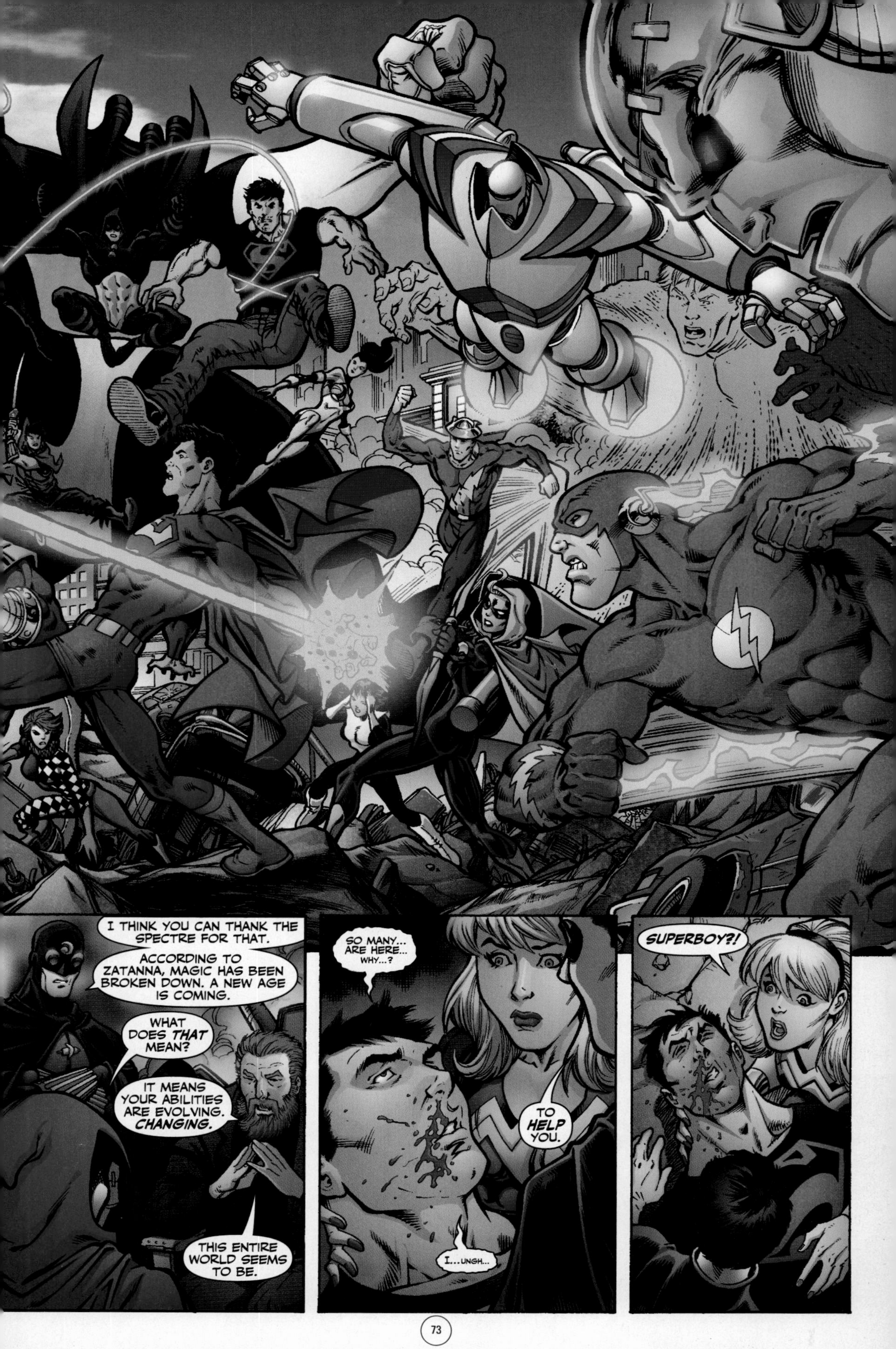

I THINK YOU CAN THANK THE SPECTRE FOR THAT.
ACCORDING TO ZATANNA, MAGIC HAS BEEN BROKEN DOWN. A NEW AGE IS COMING.
WHAT DOES *THAT* MEAN?
IT MEANS YOUR ABILITIES ARE EVOLVING. *CHANGING.*
THIS ENTIRE WORLD SEEMS TO BE.
SO MANY... ARE HERE... WHY...?
TO *HELP* YOU.
I...UNGH...
SUPERBOY?!

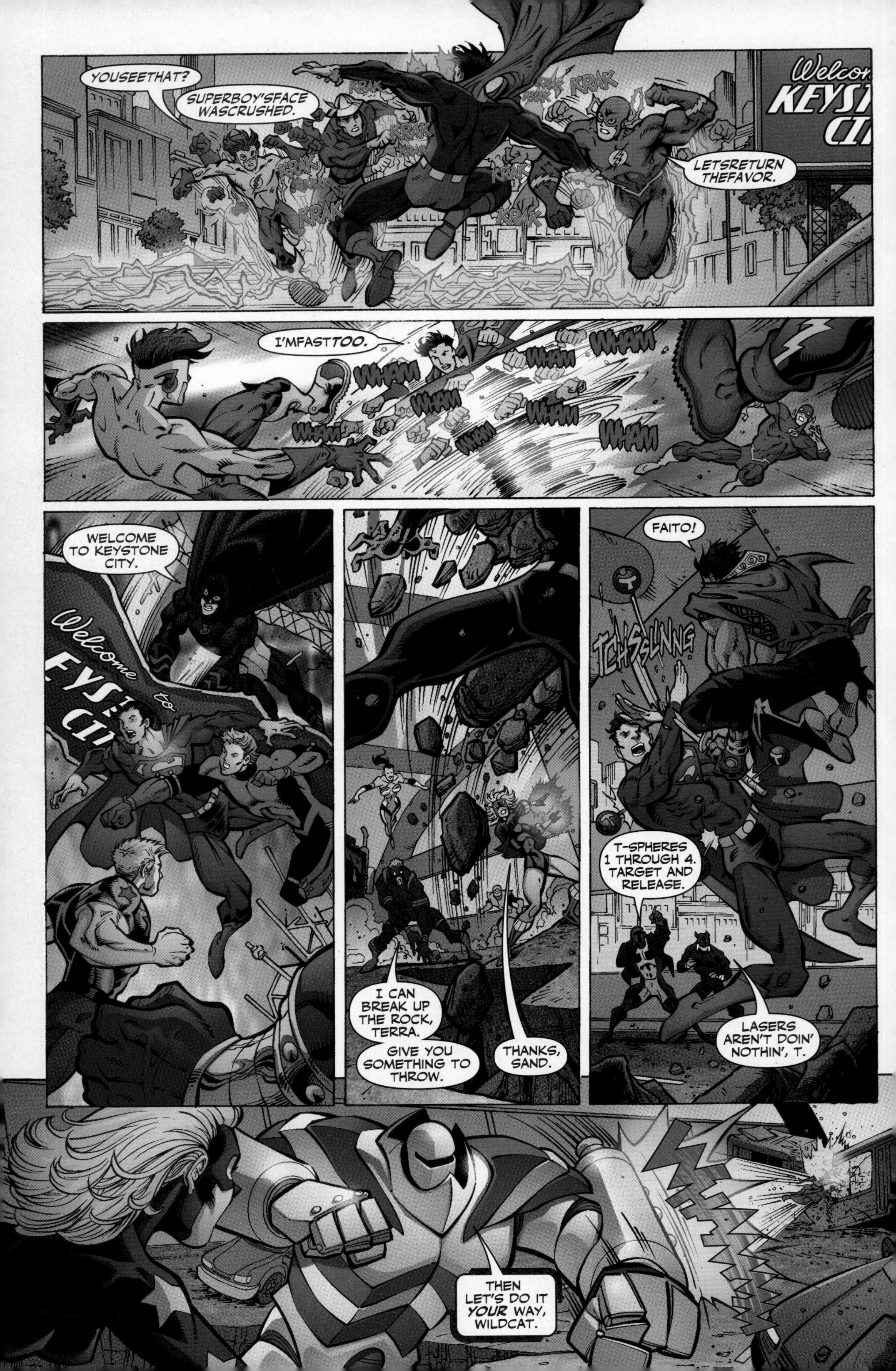
YOUSEETHAT?
SUPERBOY'SFACE WASCRUSHED.
KRAK
LETSRETURN THEFAVOR.
Welcome KEYST CITY
I'MFASTTOO.
WHAM
WELCOME TO KEYSTONE CITY.
Welcome to KEYSTONE CITY
FAITO!
TCHSLUNG
T-SPHERES 1 THROUGH 4. TARGET AND RELEASE.
I CAN BREAK UP THE ROCK, TERRA.
GIVE YOU SOMETHING TO THROW.
THANKS, SAND.
LASERS AREN'T DOIN' NOTHIN', T.
THEN LET'S DO IT YOUR WAY, WILDCAT.

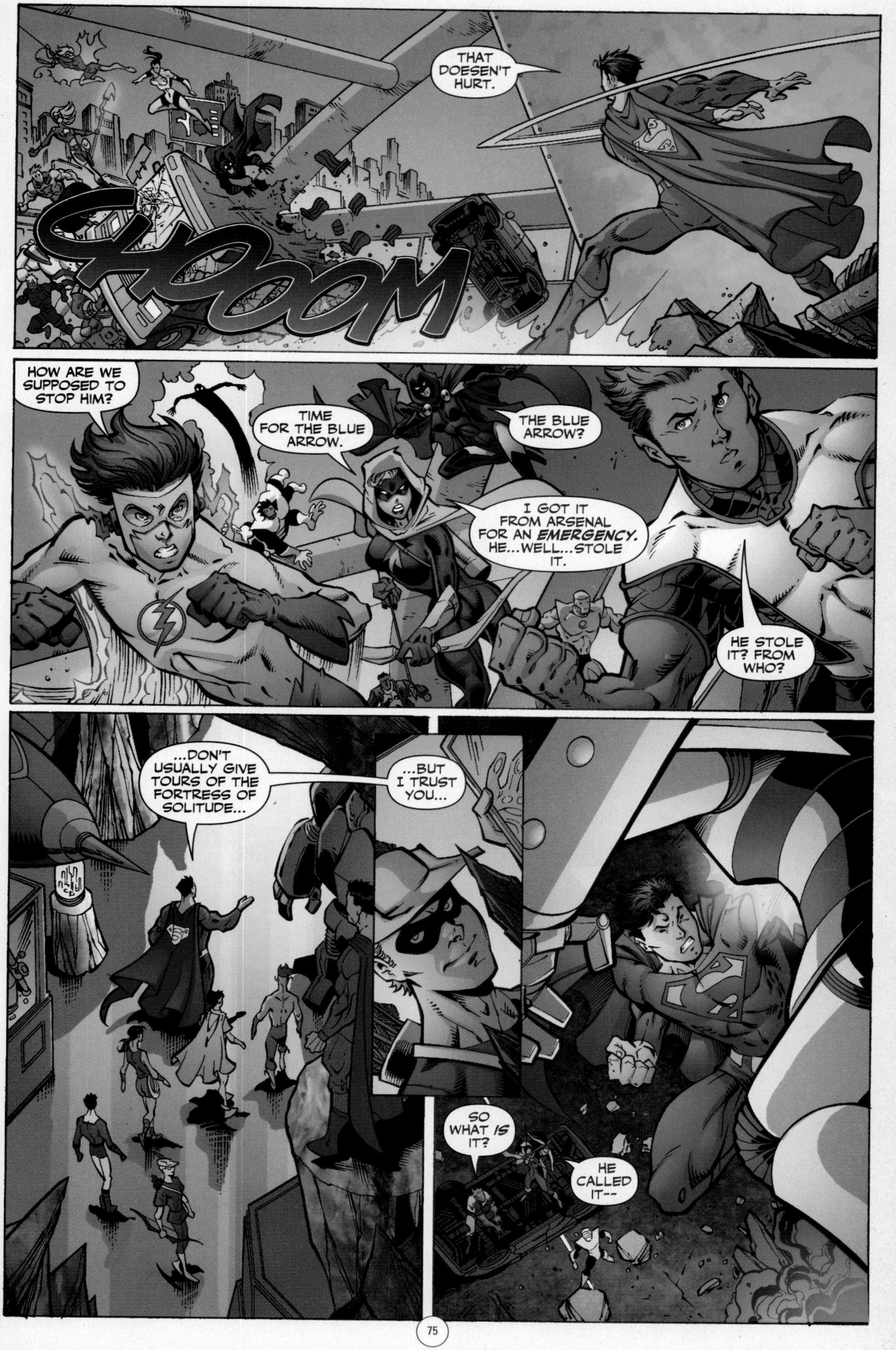
THAT DOESEN'T HURT.
CHOOOM
HOW ARE WE SUPPOSED TO STOP HIM?
TIME FOR THE BLUE ARROW.
THE BLUE ARROW?
I GOT IT FROM ARSENAL FOR AN *EMERGENCY.* HE...WELL...STOLE IT.
HE STOLE IT? FROM WHO?
...DON'T USUALLY GIVE TOURS OF THE FORTRESS OF SOLITUDE...
...BUT I TRUST YOU...
SO WHAT *IS* IT?
HE CALLED IT--

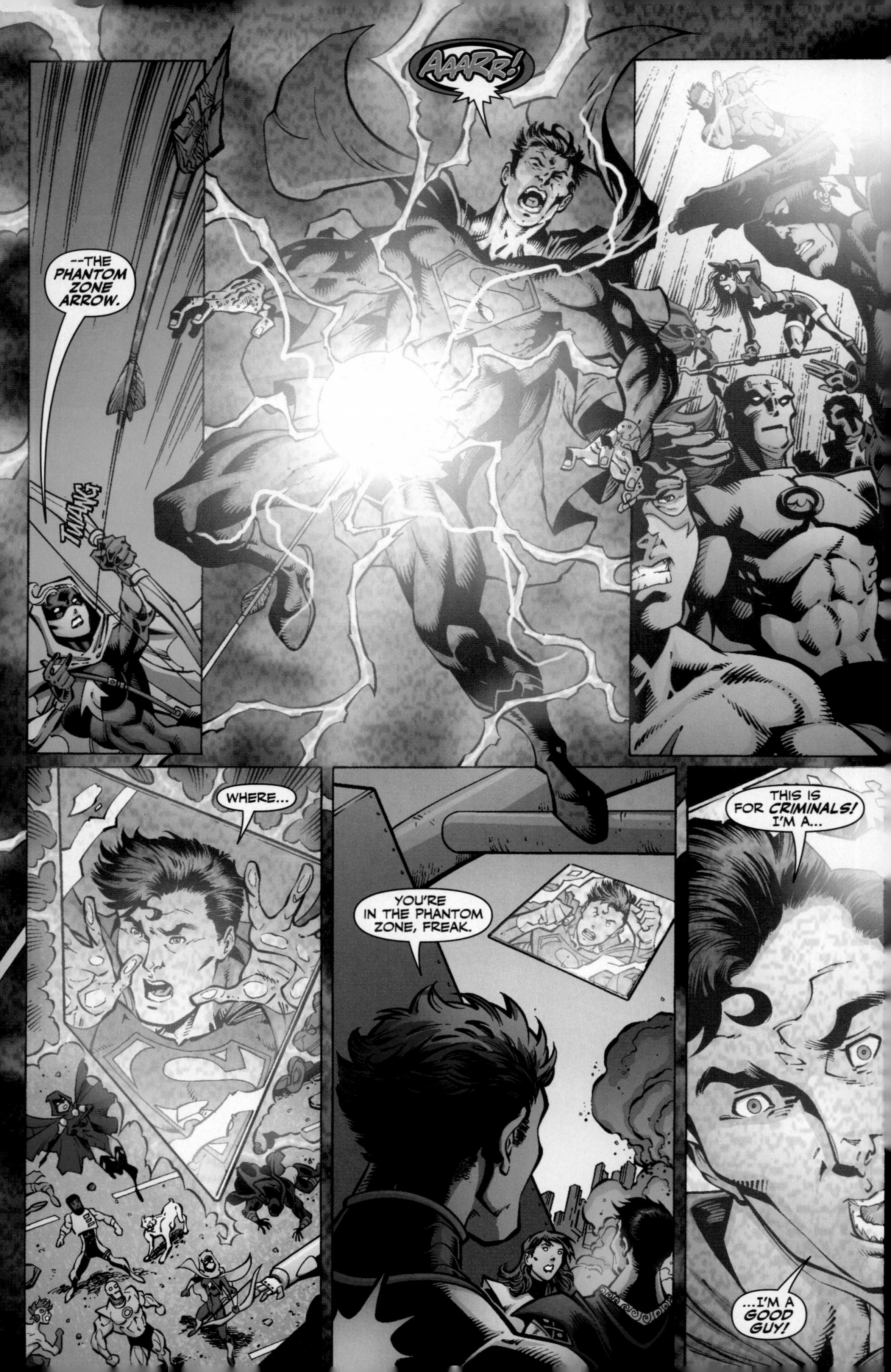
--THE PHANTOM ZONE ARROW.
TWANG
AAARR!
WHERE...
YOU'RE IN THE PHANTOM ZONE, FREAK.
THIS IS FOR CRIMINALS! I'M A...
...I'M A GOOD GUY!

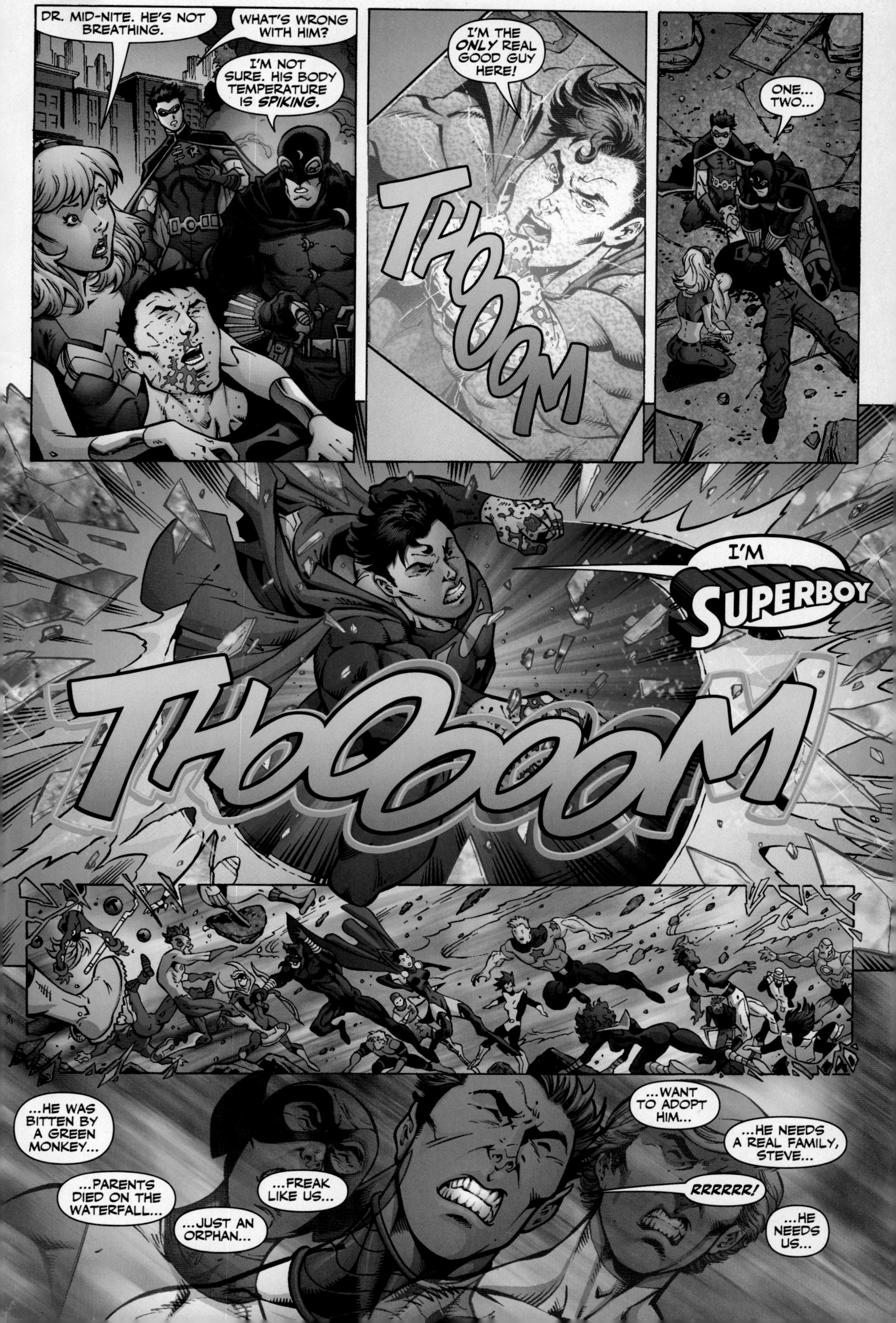
DR. MID-NITE. HE'S NOT BREATHING.
WHAT'S WRONG WITH HIM?
I'M NOT SURE. HIS BODY TEMPERATURE IS SPIKING.
I'M THE ONLY REAL GOOD GUY HERE!
THOOOM
ONE... TWO...
I'M SUPERBOY
THOOOOOM
...HE WAS BITTEN BY A GREEN MONKEY...
...PARENTS DIED ON THE WATERFALL...
...JUST AN ORPHAN...
...FREAK LIKE US...
...WANT TO ADOPT HIM...
...HE NEEDS A REAL FAMILY, STEVE...
RRRRRR!
...HE NEEDS US...

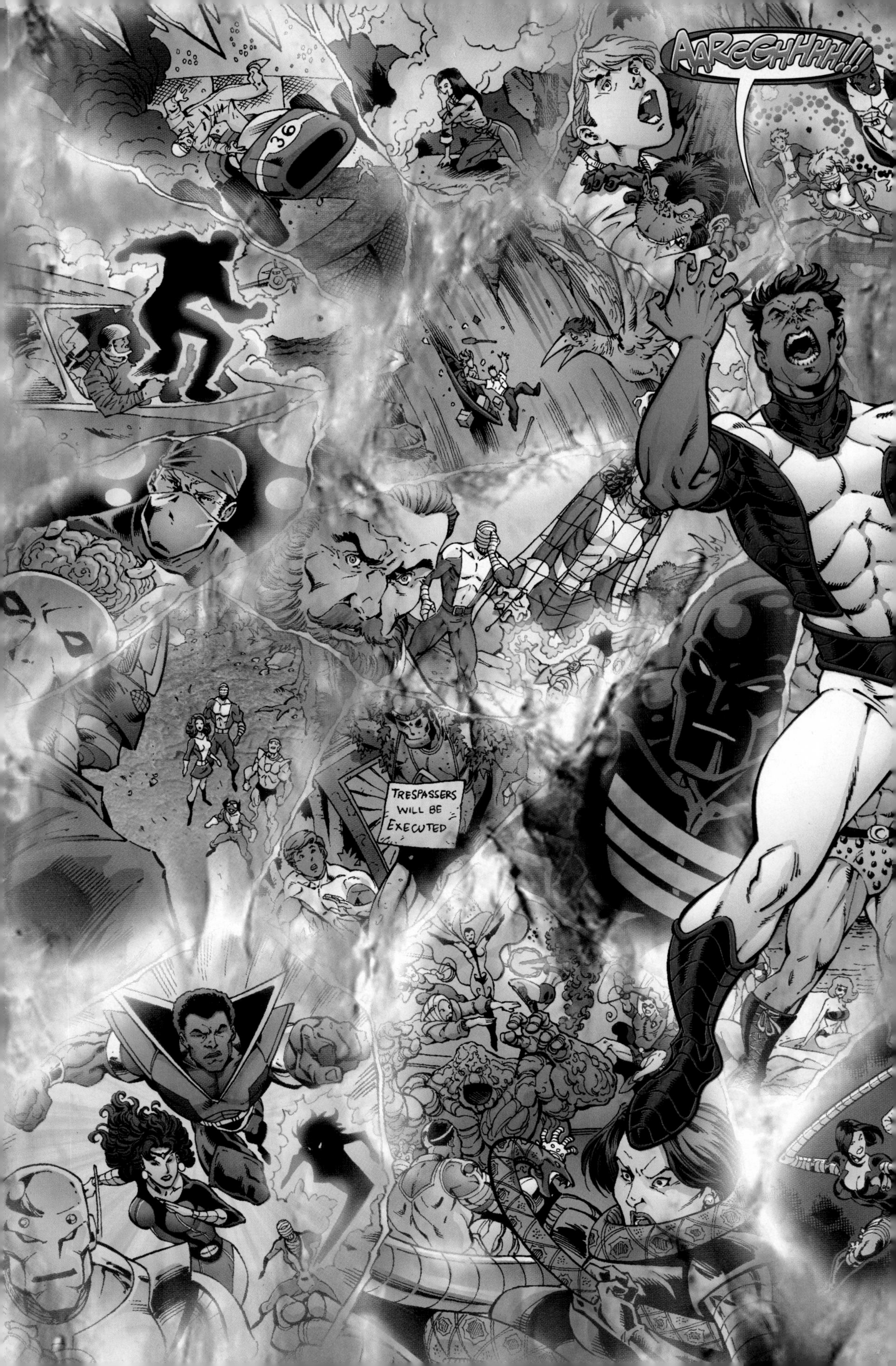
AARGGHHHH!!!
TRESPASSERS WILL BE EXECUTED

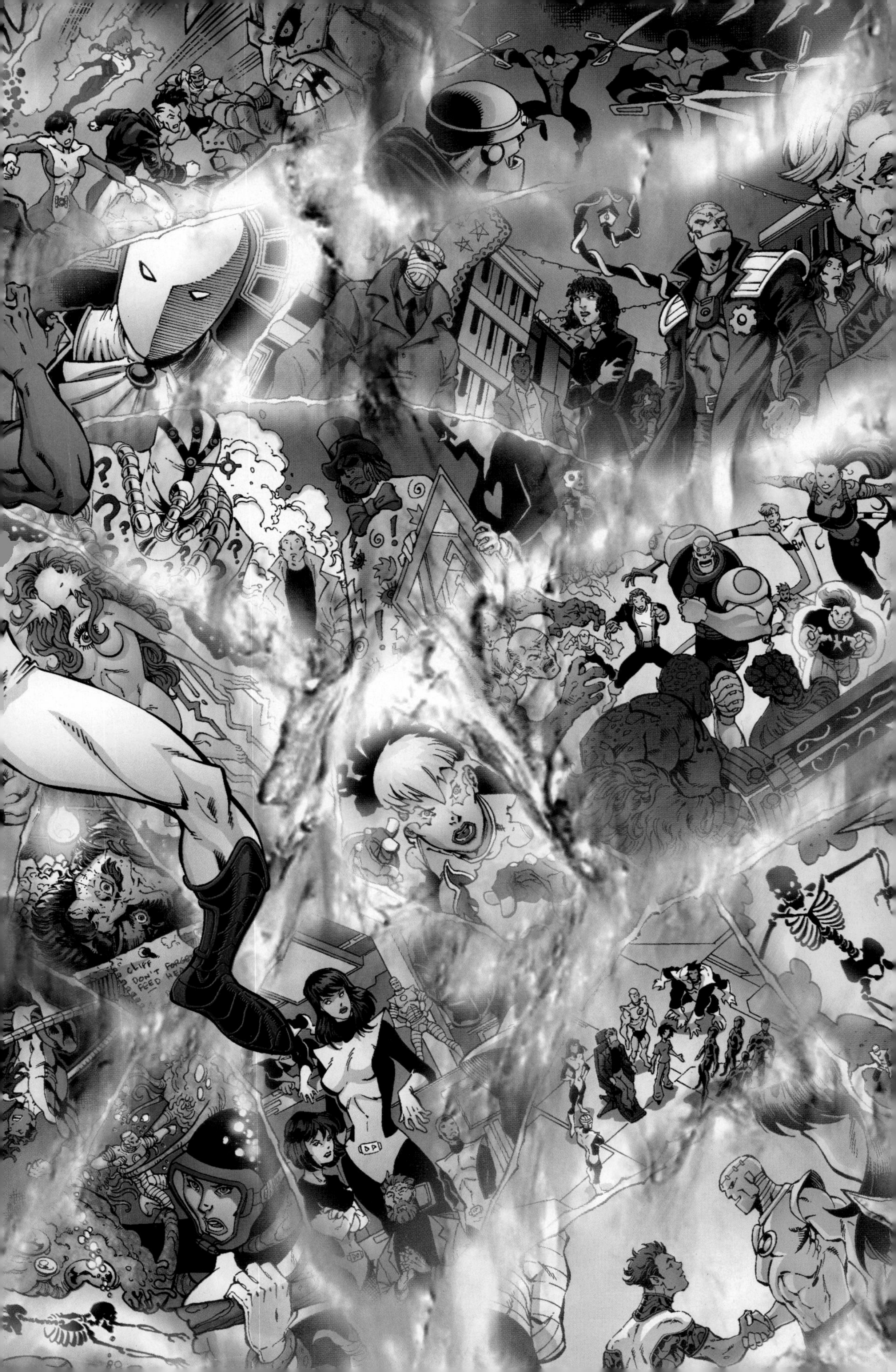
CLIFF
DON'T FEED

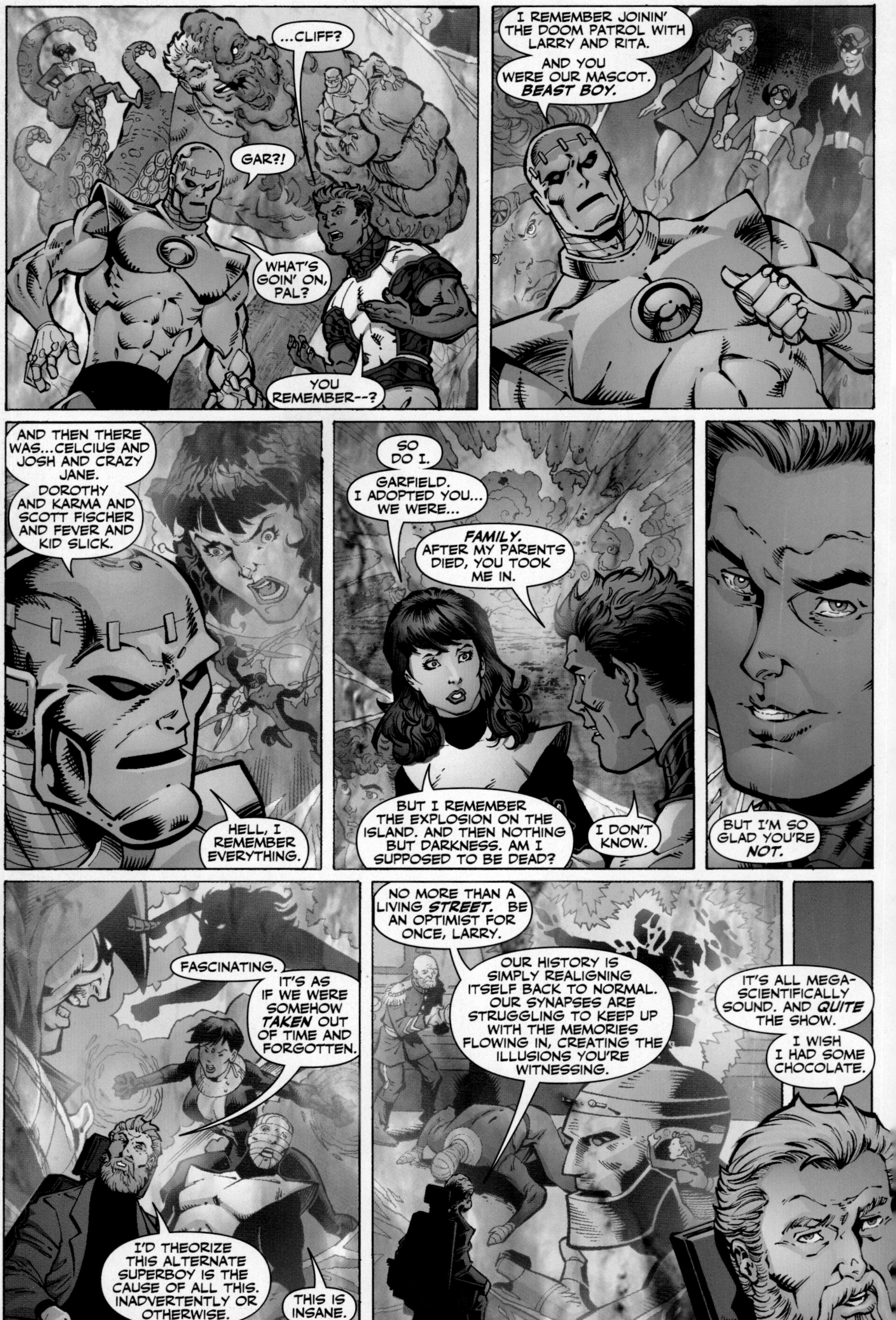
...CLIFF?
GAR?!
WHAT'S GOIN' ON, PAL?
YOU REMEMBER--?
I REMEMBER JOININ' THE DOOM PATROL WITH LARRY AND RITA.
AND YOU WERE OUR MASCOT. BEAST BOY.
AND THEN THERE WAS...CELCIUS AND JOSH AND CRAZY JANE.
DOROTHY AND KARMA AND SCOTT FISCHER AND FEVER AND KID SLICK.
HELL, I REMEMBER EVERYTHING.
SO DO I.
GARFIELD. I ADOPTED YOU... WE WERE...
FAMILY. AFTER MY PARENTS DIED, YOU TOOK ME IN.
BUT I REMEMBER THE EXPLOSION ON THE ISLAND. AND THEN NOTHING BUT DARKNESS. AM I SUPPOSED TO BE DEAD?
I DON'T KNOW.
BUT I'M SO GLAD YOU'RE NOT.
FASCINATING.
IT'S AS IF WE WERE SOMEHOW TAKEN OUT OF TIME AND FORGOTTEN.
I'D THEORIZE THIS ALTERNATE SUPERBOY IS THE CAUSE OF ALL THIS. INADVERTENTLY OR OTHERWISE.
THIS IS INSANE.
NO MORE THAN A LIVING STREET. BE AN OPTIMIST FOR ONCE, LARRY.
OUR HISTORY IS SIMPLY REALIGNING ITSELF BACK TO NORMAL. OUR SYNAPSES ARE STRUGGLING TO KEEP UP WITH THE MEMORIES FLOWING IN, CREATING THE ILLUSIONS YOU'RE WITNESSING.
IT'S ALL MEGA-SCIENTIFICALLY SOUND. AND QUITE THE SHOW.
I WISH I HAD SOME CHOCOLATE.

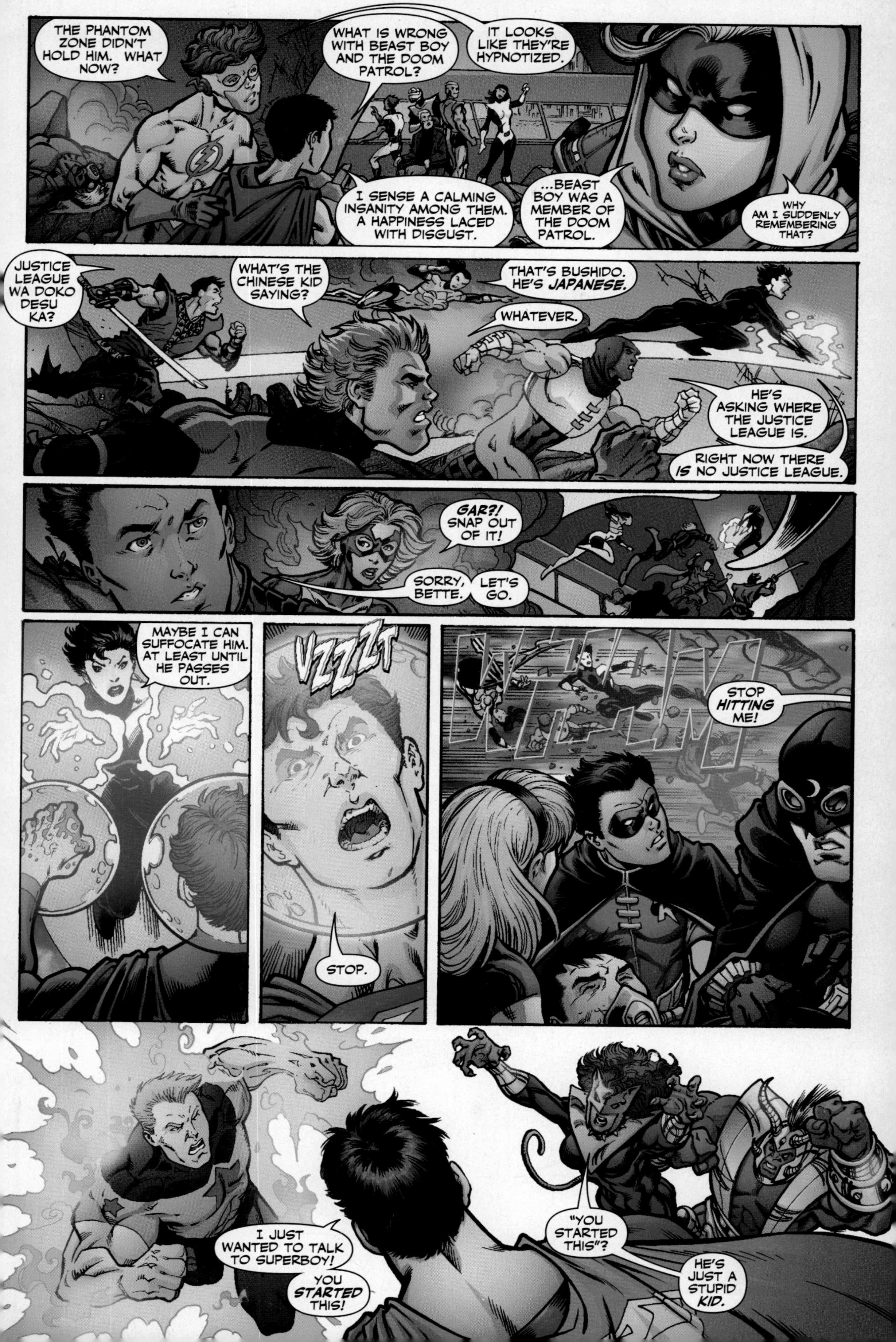
THE PHANTOM ZONE DIDN'T HOLD HIM. WHAT NOW?
WHAT IS WRONG WITH BEAST BOY AND THE DOOM PATROL?
IT LOOKS LIKE THEY'RE HYPNOTIZED.
I SENSE A CALMING INSANITY AMONG THEM. A HAPPINESS LACED WITH DISGUST.
...BEAST BOY WAS A MEMBER OF THE DOOM PATROL.
WHY AM I SUDDENLY REMEMBERING THAT?
JUSTICE LEAGUE WA DOKO DESU KA?
WHAT'S THE CHINESE KID SAYING?
THAT'S BUSHIDO. HE'S JAPANESE.
WHATEVER.
HE'S ASKING WHERE THE JUSTICE LEAGUE IS.
RIGHT NOW THERE IS NO JUSTICE LEAGUE.
GAR?! SNAP OUT OF IT!
SORRY, BETTE.
LET'S GO.
MAYBE I CAN SUFFOCATE HIM. AT LEAST UNTIL HE PASSES OUT.
VZZZZT
STOP.
STOP HITTING ME!
I JUST WANTED TO TALK TO SUPERBOY!
YOU STARTED THIS!
"YOU STARTED THIS"?
HE'S JUST A STUPID KID.

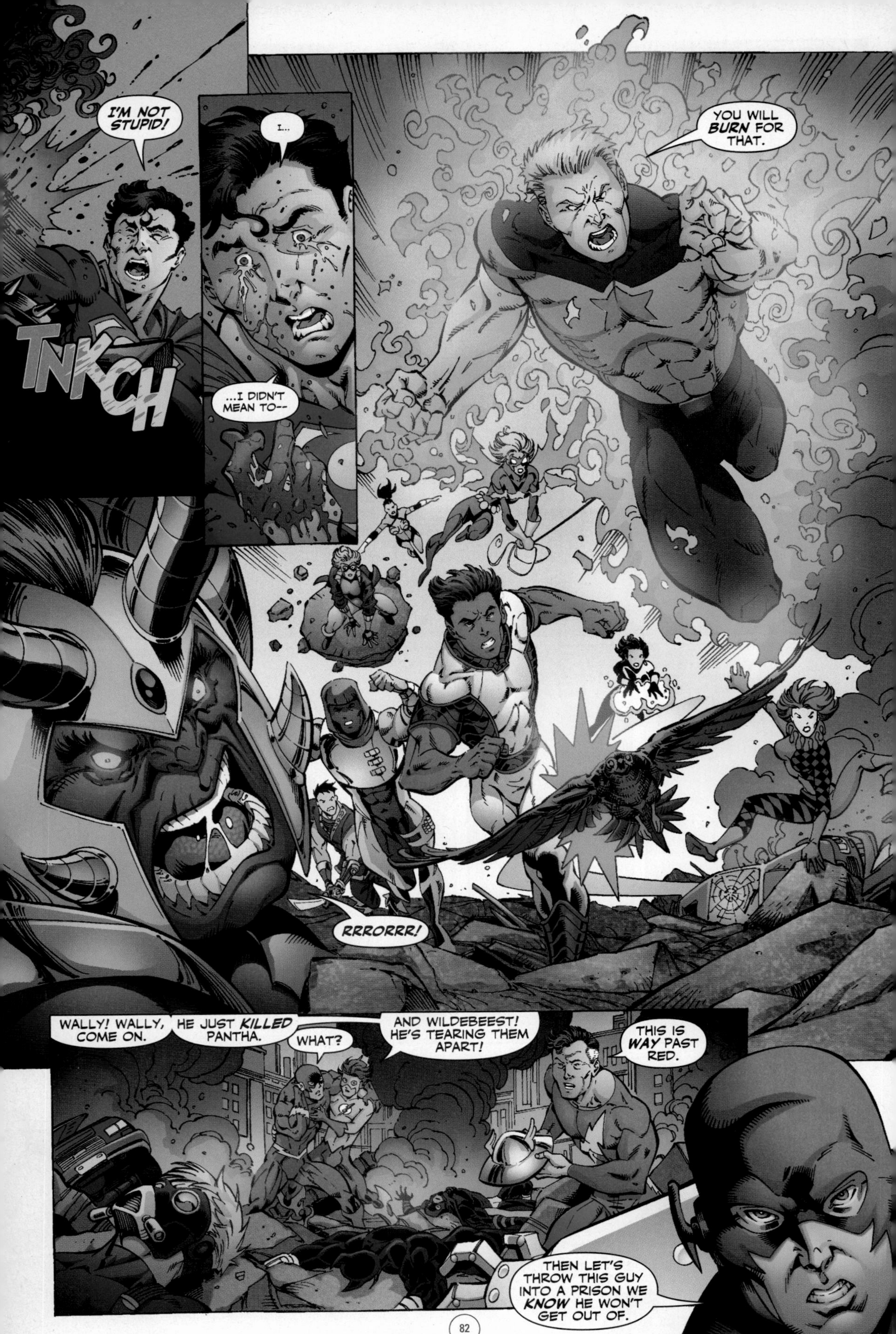
I'M NOT STUPID!
TNKCH
I...
...I DIDN'T MEAN TO--
YOU WILL BURN FOR THAT.
RRRORRR!
WALLY! WALLY, COME ON.
HE JUST KILLED PANTHA.
WHAT?
AND WILDEBEEST! HE'S TEARING THEM APART!
THIS IS WAY PAST RED.
THEN LET'S THROW THIS GUY INTO A PRISON WE KNOW HE WON'T GET OUT OF.

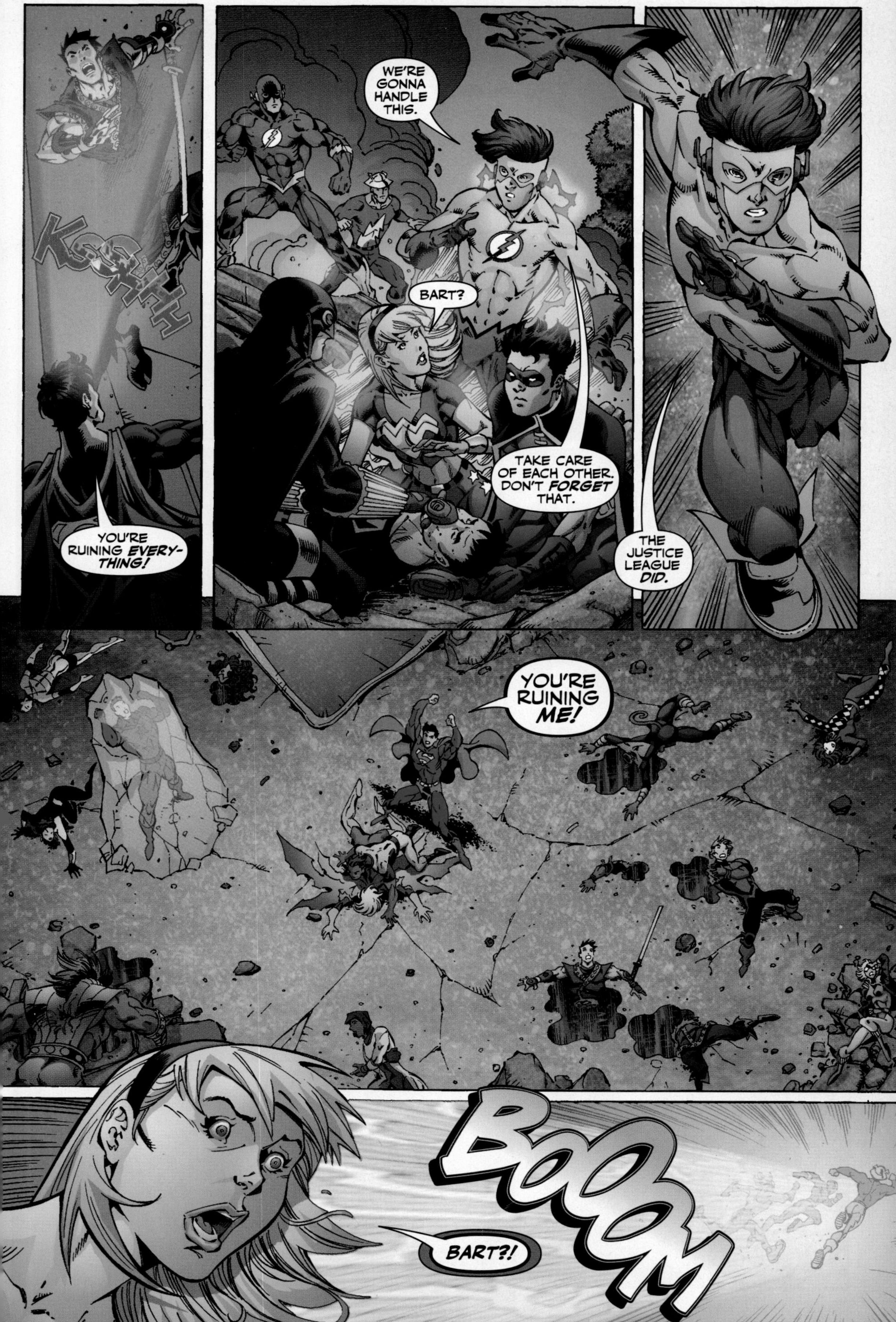
KSSHHH
YOU'RE RUINING EVERY-THING!
WE'RE GONNA HANDLE THIS.
BART?
TAKE CARE OF EACH OTHER. DON'T FORGET THAT.
THE JUSTICE LEAGUE DID.
YOU'RE RUINING ME!
BOOOM
BART?!

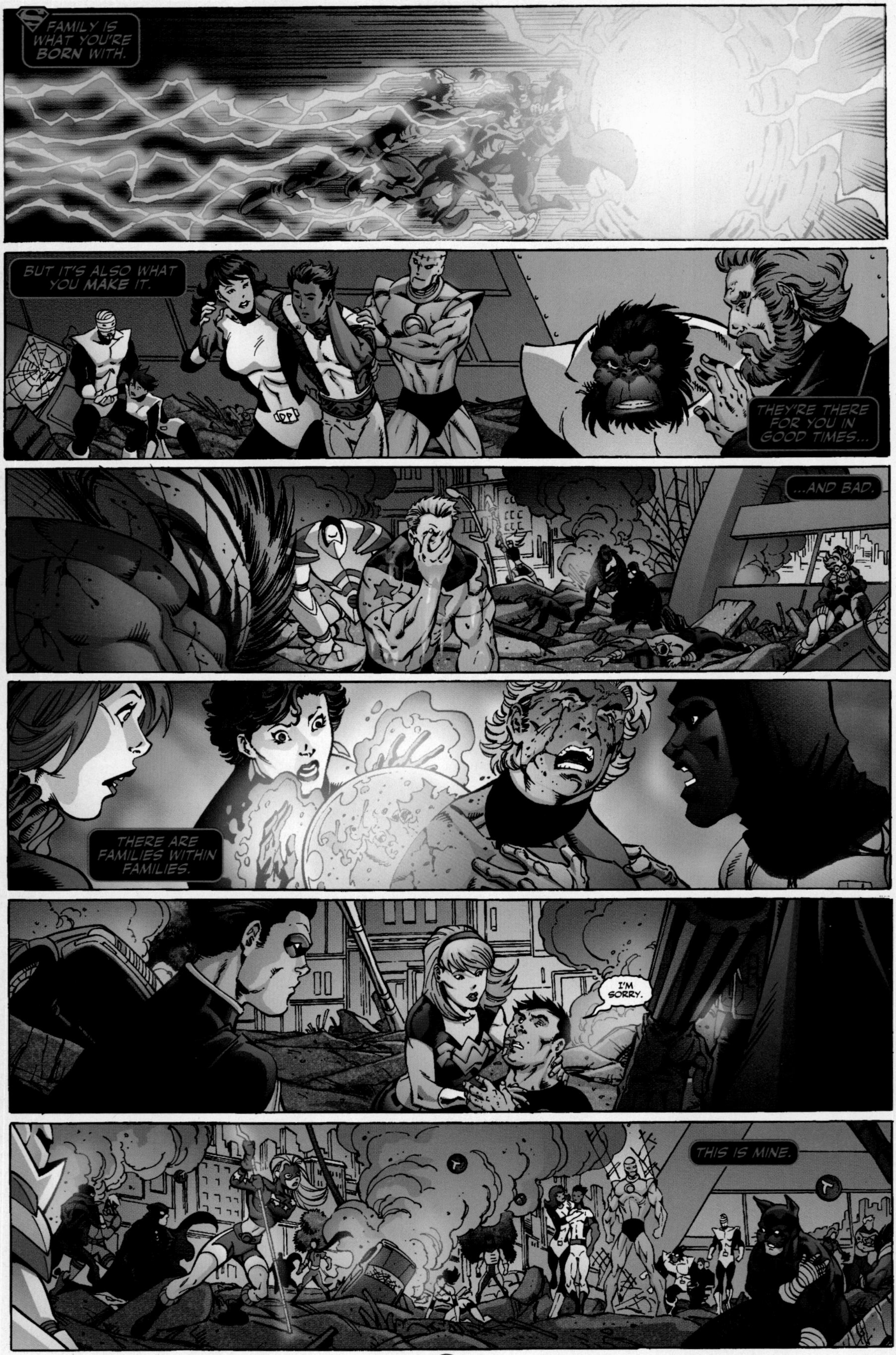
FAMILY IS WHAT YOU'RE BORN WITH.
BUT IT'S ALSO WHAT YOU MAKE IT.
THEY'RE THERE FOR YOU IN GOOD TIMES...
...AND BAD.
THERE ARE FAMILIES WITHIN FAMILIES.
I'M SORRY.
THIS IS MINE.

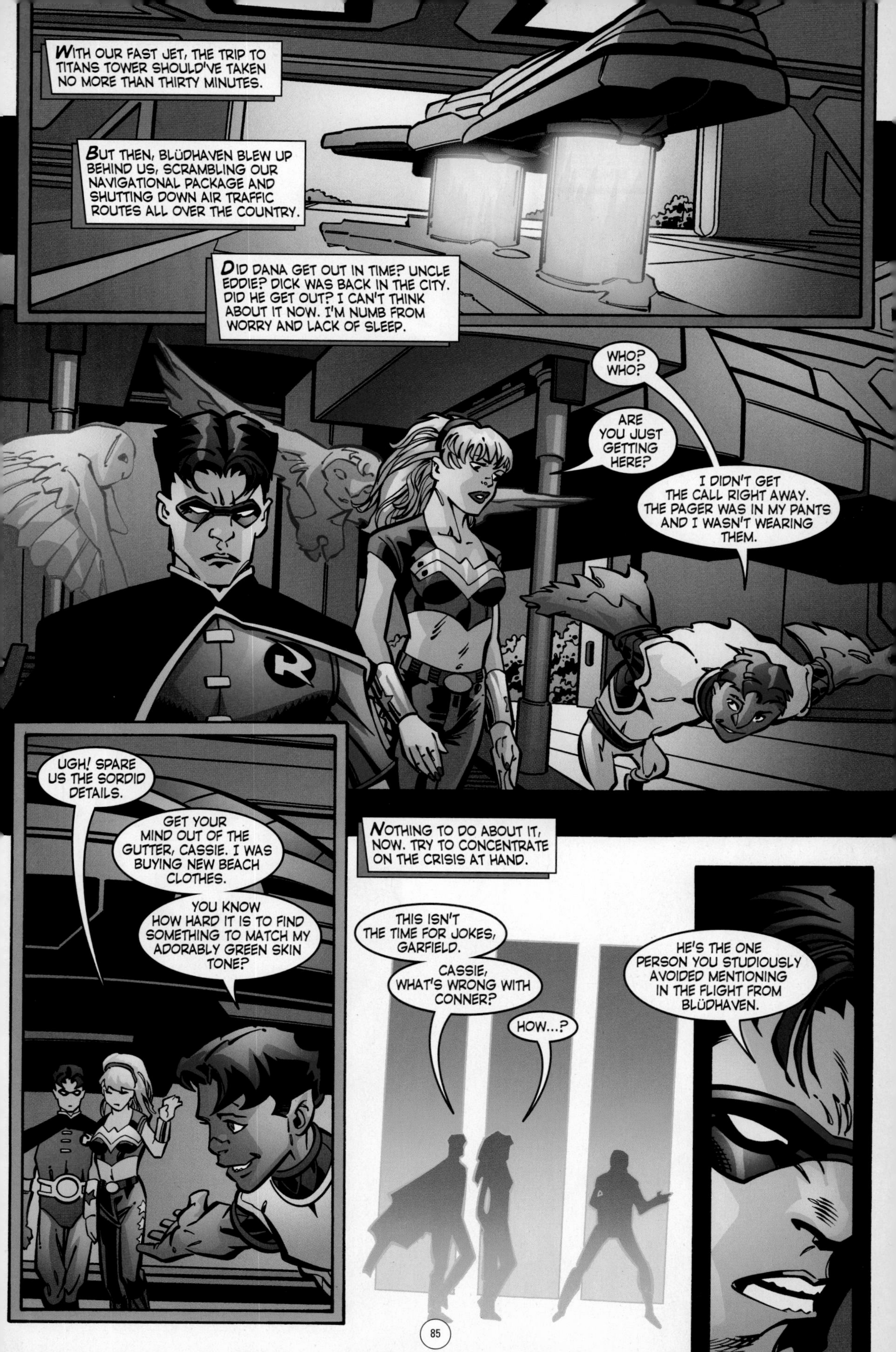
WITH OUR FAST JET, THE TRIP TO TITANS TOWER SHOULD'VE TAKEN NO MORE THAN THIRTY MINUTES.
BUT THEN, BLÜDHAVEN BLEW UP BEHIND US, SCRAMBLING OUR NAVIGATIONAL PACKAGE AND SHUTTING DOWN AIR TRAFFIC ROUTES ALL OVER THE COUNTRY.
DID DANA GET OUT IN TIME? UNCLE EDDIE? DICK WAS BACK IN THE CITY. DID HE GET OUT? I CAN'T THINK ABOUT IT NOW. I'M NUMB FROM WORRY AND LACK OF SLEEP.
WHO? WHO?
ARE YOU JUST GETTING HERE?
I DIDN'T GET THE CALL RIGHT AWAY. THE PAGER WAS IN MY PANTS AND I WASN'T WEARING THEM.
UGH! SPARE US THE SORDID DETAILS.
GET YOUR MIND OUT OF THE GUTTER, CASSIE. I WAS BUYING NEW BEACH CLOTHES.
YOU KNOW HOW HARD IT IS TO FIND SOMETHING TO MATCH MY ADORABLY GREEN SKIN TONE?
NOTHING TO DO ABOUT IT, NOW. TRY TO CONCENTRATE ON THE CRISIS AT HAND.
THIS ISN'T THE TIME FOR JOKES, GARFIELD.
CASSIE, WHAT'S WRONG WITH CONNER?
HOW...?
HE'S THE ONE PERSON YOU STUDIOUSLY AVOIDED MENTIONING IN THE FLIGHT FROM BLÜDHAVEN.

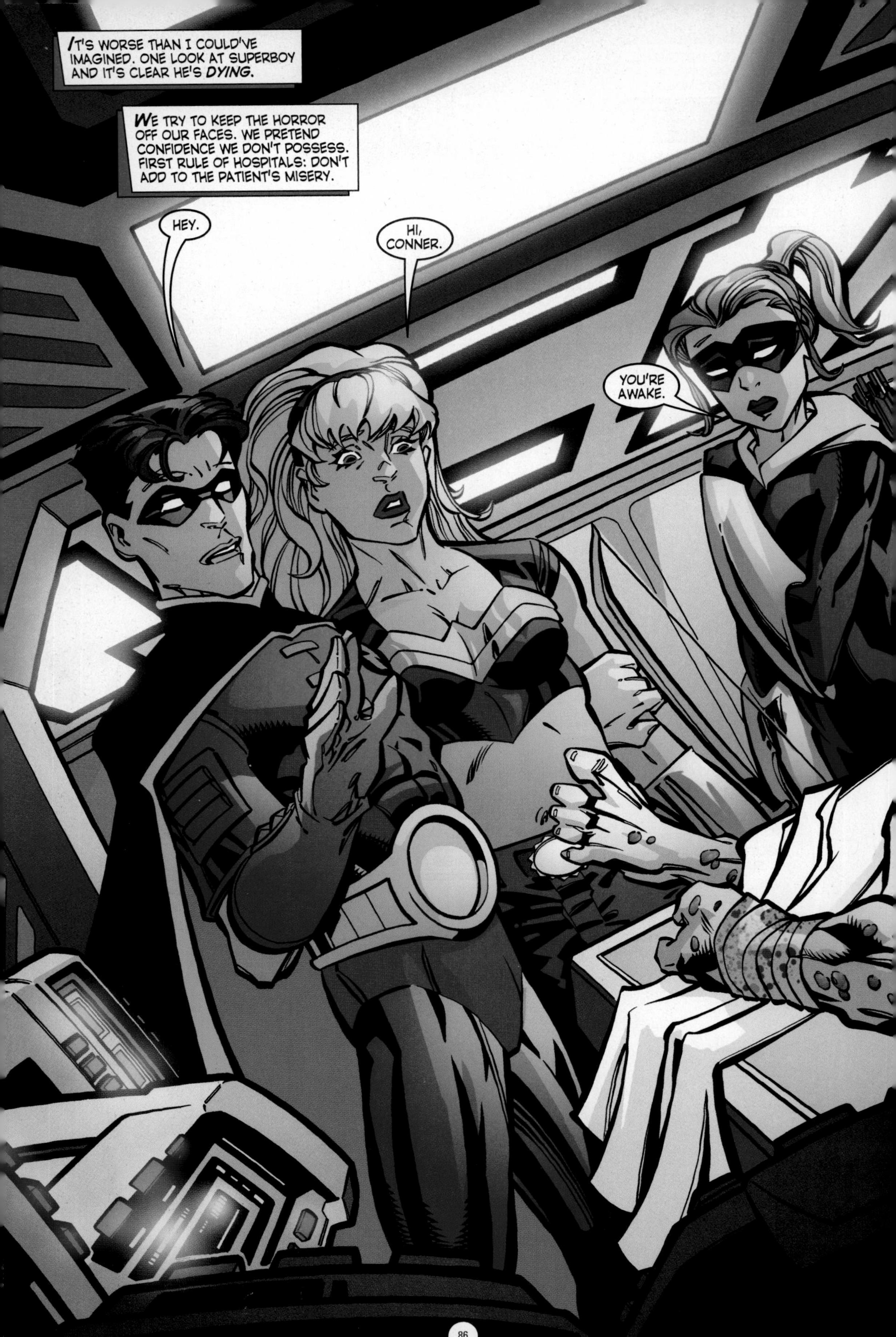
IT'S WORSE THAN I COULD'VE IMAGINED. ONE LOOK AT SUPERBOY AND IT'S CLEAR HE'S *DYING*.
WE TRY TO KEEP THE HORROR OFF OUR FACES. WE PRETEND CONFIDENCE WE DON'T POSSESS. FIRST RULE OF HOSPITALS: DON'T ADD TO THE PATIENT'S MISERY.
HEY.
HI, CONNER.
YOU'RE AWAKE.

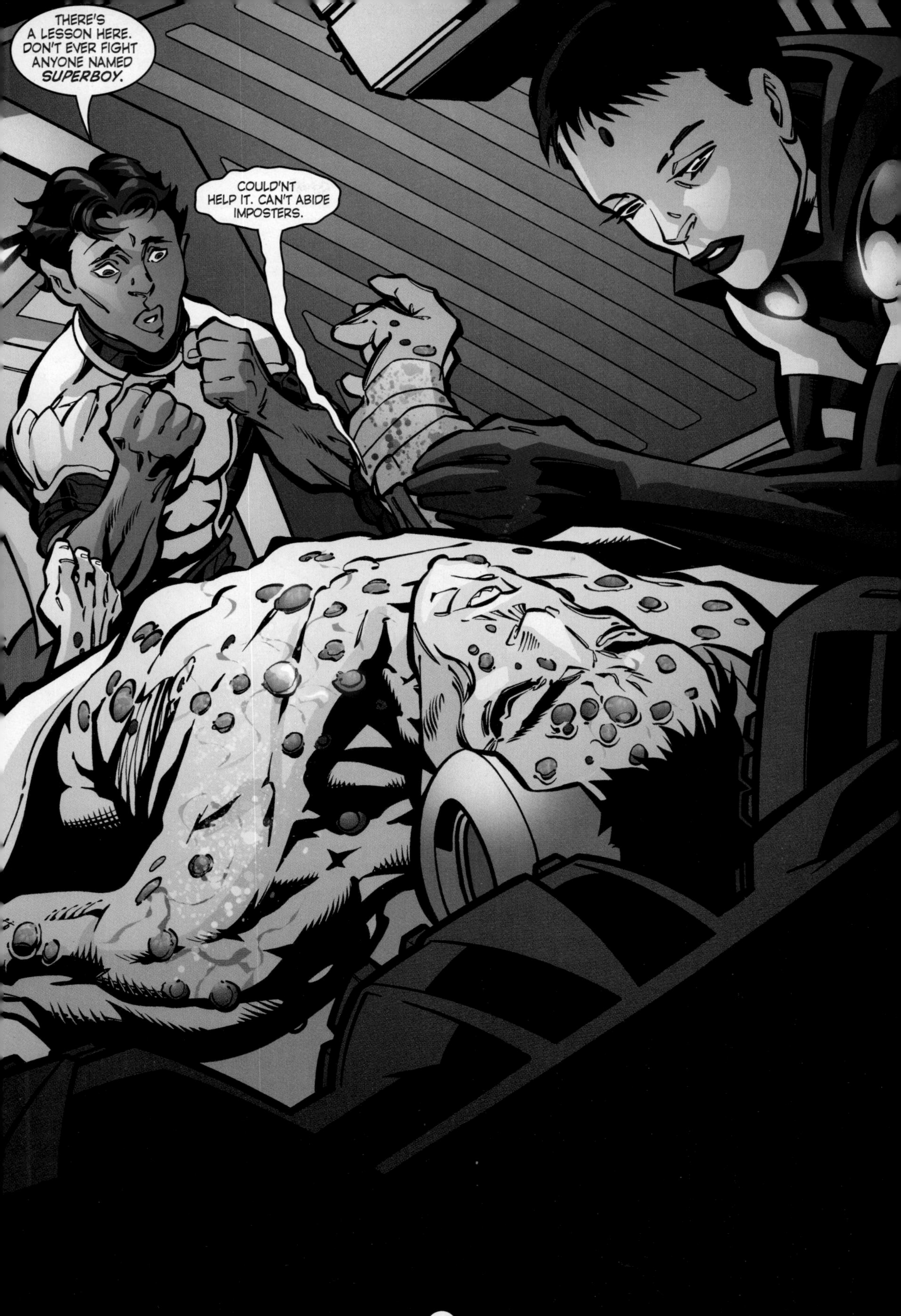
THERE'S A LESSON HERE. DON'T EVER FIGHT ANYONE NAMED SUPERBOY.
COULD'NT HELP IT. CAN'T ABIDE IMPOSTERS.

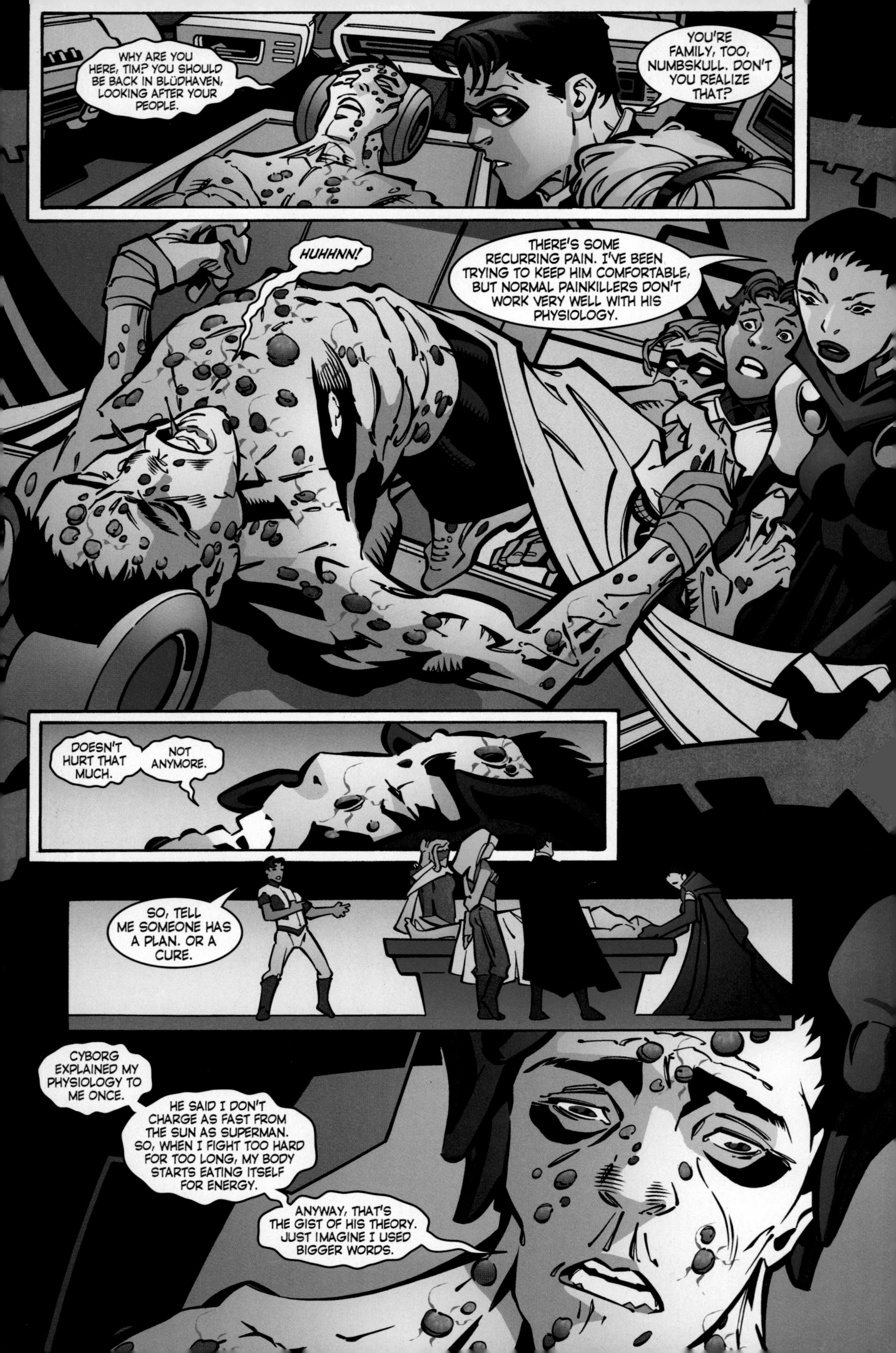
WHY ARE YOU HERE, TIM? YOU SHOULD BE BACK IN BLÜDHAVEN, LOOKING AFTER YOUR PEOPLE.
YOU'RE FAMILY, TOO, NUMBSKULL. DON'T YOU REALIZE THAT?
HUHHNN!
THERE'S SOME RECURRING PAIN. I'VE BEEN TRYING TO KEEP HIM COMFORTABLE, BUT NORMAL PAINKILLERS DON'T WORK VERY WELL WITH HIS PHYSIOLOGY.
DOESN'T HURT THAT MUCH.
NOT ANYMORE.
SO, TELL ME SOMEONE HAS A PLAN. OR A CURE.
CYBORG EXPLAINED MY PHYSIOLOGY TO ME ONCE.
HE SAID I DON'T CHARGE AS FAST FROM THE SUN AS SUPERMAN. SO, WHEN I FIGHT TOO HARD FOR TOO LONG, MY BODY STARTS EATING ITSELF FOR ENERGY.
ANYWAY, THAT'S THE GIST OF HIS THEORY. JUST IMAGINE I USED BIGGER WORDS.

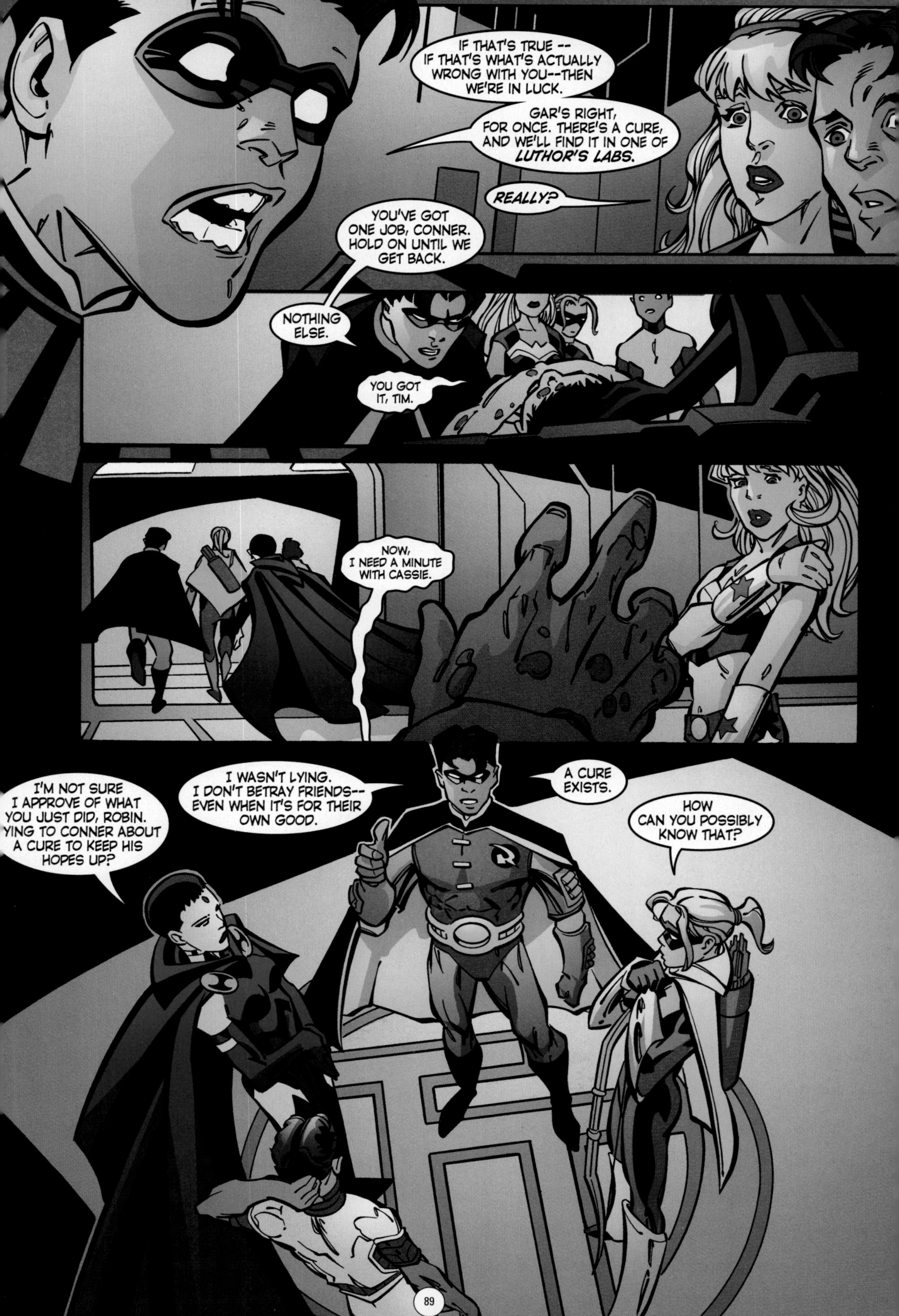
IF THAT'S TRUE -- IF THAT'S WHAT'S ACTUALLY WRONG WITH YOU--THEN WE'RE IN LUCK.
GAR'S RIGHT, FOR ONCE. THERE'S A CURE, AND WE'LL FIND IT IN ONE OF LUTHOR'S LABS.
REALLY?
YOU'VE GOT ONE JOB, CONNER. HOLD ON UNTIL WE GET BACK.
NOTHING ELSE.
YOU GOT IT, TIM.
NOW, I NEED A MINUTE WITH CASSIE.
I'M NOT SURE I APPROVE OF WHAT YOU JUST DID, ROBIN. YING TO CONNER ABOUT A CURE TO KEEP HIS HOPES UP?
I WASN'T LYING. I DON'T BETRAY FRIENDS-- EVEN WHEN IT'S FOR THEIR OWN GOOD.
A CURE EXISTS.
HOW CAN YOU POSSIBLY KNOW THAT?

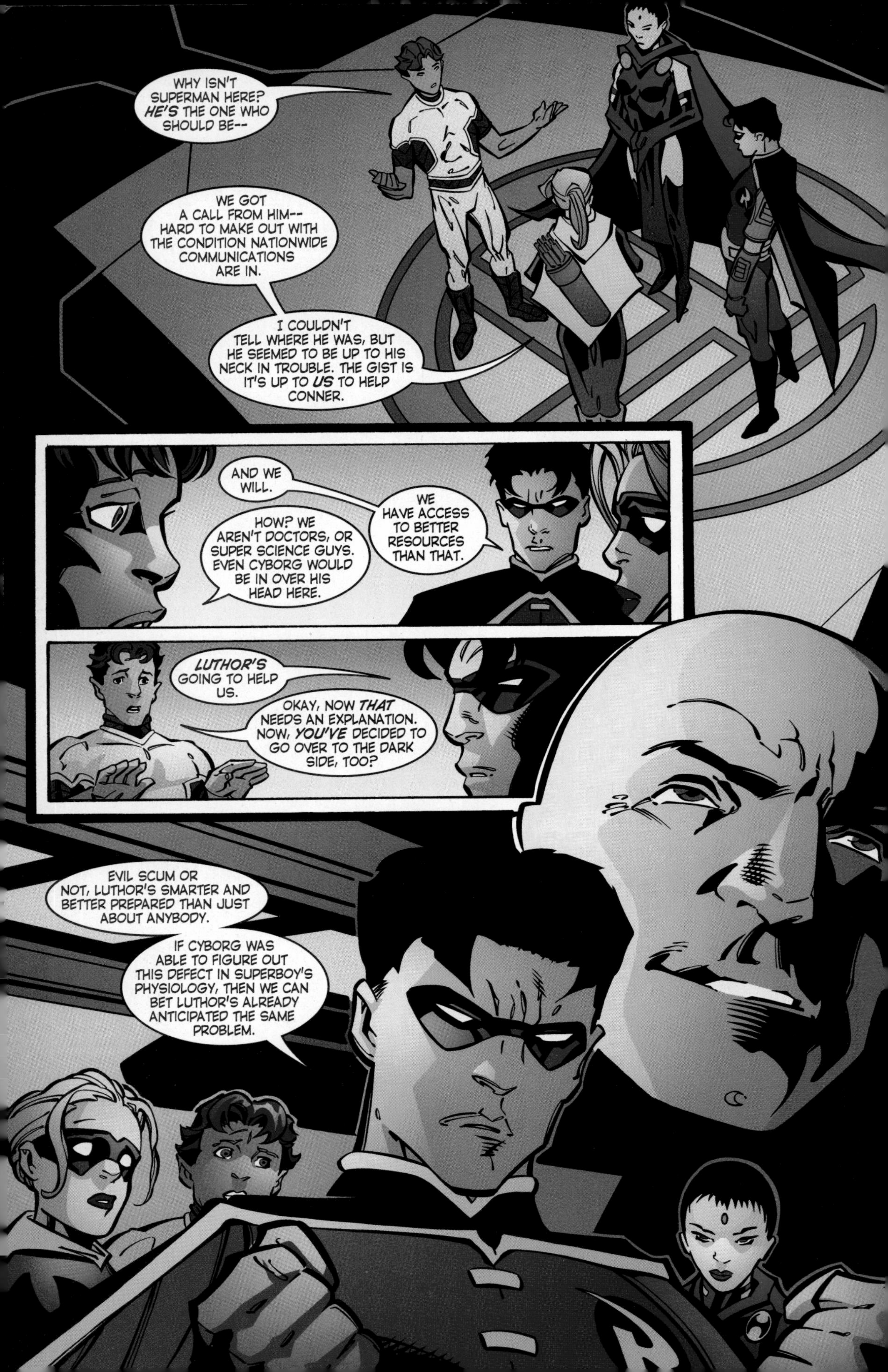
WHY ISN'T SUPERMAN HERE? *HE'S* THE ONE WHO SHOULD BE--
WE GOT A CALL FROM HIM-- HARD TO MAKE OUT WITH THE CONDITION NATIONWIDE COMMUNICATIONS ARE IN.
I COULDN'T TELL WHERE HE WAS, BUT HE SEEMED TO BE UP TO HIS NECK IN TROUBLE. THE GIST IS IT'S UP TO *US* TO HELP CONNER.
AND WE WILL.
HOW? WE AREN'T DOCTORS, OR SUPER SCIENCE GUYS. EVEN CYBORG WOULD BE IN OVER HIS HEAD HERE.
WE HAVE ACCESS TO BETTER RESOURCES THAN THAT.
LUTHOR'S GOING TO HELP US.
OKAY, NOW *THAT* NEEDS AN EXPLANATION. NOW, *YOU'VE* DECIDED TO GO OVER TO THE DARK SIDE, TOO?
EVIL SCUM OR NOT, LUTHOR'S SMARTER AND BETTER PREPARED THAN JUST ABOUT ANYBODY.
IF CYBORG WAS ABLE TO FIGURE OUT THIS DEFECT IN SUPERBOY'S PHYSIOLOGY, THEN WE CAN BET LUTHOR'S ALREADY ANTICIPATED THE SAME PROBLEM.

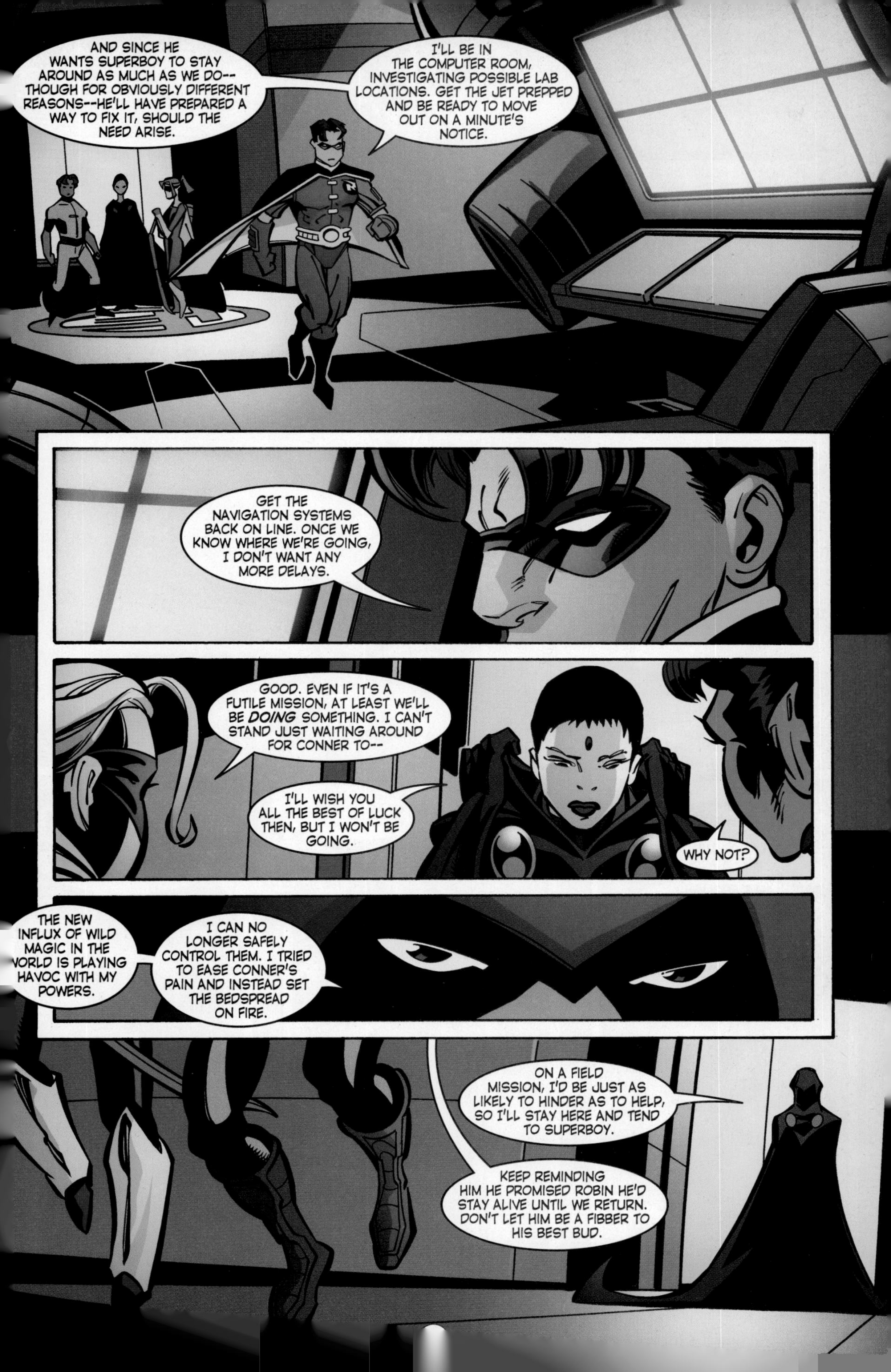
AND SINCE HE WANTS SUPERBOY TO STAY AROUND AS MUCH AS WE DO--THOUGH FOR OBVIOUSLY DIFFERENT REASONS--HE'LL HAVE PREPARED A WAY TO FIX IT, SHOULD THE NEED ARISE.
I'LL BE IN THE COMPUTER ROOM, INVESTIGATING POSSIBLE LAB LOCATIONS. GET THE JET PREPPED AND BE READY TO MOVE OUT ON A MINUTE'S NOTICE.
GET THE NAVIGATION SYSTEMS BACK ON LINE. ONCE WE KNOW WHERE WE'RE GOING, I DON'T WANT ANY MORE DELAYS.
GOOD. EVEN IF IT'S A FUTILE MISSION, AT LEAST WE'LL BE *DOING* SOMETHING. I CAN'T STAND JUST WAITING AROUND FOR CONNER TO--
I'LL WISH YOU ALL THE BEST OF LUCK THEN, BUT I WON'T BE GOING.
WHY NOT?
THE NEW INFLUX OF WILD MAGIC IN THE WORLD IS PLAYING HAVOC WITH MY POWERS.
I CAN NO LONGER SAFELY CONTROL THEM. I TRIED TO EASE CONNER'S PAIN AND INSTEAD SET THE BEDSPREAD ON FIRE.
ON A FIELD MISSION, I'D BE JUST AS LIKELY TO HINDER AS TO HELP, SO I'LL STAY HERE AND TEND TO SUPERBOY.
KEEP REMINDING HIM HE PROMISED ROBIN HE'D STAY ALIVE UNTIL WE RETURN. DON'T LET HIM BE A FIBBER TO HIS BEST BUD.

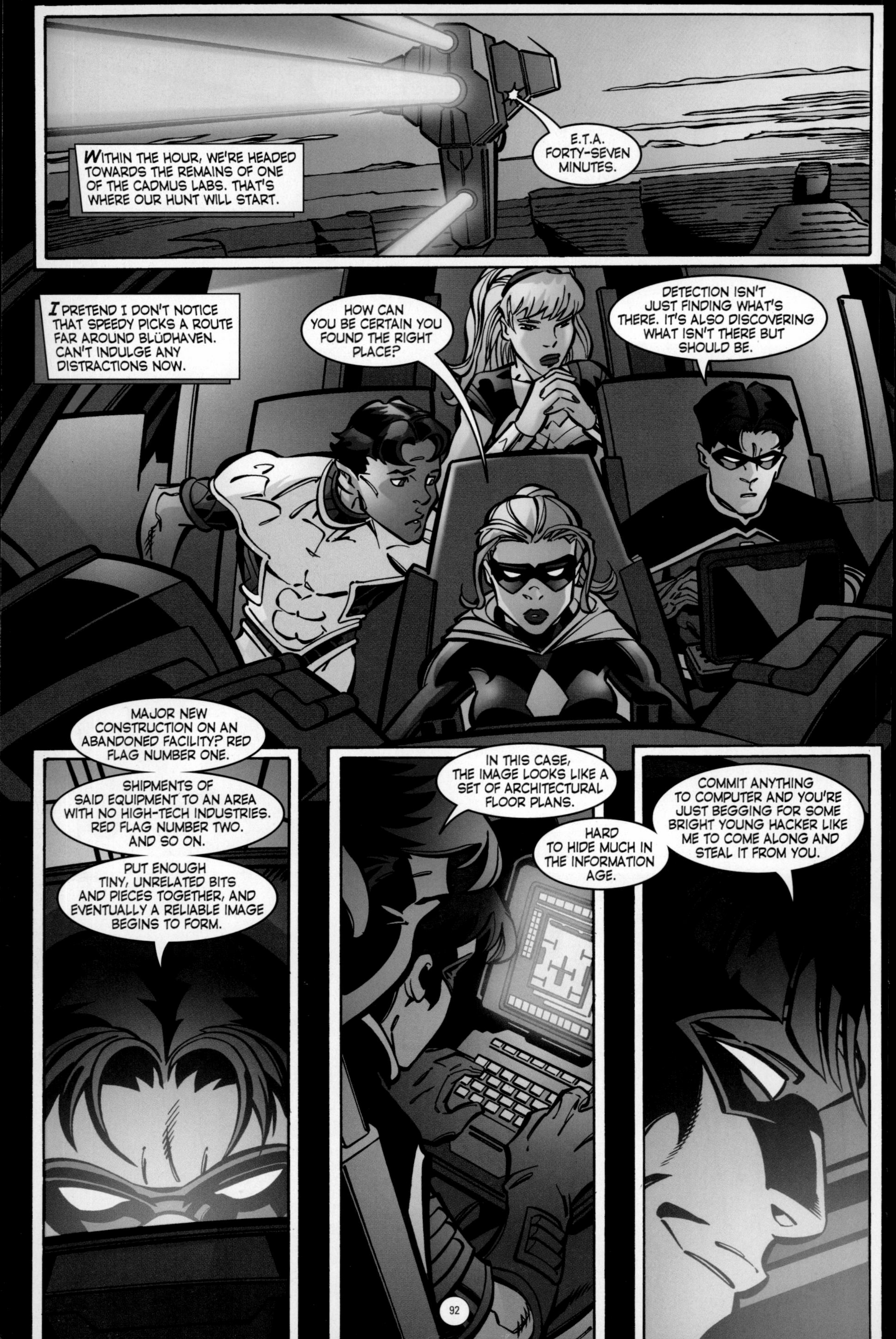
WITHIN THE HOUR, WE'RE HEADED TOWARDS THE REMAINS OF ONE OF THE CADMUS LABS. THAT'S WHERE OUR HUNT WILL START.
E.T.A. FORTY-SEVEN MINUTES.
I PRETEND I DON'T NOTICE THAT SPEEDY PICKS A ROUTE FAR AROUND BLÜDHAVEN. CAN'T INDULGE ANY DISTRACTIONS NOW.
HOW CAN YOU BE CERTAIN YOU FOUND THE RIGHT PLACE?
DETECTION ISN'T JUST FINDING WHAT'S THERE. IT'S ALSO DISCOVERING WHAT ISN'T THERE BUT SHOULD BE.
MAJOR NEW CONSTRUCTION ON AN ABANDONED FACILITY? RED FLAG NUMBER ONE.
SHIPMENTS OF SAID EQUIPMENT TO AN AREA WITH NO HIGH-TECH INDUSTRIES. RED FLAG NUMBER TWO. AND SO ON.
PUT ENOUGH TINY, UNRELATED BITS AND PIECES TOGETHER, AND EVENTUALLY A RELIABLE IMAGE BEGINS TO FORM.
IN THIS CASE, THE IMAGE LOOKS LIKE A SET OF ARCHITECTURAL FLOOR PLANS.
HARD TO HIDE MUCH IN THE INFORMATION AGE.
COMMIT ANYTHING TO COMPUTER AND YOU'RE JUST BEGGING FOR SOME BRIGHT YOUNG HACKER LIKE ME TO COME ALONG AND STEAL IT FROM YOU.

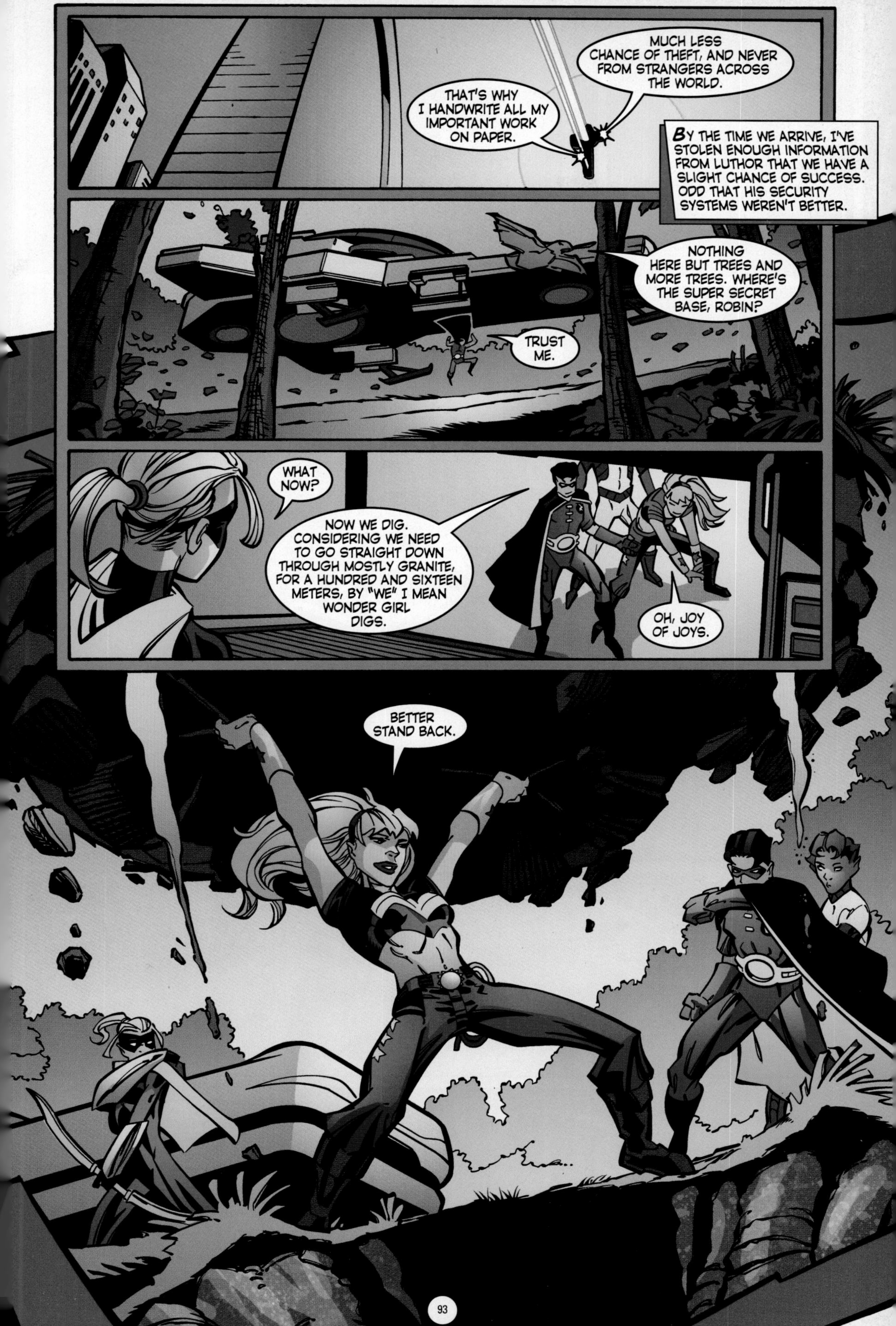
THAT'S WHY I HANDWRITE ALL MY IMPORTANT WORK ON PAPER.
MUCH LESS CHANCE OF THEFT, AND NEVER FROM STRANGERS ACROSS THE WORLD.
BY THE TIME WE ARRIVE, I'VE STOLEN ENOUGH INFORMATION FROM LUTHOR THAT WE HAVE A SLIGHT CHANCE OF SUCCESS. ODD THAT HIS SECURITY SYSTEMS WEREN'T BETTER.
NOTHING HERE BUT TREES AND MORE TREES. WHERE'S THE SUPER SECRET BASE, ROBIN?
TRUST ME.
WHAT NOW?
NOW WE DIG. CONSIDERING WE NEED TO GO STRAIGHT DOWN THROUGH MOSTLY GRANITE, FOR A HUNDRED AND SIXTEEN METERS, BY "WE" I MEAN WONDER GIRL DIGS.
OH, JOY OF JOYS.
BETTER STAND BACK.

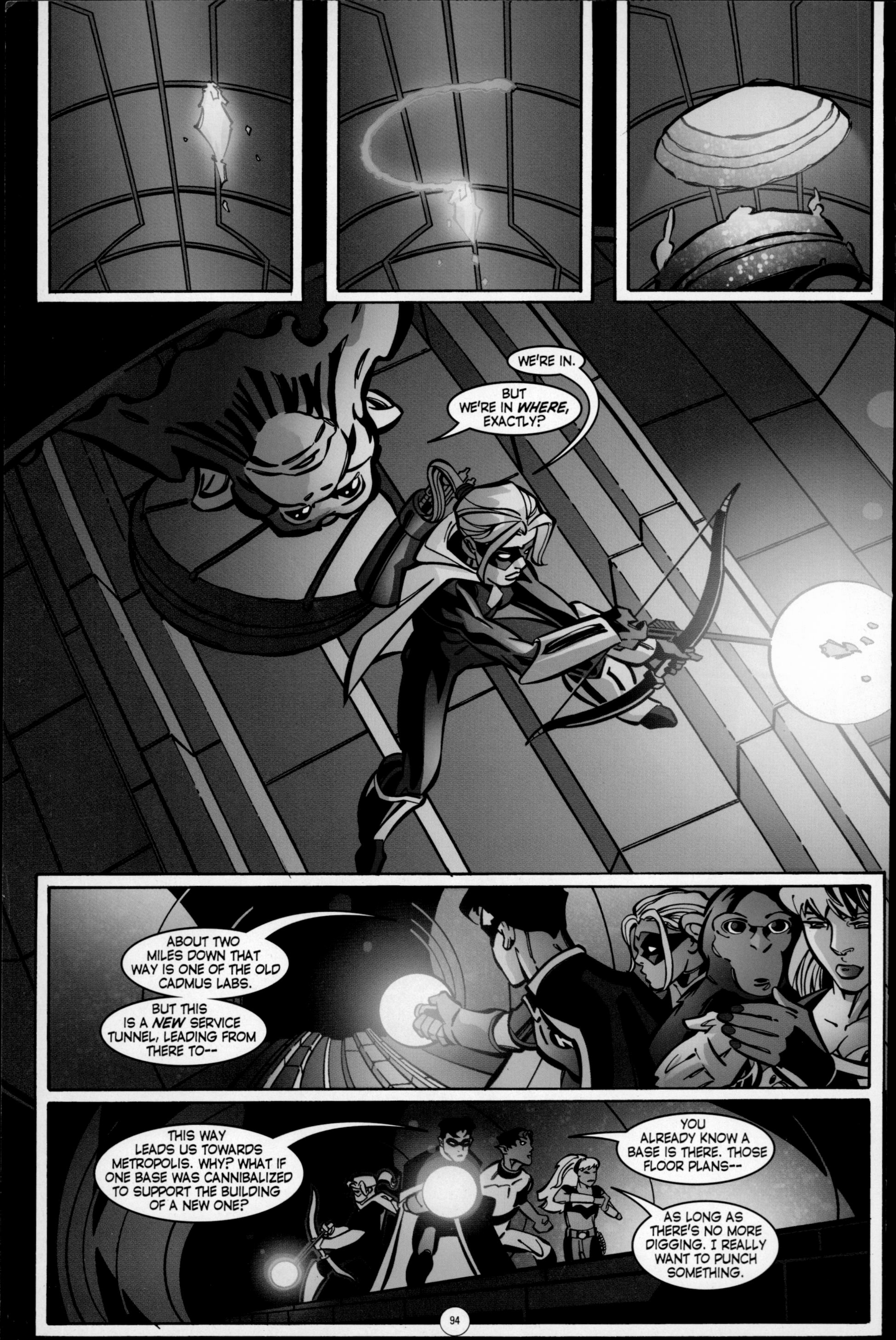
WE'RE IN.
BUT WE'RE IN *WHERE*, EXACTLY?
ABOUT TWO MILES DOWN THAT WAY IS ONE OF THE OLD CADMUS LABS.
BUT THIS IS A *NEW* SERVICE TUNNEL, LEADING FROM THERE TO--
THIS WAY LEADS US TOWARDS METROPOLIS. WHY? WHAT IF ONE BASE WAS CANNIBALIZED TO SUPPORT THE BUILDING OF A NEW ONE?
YOU ALREADY KNOW A BASE IS THERE. THOSE FLOOR PLANS--
AS LONG AS THERE'S NO MORE DIGGING. I REALLY WANT TO PUNCH SOMETHING.

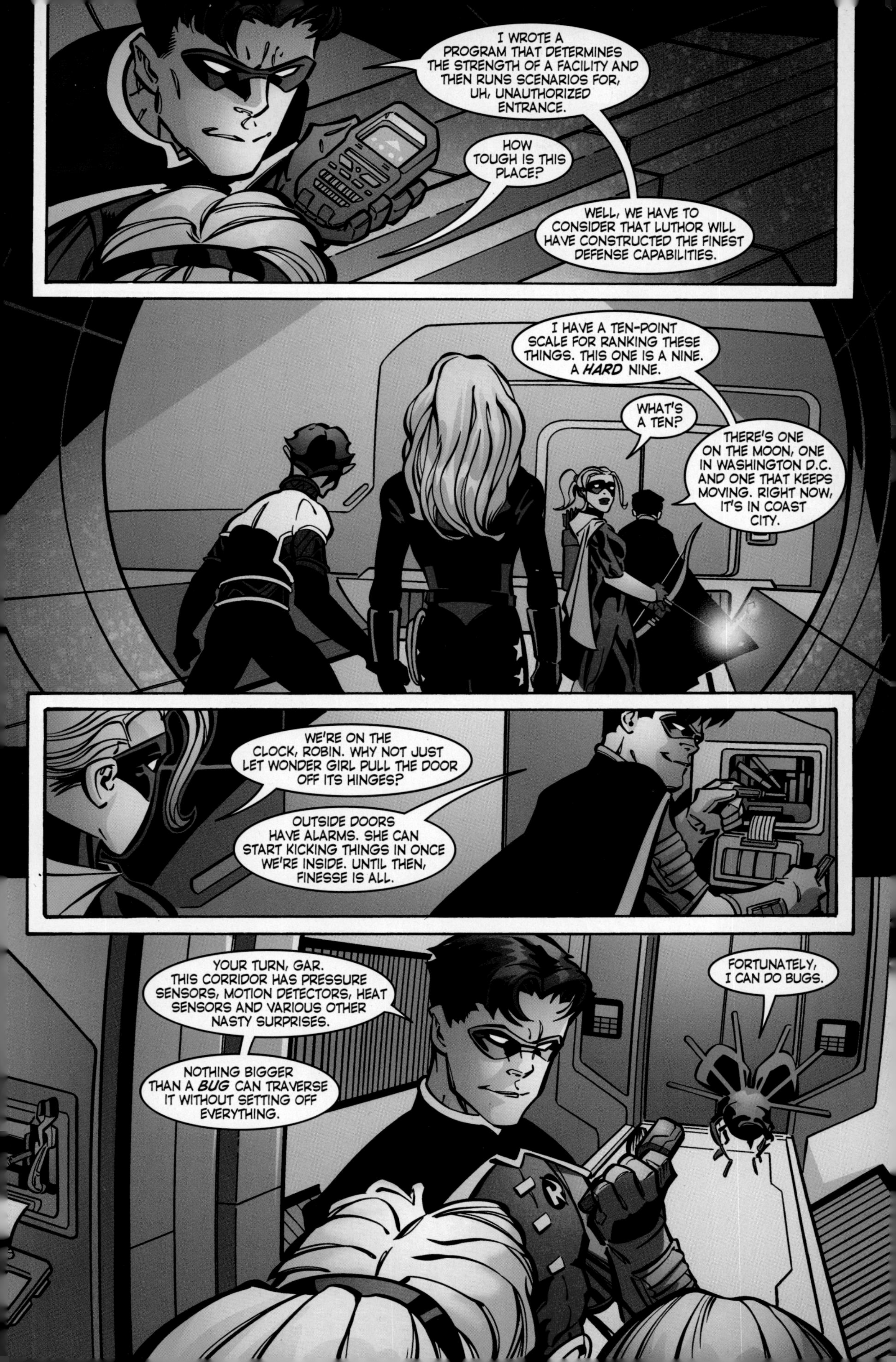
I WROTE A PROGRAM THAT DETERMINES THE STRENGTH OF A FACILITY AND THEN RUNS SCENARIOS FOR, UH, UNAUTHORIZED ENTRANCE.
HOW TOUGH IS THIS PLACE?
WELL, WE HAVE TO CONSIDER THAT LUTHOR WILL HAVE CONSTRUCTED THE FINEST DEFENSE CAPABILITIES.
I HAVE A TEN-POINT SCALE FOR RANKING THESE THINGS. THIS ONE IS A NINE. A *HARD* NINE.
WHAT'S A TEN?
THERE'S ONE ON THE MOON, ONE IN WASHINGTON D.C. AND ONE THAT KEEPS MOVING. RIGHT NOW, IT'S IN COAST CITY.
WE'RE ON THE CLOCK, ROBIN. WHY NOT JUST LET WONDER GIRL PULL THE DOOR OFF ITS HINGES?
OUTSIDE DOORS HAVE ALARMS. SHE CAN START KICKING THINGS IN ONCE WE'RE INSIDE. UNTIL THEN, FINESSE IS ALL.
YOUR TURN, GAR. THIS CORRIDOR HAS PRESSURE SENSORS, MOTION DETECTORS, HEAT SENSORS AND VARIOUS OTHER NASTY SURPRISES.
NOTHING BIGGER THAN A *BUG* CAN TRAVERSE IT WITHOUT SETTING OFF EVERYTHING.
FORTUNATELY, I CAN DO BUGS.

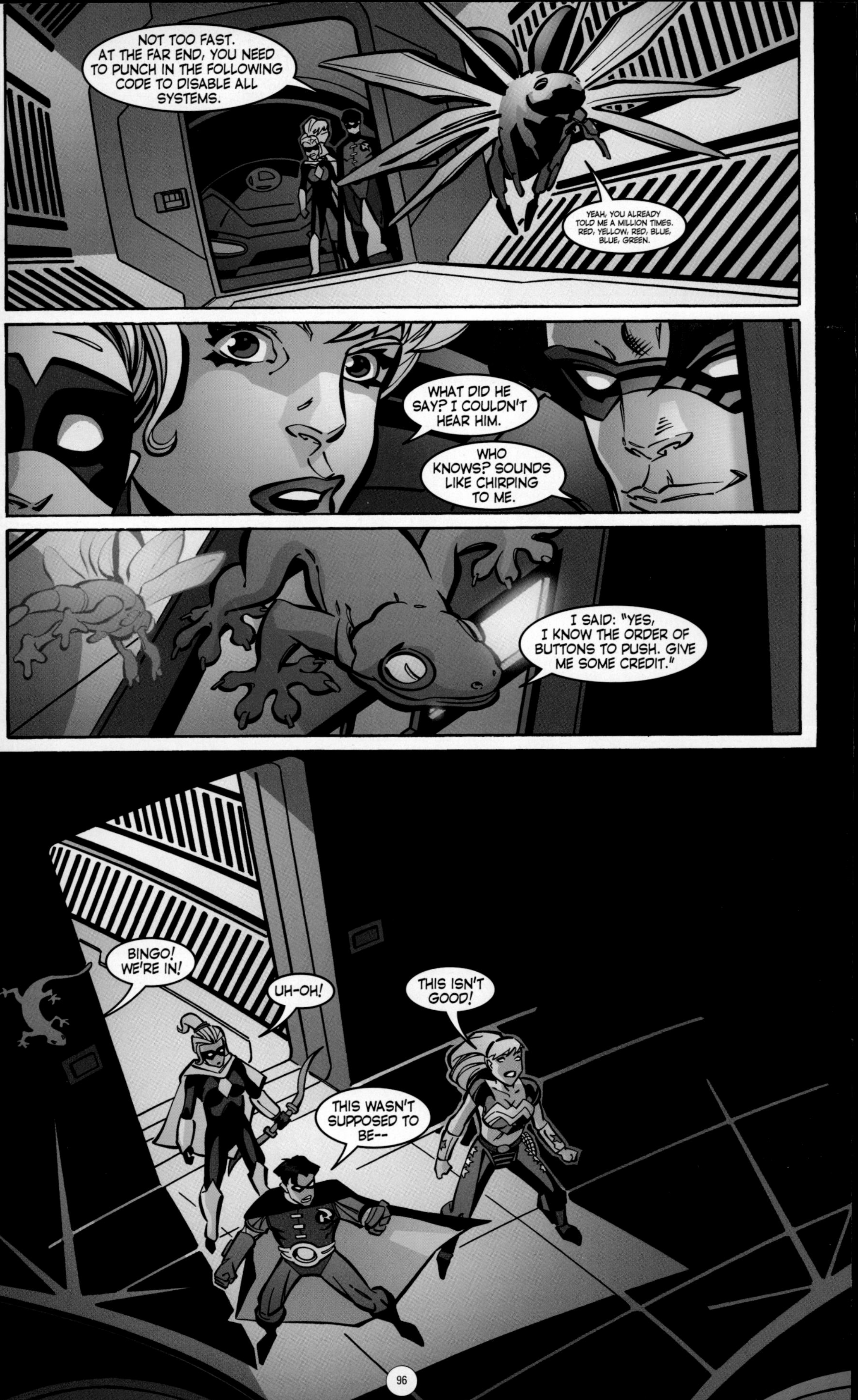
NOT TOO FAST. AT THE FAR END, YOU NEED TO PUNCH IN THE FOLLOWING CODE TO DISABLE ALL SYSTEMS.
YEAH, YOU ALREADY TOLD ME A MILLION TIMES. RED, YELLOW, RED, BLUE, BLUE, GREEN.
WHAT DID HE SAY? I COULDN'T HEAR HIM.
WHO KNOWS? SOUNDS LIKE CHIRPING TO ME.
I SAID: "YES, I KNOW THE ORDER OF BUTTONS TO PUSH. GIVE ME SOME CREDIT."
BINGO! WE'RE IN!
UH-OH!
THIS ISN'T GOOD!
THIS WASN'T SUPPOSED TO BE--

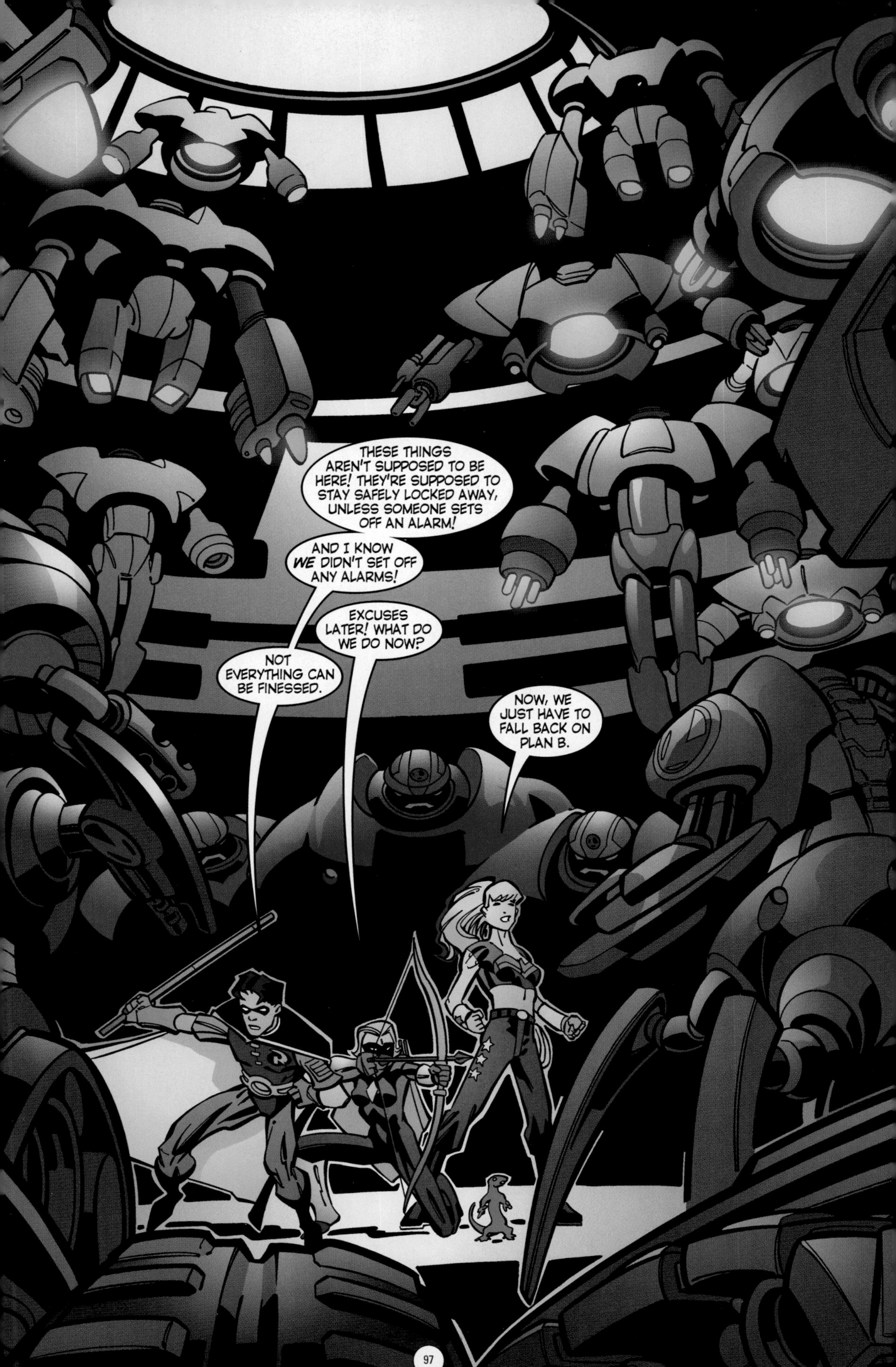
THESE THINGS AREN'T SUPPOSED TO BE HERE! THEY'RE SUPPOSED TO STAY SAFELY LOCKED AWAY, UNLESS SOMEONE SETS OFF AN ALARM!
AND I KNOW WE DIDN'T SET OFF ANY ALARMS!
EXCUSES LATER! WHAT DO WE DO NOW?
NOT EVERYTHING CAN BE FINESSED.
NOW, WE JUST HAVE TO FALL BACK ON PLAN B.

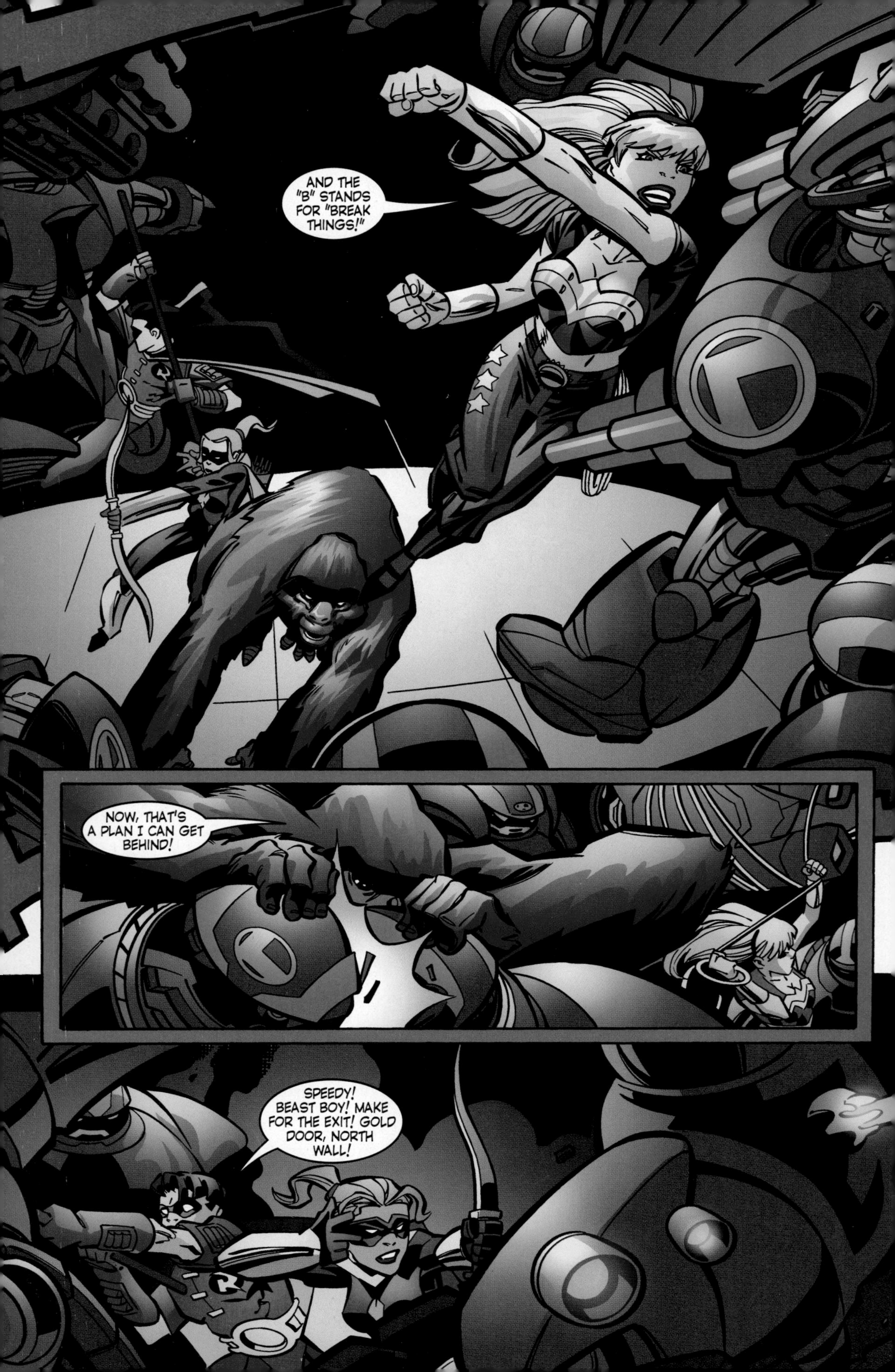
AND THE "B" STANDS FOR "BREAK THINGS!"
NOW, THAT'S A PLAN I CAN GET BEHIND!
SPEEDY! BEAST BOY! MAKE FOR THE EXIT! GOLD DOOR, NORTH WALL!

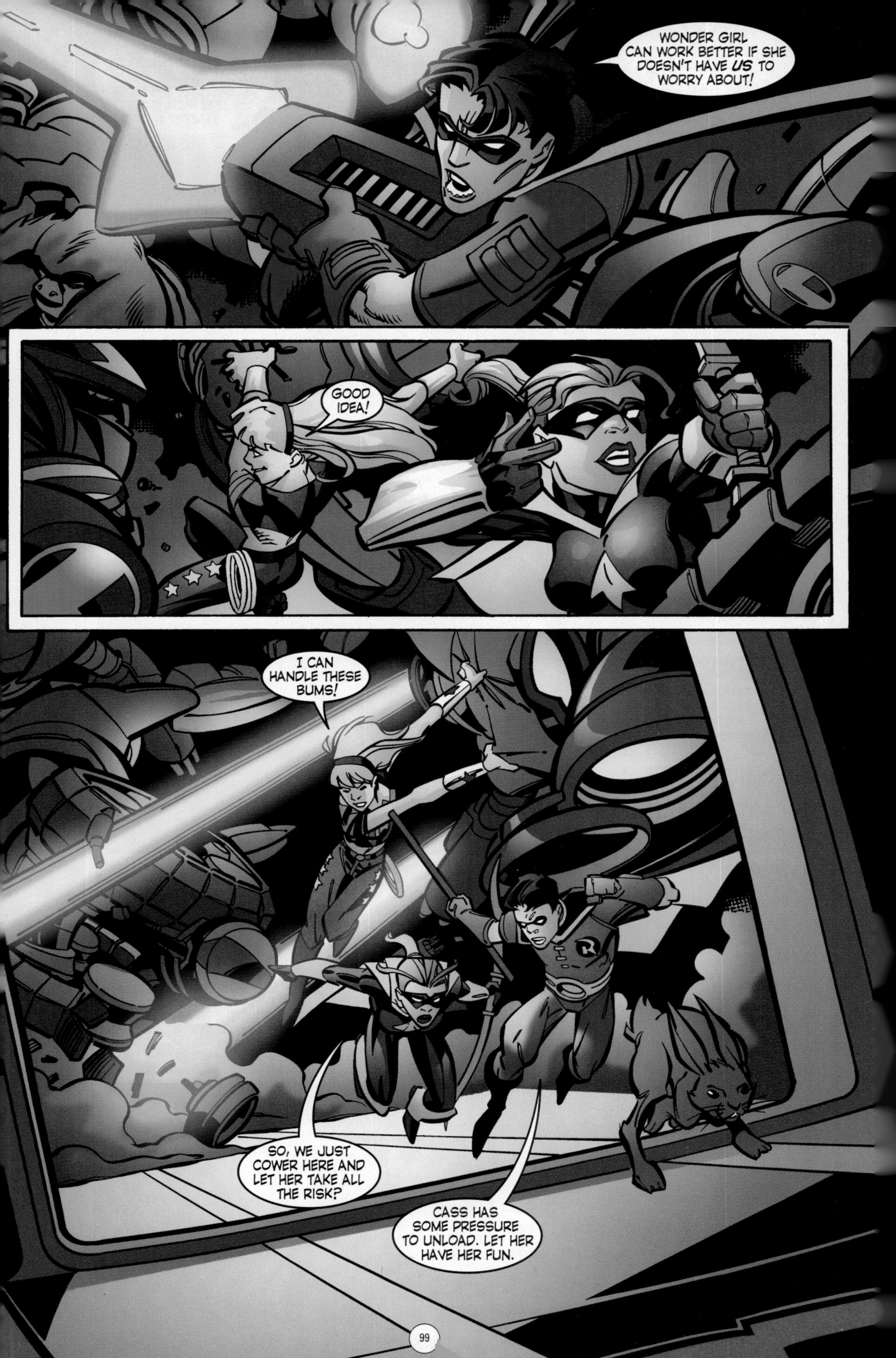
WONDER GIRL CAN WORK BETTER IF SHE DOESN'T HAVE US TO WORRY ABOUT!
GOOD IDEA!
I CAN HANDLE THESE BUMS!
SO, WE JUST COWER HERE AND LET HER TAKE ALL THE RISK?
CASS HAS SOME PRESSURE TO UNLOAD. LET HER HAVE HER FUN.

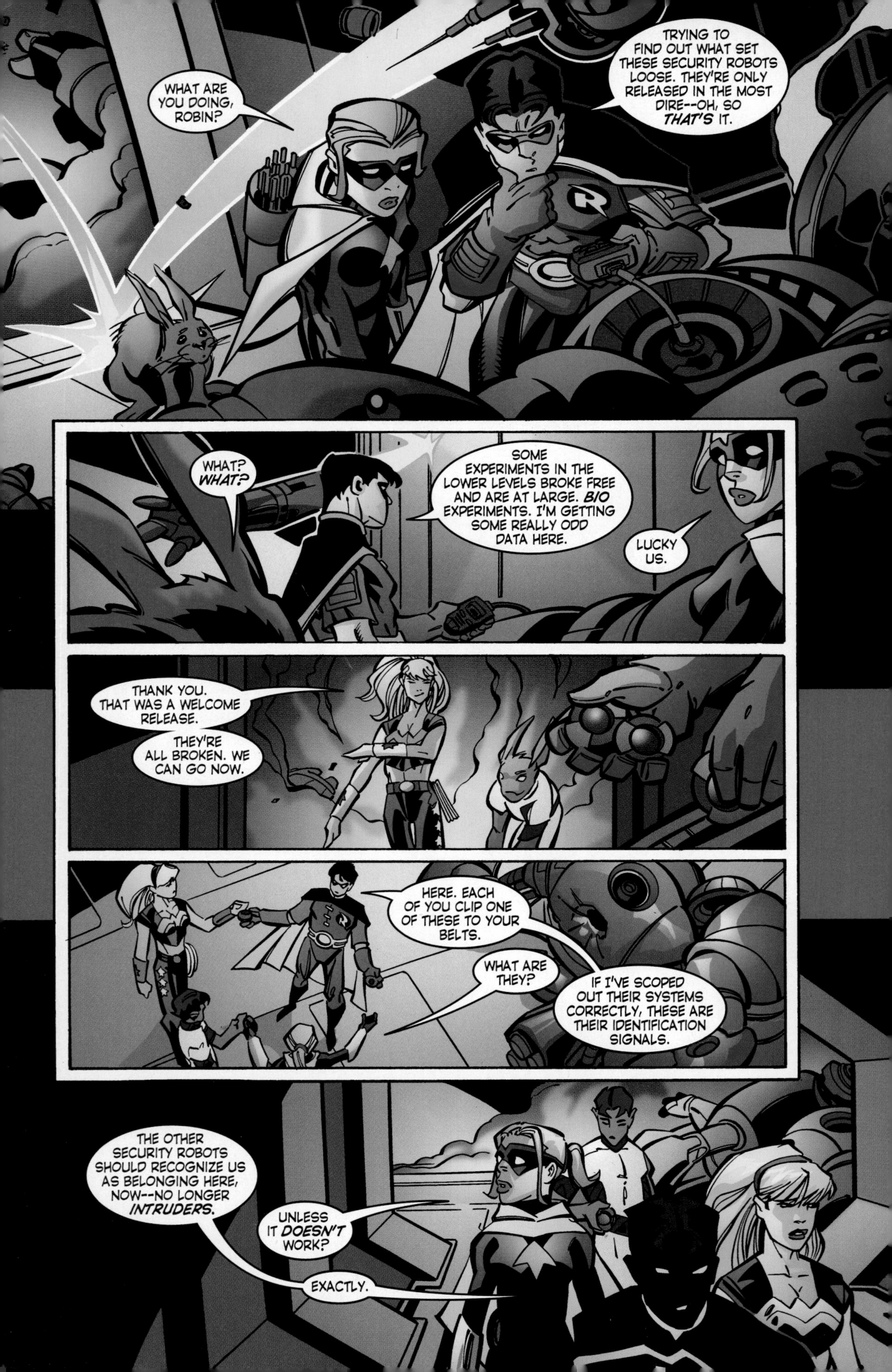
WHAT ARE YOU DOING, ROBIN?
TRYING TO FIND OUT WHAT SET THESE SECURITY ROBOTS LOOSE. THEY'RE ONLY RELEASED IN THE MOST DIRE--OH, SO *THAT'S* IT.
WHAT? *WHAT?*
SOME EXPERIMENTS IN THE LOWER LEVELS BROKE FREE AND ARE AT LARGE. *BIO* EXPERIMENTS. I'M GETTING SOME REALLY ODD DATA HERE.
LUCKY US.
THANK YOU. THAT WAS A WELCOME RELEASE.
THEY'RE ALL BROKEN. WE CAN GO NOW.
HERE. EACH OF YOU CLIP ONE OF THESE TO YOUR BELTS.
WHAT ARE THEY?
IF I'VE SCOPED OUT THEIR SYSTEMS CORRECTLY, THESE ARE THEIR IDENTIFICATION SIGNALS.
THE OTHER SECURITY ROBOTS SHOULD RECOGNIZE US AS BELONGING HERE, NOW--NO LONGER *INTRUDERS*.
UNLESS IT *DOESN'T* WORK?
EXACTLY.

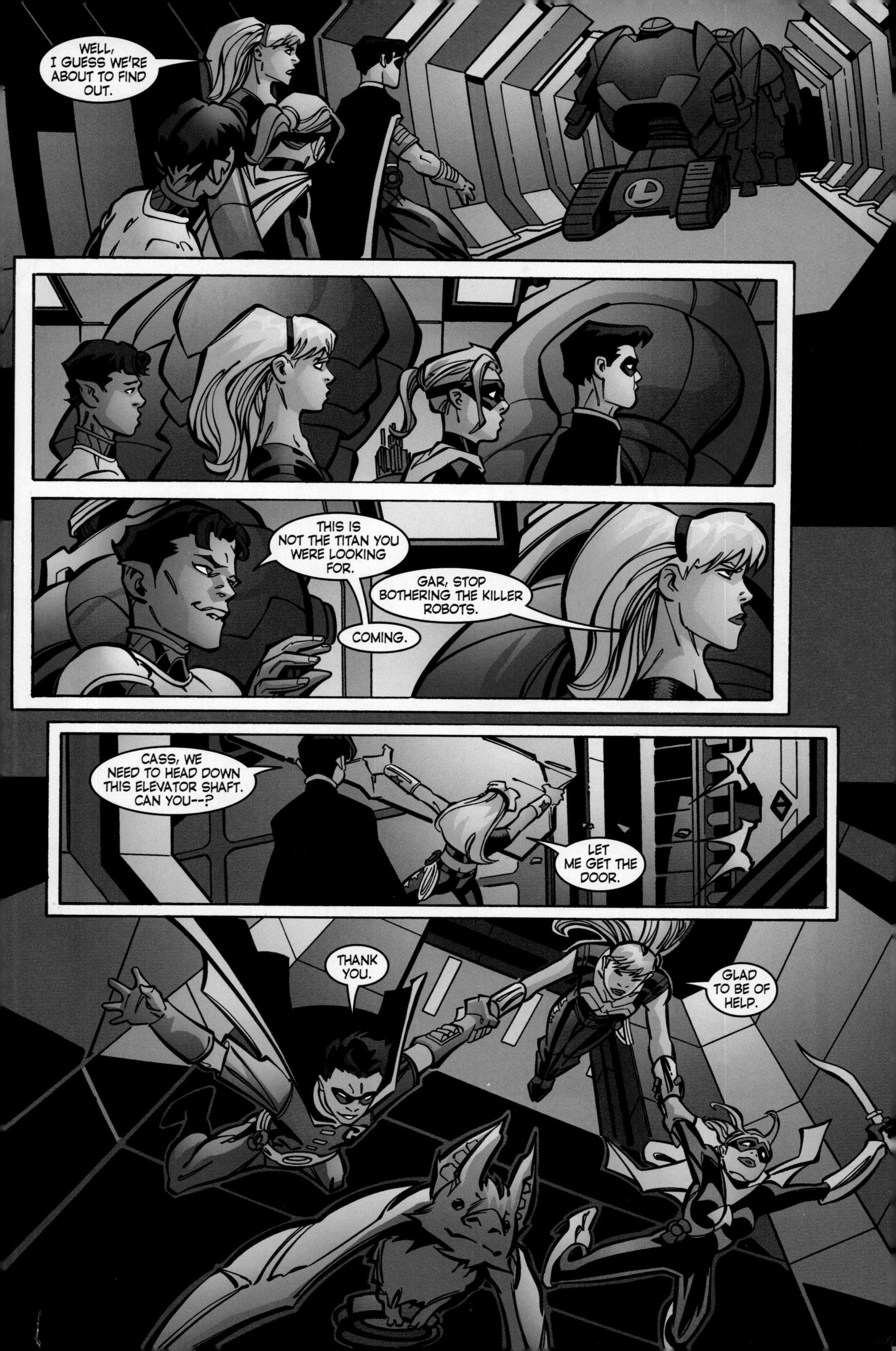
WELL, I GUESS WE'RE ABOUT TO FIND OUT.
THIS IS NOT THE TITAN YOU WERE LOOKING FOR.
GAR, STOP BOTHERING THE KILLER ROBOTS.
COMING.
CASS, WE NEED TO HEAD DOWN THIS ELEVATOR SHAFT. CAN YOU--?
LET ME GET THE DOOR.
THANK YOU.
GLAD TO BE OF HELP.

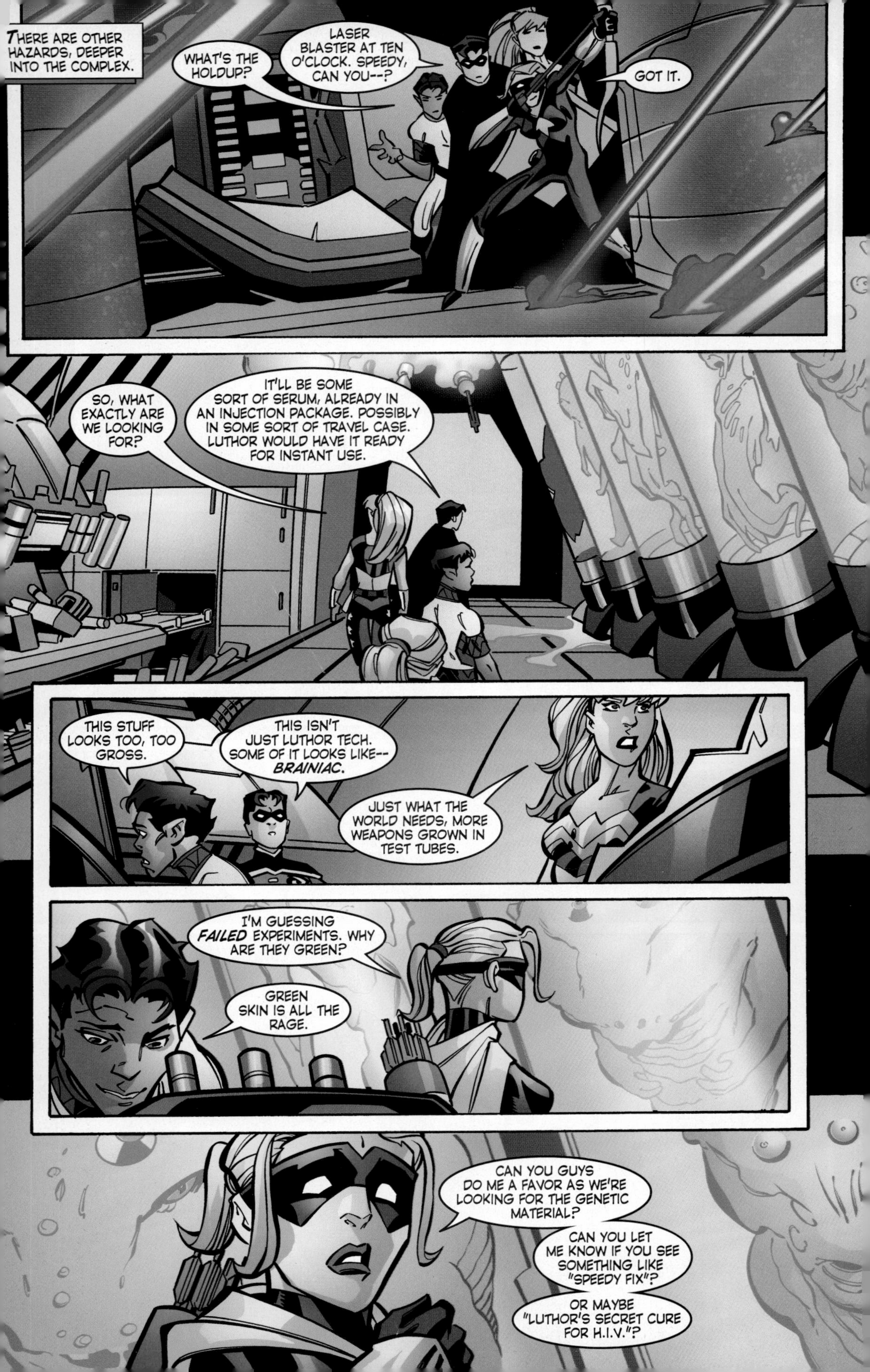
THERE ARE OTHER HAZARDS, DEEPER INTO THE COMPLEX.
WHAT'S THE HOLDUP?
LASER BLASTER AT TEN O'CLOCK. SPEEDY, CAN YOU--?
GOT IT.
SO, WHAT EXACTLY ARE WE LOOKING FOR?
IT'LL BE SOME SORT OF SERUM, ALREADY IN AN INJECTION PACKAGE. POSSIBLY IN SOME SORT OF TRAVEL CASE. LUTHOR WOULD HAVE IT READY FOR INSTANT USE.
THIS STUFF LOOKS TOO, TOO GROSS.
THIS ISN'T JUST LUTHOR TECH. SOME OF IT LOOKS LIKE-- BRAINIAC.
JUST WHAT THE WORLD NEEDS, MORE WEAPONS GROWN IN TEST TUBES.
I'M GUESSING FAILED EXPERIMENTS. WHY ARE THEY GREEN?
GREEN SKIN IS ALL THE RAGE.
CAN YOU GUYS DO ME A FAVOR AS WE'RE LOOKING FOR THE GENETIC MATERIAL?
CAN YOU LET ME KNOW IF YOU SEE SOMETHING LIKE "SPEEDY FIX"?
OR MAYBE "LUTHOR'S SECRET CURE FOR H.I.V."?

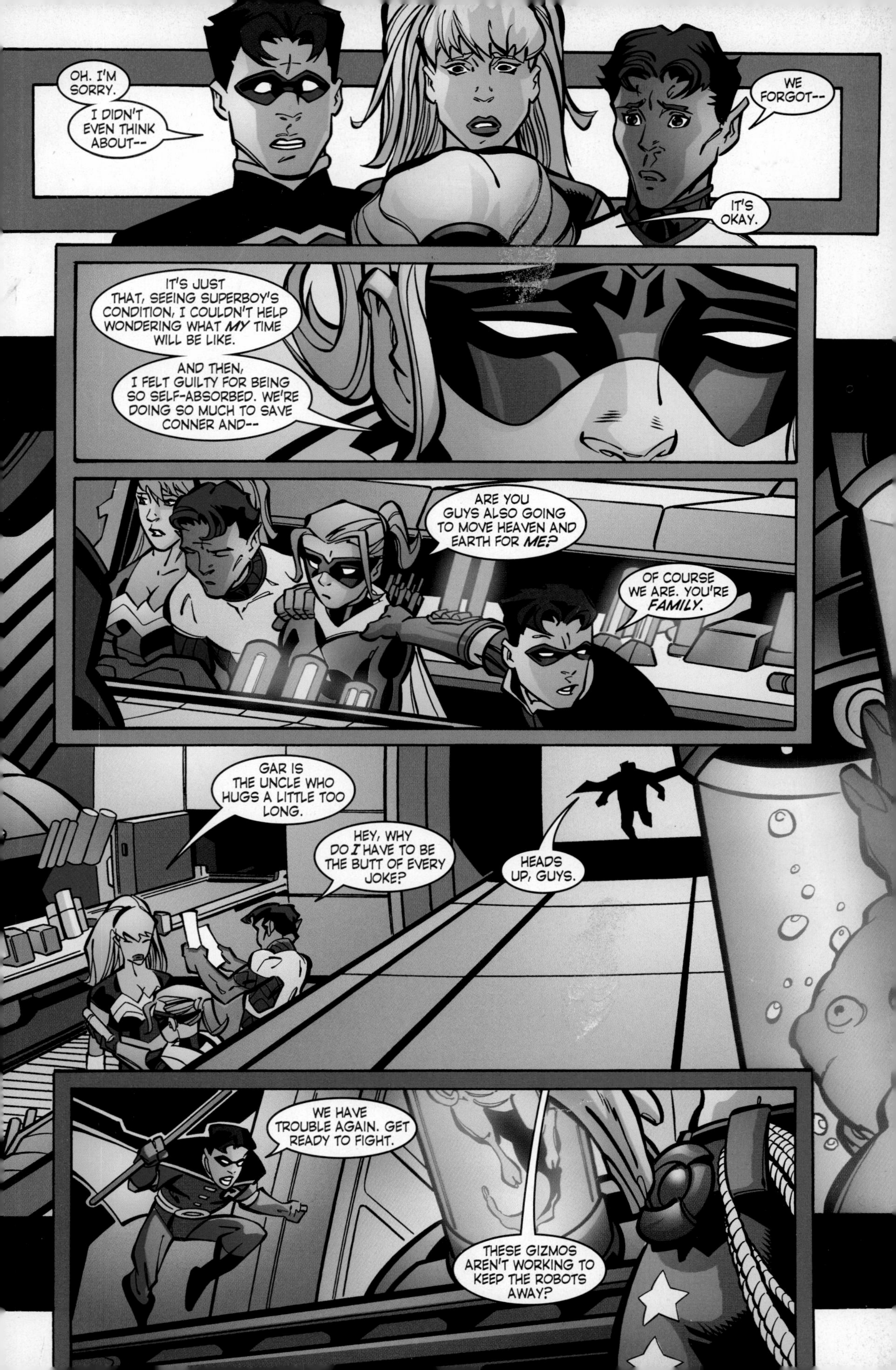
OH. I'M SORRY.
I DIDN'T EVEN THINK ABOUT--
WE FORGOT--
IT'S OKAY.
IT'S JUST THAT, SEEING SUPERBOY'S CONDITION, I COULDN'T HELP WONDERING WHAT MY TIME WILL BE LIKE.
AND THEN, I FELT GUILTY FOR BEING SO SELF-ABSORBED. WE'RE DOING SO MUCH TO SAVE CONNER AND--
ARE YOU GUYS ALSO GOING TO MOVE HEAVEN AND EARTH FOR ME?
OF COURSE WE ARE. YOU'RE FAMILY.
GAR IS THE UNCLE WHO HUGS A LITTLE TOO LONG.
HEY, WHY DO I HAVE TO BE THE BUTT OF EVERY JOKE?
HEADS UP, GUYS.
WE HAVE TROUBLE AGAIN. GET READY TO FIGHT.
THESE GIZMOS AREN'T WORKING TO KEEP THE ROBOTS AWAY?

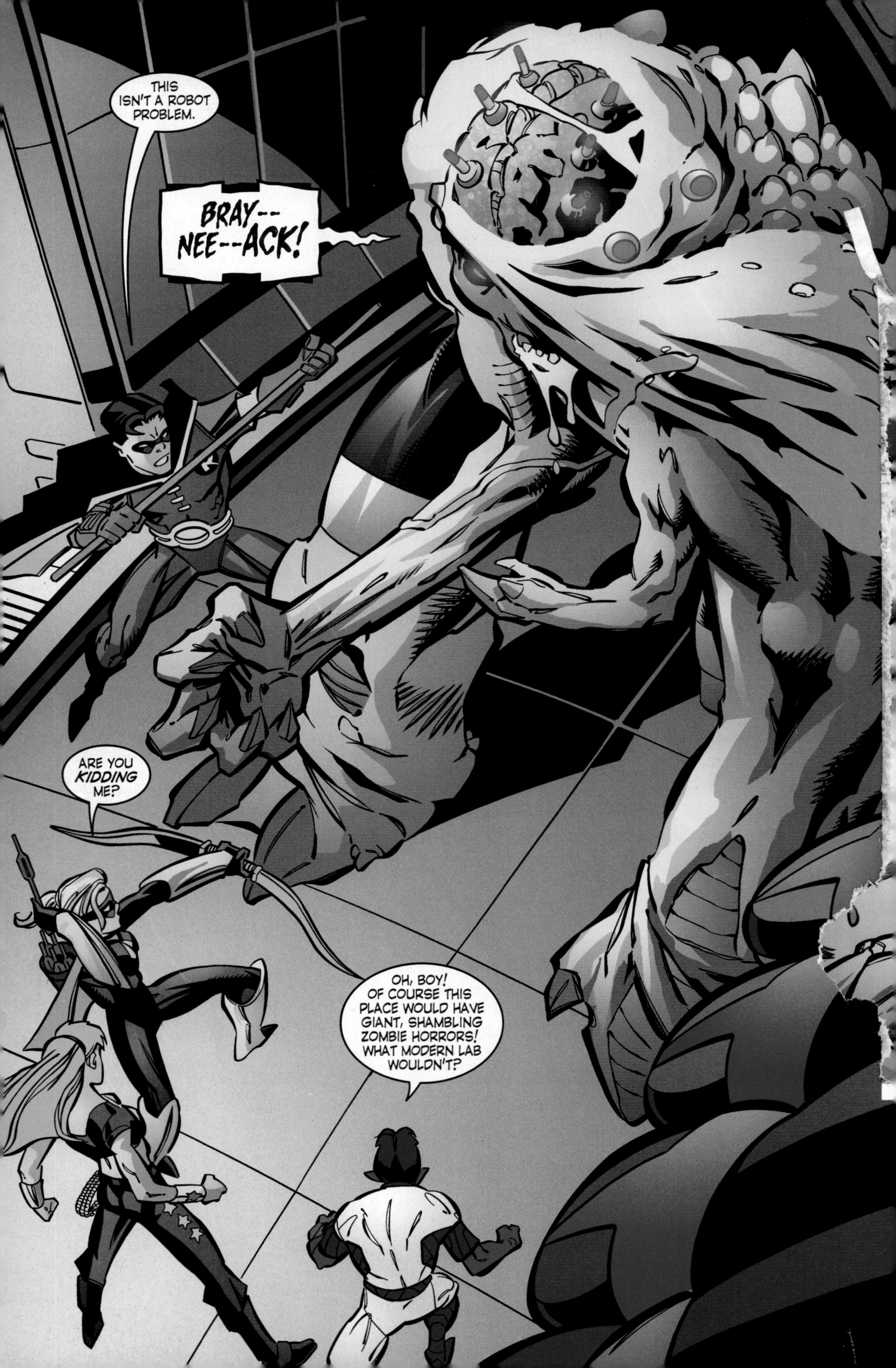

THIS ISN'T A ROBOT PROBLEM.
BRAY-- NEE--ACK!
ARE YOU *KIDDING* ME?
OH, BOY! OF COURSE THIS PLACE WOULD HAVE GIANT, SHAMBLING ZOMBIE HORRORS! WHAT MODERN LAB WOULDN'T?

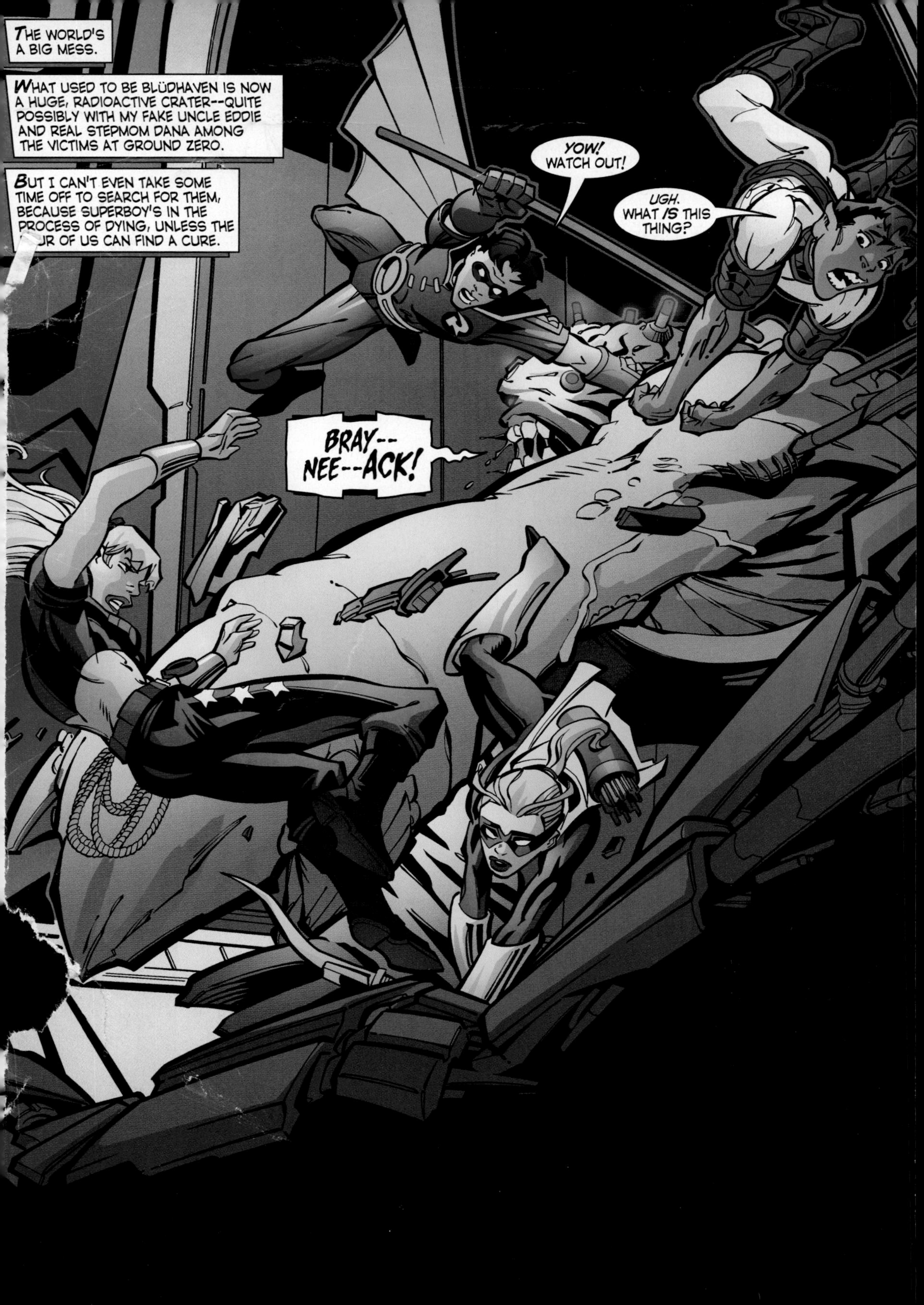
THE WORLD'S A BIG MESS.
WHAT USED TO BE BLÜDHAVEN IS NOW A HUGE, RADIOACTIVE CRATER--QUITE POSSIBLY WITH MY FAKE UNCLE EDDIE AND REAL STEPMOM DANA AMONG THE VICTIMS AT GROUND ZERO.
BUT I CAN'T EVEN TAKE SOME TIME OFF TO SEARCH FOR THEM, BECAUSE SUPERBOY'S IN THE PROCESS OF DYING, UNLESS THE UR OF US CAN FIND A CURE.
YOW! WATCH OUT!
UGH. WHAT IS THIS THING?
BRAY-- NEE--ACK!

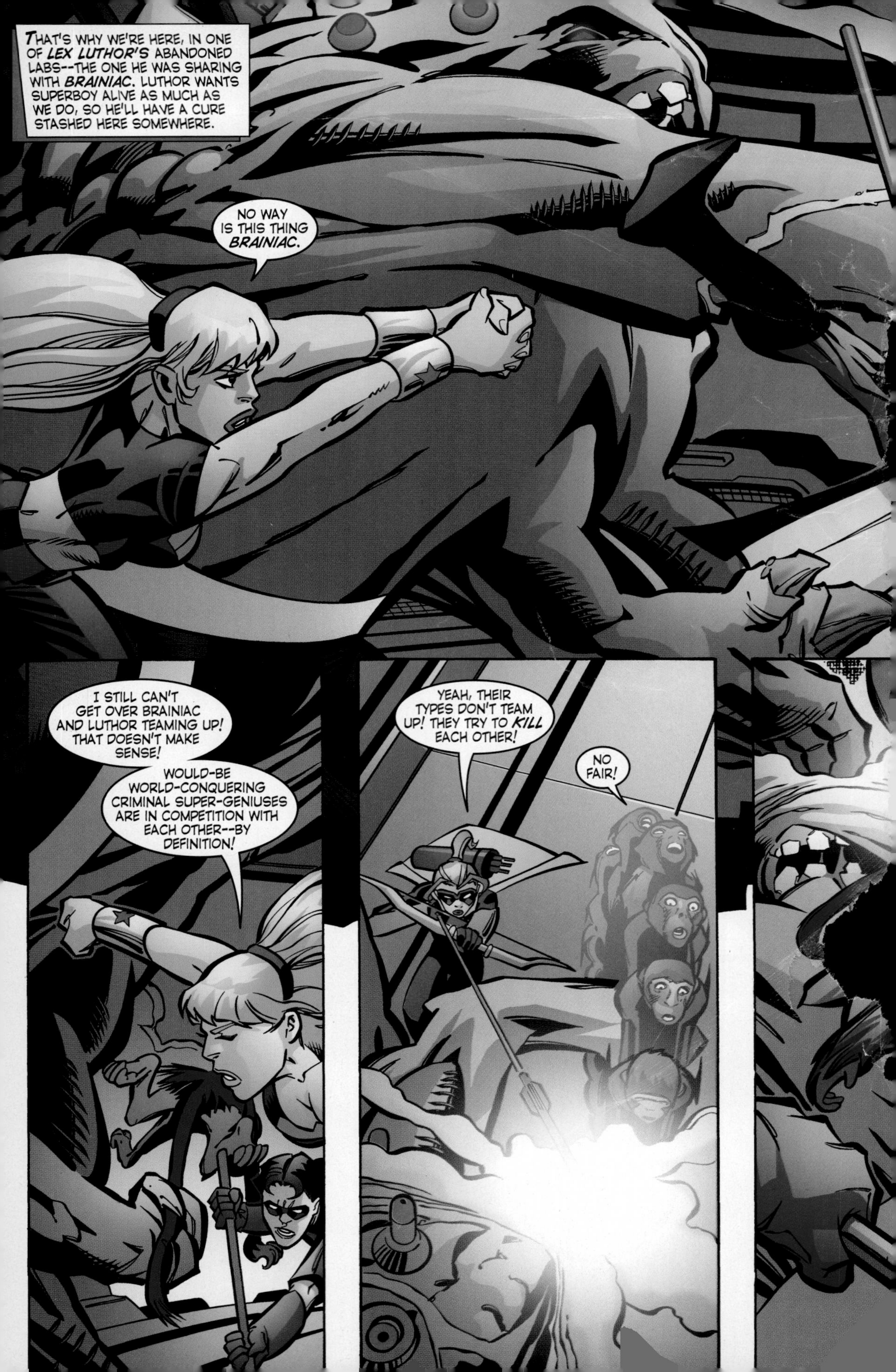
THAT'S WHY WE'RE HERE, IN ONE OF LEX LUTHOR'S ABANDONED LABS--THE ONE HE WAS SHARING WITH BRAINIAC. LUTHOR WANTS SUPERBOY ALIVE AS MUCH AS WE DO, SO HE'LL HAVE A CURE STASHED HERE SOMEWHERE.
NO WAY IS THIS THING BRAINIAC.
I STILL CAN'T GET OVER BRAINIAC AND LUTHOR TEAMING UP! THAT DOESN'T MAKE SENSE!
WOULD-BE WORLD-CONQUERING CRIMINAL SUPER-GENIUSES ARE IN COMPETITION WITH EACH OTHER--BY DEFINITION!
YEAH, THEIR TYPES DON'T TEAM UP! THEY TRY TO KILL EACH OTHER!
NO FAIR!

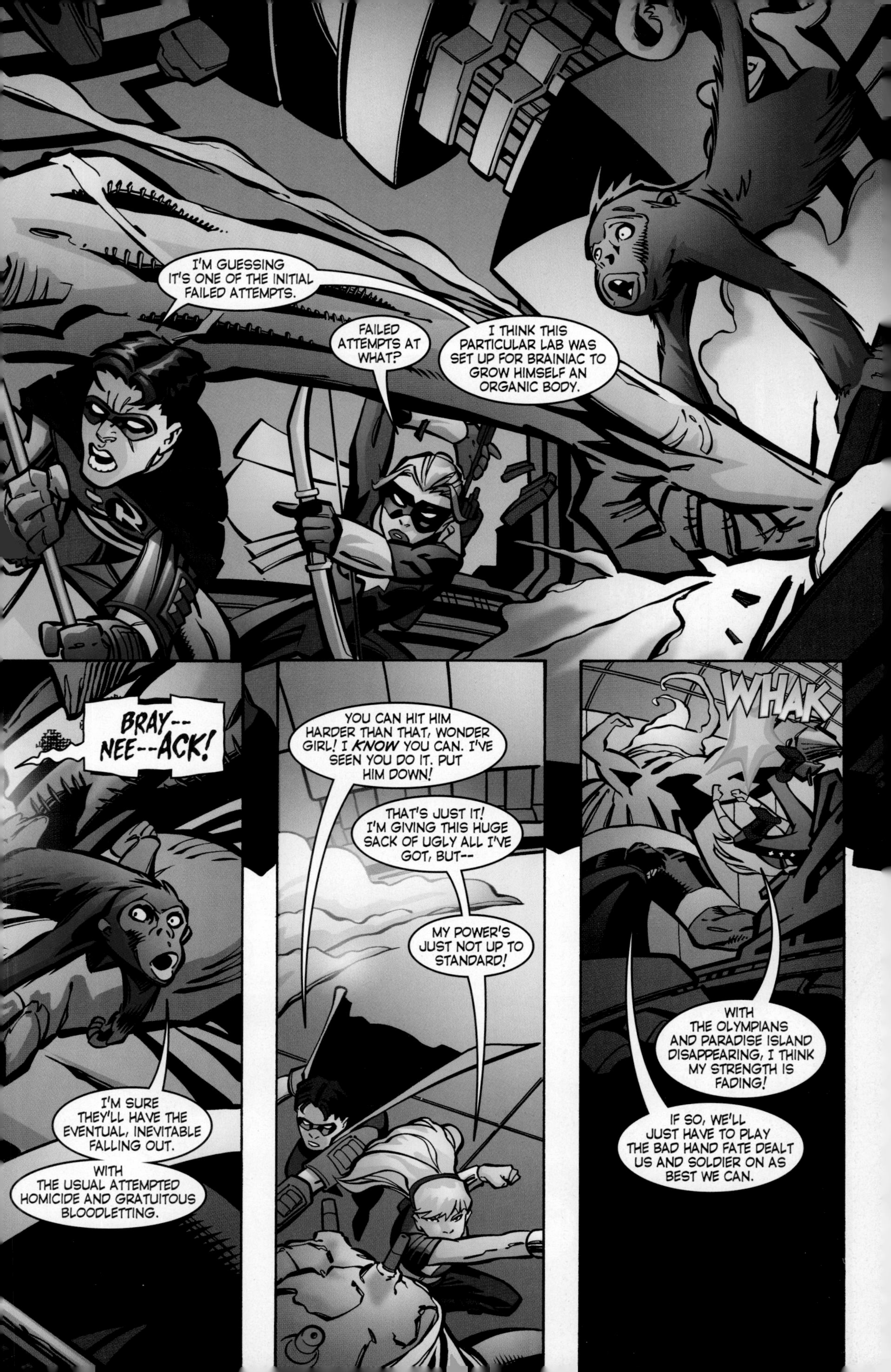

I'M GUESSING IT'S ONE OF THE INITIAL FAILED ATTEMPTS.
FAILED ATTEMPTS AT WHAT?
I THINK THIS PARTICULAR LAB WAS SET UP FOR BRAINIAC TO GROW HIMSELF AN ORGANIC BODY.
BRAY--NEE--ACK!
I'M SURE THEY'LL HAVE THE EVENTUAL, INEVITABLE FALLING OUT.
WITH THE USUAL ATTEMPTED HOMICIDE AND GRATUITOUS BLOODLETTING.
YOU CAN HIT HIM HARDER THAN THAT, WONDER GIRL! I KNOW YOU CAN. I'VE SEEN YOU DO IT. PUT HIM DOWN!
THAT'S JUST IT! I'M GIVING THIS HUGE SACK OF UGLY ALL I'VE GOT, BUT--
MY POWER'S JUST NOT UP TO STANDARD!
WHAK
WITH THE OLYMPIANS AND PARADISE ISLAND DISAPPEARING, I THINK MY STRENGTH IS FADING!
IF SO, WE'LL JUST HAVE TO PLAY THE BAD HAND FATE DEALT US AND SOLDIER ON AS BEST WE CAN.

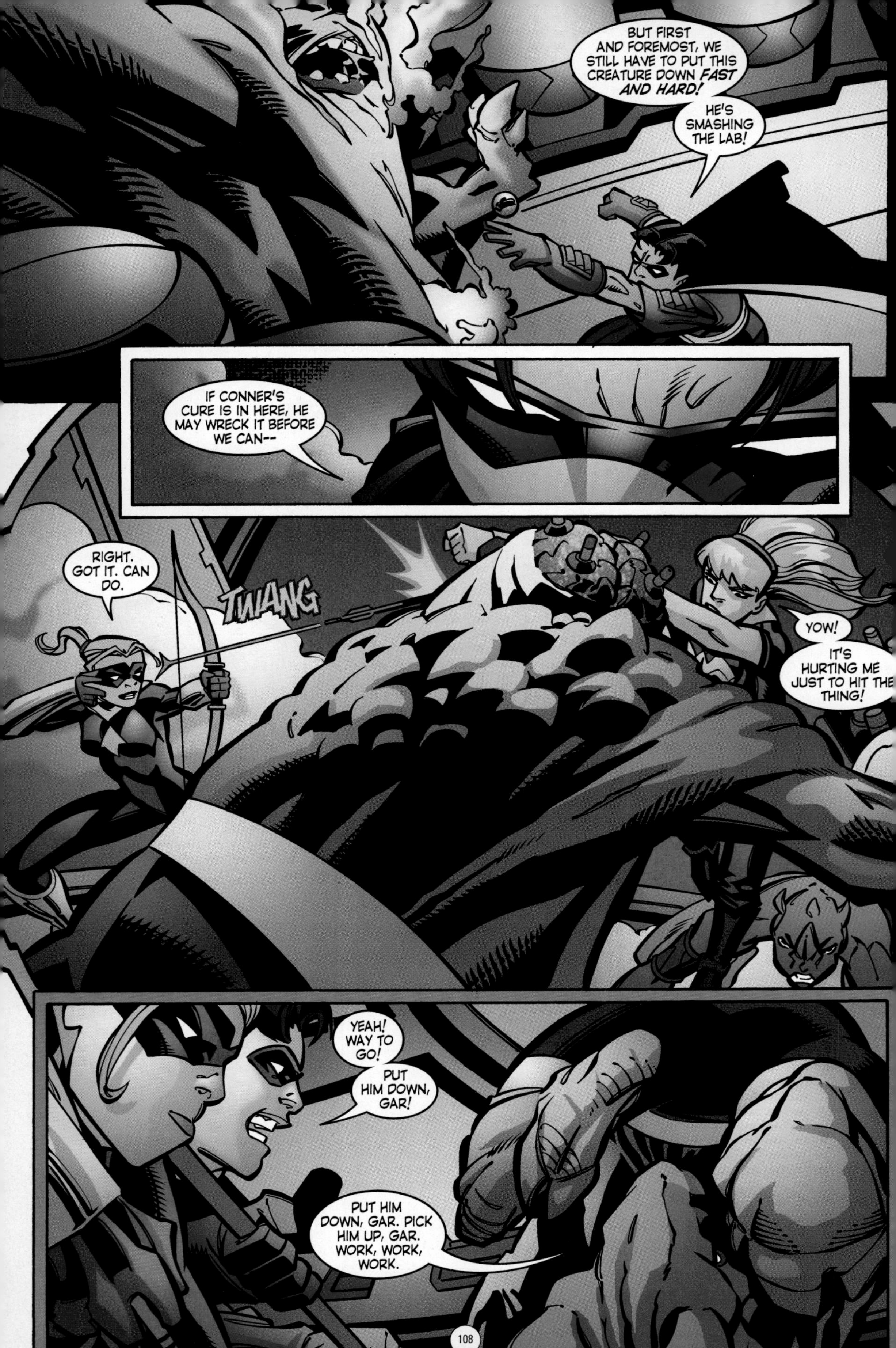

BUT FIRST AND FOREMOST, WE STILL HAVE TO PUT THIS CREATURE DOWN FAST AND HARD!
HE'S SMASHING THE LAB!
IF CONNER'S CURE IS IN HERE, HE MAY WRECK IT BEFORE WE CAN--
RIGHT. GOT IT. CAN DO.
TWANG
YOW!
IT'S HURTING ME JUST TO HIT THE THING!
YEAH! WAY TO GO!
PUT HIM DOWN, GAR!
PUT HIM DOWN, GAR. PICK HIM UP, GAR. WORK, WORK, WORK.

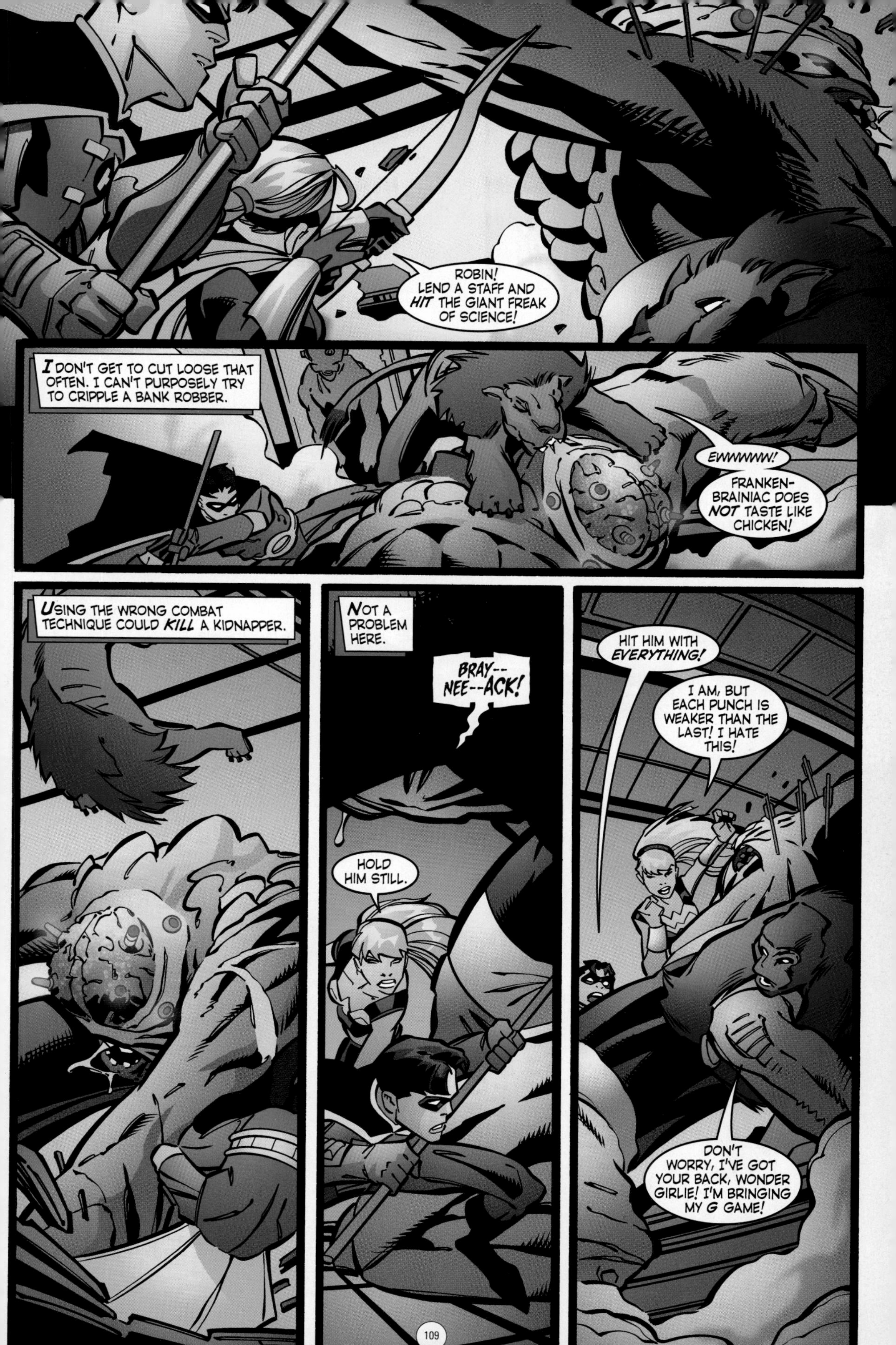

ROBIN! LEND A STAFF AND HIT THE GIANT FREAK OF SCIENCE!
I DON'T GET TO CUT LOOSE THAT OFTEN. I CAN'T PURPOSELY TRY TO CRIPPLE A BANK ROBBER.
EWWWWW!
FRANKEN-BRAINIAC DOES NOT TASTE LIKE CHICKEN!
USING THE WRONG COMBAT TECHNIQUE COULD KILL A KIDNAPPER.
NOT A PROBLEM HERE.
BRAY-- NEE--ACK!
HOLD HIM STILL.
HIT HIM WITH EVERYTHING!
I AM, BUT EACH PUNCH IS WEAKER THAN THE LAST! I HATE THIS!
DON'T WORRY, I'VE GOT YOUR BACK, WONDER GIRLIE! I'M BRINGING MY G GAME!

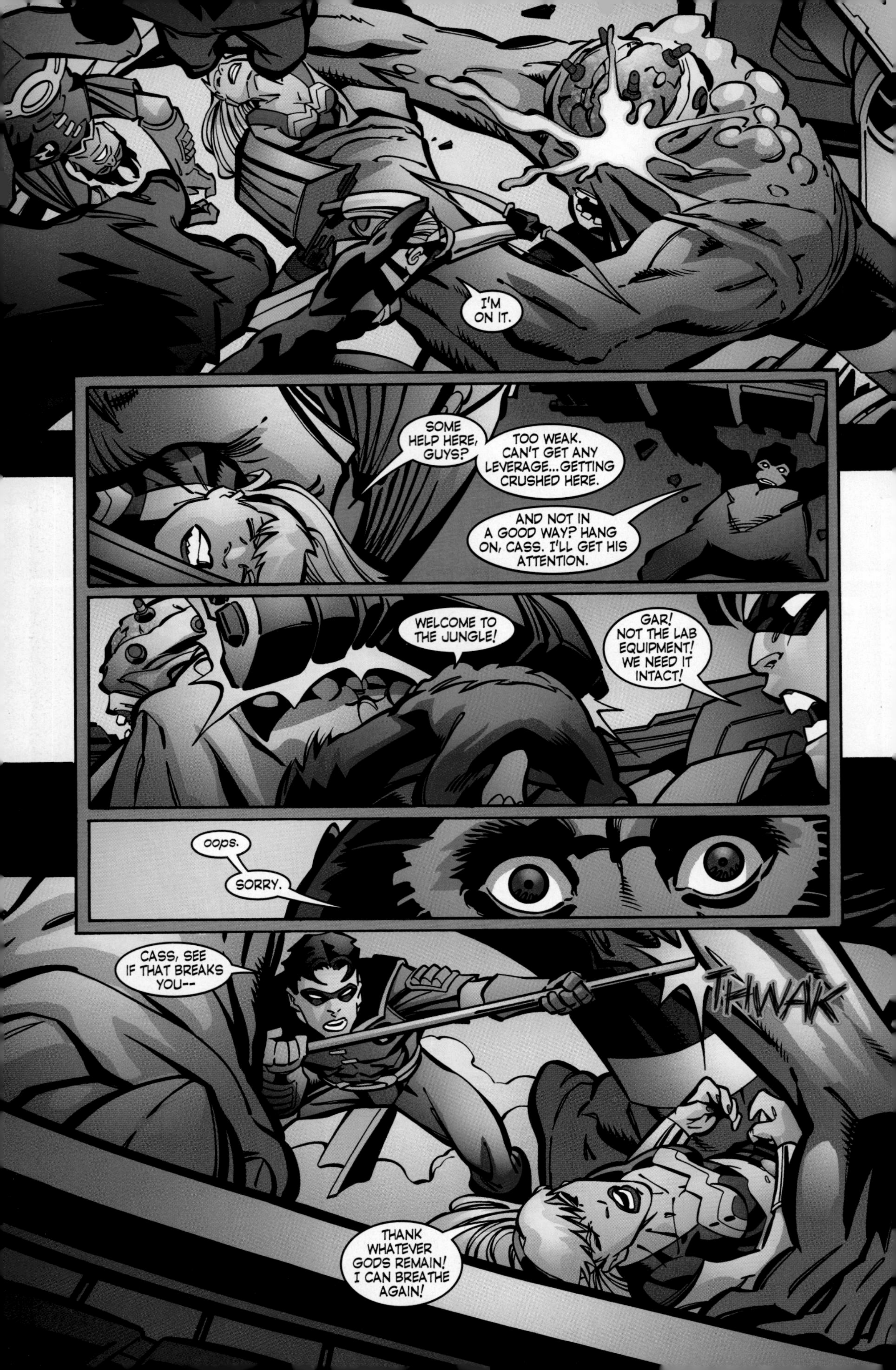
I'M ON IT.
SOME HELP HERE, GUYS?
TOO WEAK. CAN'T GET ANY LEVERAGE...GETTING CRUSHED HERE.
AND NOT IN A GOOD WAY? HANG ON, CASS. I'LL GET HIS ATTENTION.
WELCOME TO THE JUNGLE!
GAR! NOT THE LAB EQUIPMENT! WE NEED IT INTACT!
oops.
SORRY.
CASS, SEE IF THAT BREAKS YOU--
THWAK
THANK WHATEVER GODS REMAIN! I CAN BREATHE AGAIN!

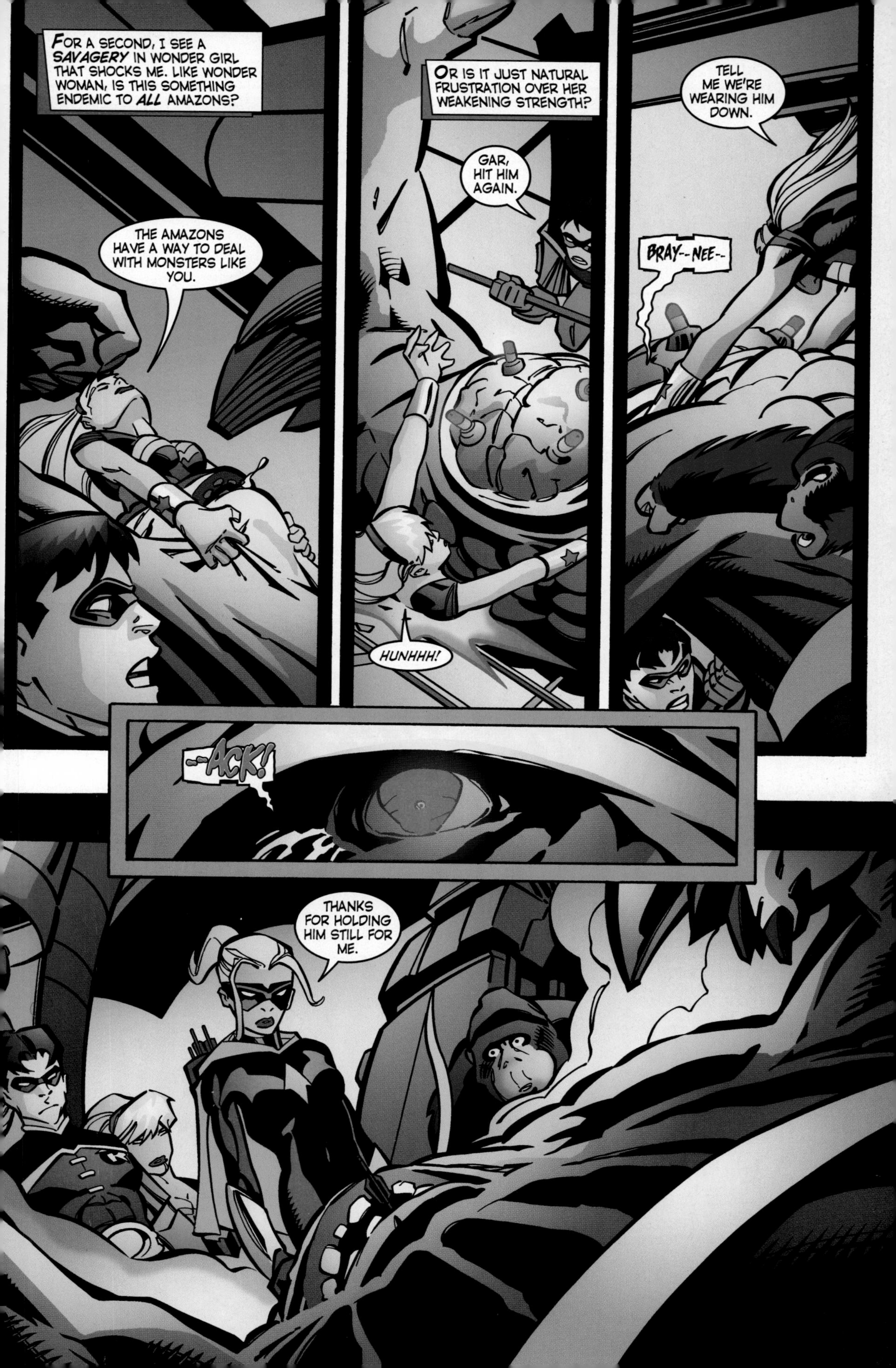

FOR A SECOND, I SEE A SAVAGERY IN WONDER GIRL THAT SHOCKS ME. LIKE WONDER WOMAN, IS THIS SOMETHING ENDEMIC TO ALL AMAZONS?
THE AMAZONS HAVE A WAY TO DEAL WITH MONSTERS LIKE YOU.
OR IS IT JUST NATURAL FRUSTRATION OVER HER WEAKENING STRENGTH?
GAR, HIT HIM AGAIN.
HUNHHH!
TELL ME WE'RE WEARING HIM DOWN.
BRAY--NEE--
--ACK!
THANKS FOR HOLDING HIM STILL FOR ME.

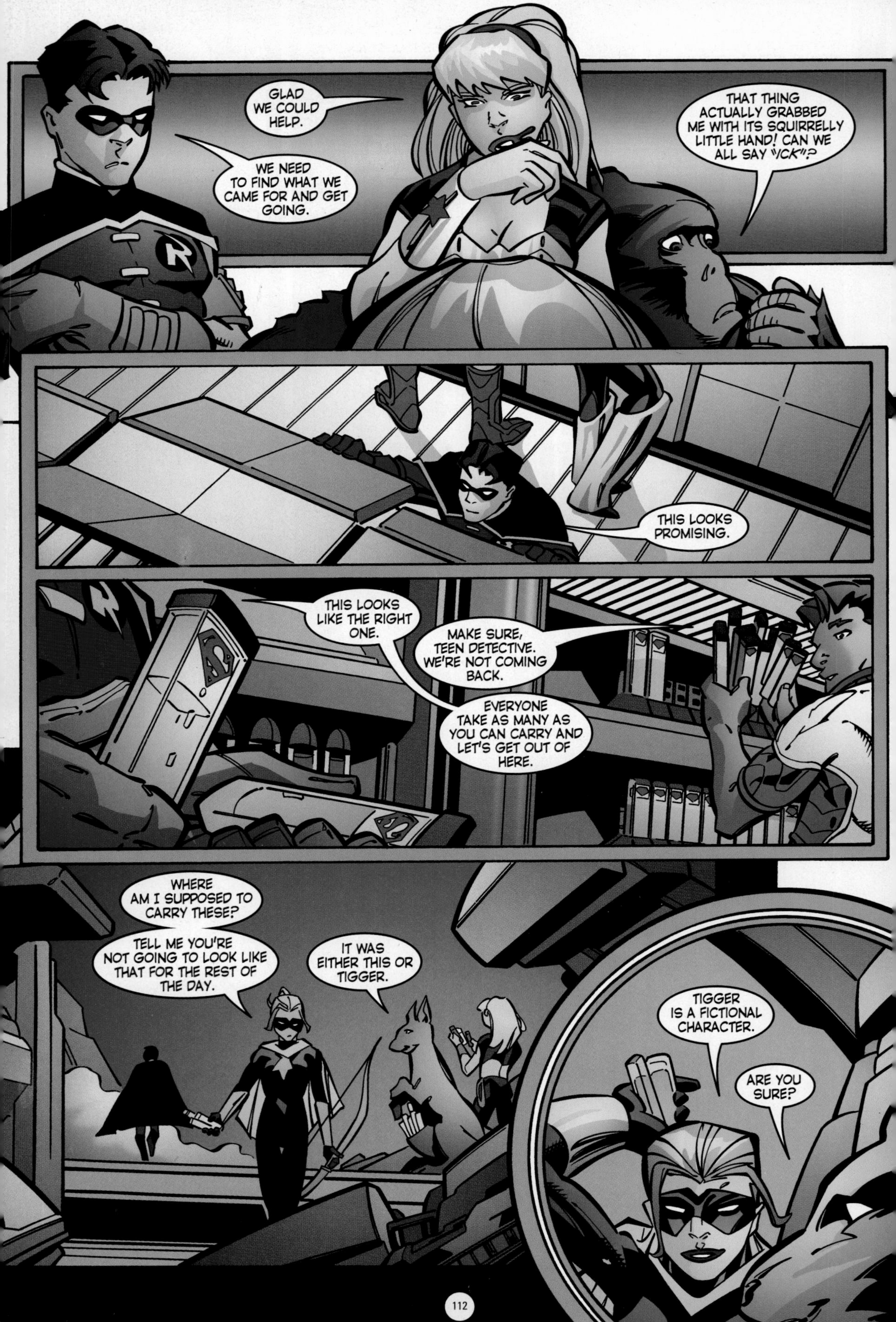
GLAD WE COULD HELP.
WE NEED TO FIND WHAT WE CAME FOR AND GET GOING.
THAT THING ACTUALLY GRABBED ME WITH ITS SQUIRRELLY LITTLE HAND! CAN WE ALL SAY "ICK"?
THIS LOOKS PROMISING.
THIS LOOKS LIKE THE RIGHT ONE.
MAKE SURE, TEEN DETECTIVE. WE'RE NOT COMING BACK.
EVERYONE TAKE AS MANY AS YOU CAN CARRY AND LET'S GET OUT OF HERE.
WHERE AM I SUPPOSED TO CARRY THESE?
TELL ME YOU'RE NOT GOING TO LOOK LIKE THAT FOR THE REST OF THE DAY.
IT WAS EITHER THIS OR TIGGER.
TIGGER IS A FICTIONAL CHARACTER.
ARE YOU SURE?

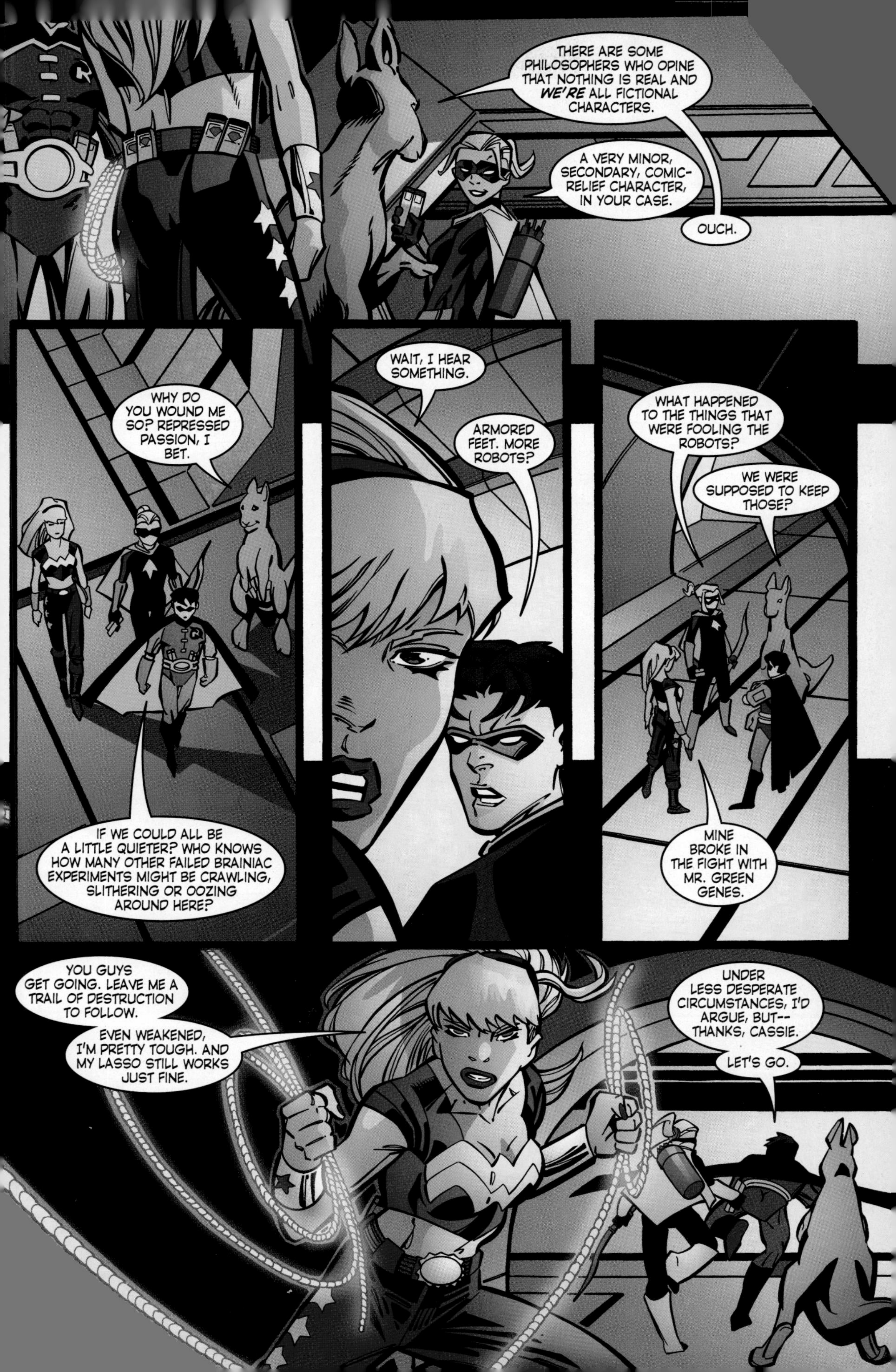
THERE ARE SOME PHILOSOPHERS WHO OPINE THAT NOTHING IS REAL AND *WE'RE* ALL FICTIONAL CHARACTERS.
A VERY MINOR, SECONDARY, COMIC-RELIEF CHARACTER, IN YOUR CASE.
OUCH.
WHY DO YOU WOUND ME SO? REPRESSED PASSION, I BET.
IF WE COULD ALL BE A LITTLE QUIETER? WHO KNOWS HOW MANY OTHER FAILED BRAINIAC EXPERIMENTS MIGHT BE CRAWLING, SLITHERING OR OOZING AROUND HERE?
WAIT, I HEAR SOMETHING.
ARMORED FEET. MORE ROBOTS?
WHAT HAPPENED TO THE THINGS THAT WERE FOOLING THE ROBOTS?
WE WERE SUPPOSED TO KEEP THOSE?
MINE BROKE IN THE FIGHT WITH MR. GREEN GENES.
YOU GUYS GET GOING. LEAVE ME A TRAIL OF DESTRUCTION TO FOLLOW.
EVEN WEAKENED, I'M PRETTY TOUGH. AND MY LASSO STILL WORKS JUST FINE.
UNDER LESS DESPERATE CIRCUMSTANCES, I'D ARGUE, BUT-- THANKS, CASSIE.
LET'S GO.

HERE, CONNER. TRY TO SIP JUST A LITTLE OF THIS BROTH.

YOU'RE NOT GOING TO MAKE ME EAT ALONE AGAIN, ARE YOU?

MAYBE A BIT LATER. NOT MUCH APPETITE JUST NOW.

YOU NEED TO KEEP YOUR STRENGTH UP. YOU MADE TIM A SOLEMN PROMISE YOU'D HANG ON UNTIL THEY RETURN.

THEY'D BEST HURRY, THEN.

DON'T TALK LIKE THAT, CONNER. IF THE DESTRUCTION OF MAGIC WEREN'T PLAYING HAVOC WITH MY POWERS, I COULD *FORCE* YOU TO EAT SOMETHING.

I KNOW.

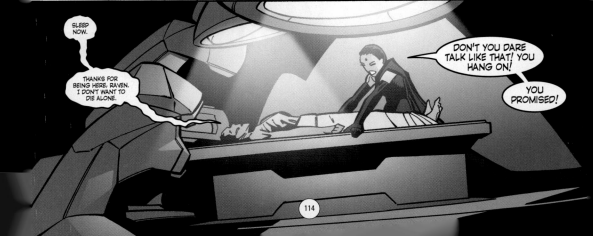

SLEEP NOW.

THANKS FOR BEING HERE, RAVEN. I DON'T WANT TO DIE ALONE.

DON'T YOU DARE TALK LIKE THAT! YOU HANG ON!

YOU PROMISED!

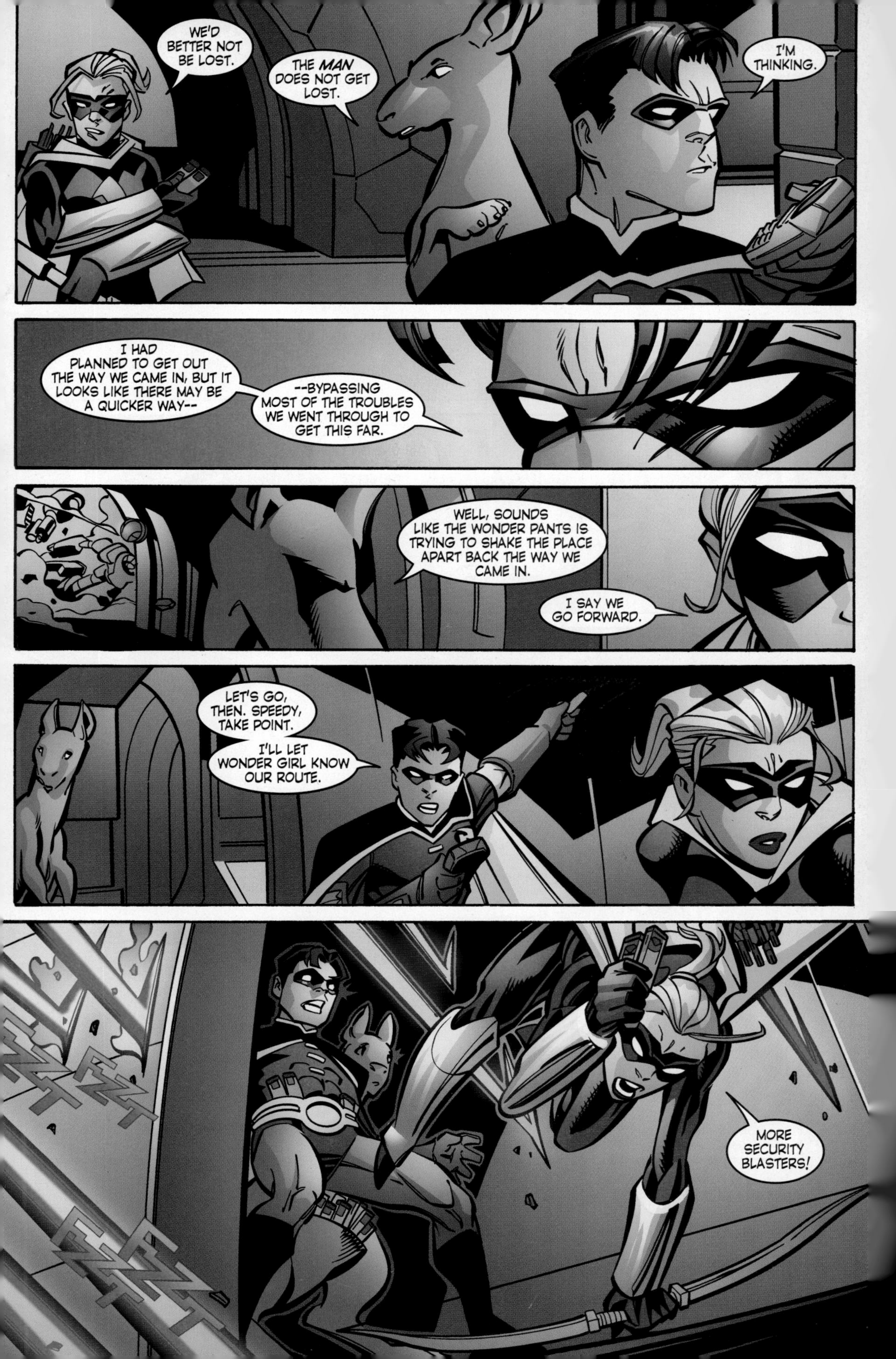
WE'D BETTER NOT BE LOST.
THE *MAN* DOES NOT GET LOST.
I'M THINKING.
I HAD PLANNED TO GET OUT THE WAY WE CAME IN, BUT IT LOOKS LIKE THERE MAY BE A QUICKER WAY--
--BYPASSING MOST OF THE TROUBLES WE WENT THROUGH TO GET THIS FAR.
WELL, SOUNDS LIKE THE WONDER PANTS IS TRYING TO SHAKE THE PLACE APART BACK THE WAY WE CAME IN.
I SAY WE GO FORWARD.
LET'S GO, THEN. SPEEDY, TAKE POINT.
I'LL LET WONDER GIRL KNOW OUR ROUTE.
MORE SECURITY BLASTERS!

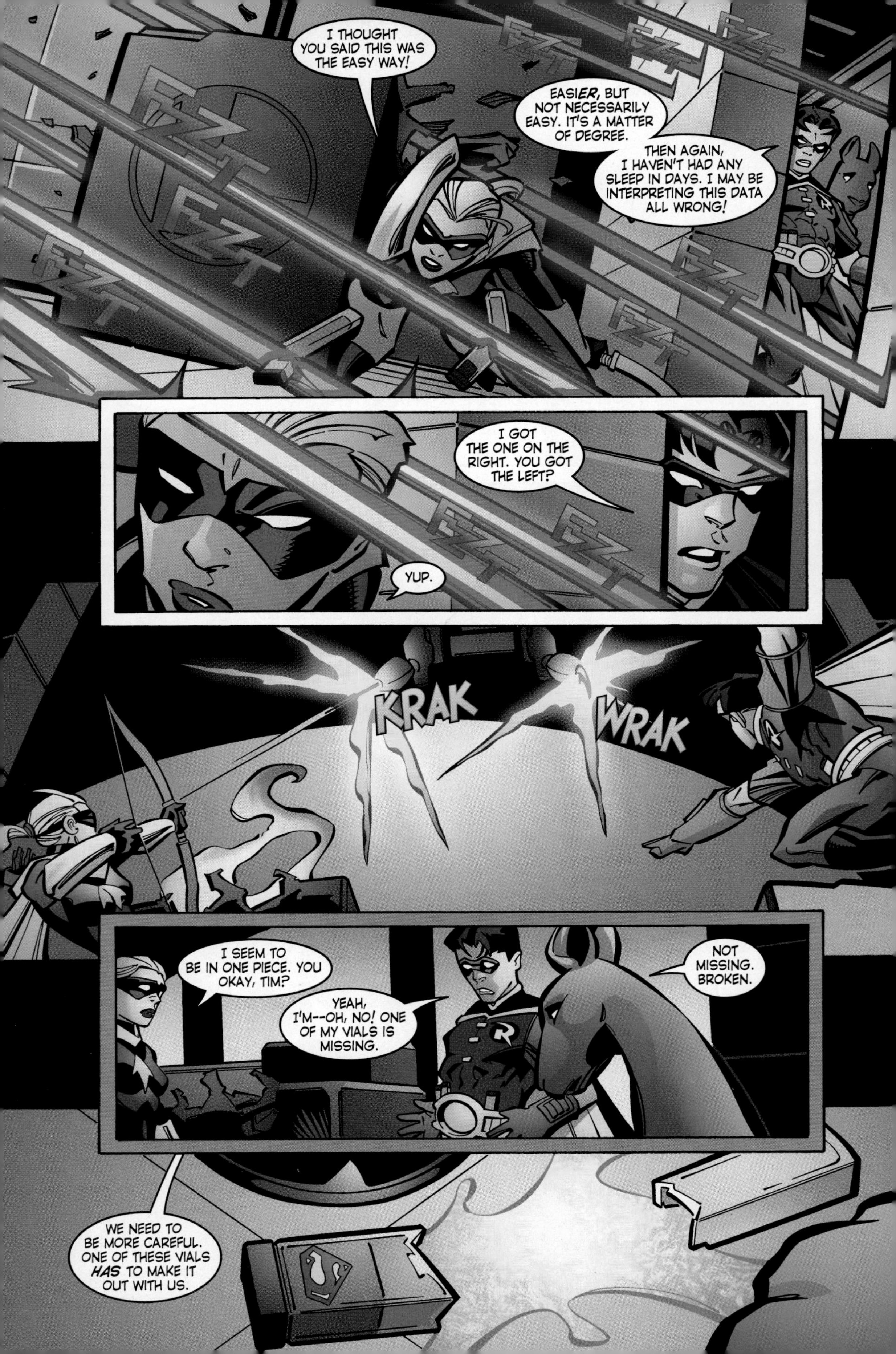

I THOUGHT YOU SAID THIS WAS THE EASY WAY!
EASIER, BUT NOT NECESSARILY EASY. IT'S A MATTER OF DEGREE.
THEN AGAIN, I HAVEN'T HAD ANY SLEEP IN DAYS. I MAY BE INTERPRETING THIS DATA ALL WRONG!
FZZT
I GOT THE ONE ON THE RIGHT. YOU GOT THE LEFT?
YUP.
KRAK
WRAK
I SEEM TO BE IN ONE PIECE. YOU OKAY, TIM?
YEAH, I'M--OH, NO! ONE OF MY VIALS IS MISSING.
NOT MISSING. BROKEN.
WE NEED TO BE MORE CAREFUL. ONE OF THESE VIALS HAS TO MAKE IT OUT WITH US.

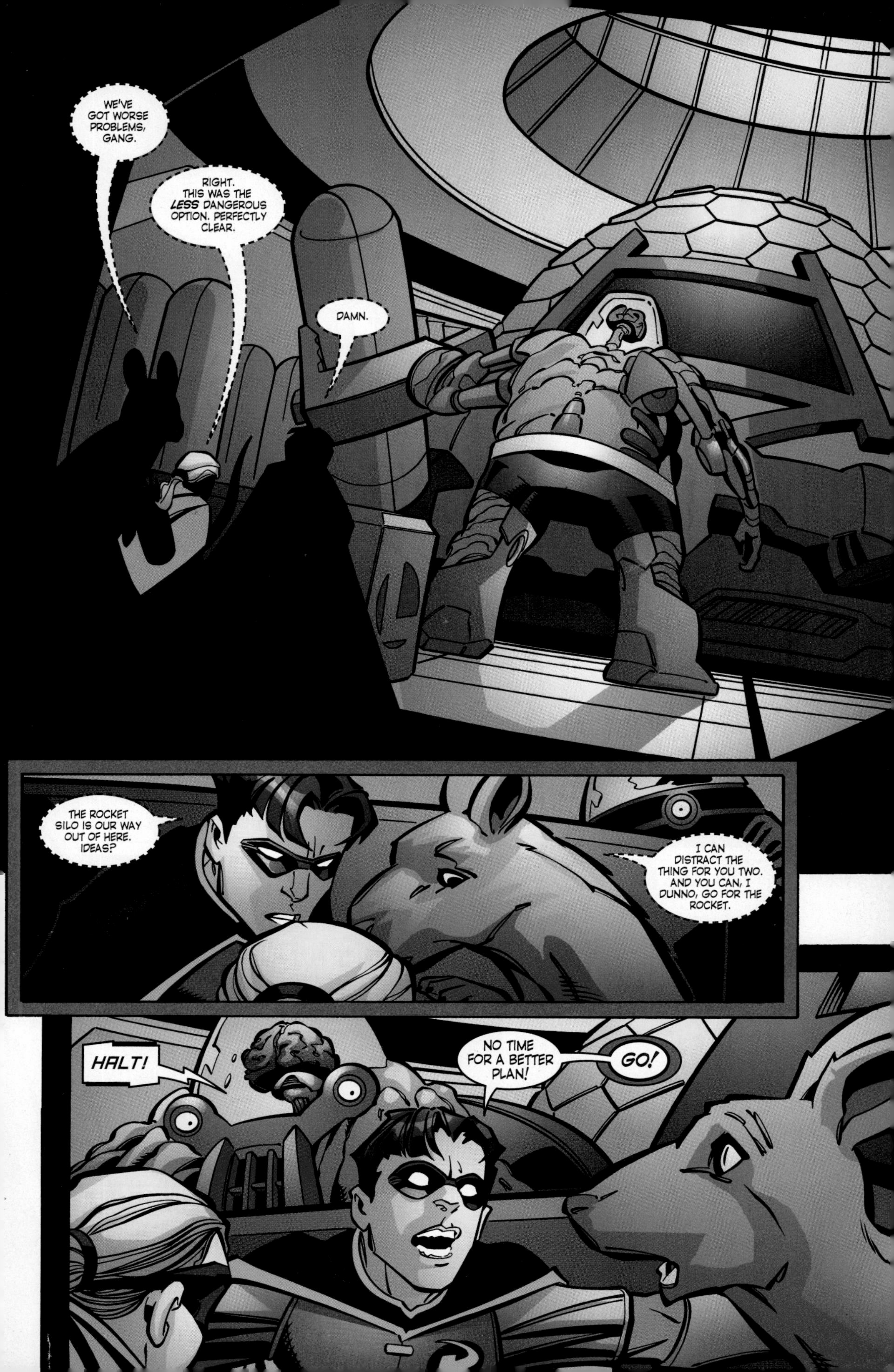
WE'VE GOT WORSE PROBLEMS, GANG.
RIGHT. THIS WAS THE LESS DANGEROUS OPTION. PERFECTLY CLEAR.
DAMN.
THE ROCKET SILO IS OUR WAY OUT OF HERE. IDEAS?
I CAN DISTRACT THE THING FOR YOU TWO. AND YOU CAN, I DUNNO, GO FOR THE ROCKET.
HALT!
NO TIME FOR A BETTER PLAN!
GO!

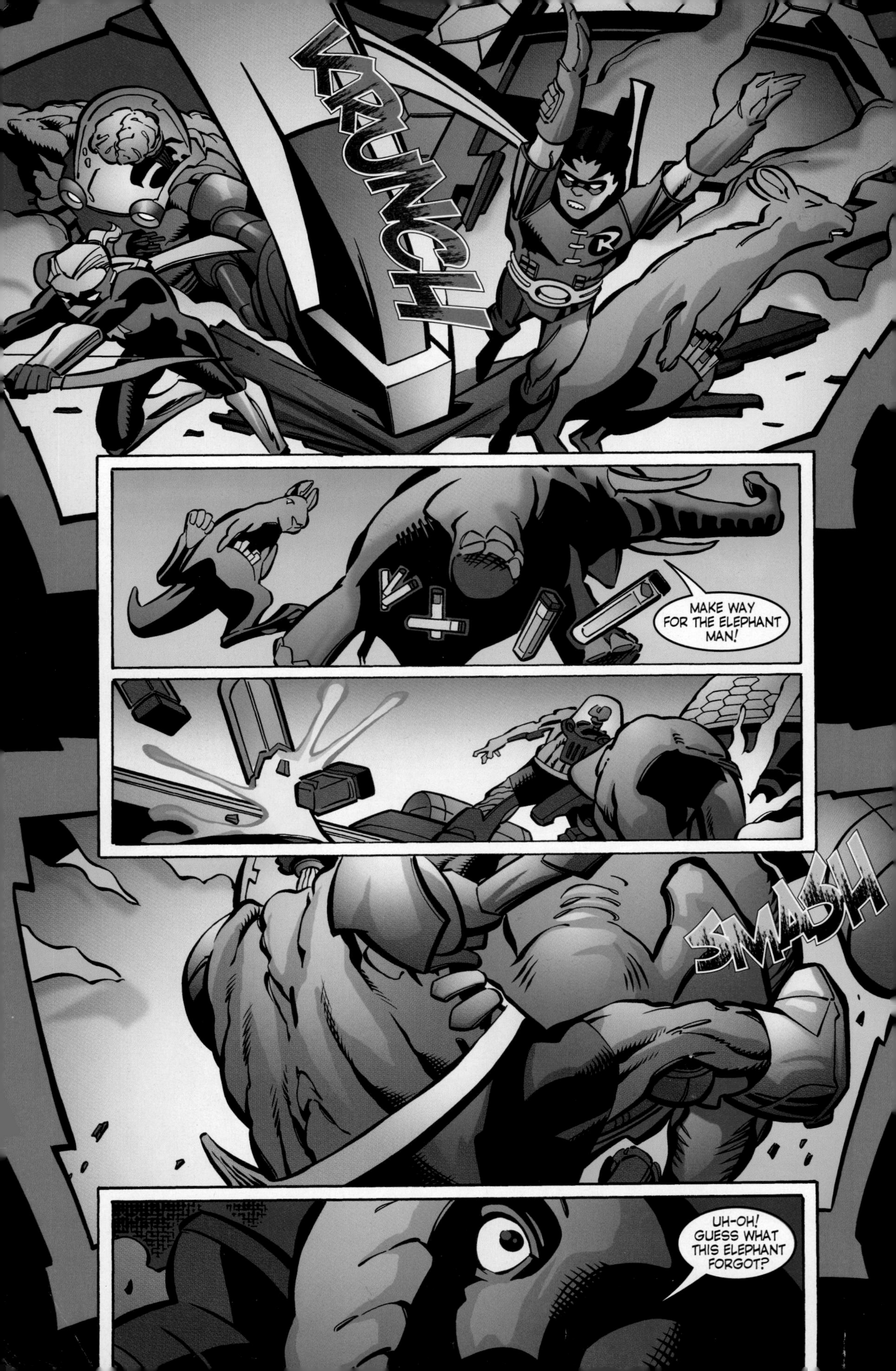
KRUNCH
MAKE WAY FOR THE ELEPHANT MAN!
SMASH
UH-OH! GUESS WHAT THIS ELEPHANT FORGOT?

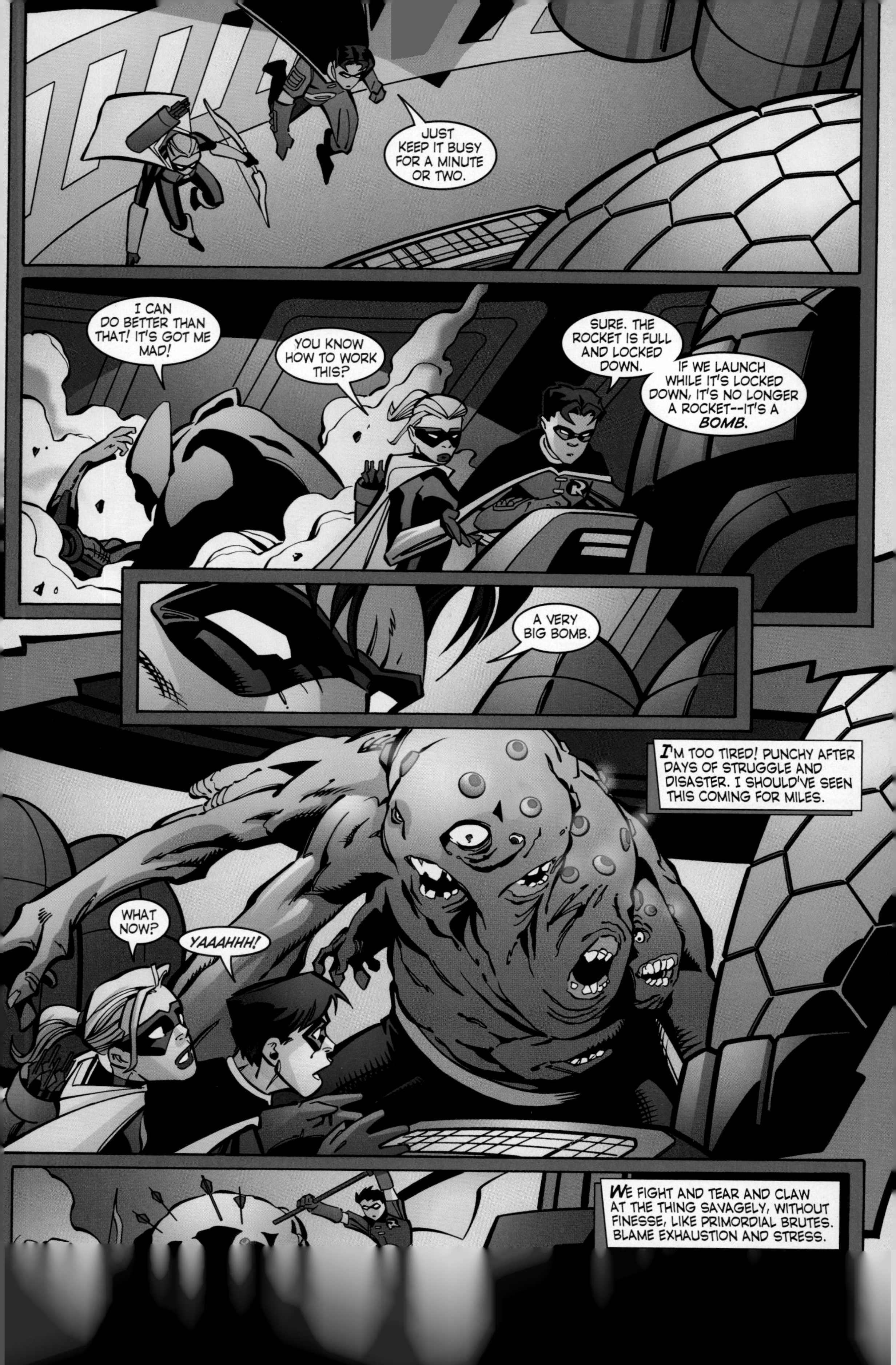
JUST KEEP IT BUSY FOR A MINUTE OR TWO.
I CAN DO BETTER THAN THAT! IT'S GOT ME MAD!
YOU KNOW HOW TO WORK THIS?
SURE. THE ROCKET IS FULL AND LOCKED DOWN.
IF WE LAUNCH WHILE IT'S LOCKED DOWN, IT'S NO LONGER A ROCKET--IT'S A ***BOMB.***
A VERY BIG BOMB.
I'M TOO TIRED! PUNCHY AFTER DAYS OF STRUGGLE AND DISASTER. I SHOULD'VE SEEN THIS COMING FOR MILES.
WHAT NOW?
YAAAHHH!
WE FIGHT AND TEAR AND CLAW AT THE THING SAVAGELY, WITHOUT FINESSE, LIKE PRIMORDIAL BRUTES. BLAME EXHAUSTION AND STRESS.

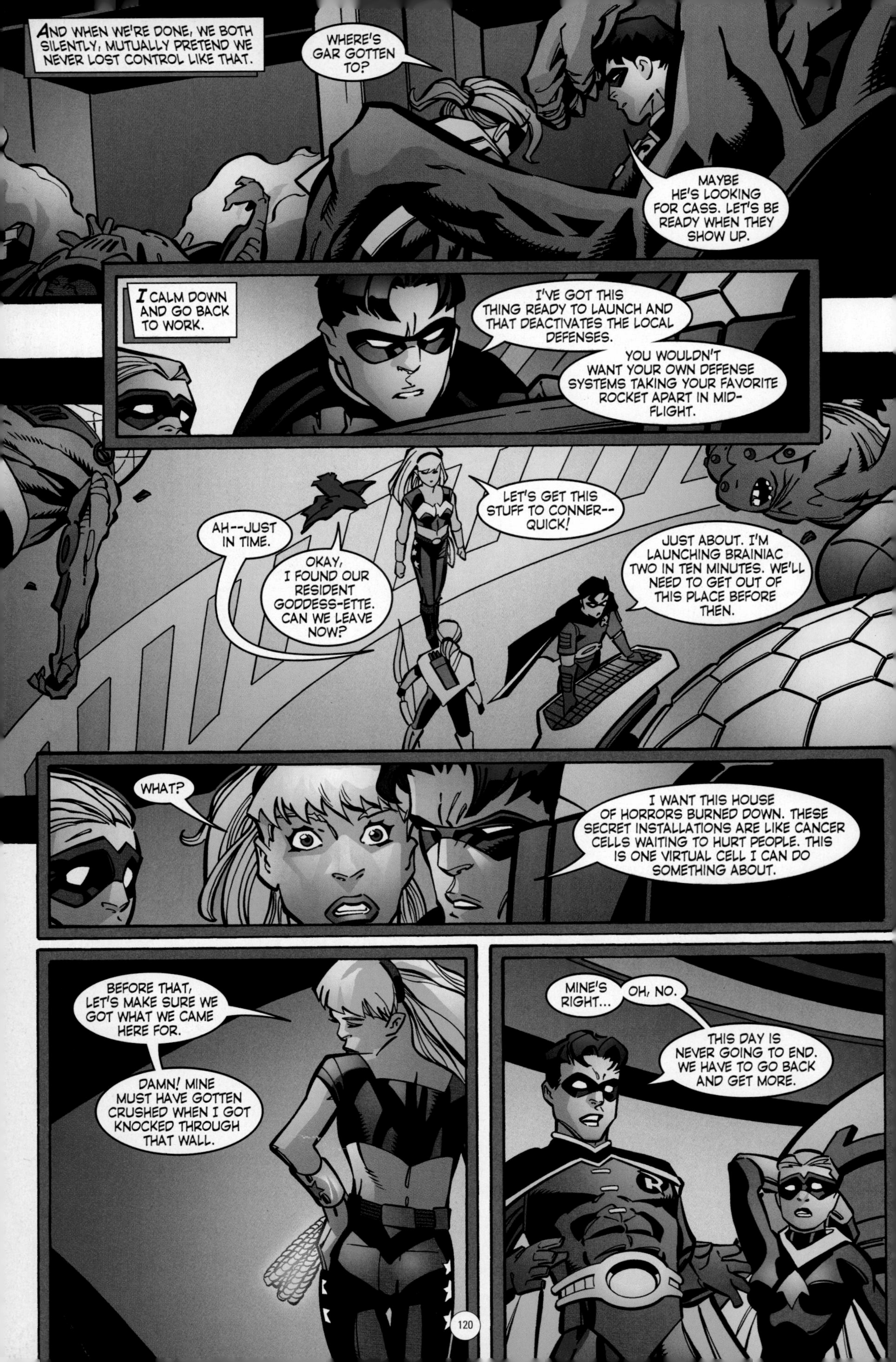
AND WHEN WE'RE DONE, WE BOTH SILENTLY, MUTUALLY PRETEND WE NEVER LOST CONTROL LIKE THAT.
WHERE'S GAR GOTTEN TO?
MAYBE HE'S LOOKING FOR CASS. LET'S BE READY WHEN THEY SHOW UP.
I CALM DOWN AND GO BACK TO WORK.
I'VE GOT THIS THING READY TO LAUNCH AND THAT DEACTIVATES THE LOCAL DEFENSES.
YOU WOULDN'T WANT YOUR OWN DEFENSE SYSTEMS TAKING YOUR FAVORITE ROCKET APART IN MID-FLIGHT.
AH--JUST IN TIME.
OKAY, I FOUND OUR RESIDENT GODDESS-ETTE. CAN WE LEAVE NOW?
LET'S GET THIS STUFF TO CONNER--QUICK!
JUST ABOUT. I'M LAUNCHING BRAINIAC TWO IN TEN MINUTES. WE'LL NEED TO GET OUT OF THIS PLACE BEFORE THEN.
WHAT?
I WANT THIS HOUSE OF HORRORS BURNED DOWN. THESE SECRET INSTALLATIONS ARE LIKE CANCER CELLS WAITING TO HURT PEOPLE. THIS IS ONE VIRTUAL CELL I CAN DO SOMETHING ABOUT.
BEFORE THAT, LET'S MAKE SURE WE GOT WHAT WE CAME HERE FOR.
DAMN! MINE MUST HAVE GOTTEN CRUSHED WHEN I GOT KNOCKED THROUGH THAT WALL.
MINE'S RIGHT...
OH, NO.
THIS DAY IS NEVER GOING TO END. WE HAVE TO GO BACK AND GET MORE.

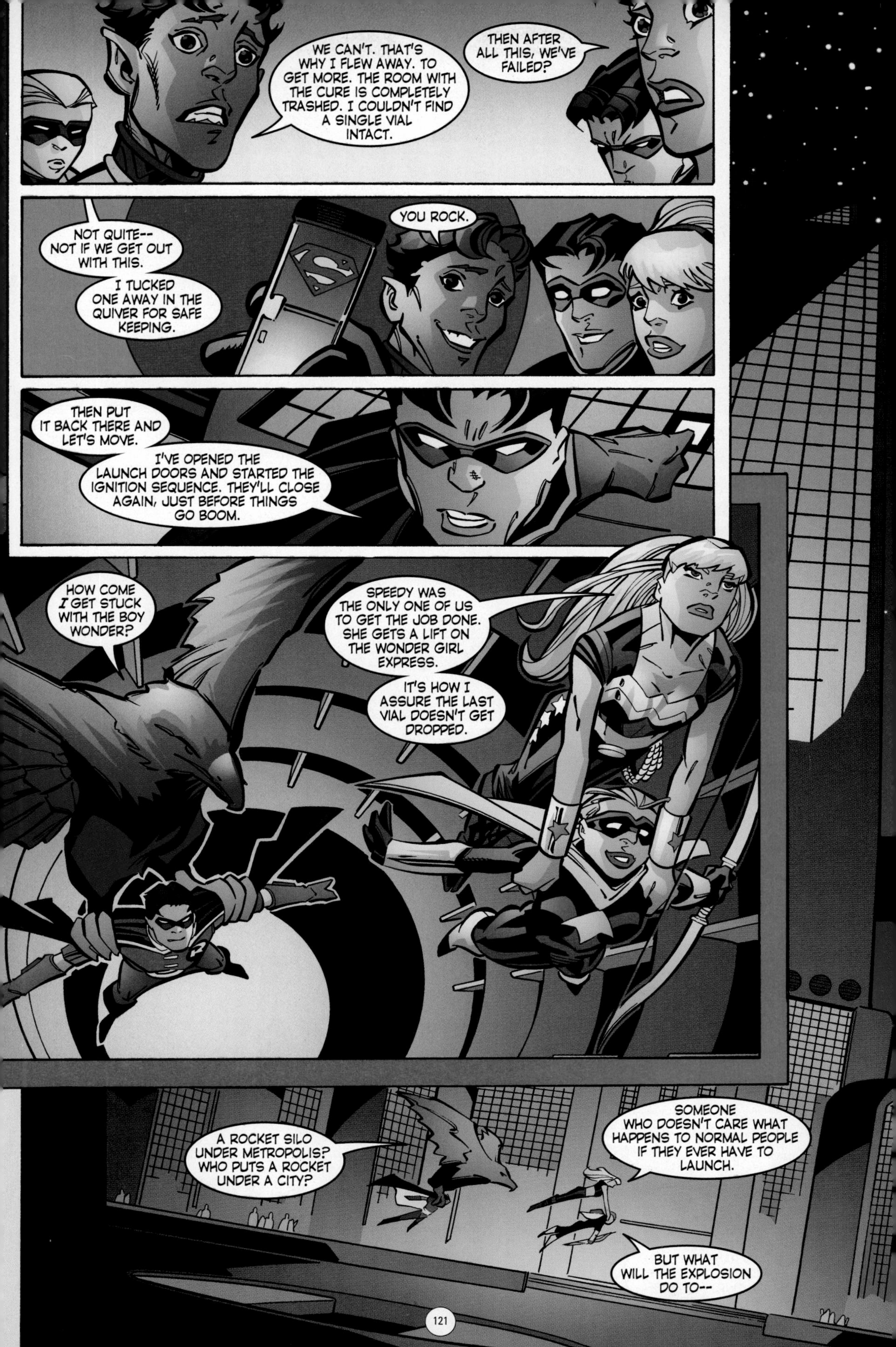

WE CAN'T. THAT'S WHY I FLEW AWAY. TO GET MORE. THE ROOM WITH THE CURE IS COMPLETELY TRASHED. I COULDN'T FIND A SINGLE VIAL INTACT.
THEN AFTER ALL THIS, WE'VE FAILED?
NOT QUITE-- NOT IF WE GET OUT WITH THIS.
I TUCKED ONE AWAY IN THE QUIVER FOR SAFE KEEPING.
YOU ROCK.
THEN PUT IT BACK THERE AND LET'S MOVE.
I'VE OPENED THE LAUNCH DOORS AND STARTED THE IGNITION SEQUENCE. THEY'LL CLOSE AGAIN, JUST BEFORE THINGS GO BOOM.
HOW COME *I* GET STUCK WITH THE BOY WONDER?
SPEEDY WAS THE ONLY ONE OF US TO GET THE JOB DONE. SHE GETS A LIFT ON THE WONDER GIRL EXPRESS.
IT'S HOW I ASSURE THE LAST VIAL DOESN'T GET DROPPED.
A ROCKET SILO UNDER METROPOLIS? WHO PUTS A ROCKET UNDER A CITY?
SOMEONE WHO DOESN'T CARE WHAT HAPPENS TO NORMAL PEOPLE IF THEY EVER HAVE TO LAUNCH.
BUT WHAT WILL THE EXPLOSION DO TO--

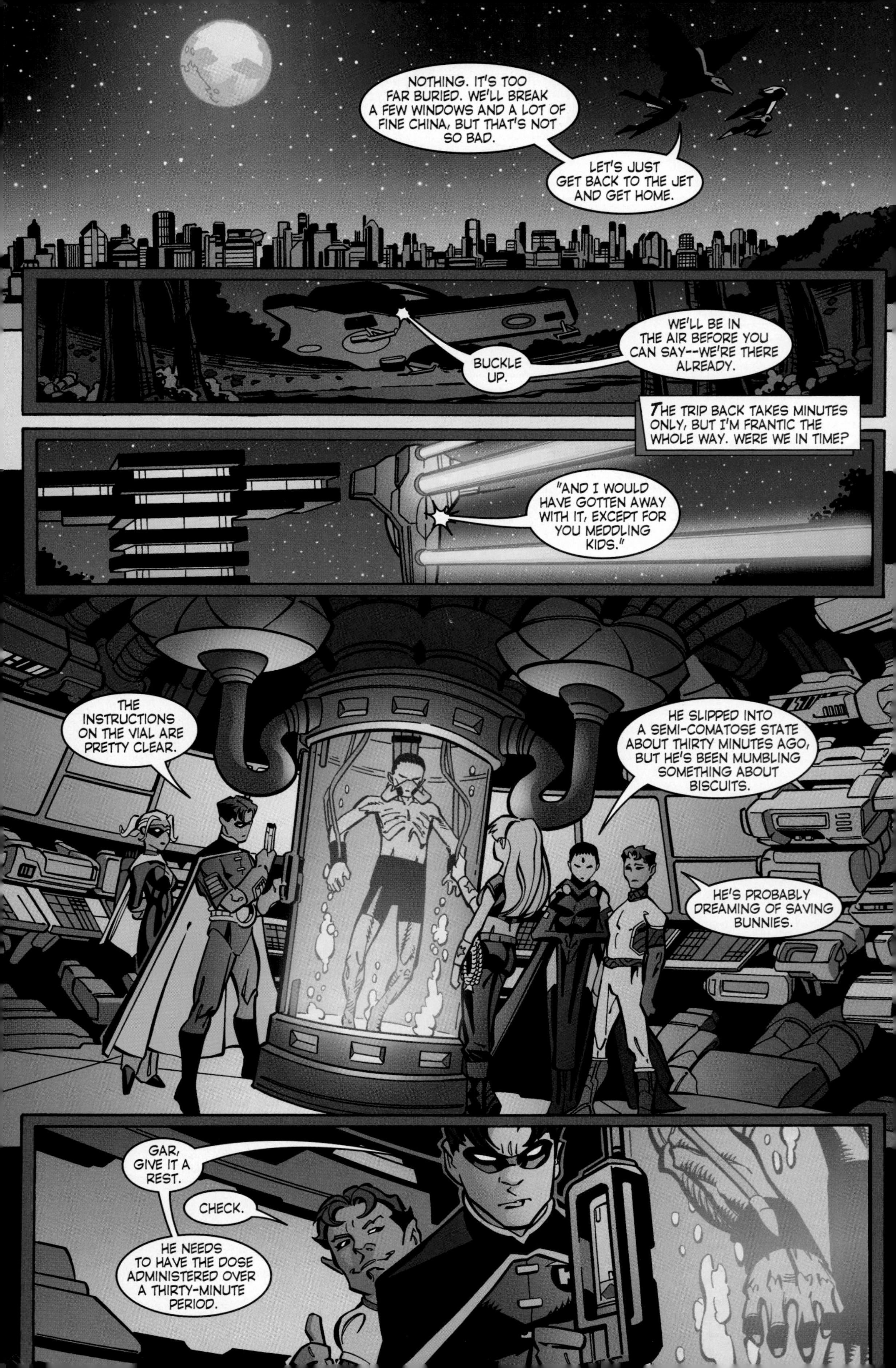
NOTHING. IT'S TOO FAR BURIED. WE'LL BREAK A FEW WINDOWS AND A LOT OF FINE CHINA, BUT THAT'S NOT SO BAD.
LET'S JUST GET BACK TO THE JET AND GET HOME.
BUCKLE UP.
WE'LL BE IN THE AIR BEFORE YOU CAN SAY--WE'RE THERE ALREADY.
THE TRIP BACK TAKES MINUTES ONLY, BUT I'M FRANTIC THE WHOLE WAY. WERE WE IN TIME?
"AND I WOULD HAVE GOTTEN AWAY WITH IT, EXCEPT FOR YOU MEDDLING KIDS."
THE INSTRUCTIONS ON THE VIAL ARE PRETTY CLEAR.
HE SLIPPED INTO A SEMI-COMATOSE STATE ABOUT THIRTY MINUTES AGO, BUT HE'S BEEN MUMBLING SOMETHING ABOUT BISCUITS.
HE'S PROBABLY DREAMING OF SAVING BUNNIES.
GAR, GIVE IT A REST.
CHECK.
HE NEEDS TO HAVE THE DOSE ADMINISTERED OVER A THIRTY-MINUTE PERIOD.

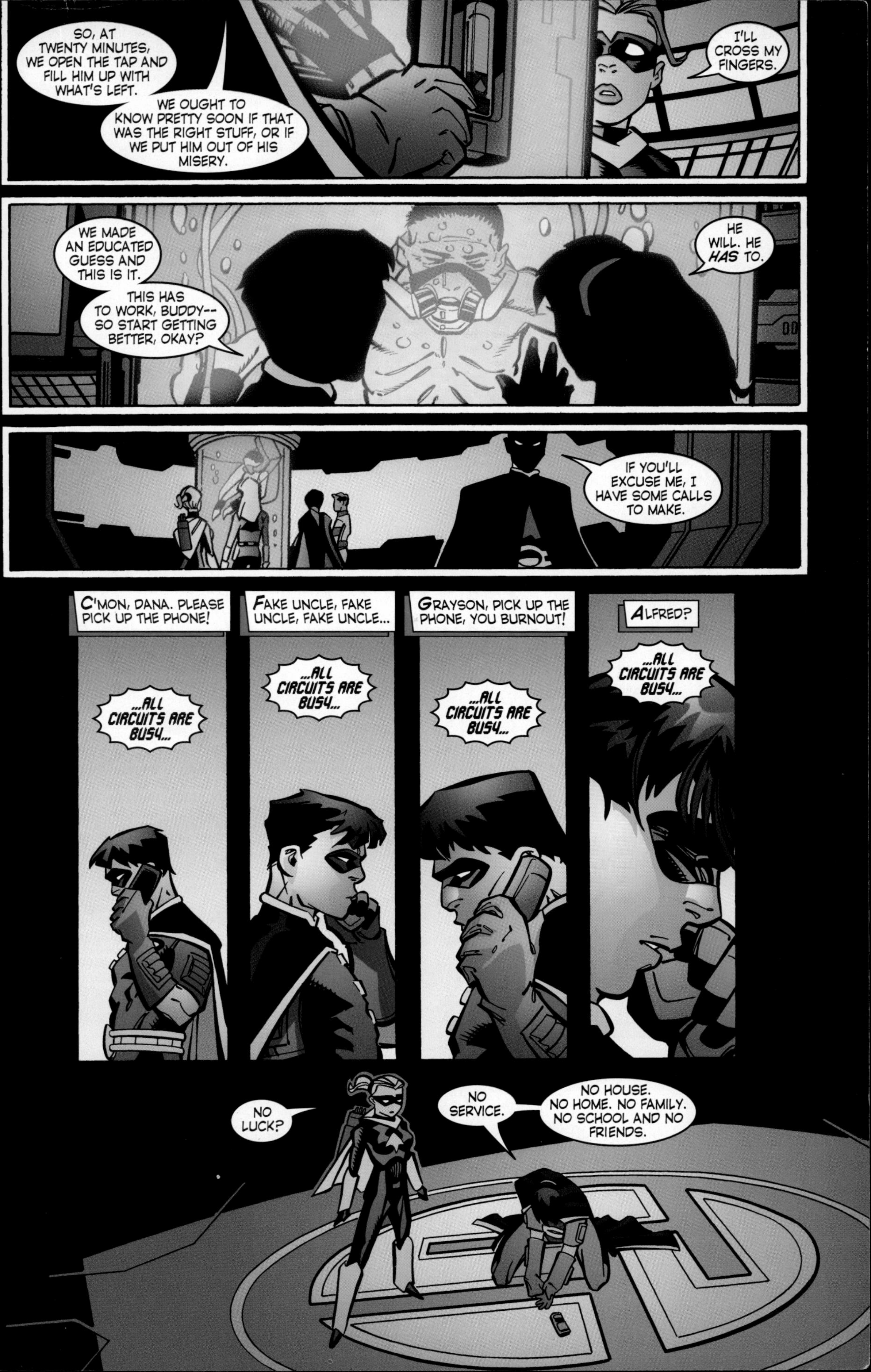
SO, AT TWENTY MINUTES, WE OPEN THE TAP AND FILL HIM UP WITH WHAT'S LEFT.
WE OUGHT TO KNOW PRETTY SOON IF THAT WAS THE RIGHT STUFF, OR IF WE PUT HIM OUT OF HIS MISERY.
I'LL CROSS MY FINGERS.
WE MADE AN EDUCATED GUESS AND THIS IS IT.
THIS HAS TO WORK, BUDDY-- SO START GETTING BETTER, OKAY?
HE WILL. HE HAS TO.
IF YOU'LL EXCUSE ME, I HAVE SOME CALLS TO MAKE.
C'MON, DANA. PLEASE PICK UP THE PHONE!
...ALL CIRCUITS ARE BUSY...
FAKE UNCLE, FAKE UNCLE, FAKE UNCLE...
...ALL CIRCUITS ARE BUSY...
GRAYSON, PICK UP THE PHONE, YOU BURNOUT!
...ALL CIRCUITS ARE BUSY...
ALFRED?
...ALL CIRCUITS ARE BUSY...
NO LUCK?
NO SERVICE.
NO HOUSE. NO HOME. NO FAMILY. NO SCHOOL AND NO FRIENDS.

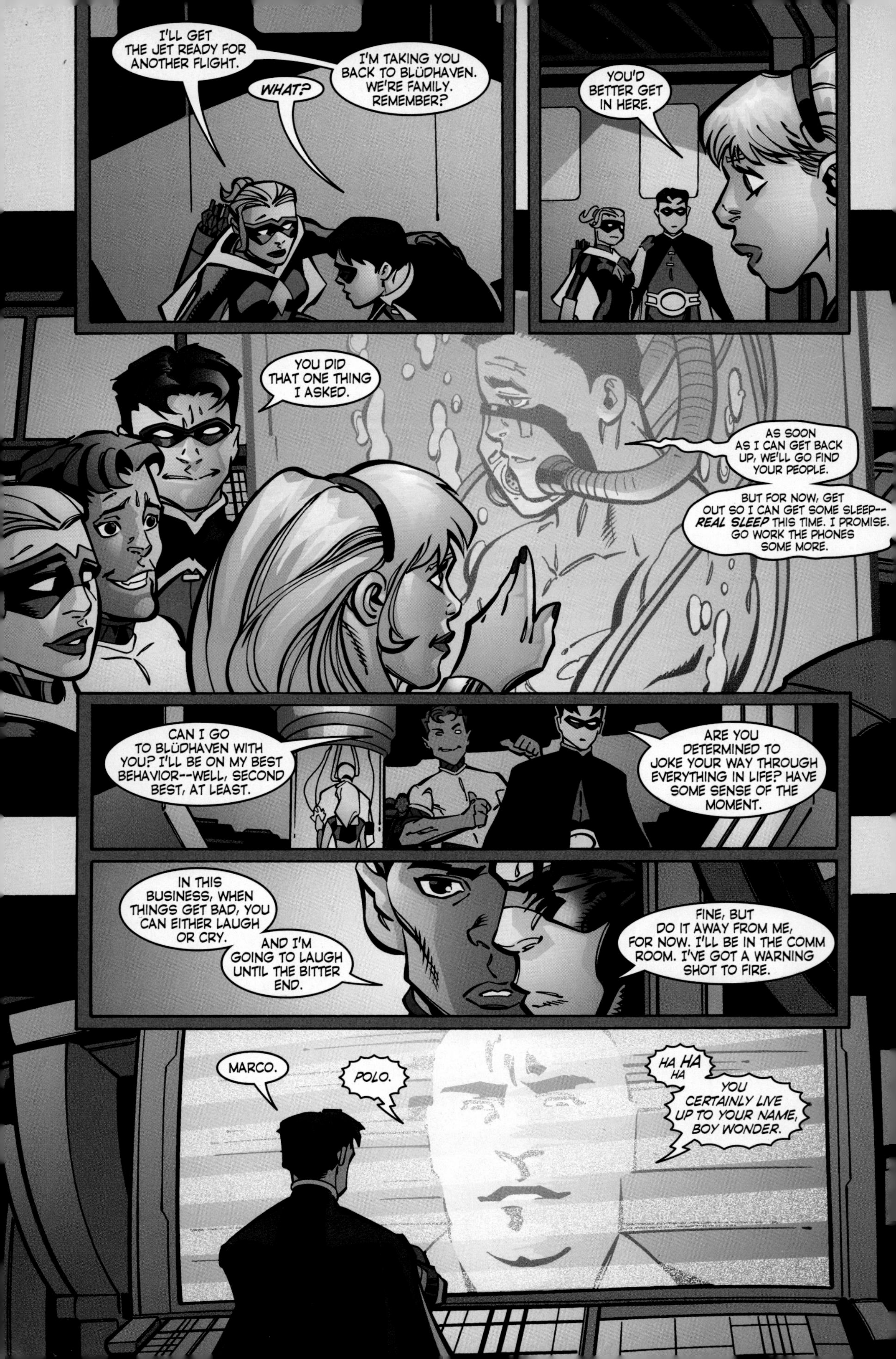

I'LL GET THE JET READY FOR ANOTHER FLIGHT.
I'M TAKING YOU BACK TO BLÜDHAVEN. WE'RE FAMILY. REMEMBER?
WHAT?
YOU'D BETTER GET IN HERE.
YOU DID THAT ONE THING I ASKED.
AS SOON AS I CAN GET BACK UP, WE'LL GO FIND YOUR PEOPLE.
BUT FOR NOW, GET OUT SO I CAN GET SOME SLEEP--REAL SLEEP THIS TIME. I PROMISE. GO WORK THE PHONES SOME MORE.
CAN I GO TO BLÜDHAVEN WITH YOU? I'LL BE ON MY BEST BEHAVIOR--WELL, SECOND BEST, AT LEAST.
ARE YOU DETERMINED TO JOKE YOUR WAY THROUGH EVERYTHING IN LIFE? HAVE SOME SENSE OF THE MOMENT.
IN THIS BUSINESS, WHEN THINGS GET BAD, YOU CAN EITHER LAUGH OR CRY.
AND I'M GOING TO LAUGH UNTIL THE BITTER END.
FINE, BUT DO IT AWAY FROM ME, FOR NOW. I'LL BE IN THE COMM ROOM. I'VE GOT A WARNING SHOT TO FIRE.
MARCO.
POLO.
HA HA HA
YOU CERTAINLY LIVE UP TO YOUR NAME, BOY WONDER.

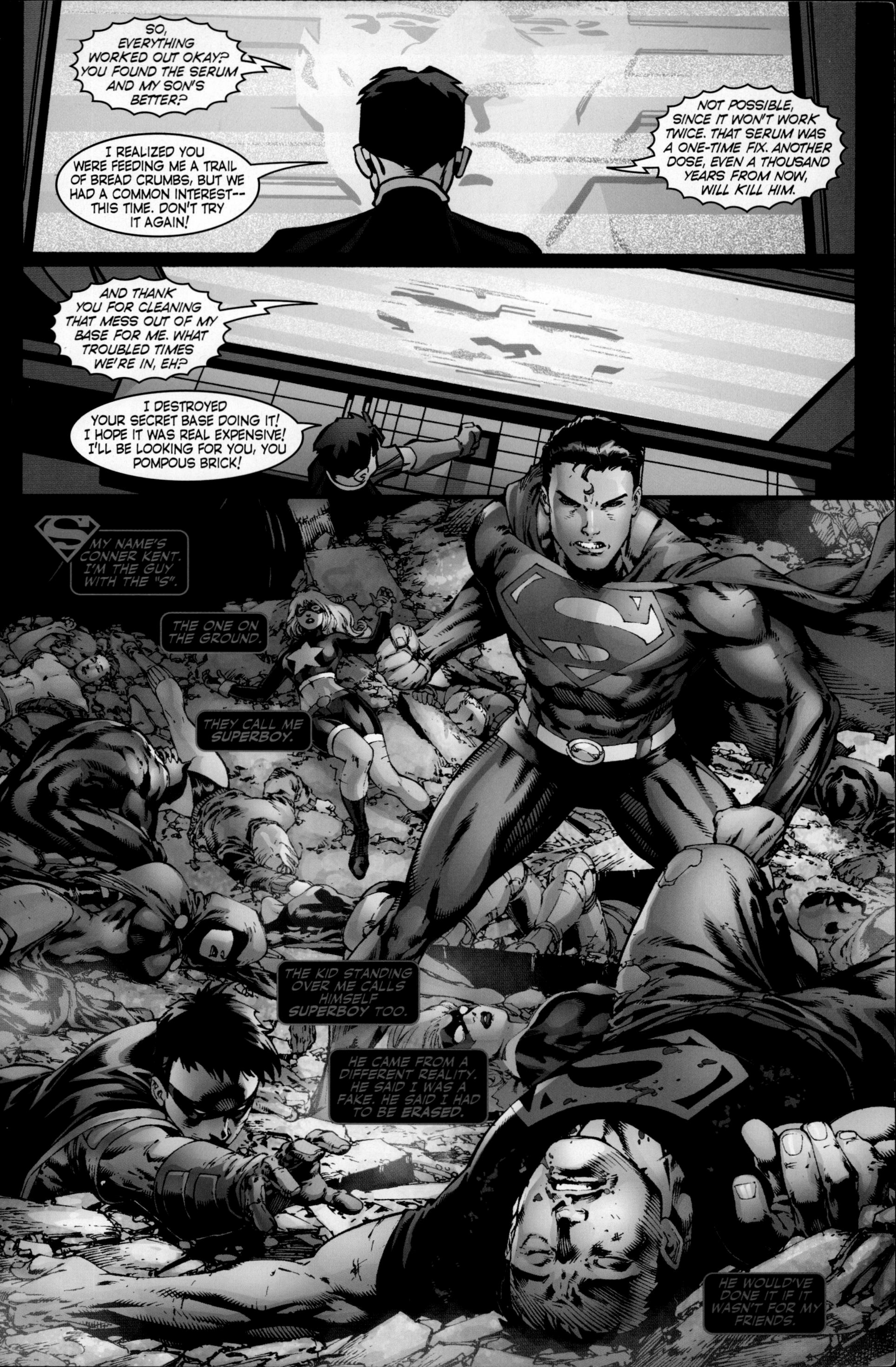
SO, EVERYTHING WORKED OUT OKAY? YOU FOUND THE SERUM AND MY SON'S BETTER?
I REALIZED YOU WERE FEEDING ME A TRAIL OF BREAD CRUMBS, BUT WE HAD A COMMON INTEREST-- THIS TIME. DON'T TRY IT AGAIN!
NOT POSSIBLE, SINCE IT WON'T WORK TWICE. THAT SERUM WAS A ONE-TIME FIX. ANOTHER DOSE, EVEN A THOUSAND YEARS FROM NOW, WILL KILL HIM.
AND THANK YOU FOR CLEANING THAT MESS OUT OF MY BASE FOR ME. WHAT TROUBLED TIMES WE'RE IN, EH?
I DESTROYED YOUR SECRET BASE DOING IT! I HOPE IT WAS REAL EXPENSIVE! I'LL BE LOOKING FOR YOU, YOU POMPOUS BRICK!
MY NAME'S CONNER KENT. I'M THE GUY WITH THE "S".
THE ONE ON THE GROUND.
THEY CALL ME SUPERBOY.
THE KID STANDING OVER ME CALLS HIMSELF SUPERBOY TOO.
HE CAME FROM A DIFFERENT REALITY. HE SAID I WAS A FAKE. HE SAID I HAD TO BE ERASED.
HE WOULD'VE DONE IT IF IT WASN'T FOR MY FRIENDS.

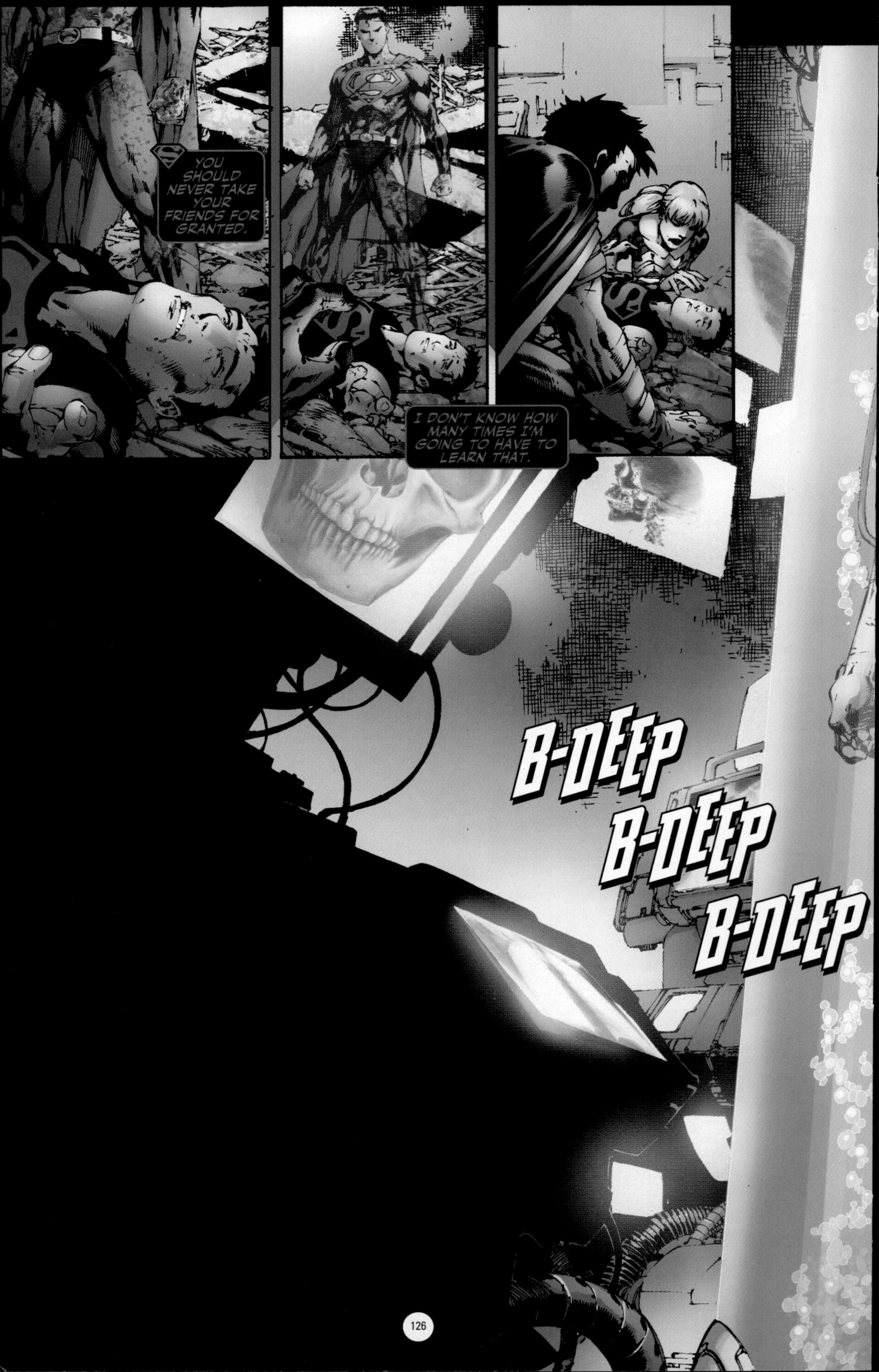
YOU SHOULD NEVER TAKE YOUR FRIENDS FOR GRANTED.
I DON'T KNOW HOW MANY TIMES I'M GOING TO HAVE TO LEARN THAT.
B-DEEP
B-DEEP
B-DEEP

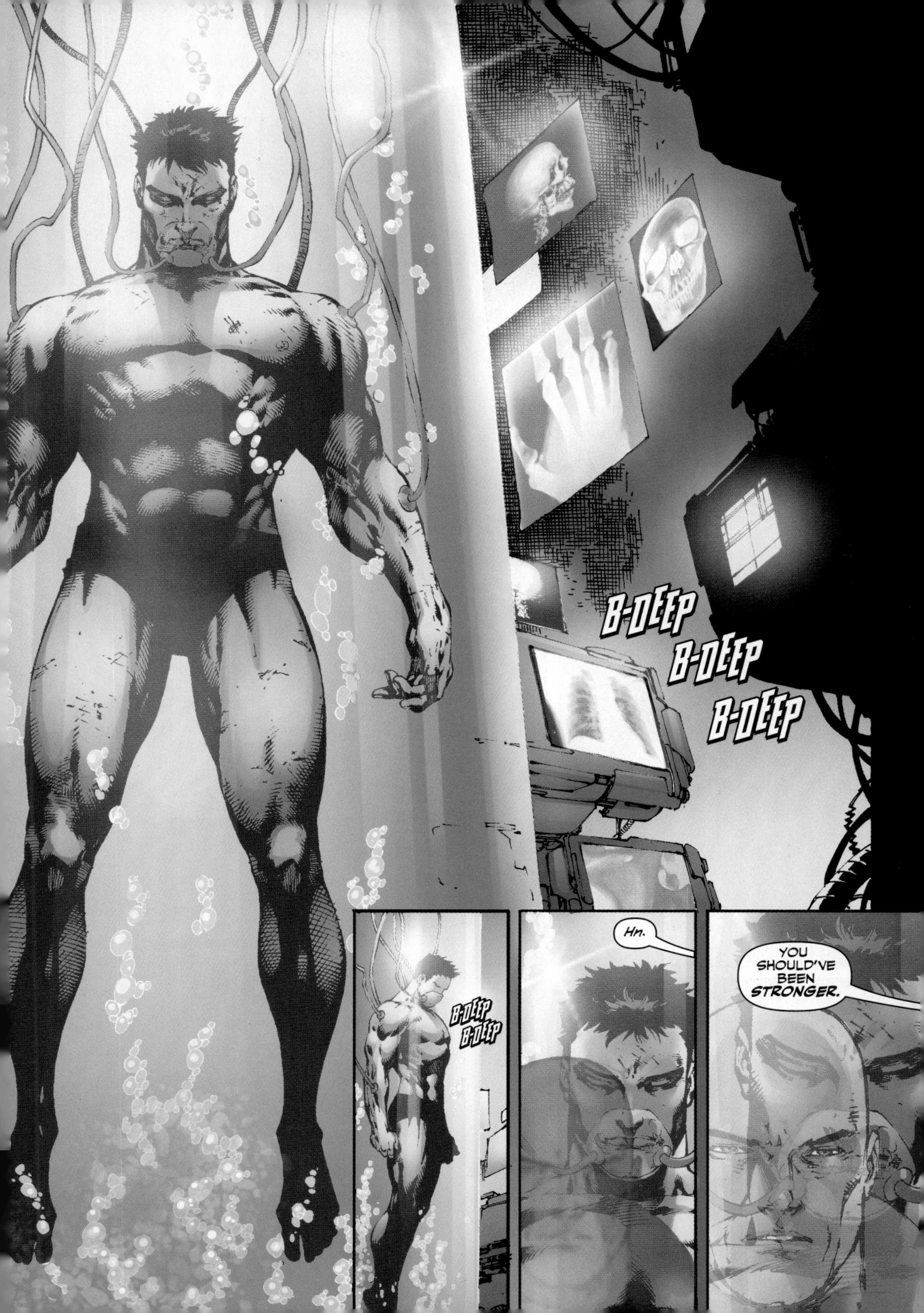
B-DEEP
B-DEEP
B-DEEP
B-DEEP
B-DEEP
Hn.
YOU SHOULD'VE BEEN STRONGER.

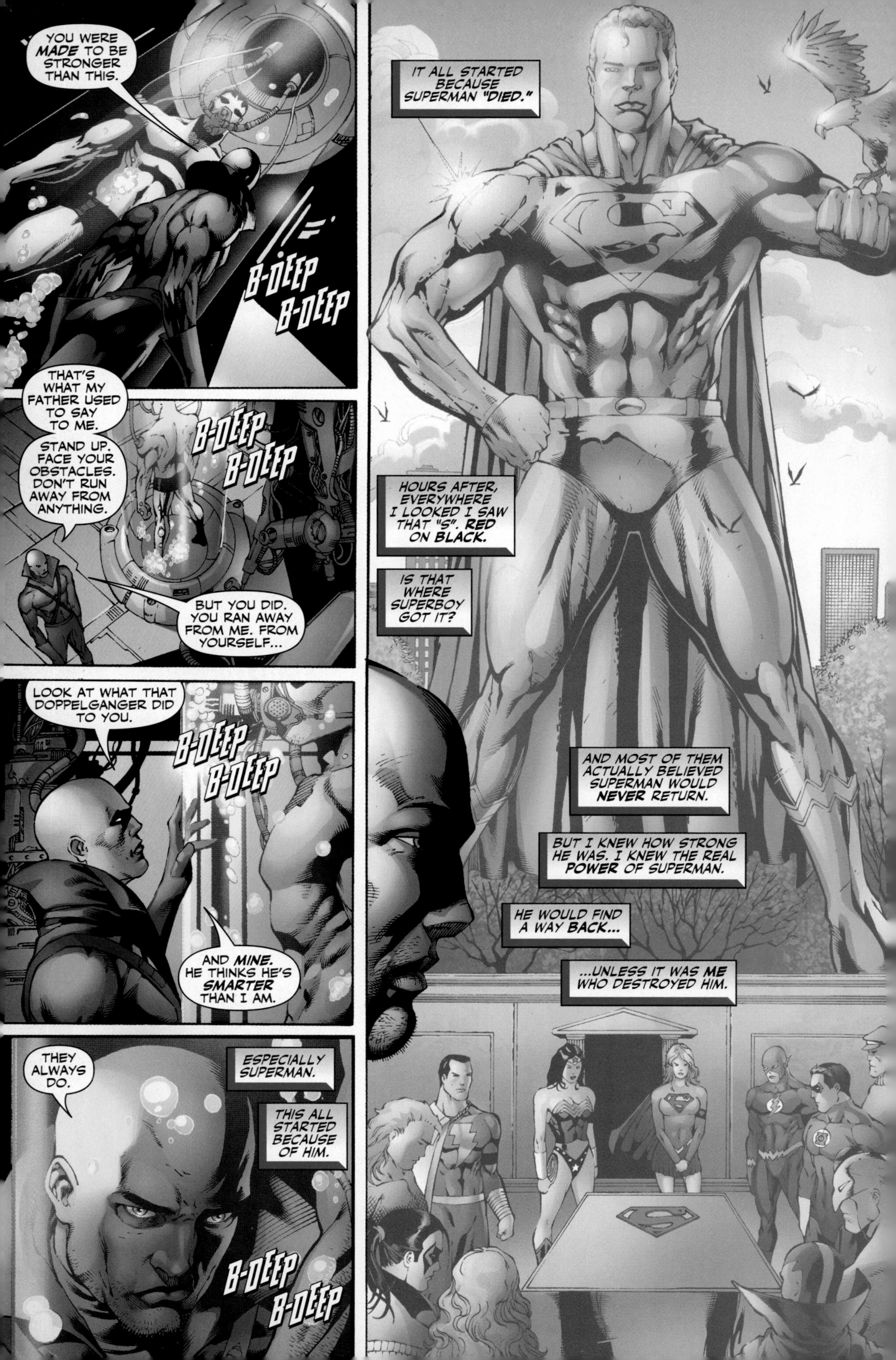
YOU WERE MADE TO BE STRONGER THAN THIS.
B-DEEP B-DEEP
THAT'S WHAT MY FATHER USED TO SAY TO ME.
STAND UP. FACE YOUR OBSTACLES. DON'T RUN AWAY FROM ANYTHING.
B-DEEP B-DEEP
BUT YOU DID. YOU RAN AWAY FROM ME. FROM YOURSELF...
LOOK AT WHAT THAT DOPPELGANGER DID TO YOU.
B-DEEP B-DEEP
AND MINE. HE THINKS HE'S SMARTER THAN I AM.
THEY ALWAYS DO.
ESPECIALLY SUPERMAN.
THIS ALL STARTED BECAUSE OF HIM.
B-DEEP B-DEEP
IT ALL STARTED BECAUSE SUPERMAN "DIED."
HOURS AFTER, EVERYWHERE I LOOKED I SAW THAT "S". RED ON BLACK.
IS THAT WHERE SUPERBOY GOT IT?
AND MOST OF THEM ACTUALLY BELIEVED SUPERMAN WOULD NEVER RETURN.
BUT I KNEW HOW STRONG HE WAS. I KNEW THE REAL POWER OF SUPERMAN.
HE WOULD FIND A WAY BACK...
...UNLESS IT WAS ME WHO DESTROYED HIM.

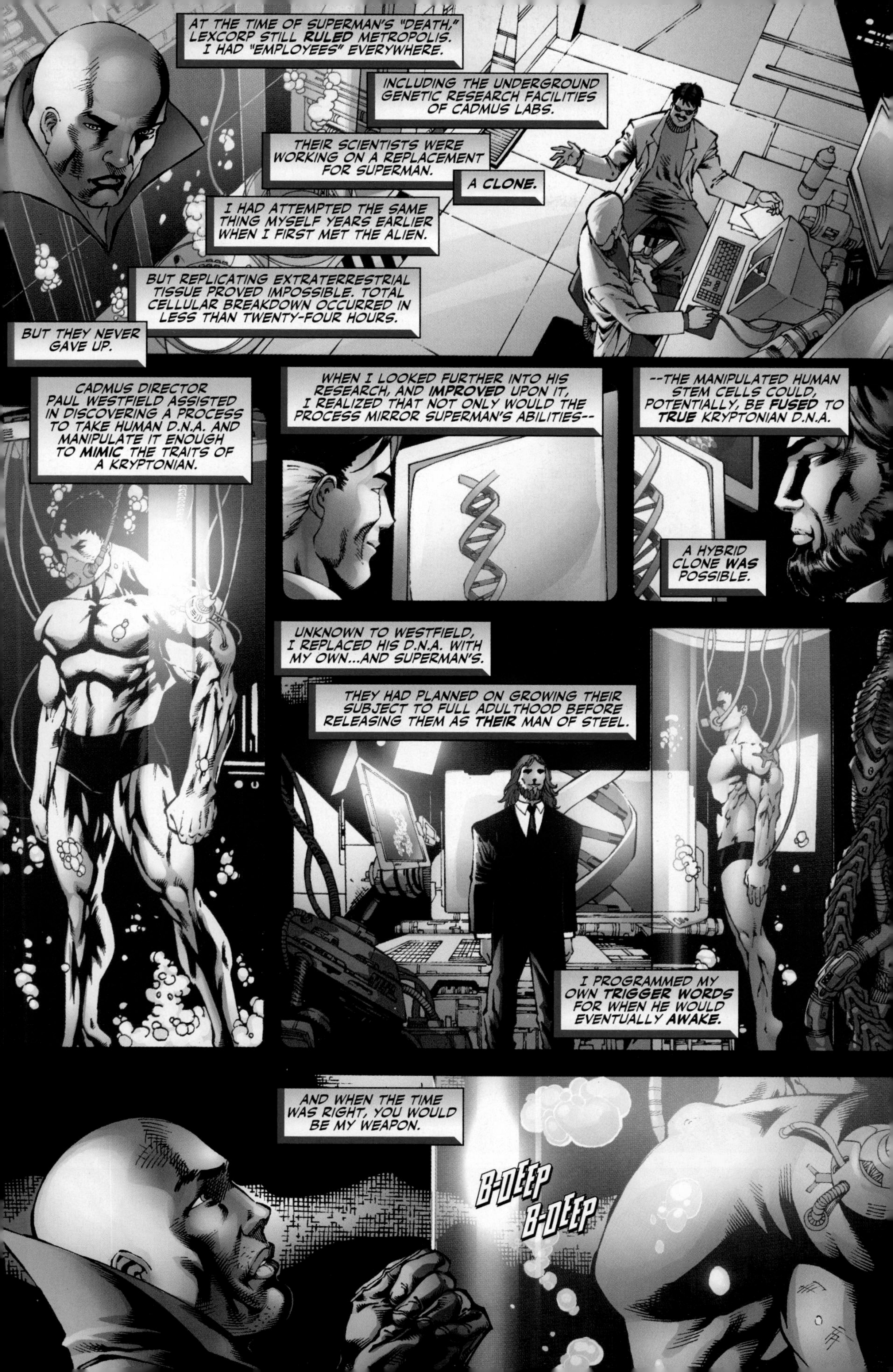

AT THE TIME OF SUPERMAN'S "DEATH," LEXCORP STILL RULED METROPOLIS. I HAD "EMPLOYEES" EVERYWHERE.
INCLUDING THE UNDERGROUND GENETIC RESEARCH FACILITIES OF CADMUS LABS.
THEIR SCIENTISTS WERE WORKING ON A REPLACEMENT FOR SUPERMAN.
A CLONE.
I HAD ATTEMPTED THE SAME THING MYSELF YEARS EARLIER WHEN I FIRST MET THE ALIEN.
BUT REPLICATING EXTRATERRESTRIAL TISSUE PROVED IMPOSSIBLE. TOTAL CELLULAR BREAKDOWN OCCURRED IN LESS THAN TWENTY-FOUR HOURS.
BUT THEY NEVER GAVE UP.
CADMUS DIRECTOR PAUL WESTFIELD ASSISTED IN DISCOVERING A PROCESS TO TAKE HUMAN D.N.A. AND MANIPULATE IT ENOUGH TO MIMIC THE TRAITS OF A KRYPTONIAN.
WHEN I LOOKED FURTHER INTO HIS RESEARCH, AND IMPROVED UPON IT, I REALIZED THAT NOT ONLY WOULD THE PROCESS MIRROR SUPERMAN'S ABILITIES--
--THE MANIPULATED HUMAN STEM CELLS COULD, POTENTIALLY, BE FUSED TO TRUE KRYPTONIAN D.N.A.
A HYBRID CLONE WAS POSSIBLE.
UNKNOWN TO WESTFIELD, I REPLACED HIS D.N.A. WITH MY OWN...AND SUPERMAN'S.
THEY HAD PLANNED ON GROWING THEIR SUBJECT TO FULL ADULTHOOD BEFORE RELEASING THEM AS THEIR MAN OF STEEL.
I PROGRAMMED MY OWN TRIGGER WORDS FOR WHEN HE WOULD EVENTUALLY AWAKE.
AND WHEN THE TIME WAS RIGHT, YOU WOULD BE MY WEAPON.
B-DEEP
B-DEEP

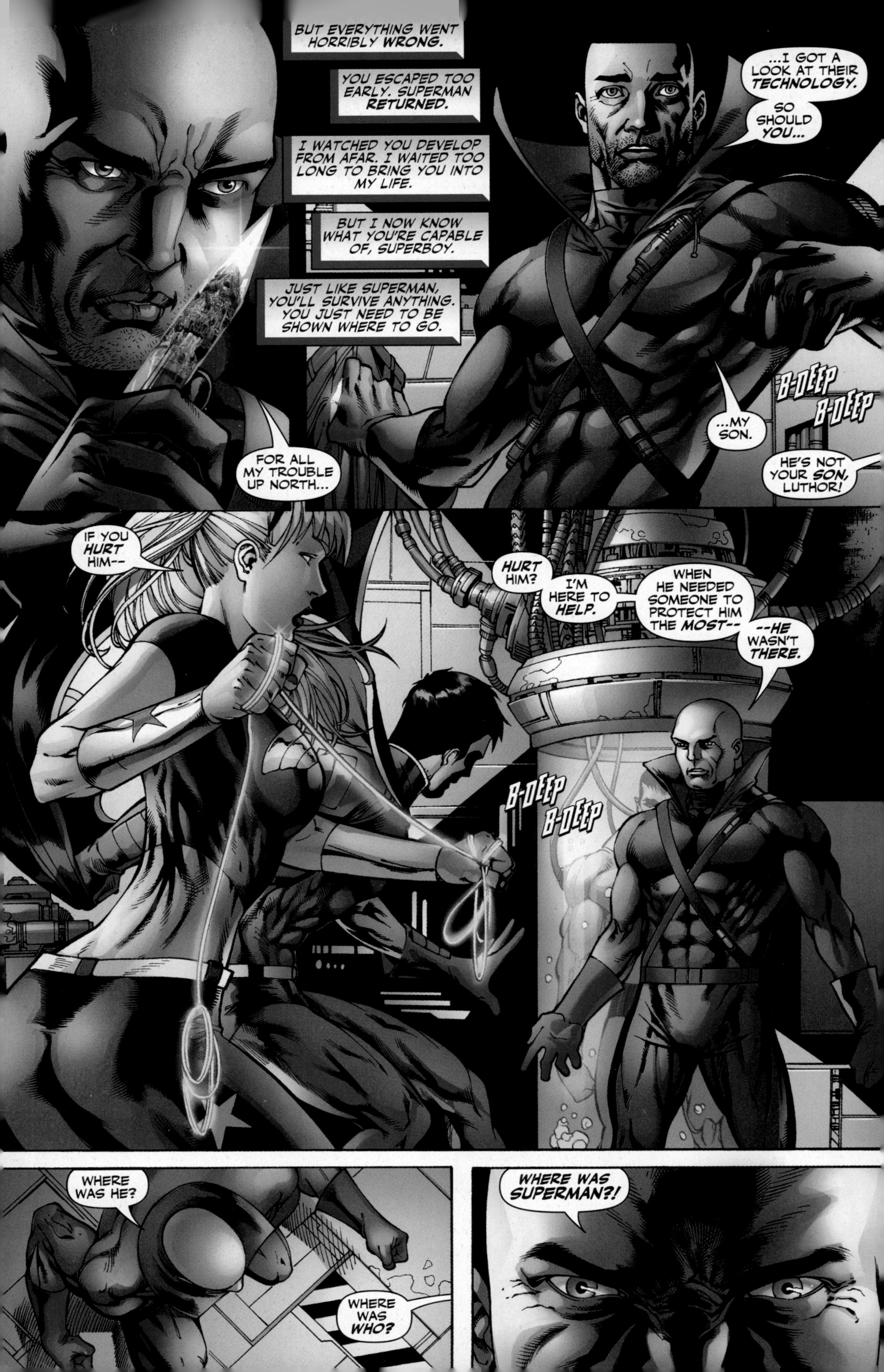
BUT EVERYTHING WENT HORRIBLY WRONG.
YOU ESCAPED TOO EARLY. SUPERMAN RETURNED.
I WATCHED YOU DEVELOP FROM AFAR. I WAITED TOO LONG TO BRING YOU INTO MY LIFE.
BUT I NOW KNOW WHAT YOU'RE CAPABLE OF, SUPERBOY.
JUST LIKE SUPERMAN, YOU'LL SURVIVE ANYTHING. YOU JUST NEED TO BE SHOWN WHERE TO GO.
FOR ALL MY TROUBLE UP NORTH...
...I GOT A LOOK AT THEIR TECHNOLOGY.
SO SHOULD YOU...
...MY SON.
B-DEEP
B-DEEP
HE'S NOT YOUR SON, LUTHOR!
IF YOU HURT HIM--
HURT HIM?
I'M HERE TO HELP.
WHEN HE NEEDED SOMEONE TO PROTECT HIM THE MOST--
--HE WASN'T THERE.
B-DEEP
B-DEEP
WHERE WAS HE?
WHERE WAS WHO?
WHERE WAS SUPERMAN?!

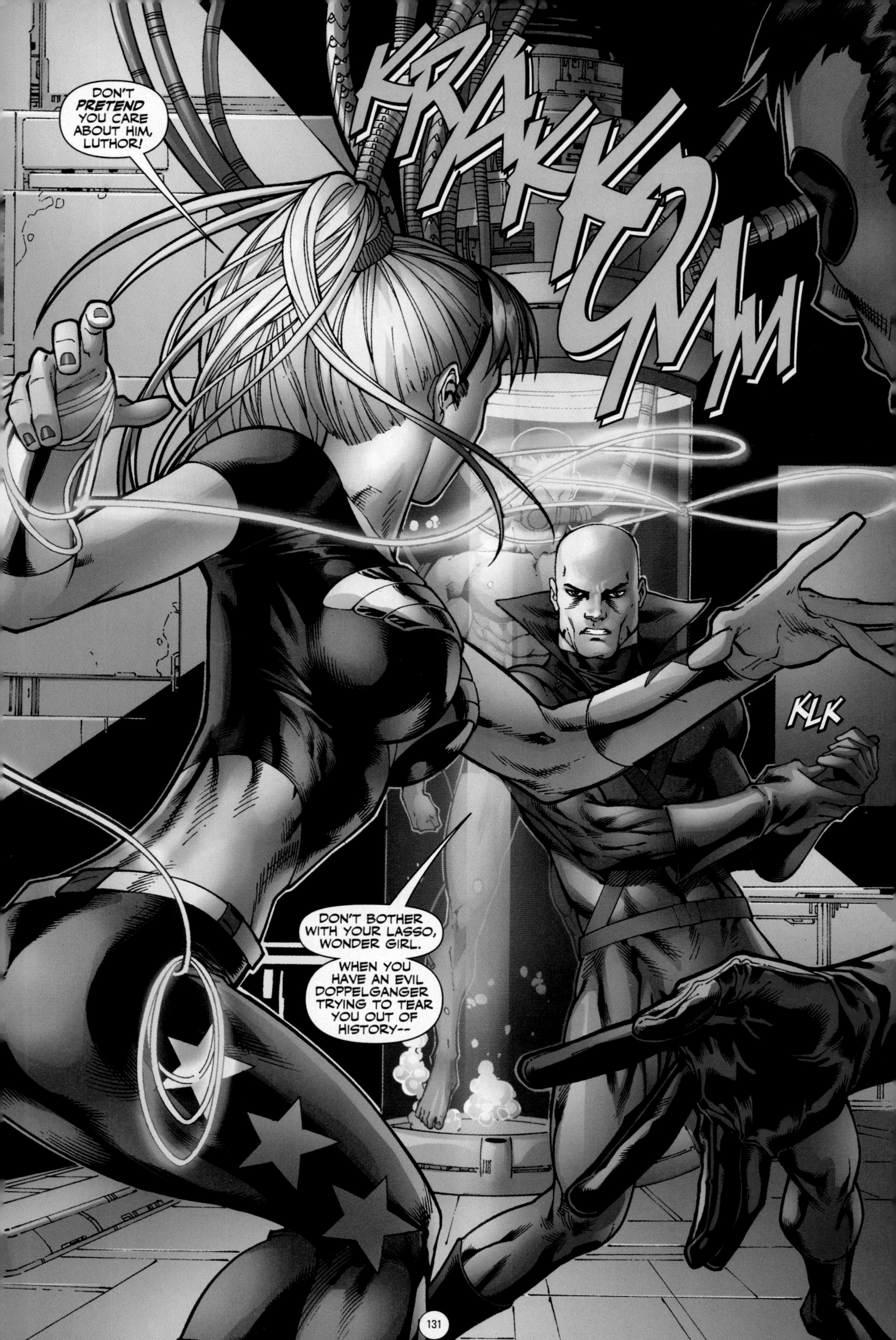
KRAKOOM
DON'T PRETEND YOU CARE ABOUT HIM, LUTHOR!
KLK
DON'T BOTHER WITH YOUR LASSO, WONDER GIRL.
WHEN YOU HAVE AN EVIL DOPPELGANGER TRYING TO TEAR YOU OUT OF HISTORY--

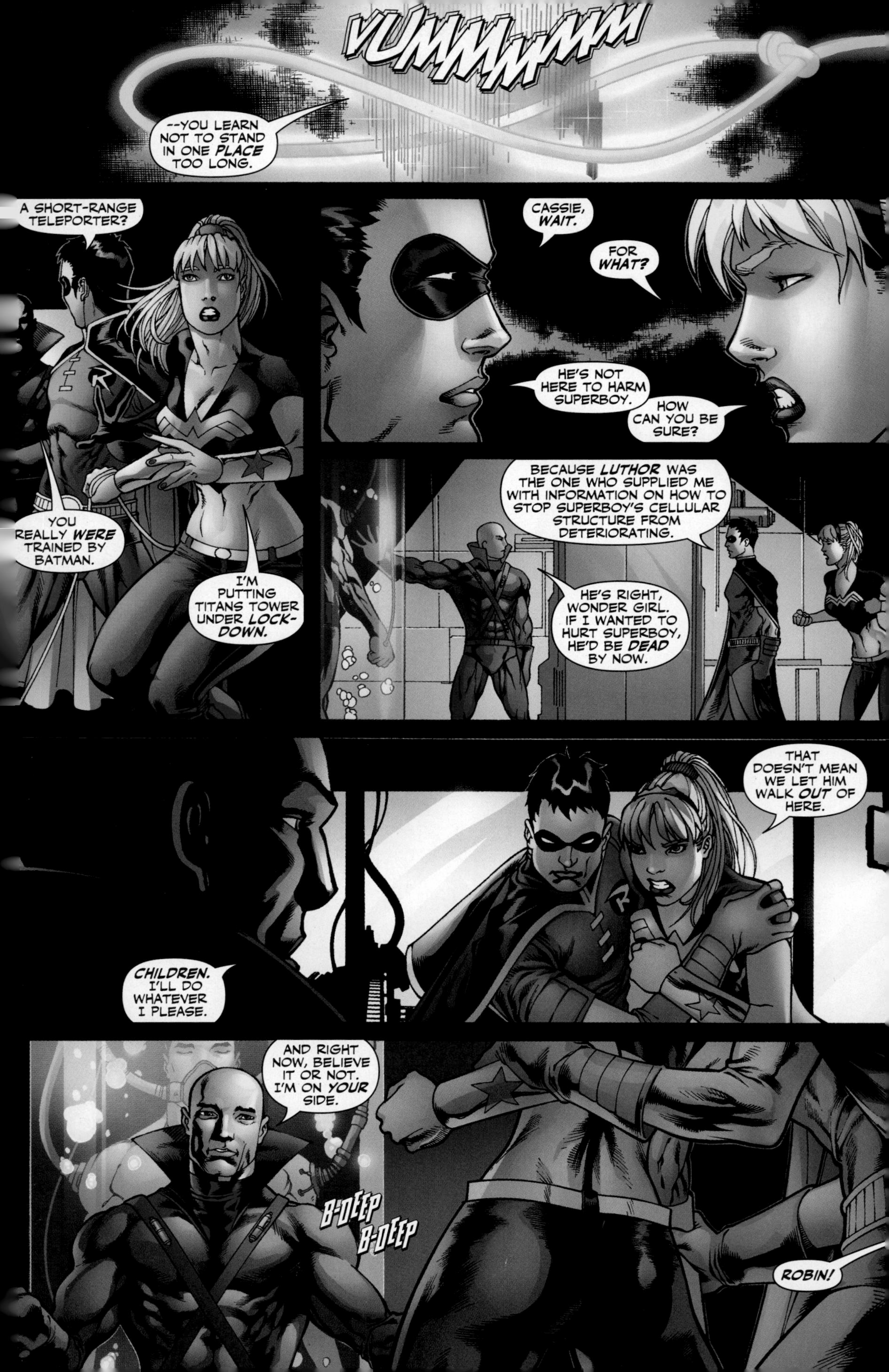

VUMMMMMM
--YOU LEARN NOT TO STAND IN ONE PLACE TOO LONG.
A SHORT-RANGE TELEPORTER?
YOU REALLY WERE TRAINED BY BATMAN.
I'M PUTTING TITANS TOWER UNDER LOCK-DOWN.
CASSIE, WAIT.
FOR WHAT?
HE'S NOT HERE TO HARM SUPERBOY.
HOW CAN YOU BE SURE?
BECAUSE LUTHOR WAS THE ONE WHO SUPPLIED ME WITH INFORMATION ON HOW TO STOP SUPERBOY'S CELLULAR STRUCTURE FROM DETERIORATING.
HE'S RIGHT, WONDER GIRL. IF I WANTED TO HURT SUPERBOY, HE'D BE DEAD BY NOW.
THAT DOESN'T MEAN WE LET HIM WALK OUT OF HERE.
CHILDREN. I'LL DO WHATEVER I PLEASE.
AND RIGHT NOW, BELIEVE IT OR NOT. I'M ON YOUR SIDE.
B-DEEP B-DEEP
ROBIN!

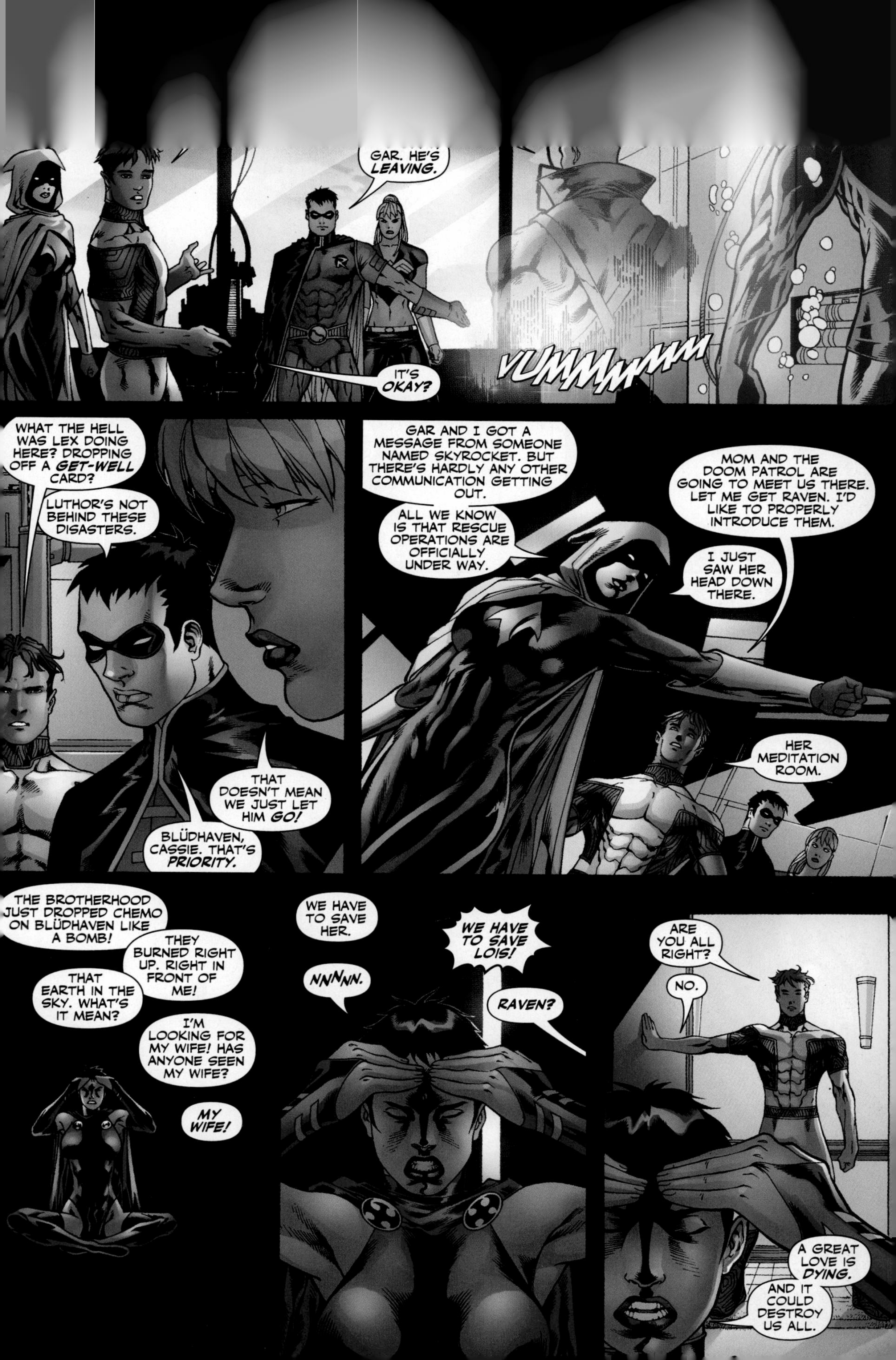
GAR. HE'S LEAVING.
IT'S OKAY?
VUMMMMMMM
WHAT THE HELL WAS LEX DOING HERE? DROPPING OFF A GET-WELL CARD?
LUTHOR'S NOT BEHIND THESE DISASTERS.
THAT DOESN'T MEAN WE JUST LET HIM GO!
BLÜDHAVEN, CASSIE. THAT'S PRIORITY.
GAR AND I GOT A MESSAGE FROM SOMEONE NAMED SKYROCKET. BUT THERE'S HARDLY ANY OTHER COMMUNICATION GETTING OUT.
ALL WE KNOW IS THAT RESCUE OPERATIONS ARE OFFICIALLY UNDER WAY.
MOM AND THE DOOM PATROL ARE GOING TO MEET US THERE. LET ME GET RAVEN. I'D LIKE TO PROPERLY INTRODUCE THEM.
I JUST SAW HER HEAD DOWN THERE.
HER MEDITATION ROOM.
THE BROTHERHOOD JUST DROPPED CHEMO ON BLÜDHAVEN LIKE A BOMB!
THEY BURNED RIGHT UP. RIGHT IN FRONT OF ME!
THAT EARTH IN THE SKY. WHAT'S IT MEAN?
I'M LOOKING FOR MY WIFE! HAS ANYONE SEEN MY WIFE?
MY WIFE!
WE HAVE TO SAVE HER.
WE HAVE TO SAVE LOIS!
NNNNN.
RAVEN?
ARE YOU ALL RIGHT?
NO.
A GREAT LOVE IS DYING.
AND IT COULD DESTROY US ALL.

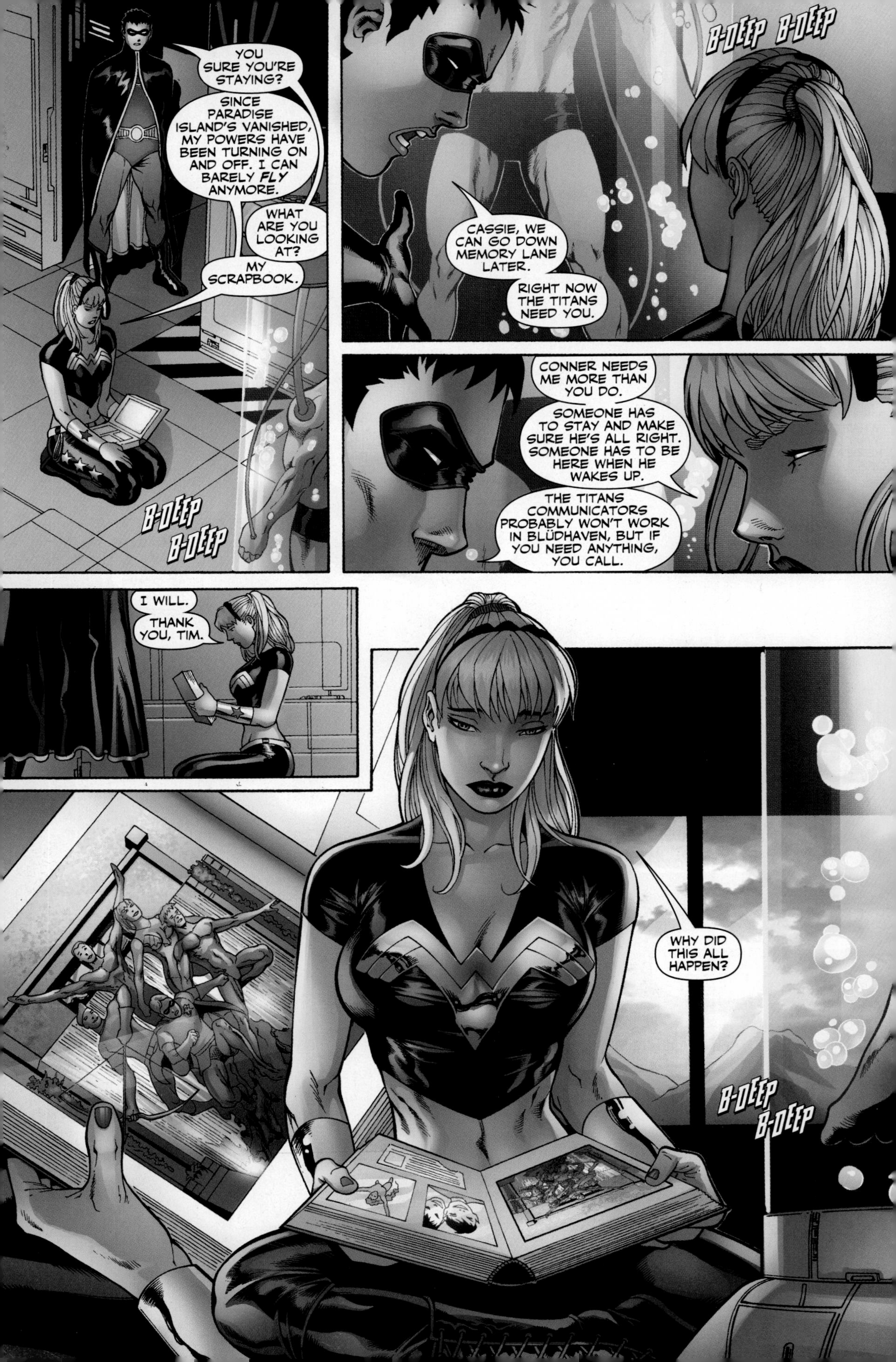
YOU SURE YOU'RE STAYING?
SINCE PARADISE ISLAND'S VANISHED, MY POWERS HAVE BEEN TURNING ON AND OFF. I CAN BARELY FLY ANYMORE.
WHAT ARE YOU LOOKING AT?
MY SCRAPBOOK.
B-DEEP B-DEEP
B-DEEP B-DEEP
CASSIE, WE CAN GO DOWN MEMORY LANE LATER.
RIGHT NOW THE TITANS NEED YOU.
CONNER NEEDS ME MORE THAN YOU DO.
SOMEONE HAS TO STAY AND MAKE SURE HE'S ALL RIGHT. SOMEONE HAS TO BE HERE WHEN HE WAKES UP.
THE TITANS COMMUNICATORS PROBABLY WON'T WORK IN BLÜDHAVEN, BUT IF YOU NEED ANYTHING, YOU CALL.
I WILL.
THANK YOU, TIM.
WHY DID THIS ALL HAPPEN?
B-DEEP B-DEEP

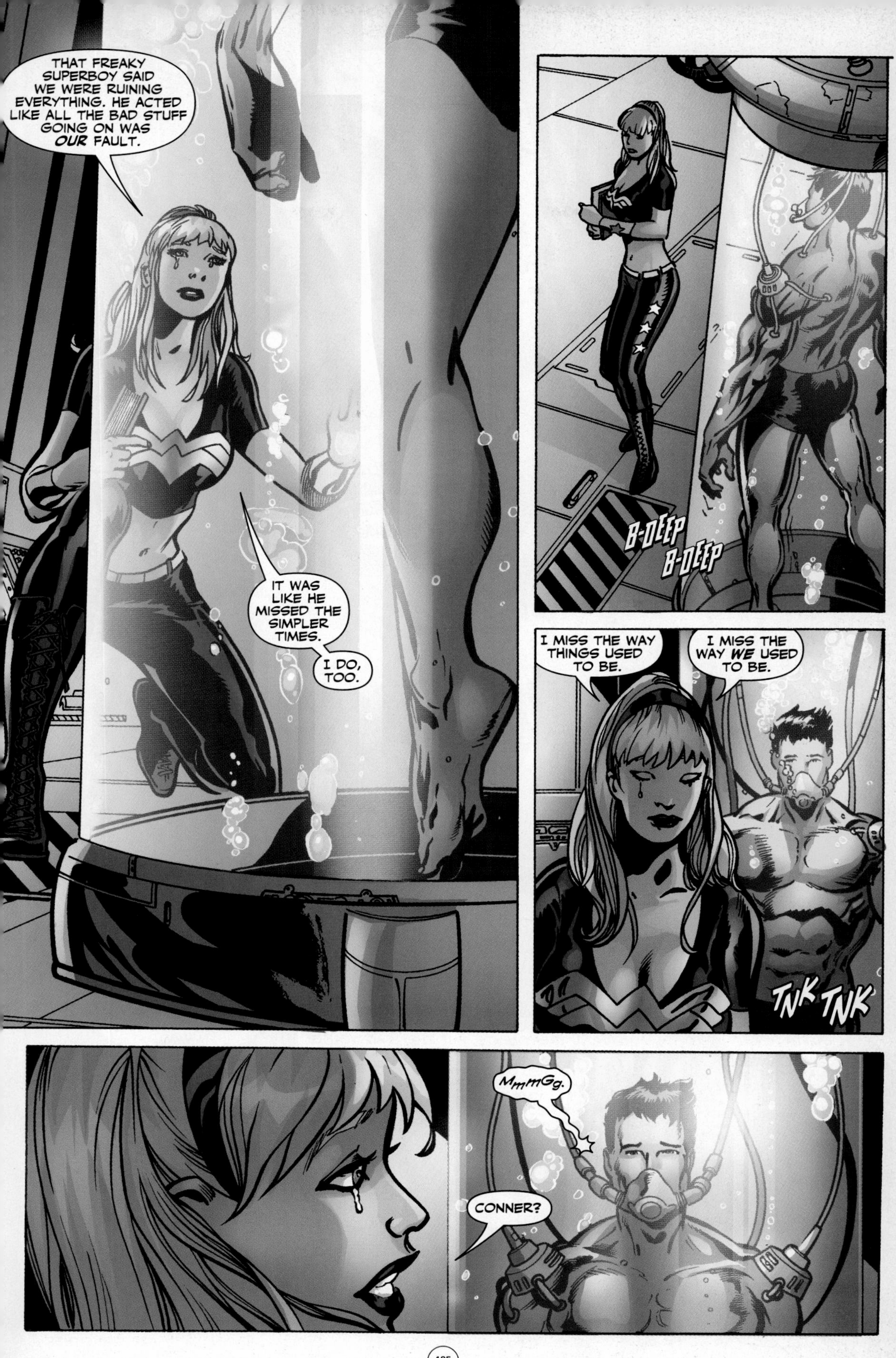

THAT FREAKY SUPERBOY SAID WE WERE RUINING EVERYTHING. HE ACTED LIKE ALL THE BAD STUFF GOING ON WAS OUR FAULT.
IT WAS LIKE HE MISSED THE SIMPLER TIMES.
I DO, TOO.
B-DEEP
B-DEEP
I MISS THE WAY THINGS USED TO BE.
I MISS THE WAY WE USED TO BE.
TNK TNK
MmmGg.
CONNER?

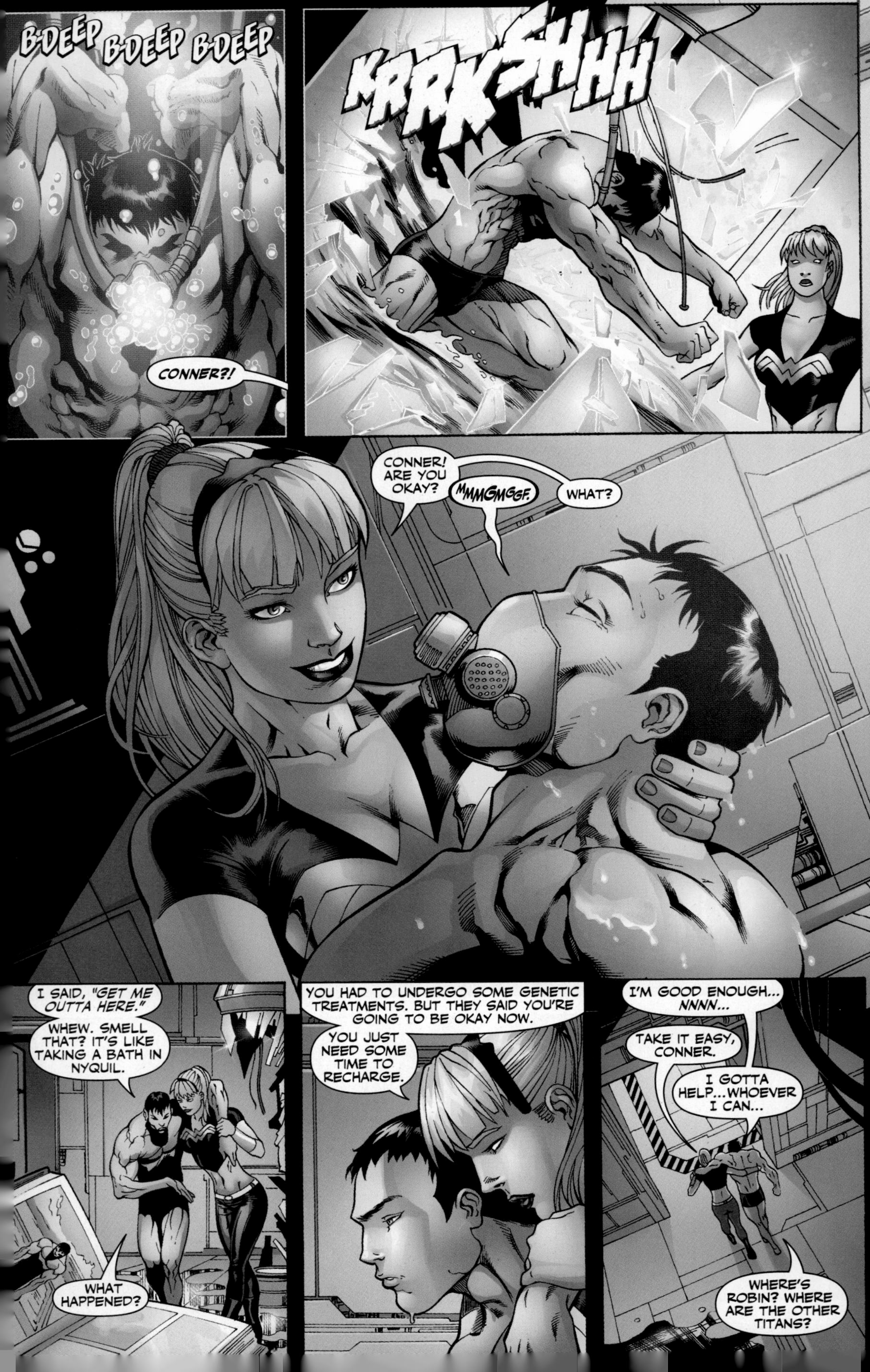
B-DEEP B-DEEP B-DEEP
CONNER?!
KRRKSHHH
CONNER! ARE YOU OKAY?
MMMGMGGF.
WHAT?
I SAID, "GET ME OUTTA HERE."
WHEW. SMELL THAT? IT'S LIKE TAKING A BATH IN NYQUIL.
WHAT HAPPENED?
YOU HAD TO UNDERGO SOME GENETIC TREATMENTS. BUT THEY SAID YOU'RE GOING TO BE OKAY NOW.
YOU JUST NEED SOME TIME TO RECHARGE.
I'M GOOD ENOUGH... NNNN...
TAKE IT EASY, CONNER.
I GOTTA HELP...WHOEVER I CAN...
WHERE'S ROBIN? WHERE ARE THE OTHER TITANS?

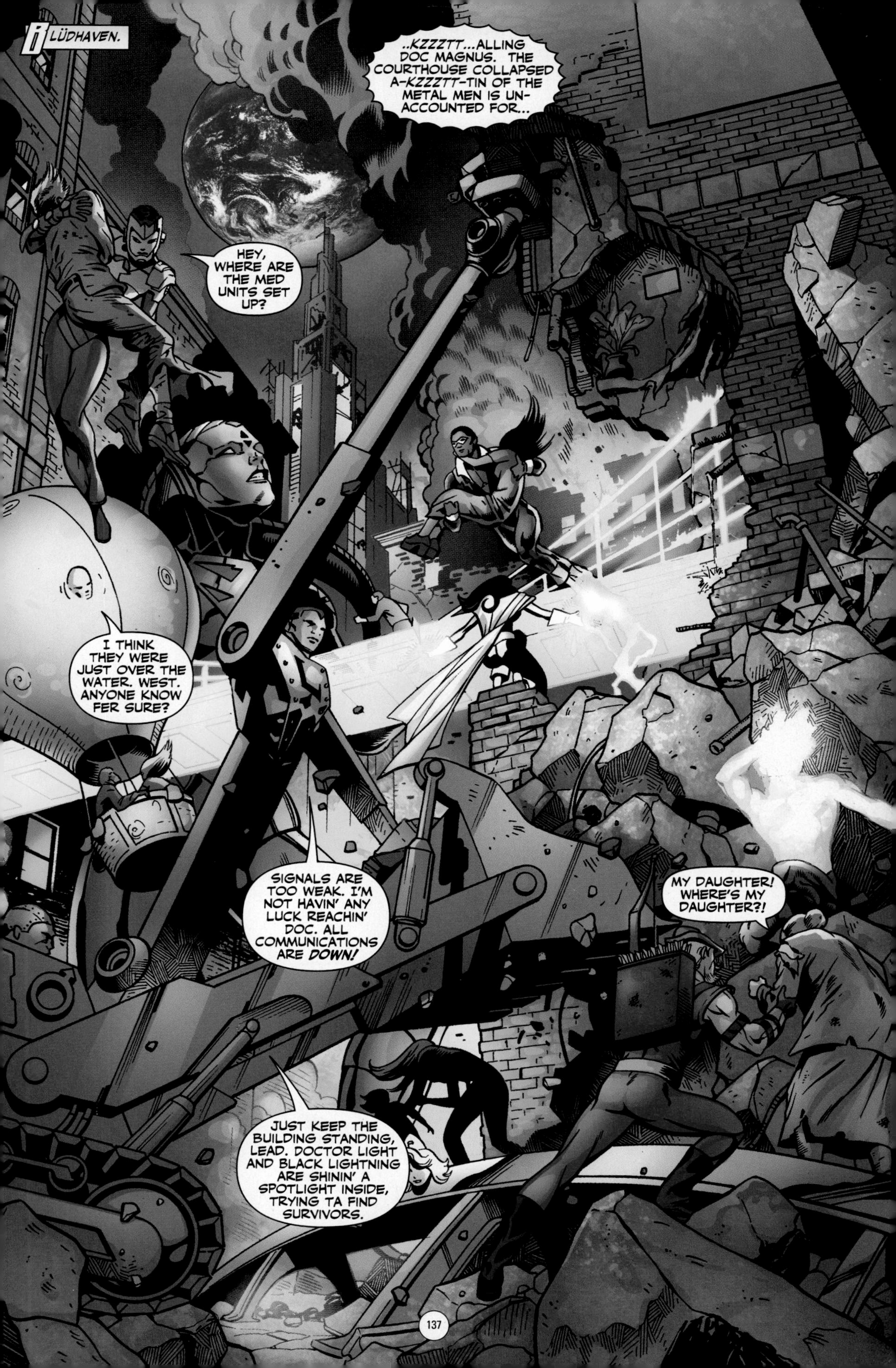
BLÜDHAVEN.
..KZZZTT...ALLING DOC MAGNUS. THE COURTHOUSE COLLAPSED A-KZZZTT-TIN OF THE METAL MEN IS UN-ACCOUNTED FOR...
HEY, WHERE ARE THE MED UNITS SET UP?
I THINK THEY WERE JUST OVER THE WATER. WEST. ANYONE KNOW FER SURE?
SIGNALS ARE TOO WEAK. I'M NOT HAVIN' ANY LUCK REACHIN' DOC. ALL COMMUNICATIONS ARE DOWN!
MY DAUGHTER! WHERE'S MY DAUGHTER?!
JUST KEEP THE BUILDING STANDING, LEAD. DOCTOR LIGHT AND BLACK LIGHTNING ARE SHININ' A SPOTLIGHT INSIDE, TRYING TA FIND SURVIVORS.

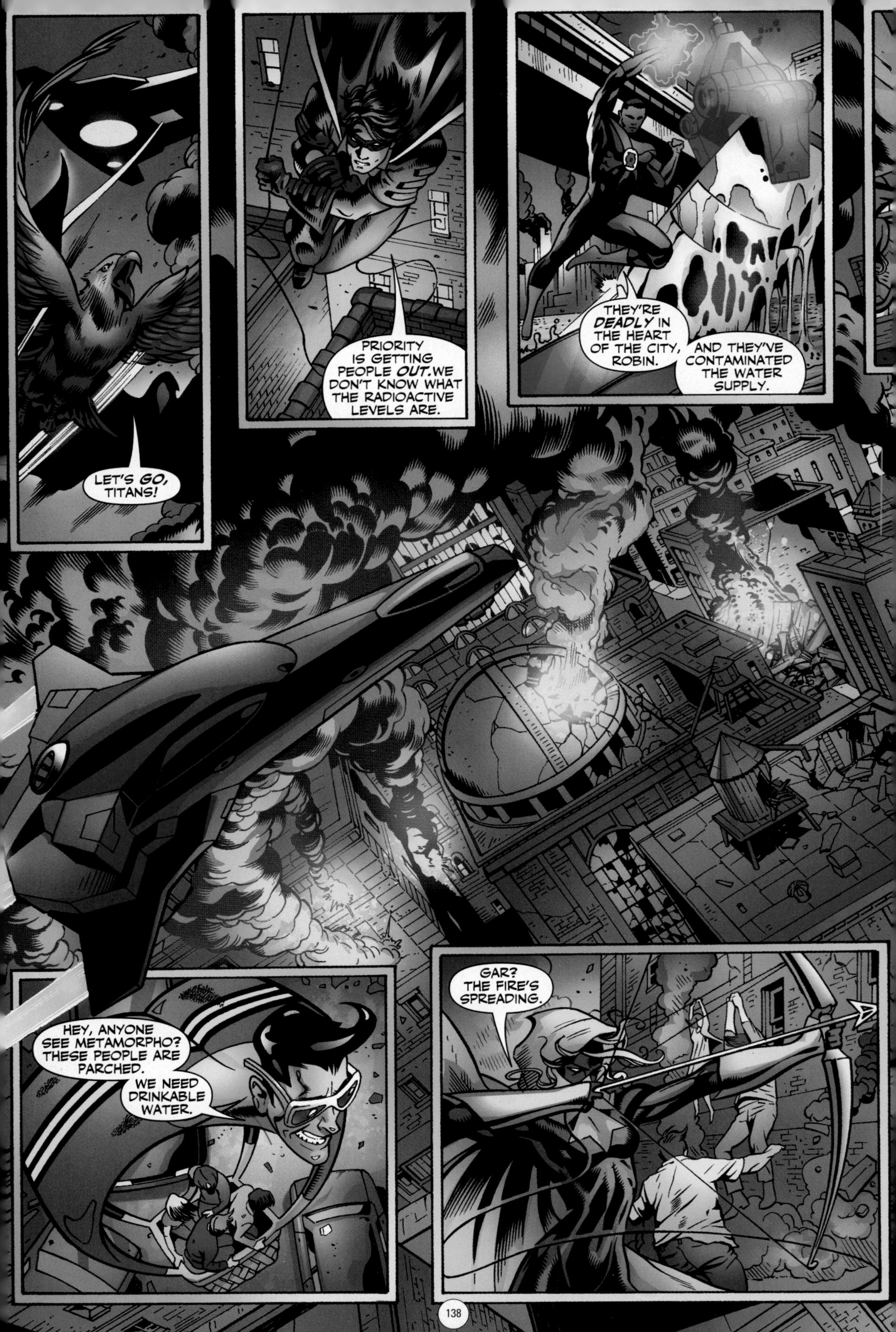

LET'S GO, TITANS!
PRIORITY IS GETTING PEOPLE OUT. WE DON'T KNOW WHAT THE RADIOACTIVE LEVELS ARE.
THEY'RE DEADLY IN THE HEART OF THE CITY, ROBIN.
AND THEY'VE CONTAMINATED THE WATER SUPPLY.
HEY, ANYONE SEE METAMORPHO? THESE PEOPLE ARE PARCHED.
WE NEED DRINKABLE WATER.
GAR? THE FIRE'S SPREADING.

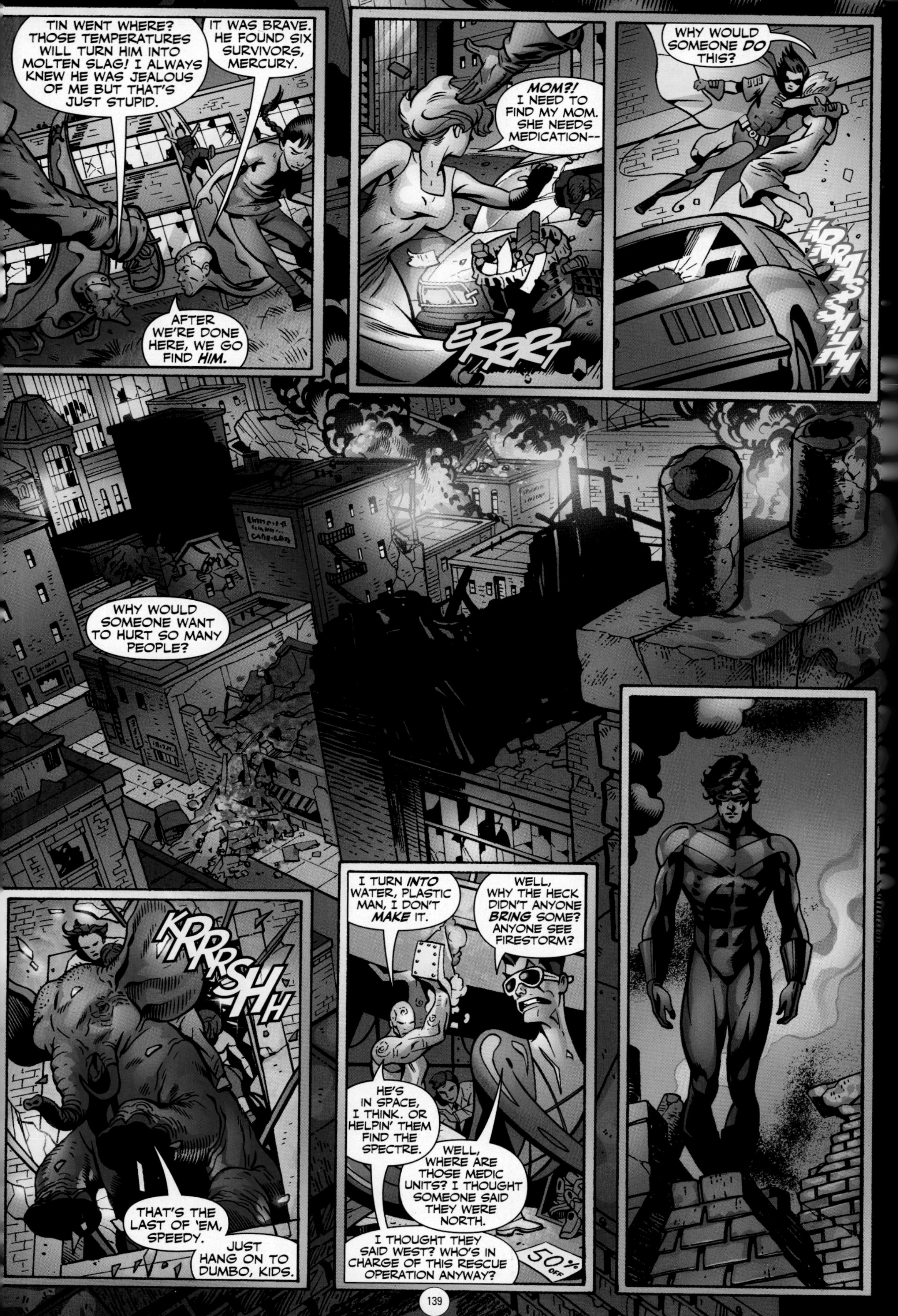
TIN WENT WHERE? THOSE TEMPERATURES WILL TURN HIM INTO MOLTEN SLAG! I ALWAYS KNEW HE WAS JEALOUS OF ME BUT THAT'S JUST STUPID.
IT WAS BRAVE. HE FOUND SIX SURVIVORS, MERCURY.
AFTER WE'RE DONE HERE, WE GO FIND HIM.
MOM?! I NEED TO FIND MY MOM. SHE NEEDS MEDICATION--
ERRRT
WHY WOULD SOMEONE DO THIS?
KRRASSHHH
WHY WOULD SOMEONE WANT TO HURT SO MANY PEOPLE?
KRRRSHH
THAT'S THE LAST OF 'EM, SPEEDY.
JUST HANG ON TO DUMBO, KIDS.
I TURN INTO WATER, PLASTIC MAN, I DON'T MAKE IT.
WELL, WHY THE HECK DIDN'T ANYONE BRING SOME? ANYONE SEE FIRESTORM?
HE'S IN SPACE, I THINK. OR HELPIN' THEM FIND THE SPECTRE.
WELL, WHERE ARE THOSE MEDIC UNITS? I THOUGHT SOMEONE SAID THEY WERE NORTH.
I THOUGHT THEY SAID WEST? WHO'S IN CHARGE OF THIS RESCUE OPERATION ANYWAY?
50% OFF

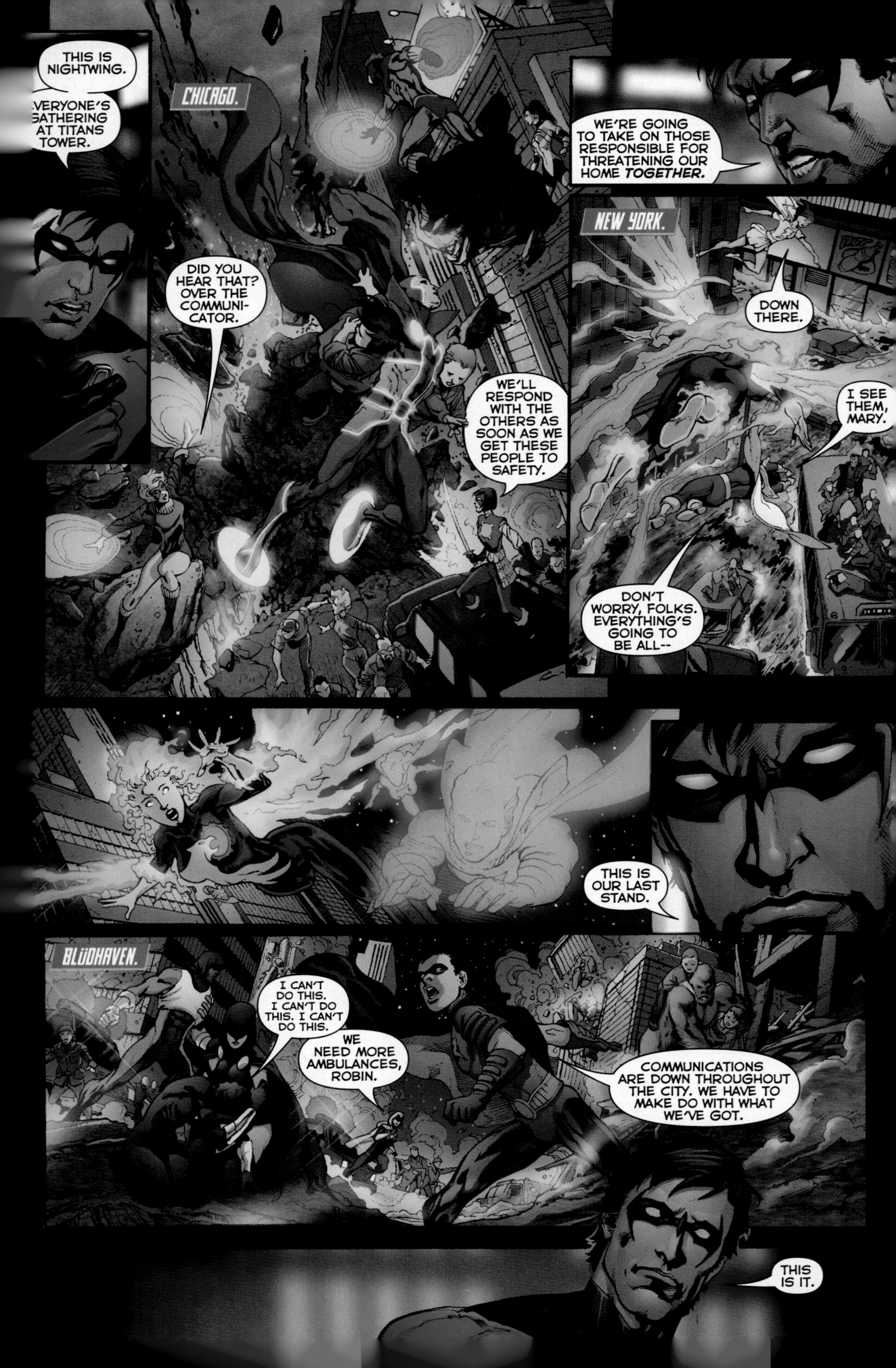
THIS IS NIGHTWING.
EVERYONE'S GATHERING AT TITANS TOWER.
CHICAGO.
WE'RE GOING TO TAKE ON THOSE RESPONSIBLE FOR THREATENING OUR HOME TOGETHER.
DID YOU HEAR THAT? OVER THE COMMUNICATOR.
WE'LL RESPOND WITH THE OTHERS AS SOON AS WE GET THESE PEOPLE TO SAFETY.
NEW YORK.
DOWN THERE.
I SEE THEM, MARY.
DON'T WORRY, FOLKS. EVERYTHING'S GOING TO BE ALL--
THIS IS OUR LAST STAND.
BLÜDHAVEN.
I CAN'T DO THIS. I CAN'T DO THIS. I CAN'T DO THIS.
WE NEED MORE AMBULANCES, ROBIN.
COMMUNICATIONS ARE DOWN THROUGHOUT THE CITY. WE HAVE TO MAKE DO WITH WHAT WE'VE GOT.
THIS IS IT.

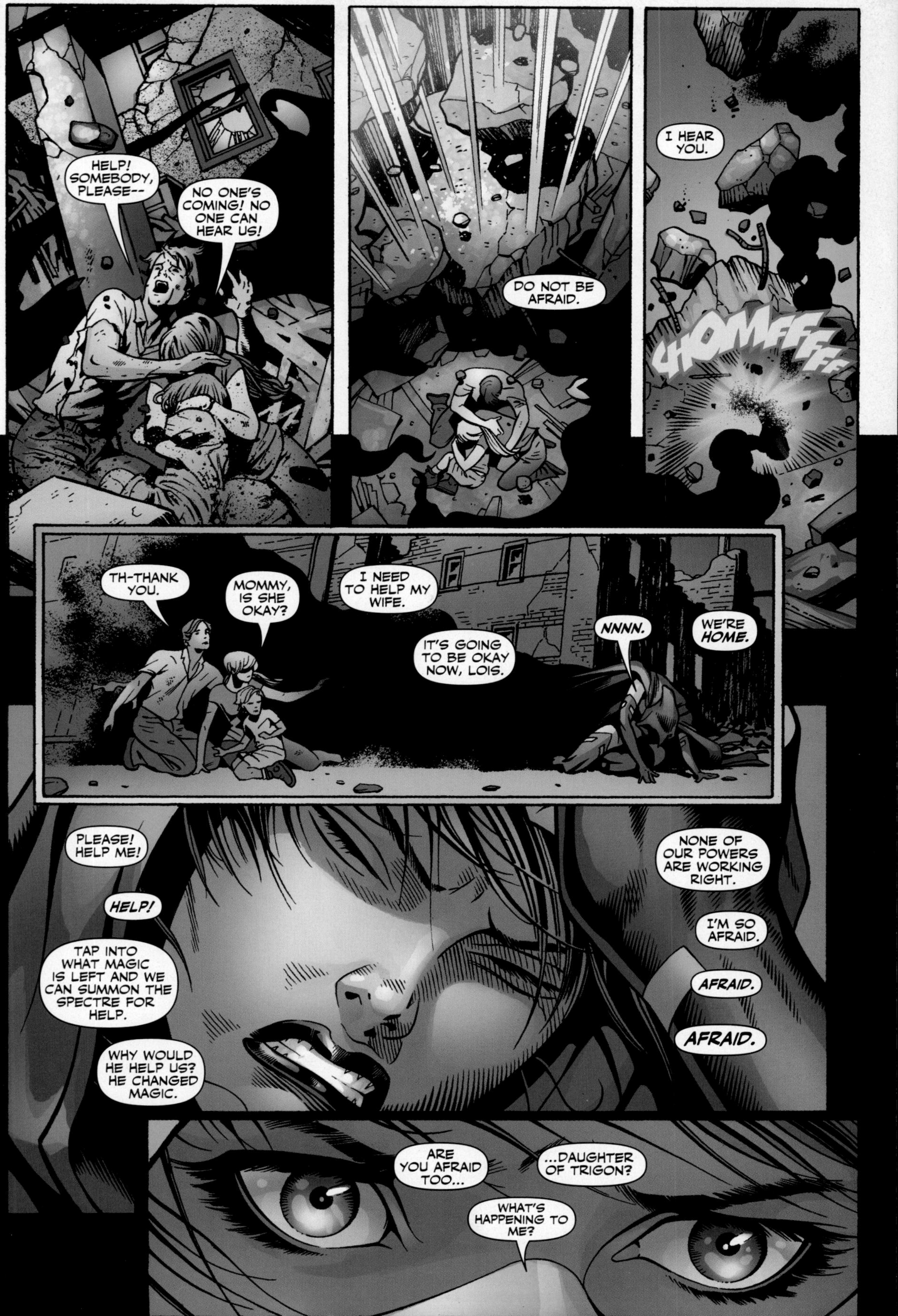
HELP! SOMEBODY, PLEASE--
NO ONE'S COMING! NO ONE CAN HEAR US!
DO NOT BE AFRAID.
I HEAR YOU.
CHOMFFFFF
TH-THANK YOU.
MOMMY, IS SHE OKAY?
I NEED TO HELP MY WIFE.
IT'S GOING TO BE OKAY NOW, LOIS.
NNNN.
WE'RE HOME.
PLEASE! HELP ME!
HELP!
TAP INTO WHAT MAGIC IS LEFT AND WE CAN SUMMON THE SPECTRE FOR HELP.
WHY WOULD HE HELP US? HE CHANGED MAGIC.
NONE OF OUR POWERS ARE WORKING RIGHT.
I'M SO AFRAID.
AFRAID.
AFRAID.
ARE YOU AFRAID TOO...
...DAUGHTER OF TRIGON?
WHAT'S HAPPENING TO ME?

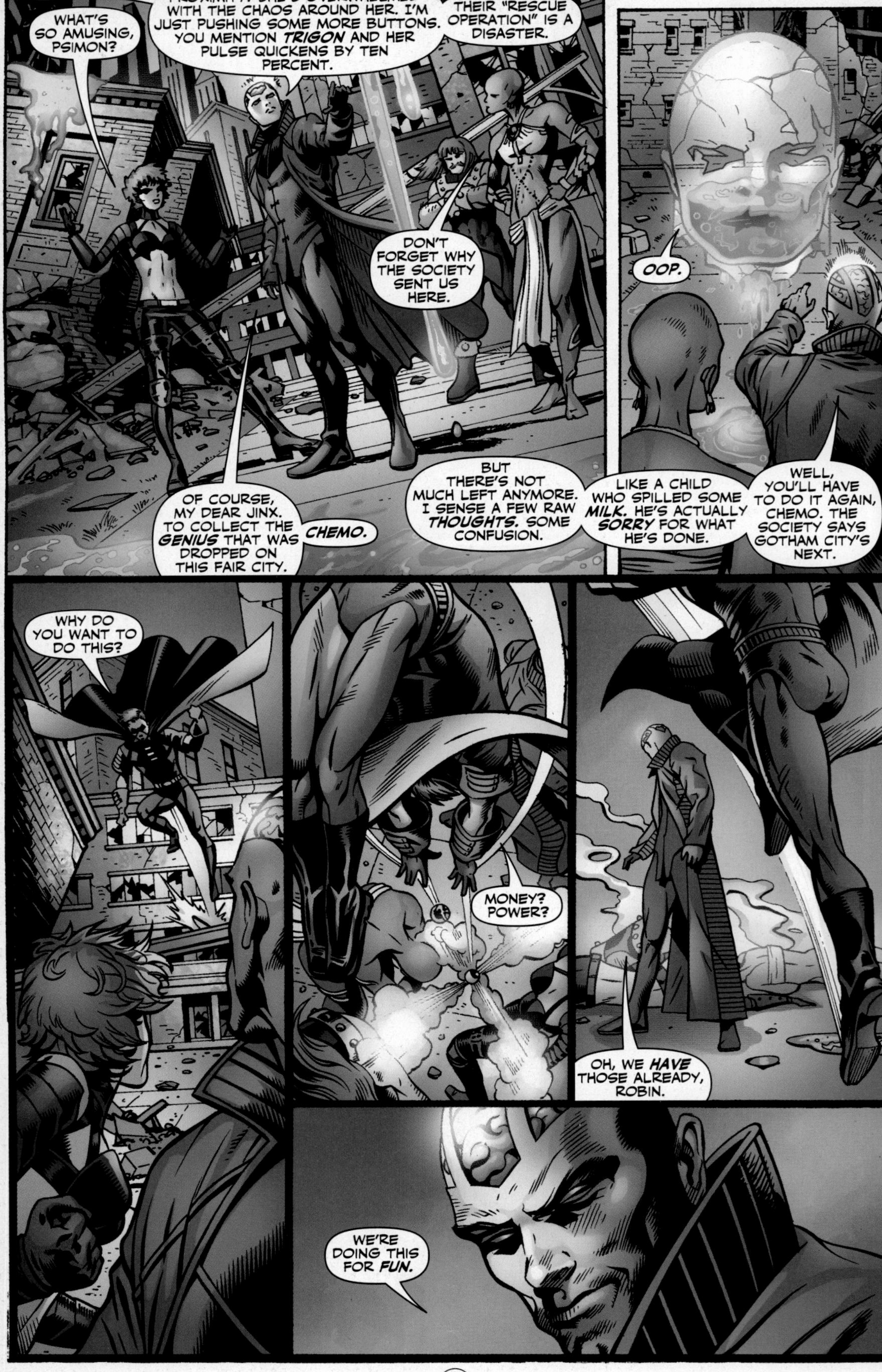
HEH.
WHAT'S SO AMUSING, PSIMON?
I CAN SENSE RAVEN IN PROXIMITY. SHE'S OVERWHELMED WITH THE CHAOS AROUND HER. I'M JUST PUSHING SOME MORE BUTTONS. YOU MENTION TRIGON AND HER PULSE QUICKENS BY TEN PERCENT.
THEIR "RESCUE OPERATION" IS A DISASTER.
DON'T FORGET WHY THE SOCIETY SENT US HERE.
OF COURSE, MY DEAR JINX. TO COLLECT THE GENIUS THAT WAS DROPPED ON THIS FAIR CITY.
CHEMO.
OOP.
BUT THERE'S NOT MUCH LEFT ANYMORE. I SENSE A FEW RAW THOUGHTS. SOME CONFUSION.
LIKE A CHILD WHO SPILLED SOME MILK. HE'S ACTUALLY SORRY FOR WHAT HE'S DONE.
WELL, YOU'LL HAVE TO DO IT AGAIN, CHEMO. THE SOCIETY SAYS GOTHAM CITY'S NEXT.
WHY DO YOU WANT TO DO THIS?
MONEY? POWER?
OH, WE HAVE THOSE ALREADY, ROBIN.
WE'RE DOING THIS FOR FUN.

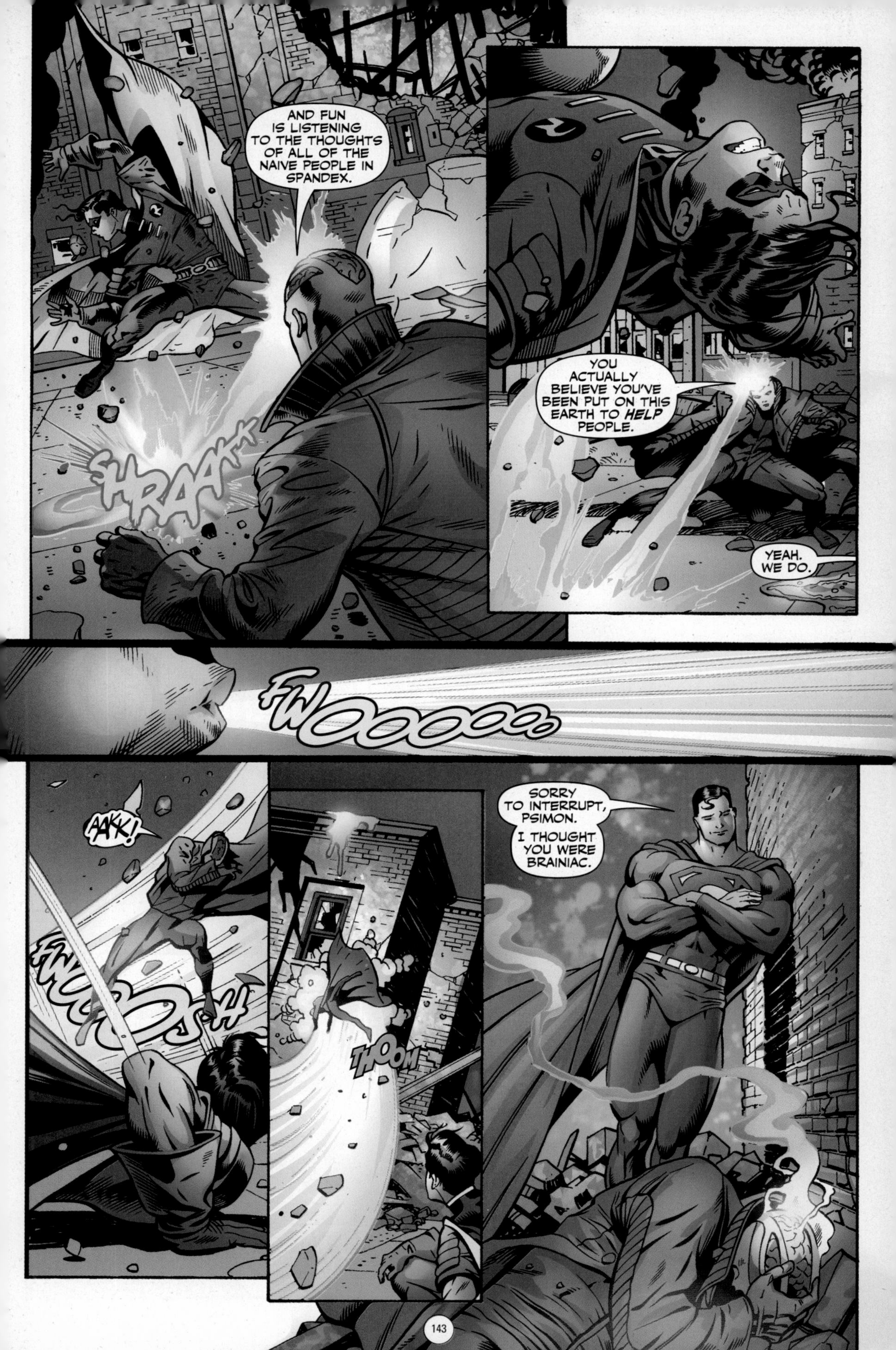
AND FUN IS LISTENING TO THE THOUGHTS OF ALL OF THE NAIVE PEOPLE IN SPANDEX.
SHRAAKK
YOU ACTUALLY BELIEVE YOU'VE BEEN PUT ON THIS EARTH TO HELP PEOPLE.
YEAH. WE DO.
FWOOOOOO
AAKK!
FWOOSH
THOOM
SORRY TO INTERRUPT, PSIMON.
I THOUGHT YOU WERE BRAINIAC.

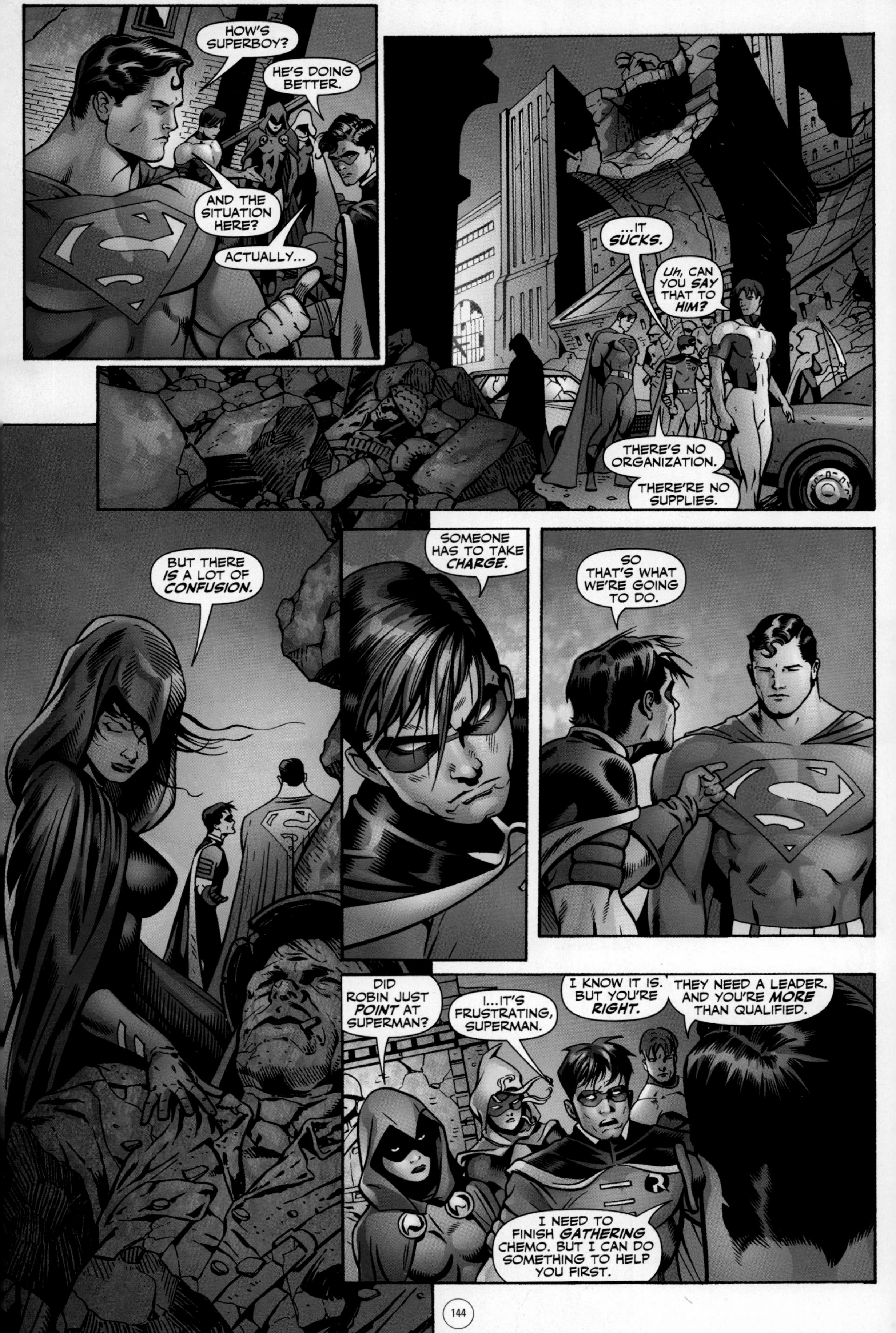
HOW'S SUPERBOY?
HE'S DOING BETTER.
AND THE SITUATION HERE?
ACTUALLY...
...IT SUCKS.
Uh, CAN YOU SAY THAT TO HIM?
THERE'S NO ORGANIZATION.
THERE'RE NO SUPPLIES.
BUT THERE IS A LOT OF CONFUSION.
SOMEONE HAS TO TAKE CHARGE.
SO THAT'S WHAT WE'RE GOING TO DO.
DID ROBIN JUST POINT AT SUPERMAN?
I...IT'S FRUSTRATING, SUPERMAN.
I KNOW IT IS. BUT YOU'RE RIGHT.
THEY NEED A LEADER. AND YOU'RE MORE THAN QUALIFIED.
I NEED TO FINISH GATHERING CHEMO. BUT I CAN DO SOMETHING TO HELP YOU FIRST.

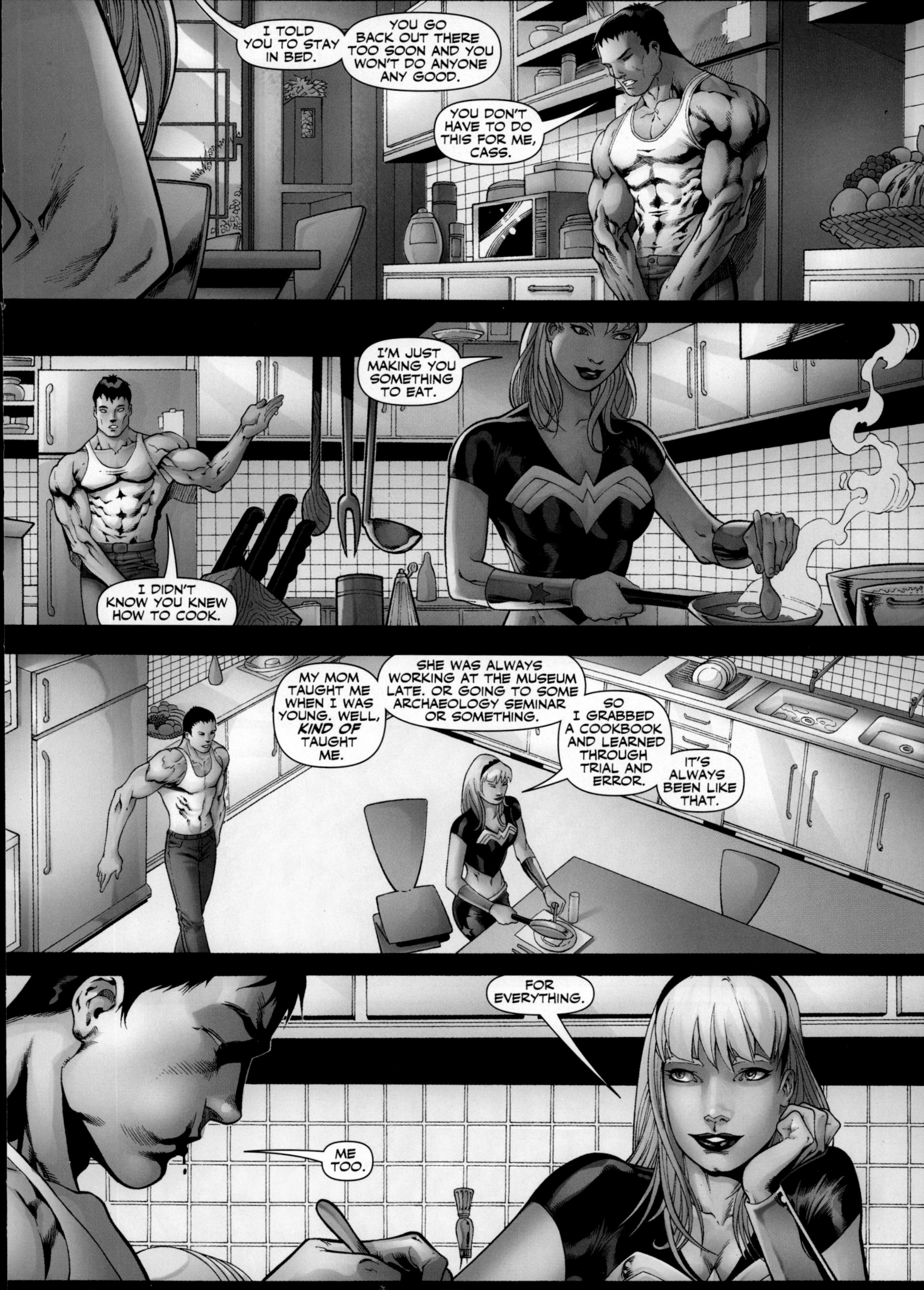
I TOLD YOU TO STAY IN BED.
YOU GO BACK OUT THERE TOO SOON AND YOU WON'T DO ANYONE ANY GOOD.
YOU DON'T HAVE TO DO THIS FOR ME, CASS.
I'M JUST MAKING YOU SOMETHING TO EAT.
I DIDN'T KNOW YOU KNEW HOW TO COOK.
MY MOM TAUGHT ME WHEN I WAS YOUNG. WELL, *KIND OF* TAUGHT ME.
SHE WAS ALWAYS WORKING AT THE MUSEUM LATE. OR GOING TO SOME ARCHAEOLOGY SEMINAR OR SOMETHING.
SO I GRABBED A COOKBOOK AND LEARNED THROUGH TRIAL AND ERROR.
IT'S ALWAYS BEEN LIKE THAT.
FOR EVERYTHING.
ME TOO.

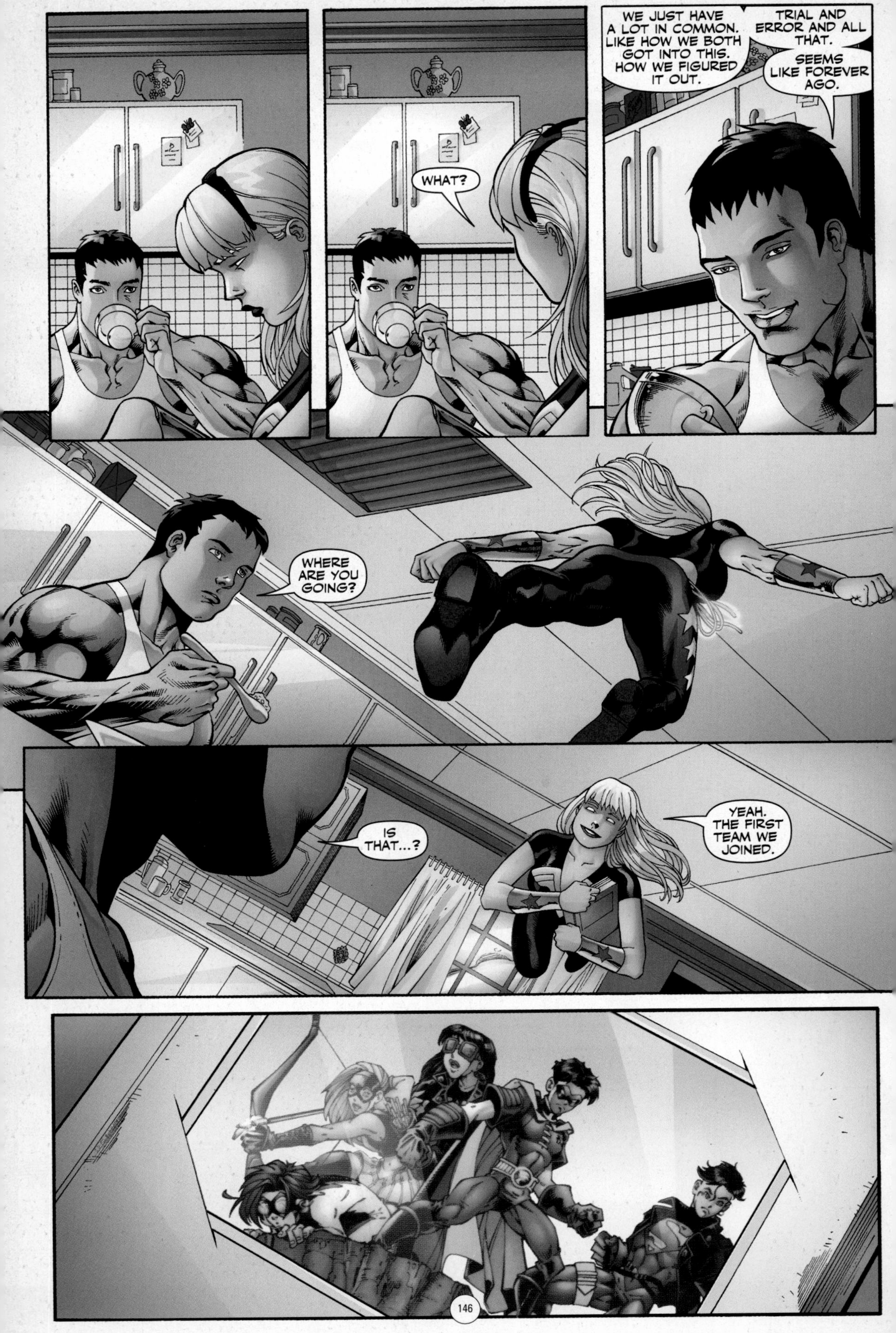
WHAT?
WE JUST HAVE A LOT IN COMMON. LIKE HOW WE BOTH GOT INTO THIS. HOW WE FIGURED IT OUT.
TRIAL AND ERROR AND ALL THAT.
SEEMS LIKE FOREVER AGO.
WHERE ARE YOU GOING?
IS THAT...?
YEAH. THE FIRST TEAM WE JOINED.

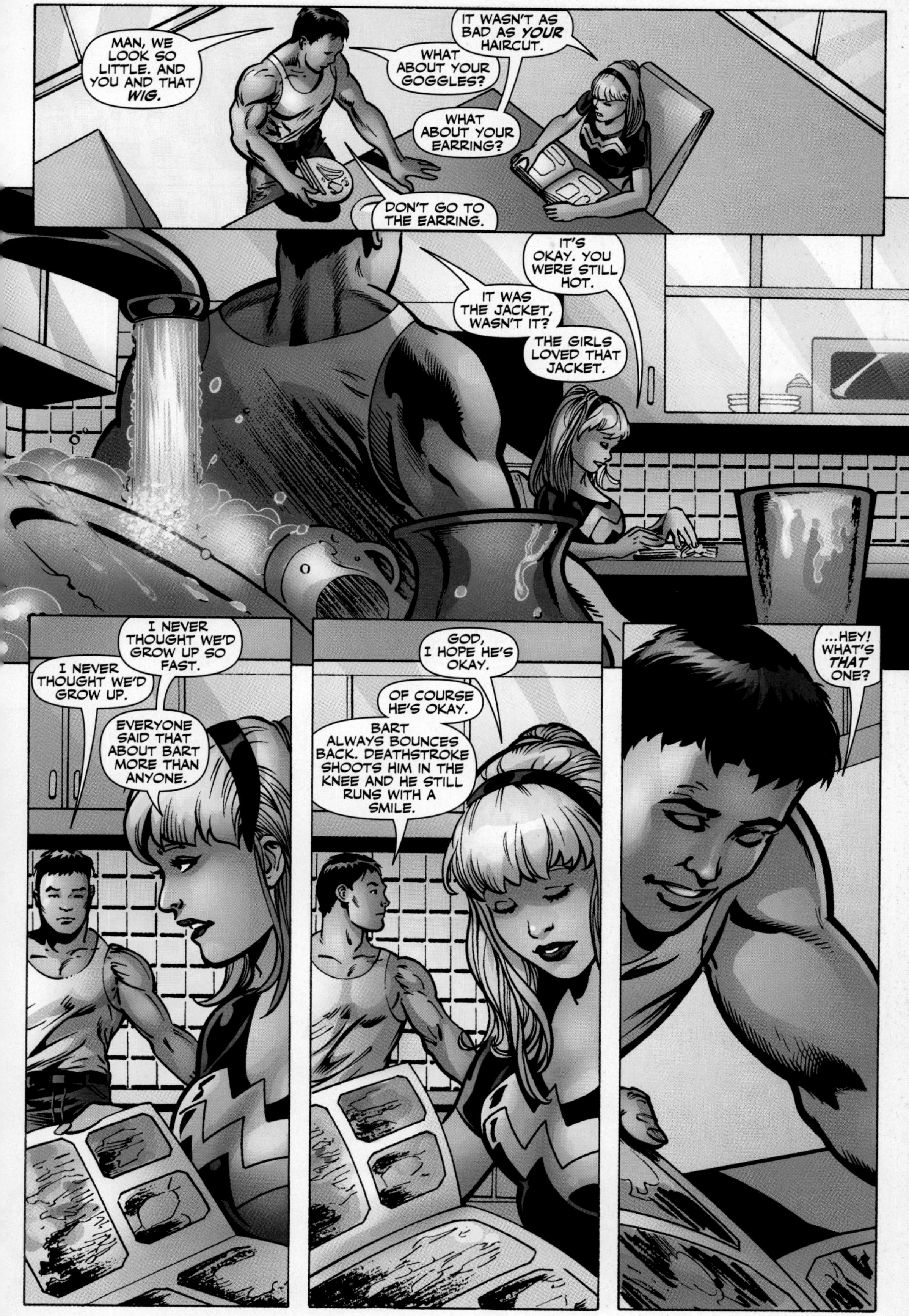

MAN, WE LOOK SO LITTLE. AND YOU AND THAT WIG.
WHAT ABOUT YOUR GOGGLES?
IT WASN'T AS BAD AS YOUR HAIRCUT.
WHAT ABOUT YOUR EARRING?
DON'T GO TO THE EARRING.
IT WAS THE JACKET, WASN'T IT?
THE GIRLS LOVED THAT JACKET.
IT'S OKAY. YOU WERE STILL HOT.
I NEVER THOUGHT WE'D GROW UP.
I NEVER THOUGHT WE'D GROW UP SO FAST.
EVERYONE SAID THAT ABOUT BART MORE THAN ANYONE.
GOD, I HOPE HE'S OKAY.
OF COURSE HE'S OKAY.
BART ALWAYS BOUNCES BACK. DEATHSTROKE SHOOTS HIM IN THE KNEE AND HE STILL RUNS WITH A SMILE.
...HEY! WHAT'S THAT ONE?

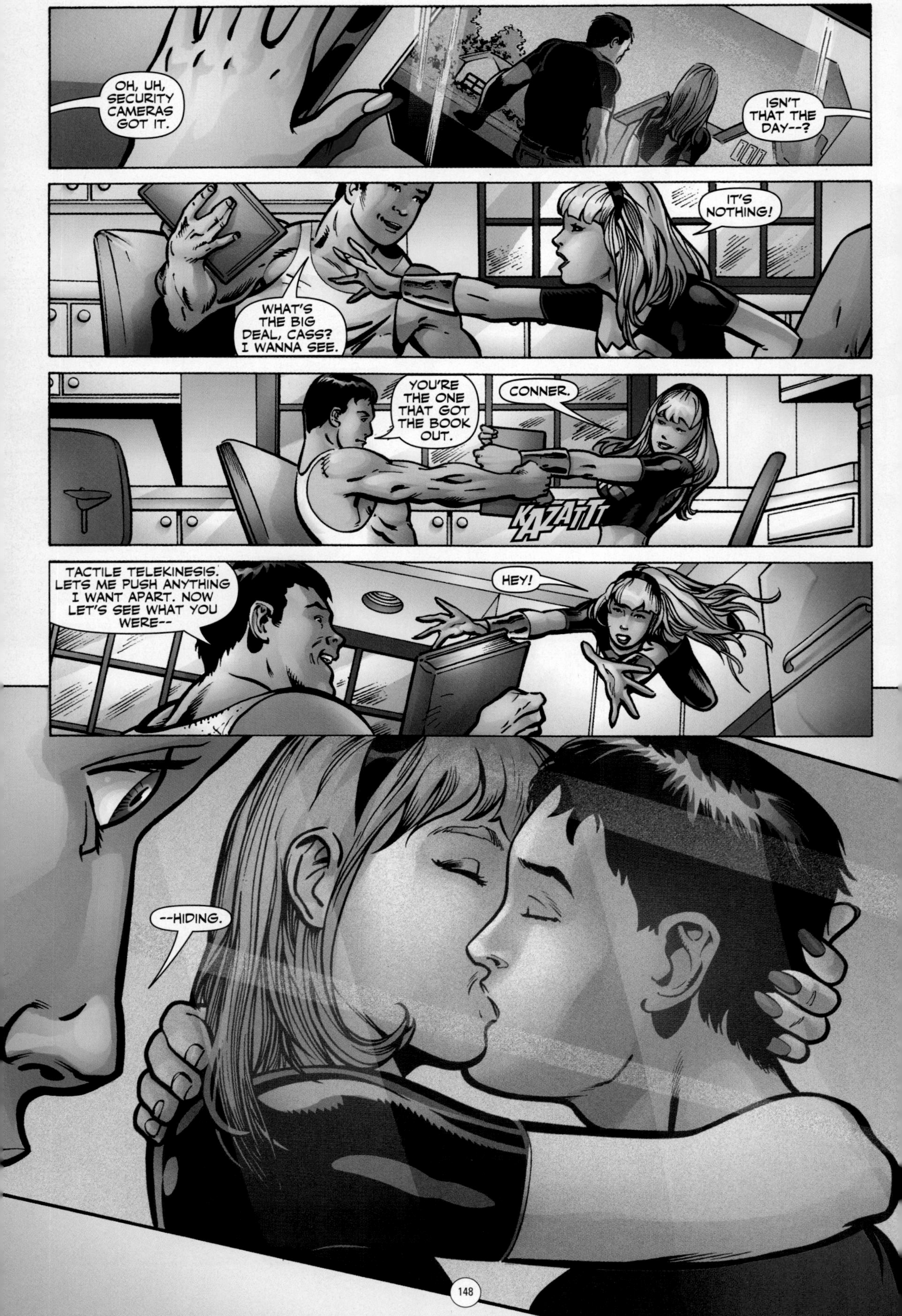
OH, UH, SECURITY CAMERAS GOT IT.
ISN'T THAT THE DAY--?
IT'S NOTHING!
WHAT'S THE BIG DEAL, CASS? I WANNA SEE.
YOU'RE THE ONE THAT GOT THE BOOK OUT.
CONNER.
KAZATT
TACTILE TELEKINESIS. LETS ME PUSH ANYTHING I WANT APART. NOW LET'S SEE WHAT YOU WERE--
HEY!
--HIDING.

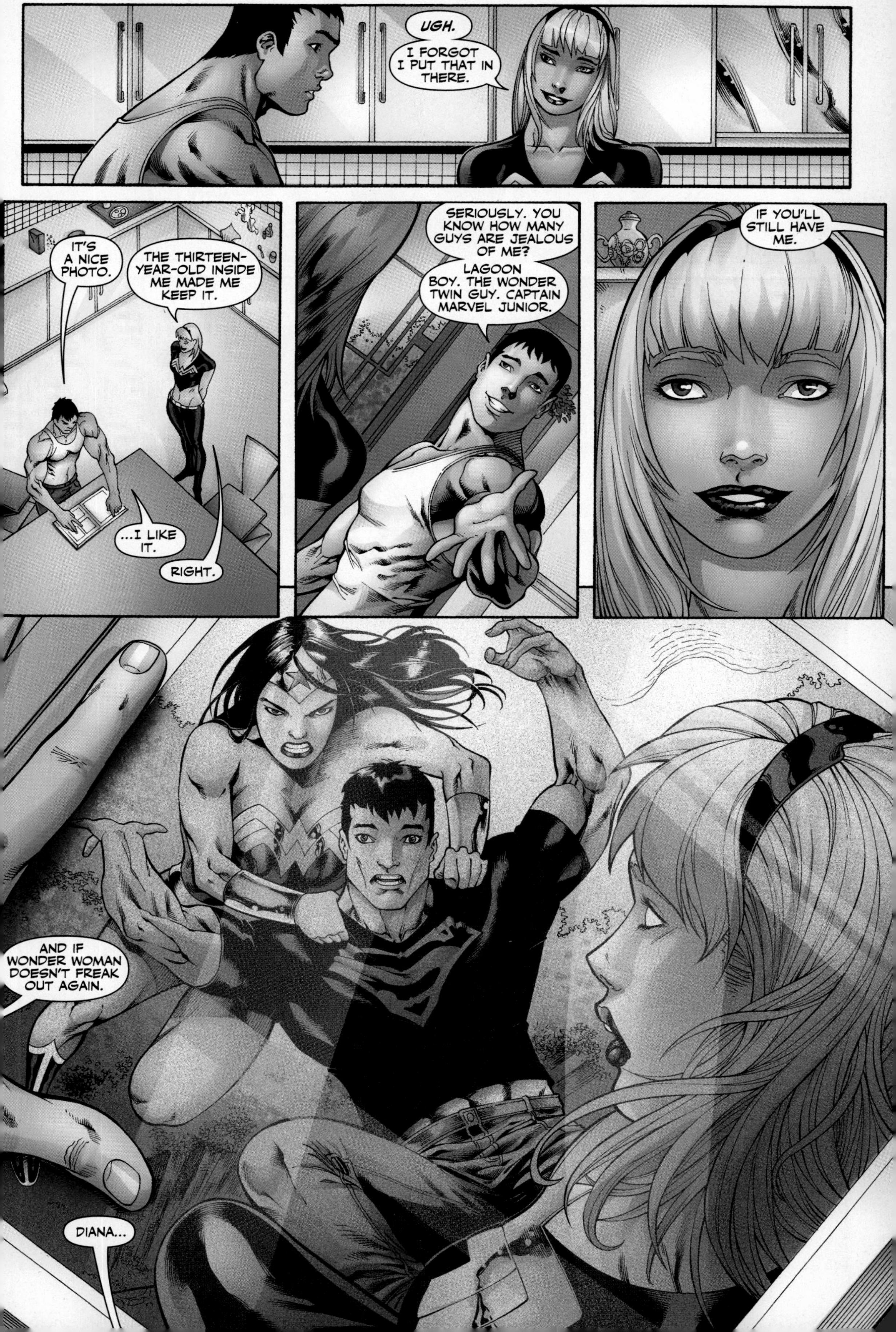
UGH.
I FORGOT I PUT THAT IN THERE.
IT'S A NICE PHOTO.
THE THIRTEEN-YEAR-OLD INSIDE ME MADE ME KEEP IT.
...I LIKE IT.
RIGHT.
SERIOUSLY. YOU KNOW HOW MANY GUYS ARE JEALOUS OF ME?
LAGOON BOY. THE WONDER TWIN GUY. CAPTAIN MARVEL JUNIOR.
IF YOU'LL STILL HAVE ME.
AND IF WONDER WOMAN DOESN'T FREAK OUT AGAIN.
DIANA...

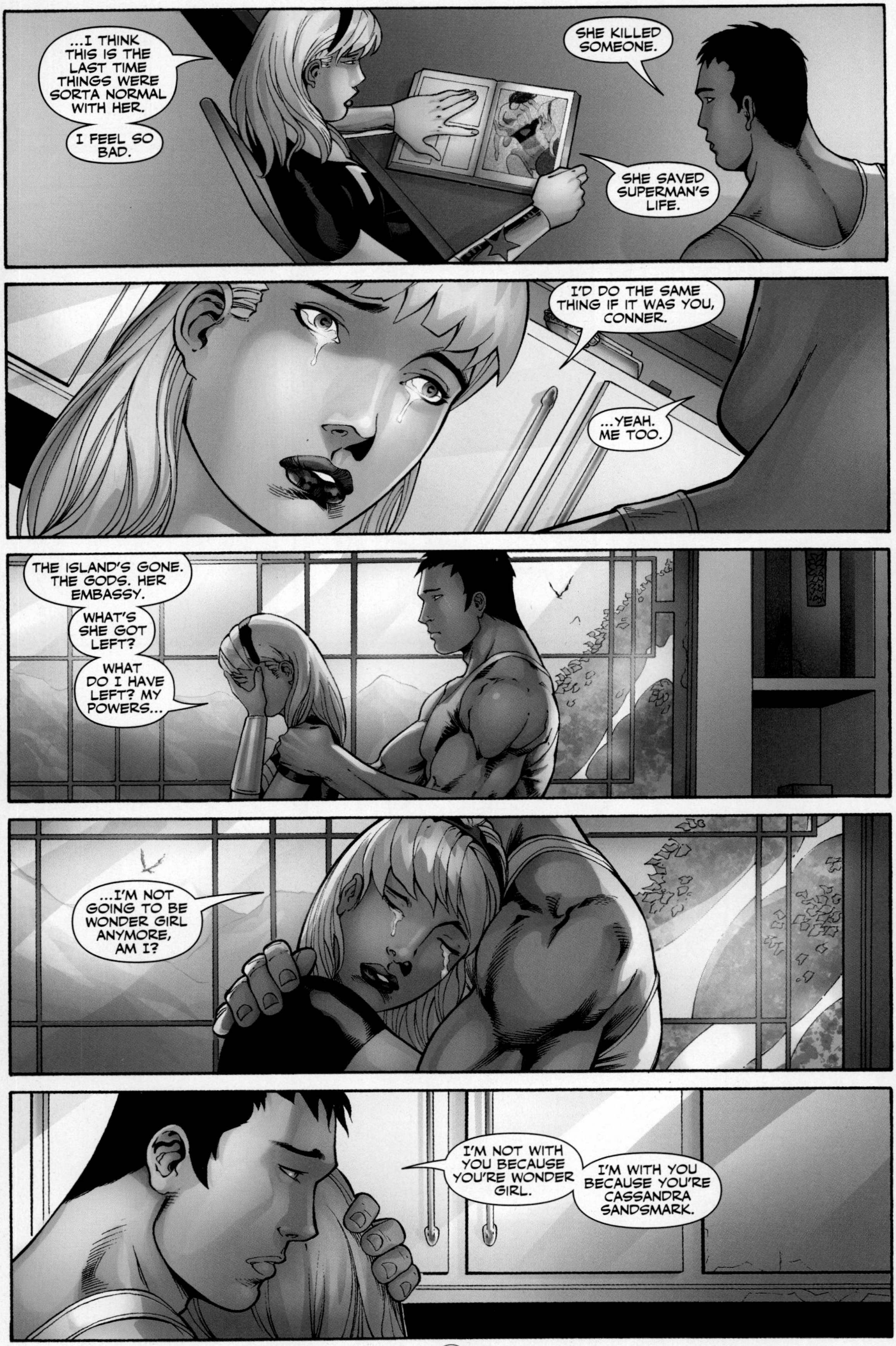

...I THINK THIS IS THE LAST TIME THINGS WERE SORTA NORMAL WITH HER.
I FEEL SO BAD.
SHE KILLED SOMEONE.
SHE SAVED SUPERMAN'S LIFE.
I'D DO THE SAME THING IF IT WAS YOU, CONNER.
...YEAH. ME TOO.
THE ISLAND'S GONE. THE GODS. HER EMBASSY.
WHAT'S SHE GOT LEFT?
WHAT DO I HAVE LEFT? MY POWERS...
...I'M NOT GOING TO BE WONDER GIRL ANYMORE, AM I?
I'M NOT WITH YOU BECAUSE YOU'RE WONDER GIRL.
I'M WITH YOU BECAUSE YOU'RE CASSANDRA SANDSMARK.

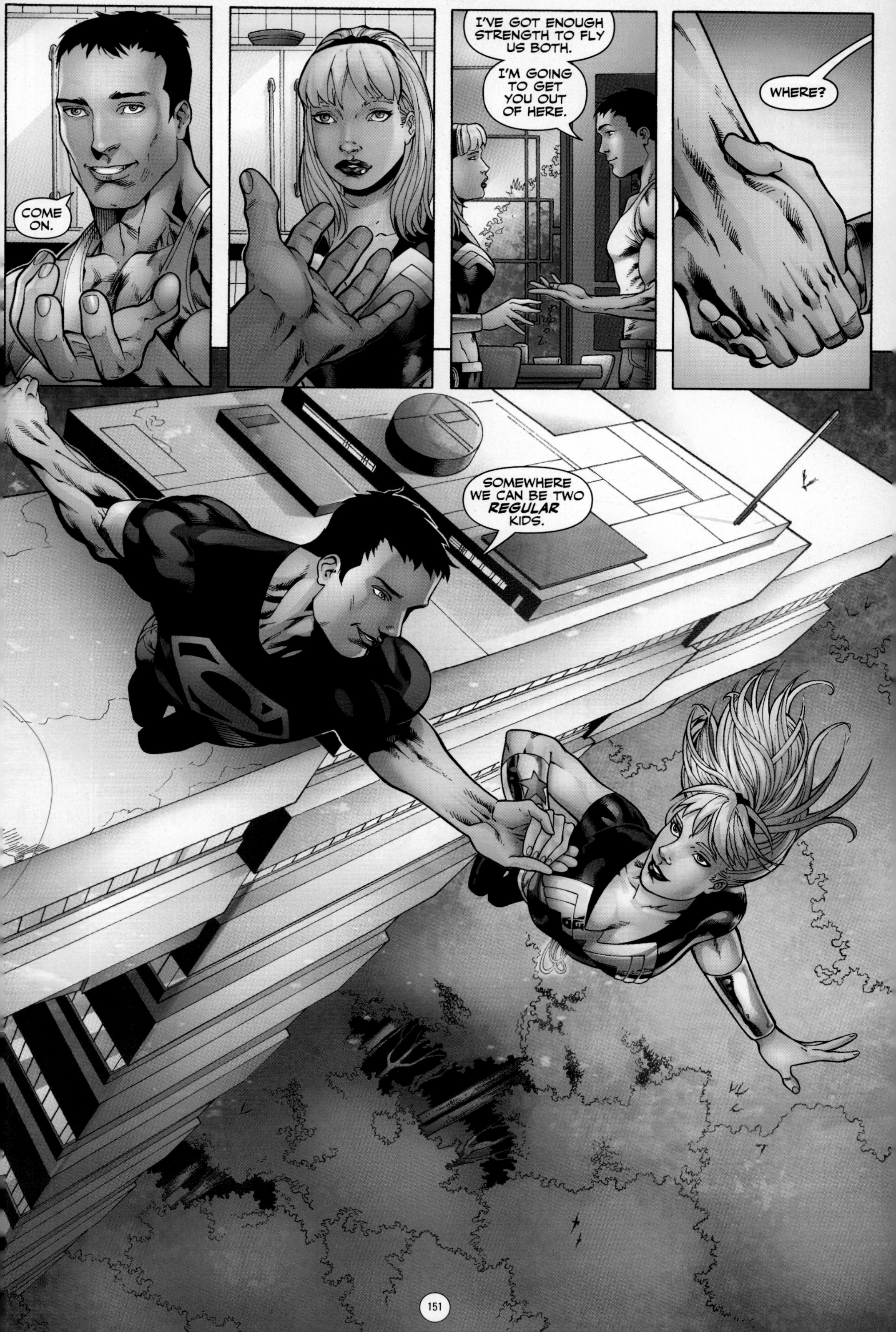
COME ON.
I'VE GOT ENOUGH STRENGTH TO FLY US BOTH.
I'M GOING TO GET YOU OUT OF HERE.
WHERE?
SOMEWHERE WE CAN BE TWO *REGULAR* KIDS.

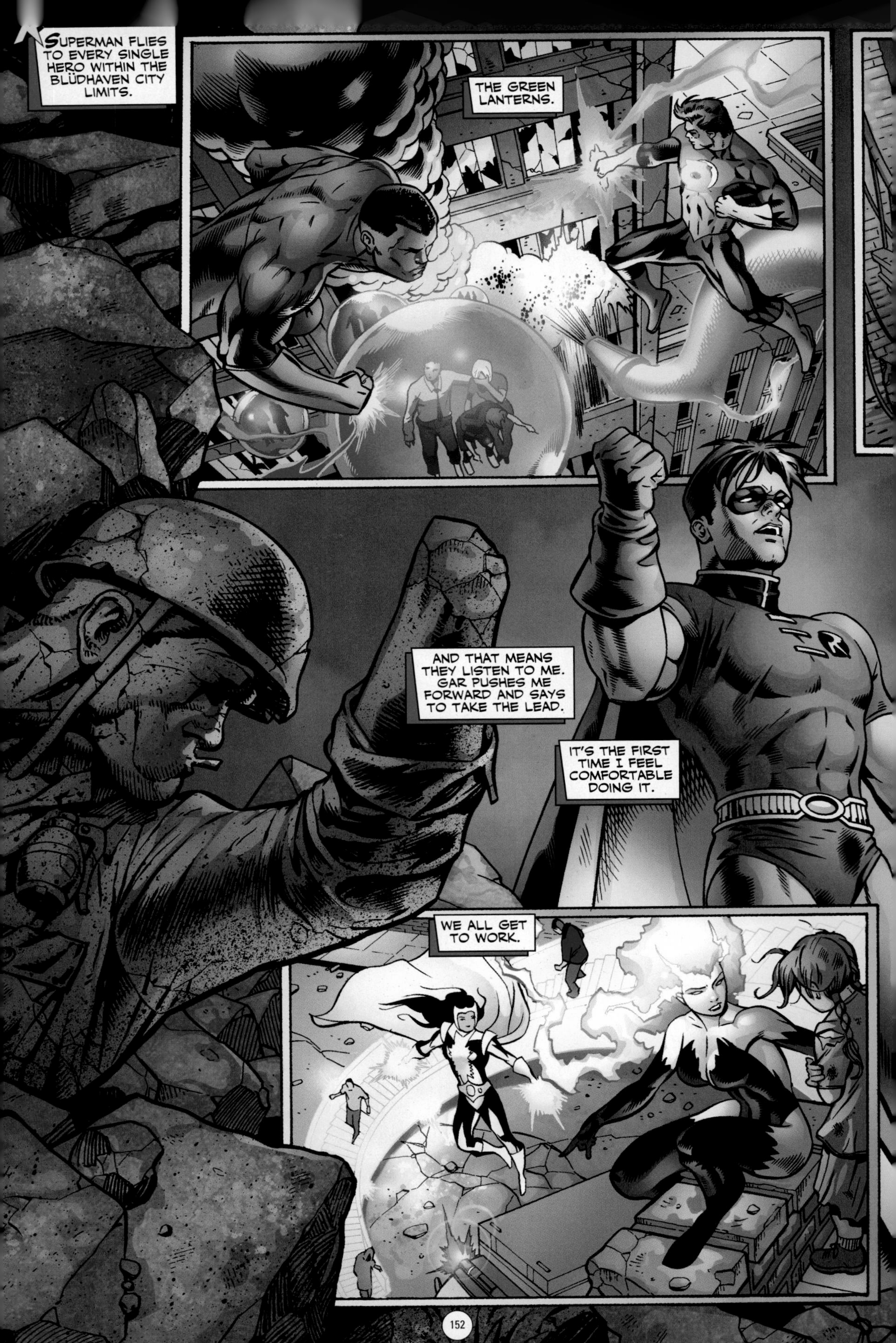
SUPERMAN FLIES TO EVERY SINGLE HERO WITHIN THE BLÜDHAVEN CITY LIMITS.
THE GREEN LANTERNS.
AND THAT MEANS THEY LISTEN TO ME. GAR PUSHES ME FORWARD AND SAYS TO TAKE THE LEAD.
IT'S THE FIRST TIME I FEEL COMFORTABLE DOING IT.
WE ALL GET TO WORK.

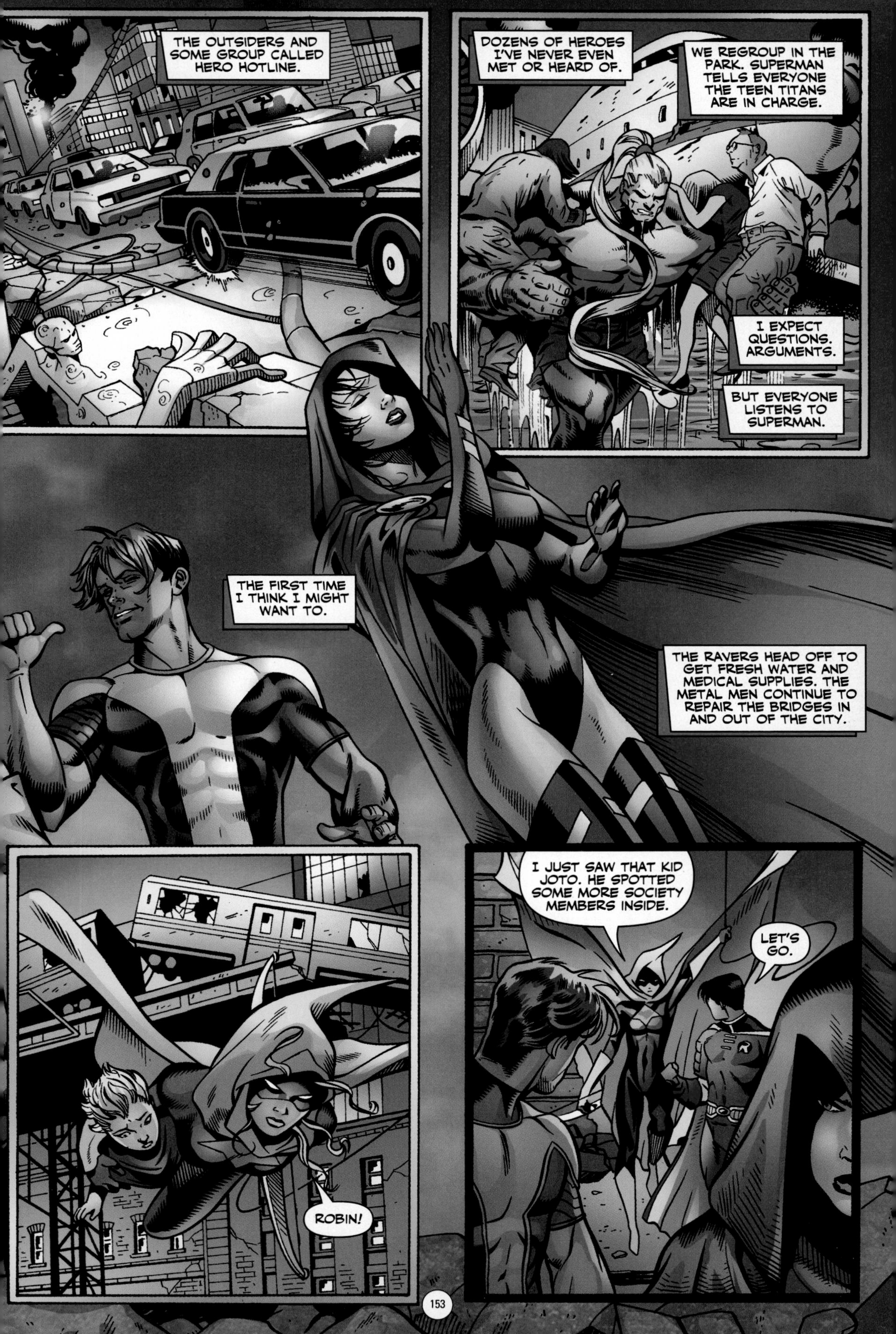
THE OUTSIDERS AND SOME GROUP CALLED HERO HOTLINE.
DOZENS OF HEROES I'VE NEVER EVEN MET OR HEARD OF.
WE REGROUP IN THE PARK. SUPERMAN TELLS EVERYONE THE TEEN TITANS ARE IN CHARGE.
I EXPECT QUESTIONS. ARGUMENTS.
BUT EVERYONE LISTENS TO SUPERMAN.
THE FIRST TIME I THINK I MIGHT WANT TO.
THE RAVERS HEAD OFF TO GET FRESH WATER AND MEDICAL SUPPLIES. THE METAL MEN CONTINUE TO REPAIR THE BRIDGES IN AND OUT OF THE CITY.
ROBIN!
I JUST SAW THAT KID JOTO. HE SPOTTED SOME MORE SOCIETY MEMBERS INSIDE.
LET'S GO.

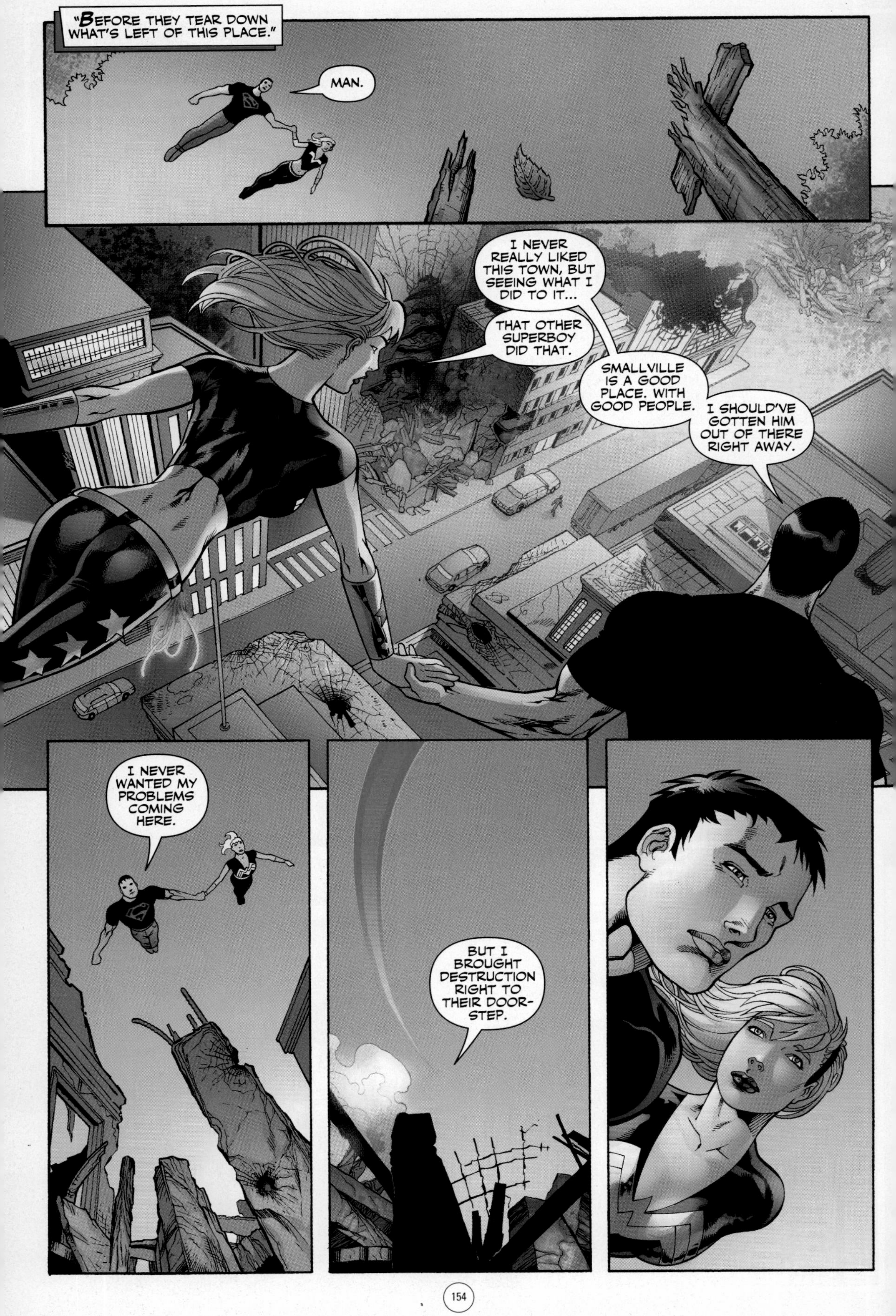

"BEFORE THEY TEAR DOWN WHAT'S LEFT OF THIS PLACE."
MAN.
I NEVER REALLY LIKED THIS TOWN, BUT SEEING WHAT I DID TO IT...
THAT OTHER SUPERBOY DID THAT.
SMALLVILLE IS A GOOD PLACE. WITH GOOD PEOPLE.
I SHOULD'VE GOTTEN HIM OUT OF THERE RIGHT AWAY.
I NEVER WANTED MY PROBLEMS COMING HERE.
BUT I BROUGHT DESTRUCTION RIGHT TO THEIR DOOR-STEP.

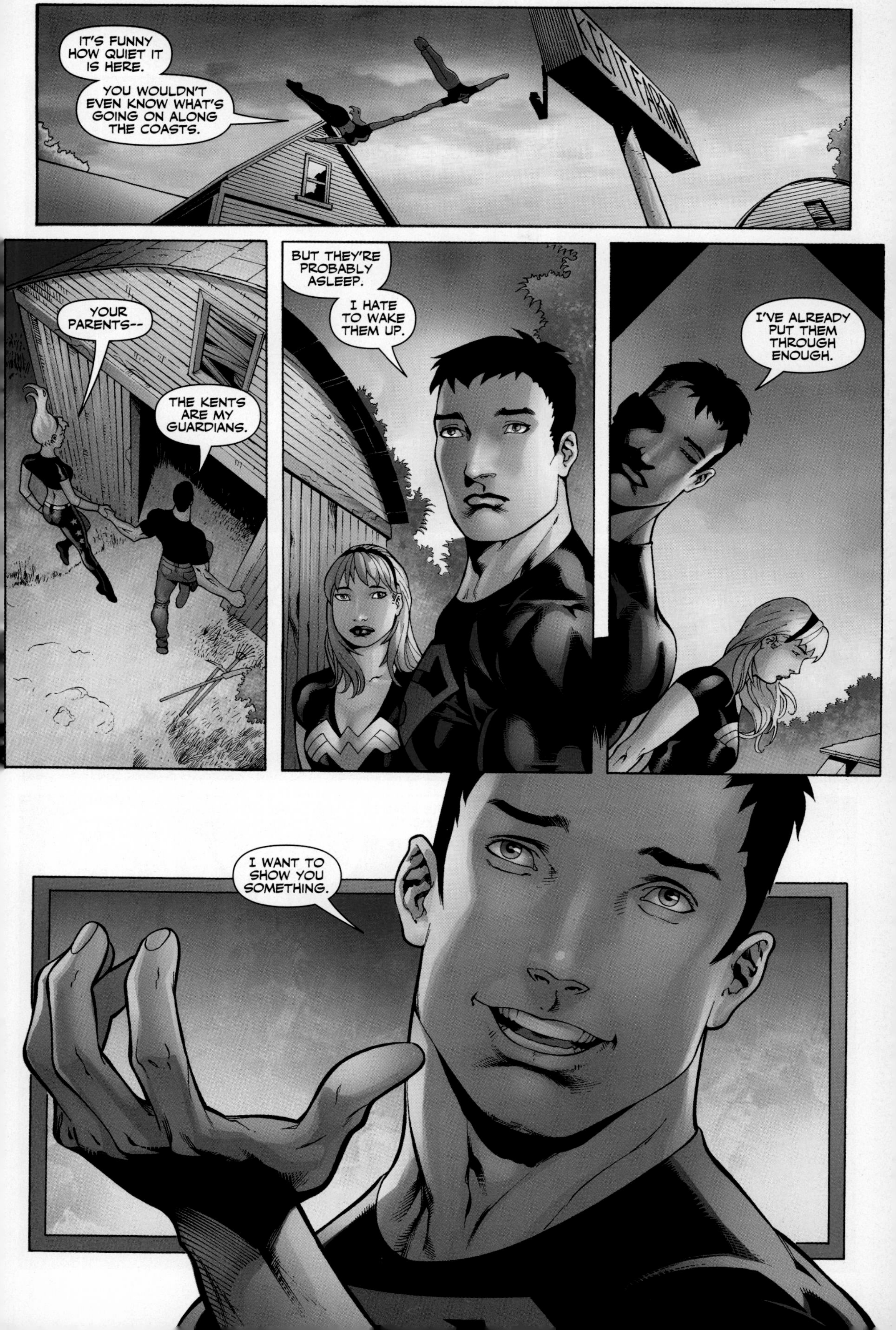

IT'S FUNNY HOW QUIET IT IS HERE.
YOU WOULDN'T EVEN KNOW WHAT'S GOING ON ALONG THE COASTS.
KENT FARM
YOUR PARENTS--
THE KENTS ARE MY GUARDIANS.
BUT THEY'RE PROBABLY ASLEEP.
I HATE TO WAKE THEM UP.
I'VE ALREADY PUT THEM THROUGH ENOUGH.
I WANT TO SHOW YOU SOMETHING.

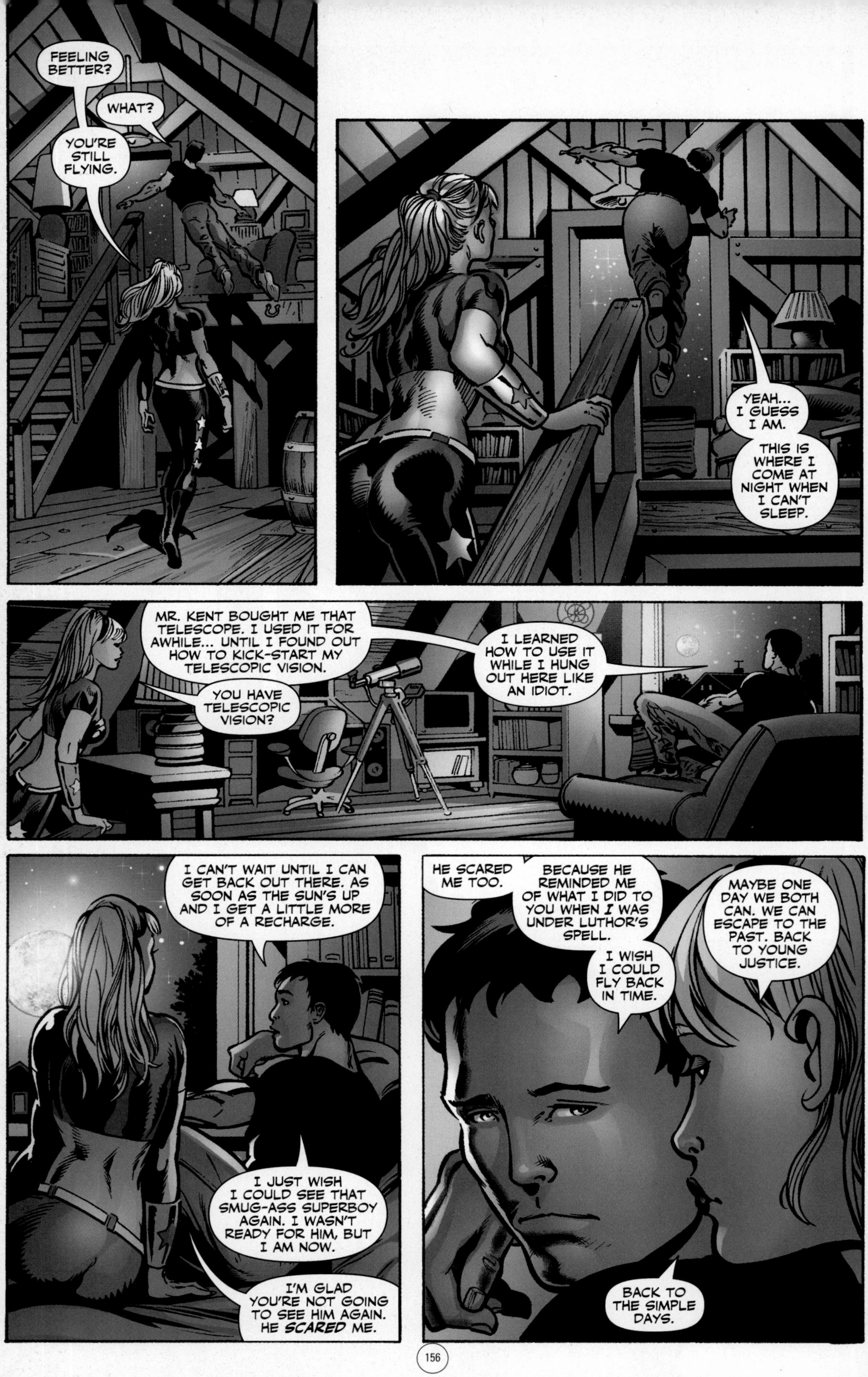
FEELING BETTER?
WHAT?
YOU'RE STILL FLYING.
YEAH... I GUESS I AM.
THIS IS WHERE I COME AT NIGHT WHEN I CAN'T SLEEP.
MR. KENT BOUGHT ME THAT TELESCOPE. I USED IT FOR AWHILE... UNTIL I FOUND OUT HOW TO KICK-START MY TELESCOPIC VISION.
YOU HAVE TELESCOPIC VISION?
I LEARNED HOW TO USE IT WHILE I HUNG OUT HERE LIKE AN IDIOT.
I CAN'T WAIT UNTIL I CAN GET BACK OUT THERE. AS SOON AS THE SUN'S UP AND I GET A LITTLE MORE OF A RECHARGE.
I JUST WISH I COULD SEE THAT SMUG-ASS SUPERBOY AGAIN. I WASN'T READY FOR HIM, BUT I AM NOW.
I'M GLAD YOU'RE NOT GOING TO SEE HIM AGAIN. HE *SCARED* ME.
HE SCARED ME TOO.
BECAUSE HE REMINDED ME OF WHAT I DID TO YOU WHEN *I* WAS UNDER LUTHOR'S SPELL.
I WISH I COULD FLY BACK IN TIME.
MAYBE ONE DAY WE BOTH CAN. WE CAN ESCAPE TO THE PAST. BACK TO YOUNG JUSTICE.
BACK TO THE SIMPLE DAYS.

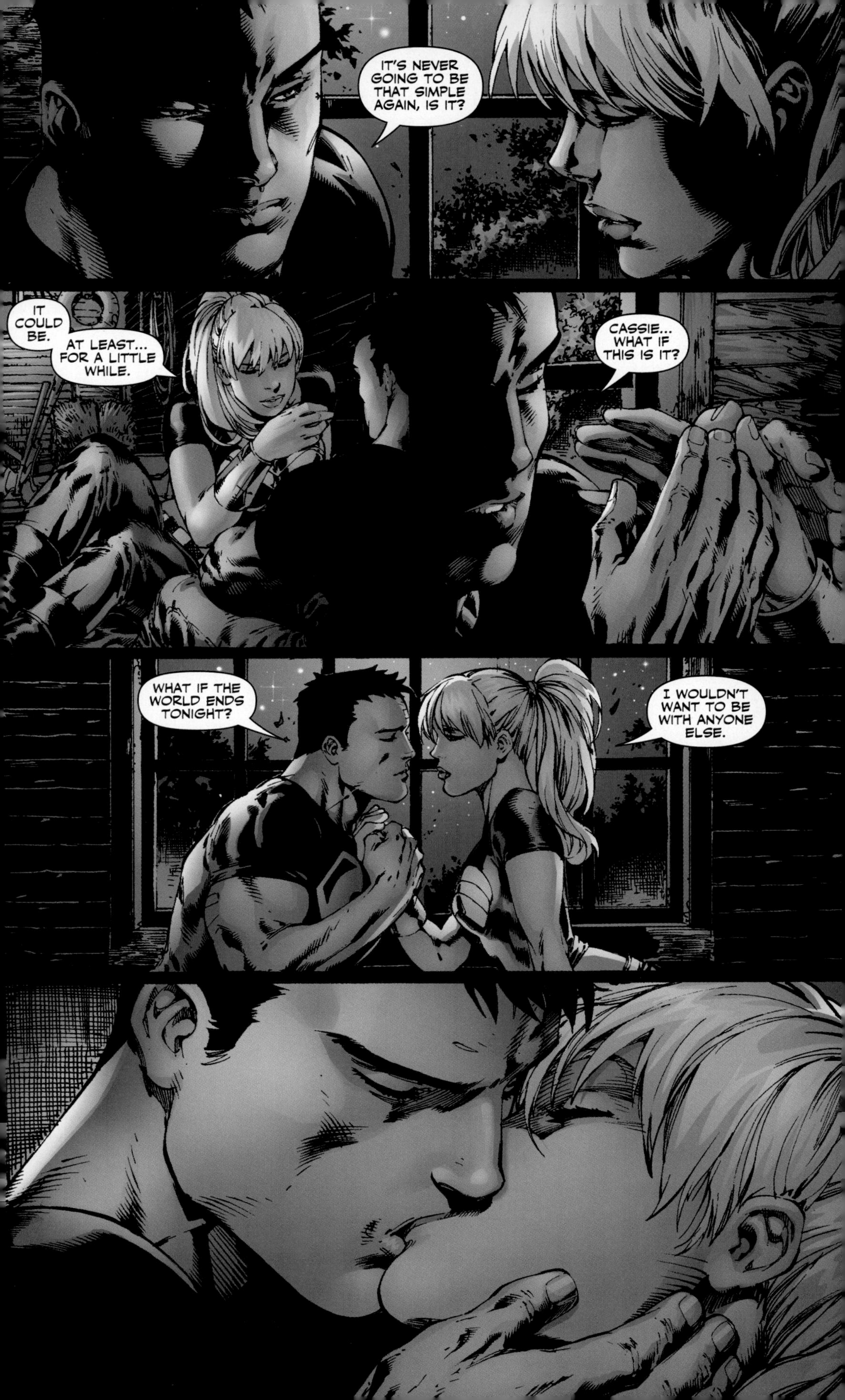
IT'S NEVER GOING TO BE THAT SIMPLE AGAIN, IS IT?
IT COULD BE.
AT LEAST... FOR A LITTLE WHILE.
CASSIE... WHAT IF THIS IS IT?
WHAT IF THE WORLD ENDS TONIGHT?
I WOULDN'T WANT TO BE WITH ANYONE ELSE.

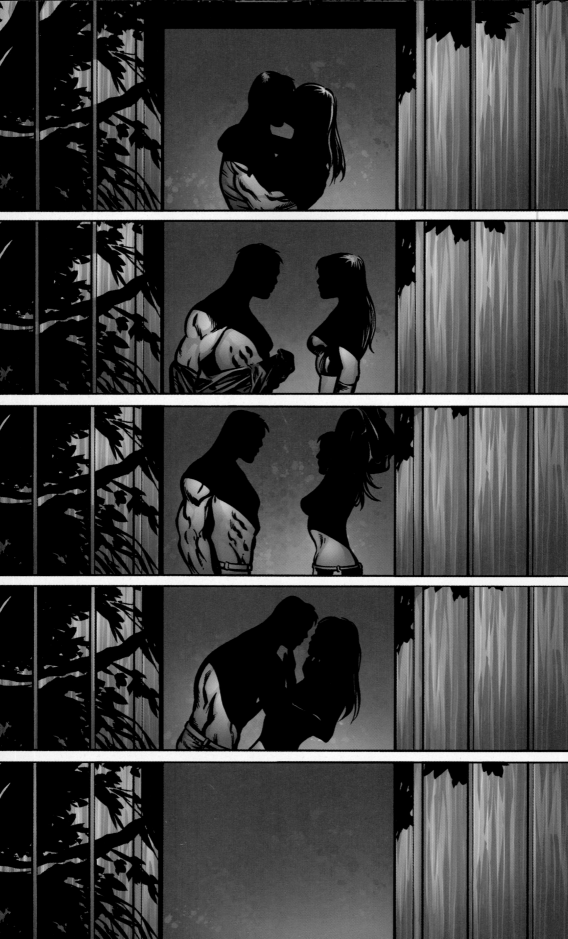

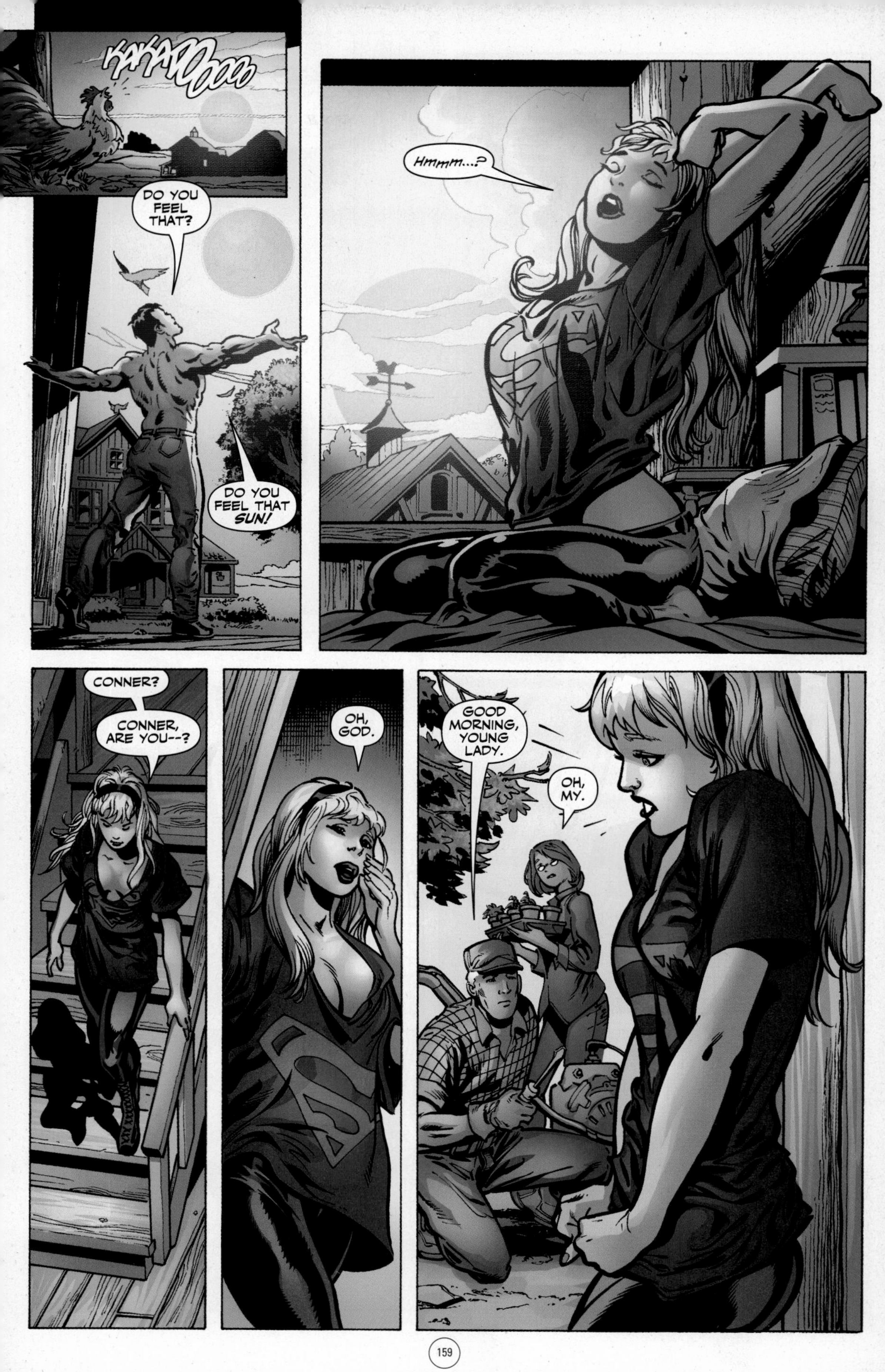
KAKAWOOooo
DO YOU FEEL THAT?
DO YOU FEEL THAT SUN!
Hmmm...?
CONNER?
CONNER, ARE YOU--?
OH, GOD.
GOOD MORNING, YOUNG LADY.
OH, MY.

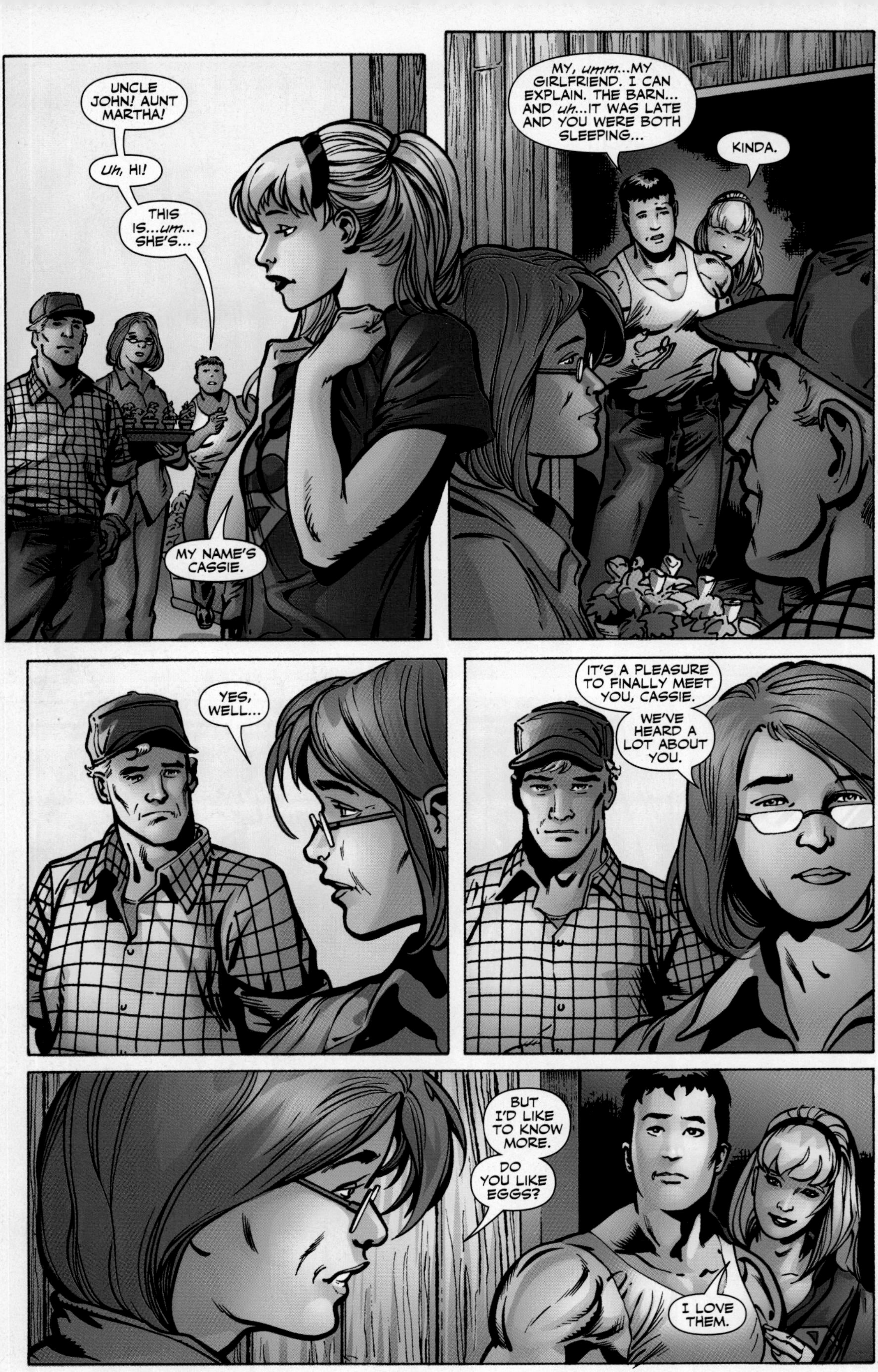
UNCLE JOHN! AUNT MARTHA!
Uh, HI!
THIS IS...*um*... SHE'S...
MY NAME'S CASSIE.
MY, *umm*...MY GIRLFRIEND. I CAN EXPLAIN. THE BARN... AND *uh*...IT WAS LATE AND YOU WERE BOTH SLEEPING...
KINDA.
YES, WELL...
IT'S A PLEASURE TO FINALLY MEET YOU, CASSIE.
WE'VE HEARD A LOT ABOUT YOU.
BUT I'D LIKE TO KNOW MORE.
DO YOU LIKE EGGS?
I LOVE THEM.

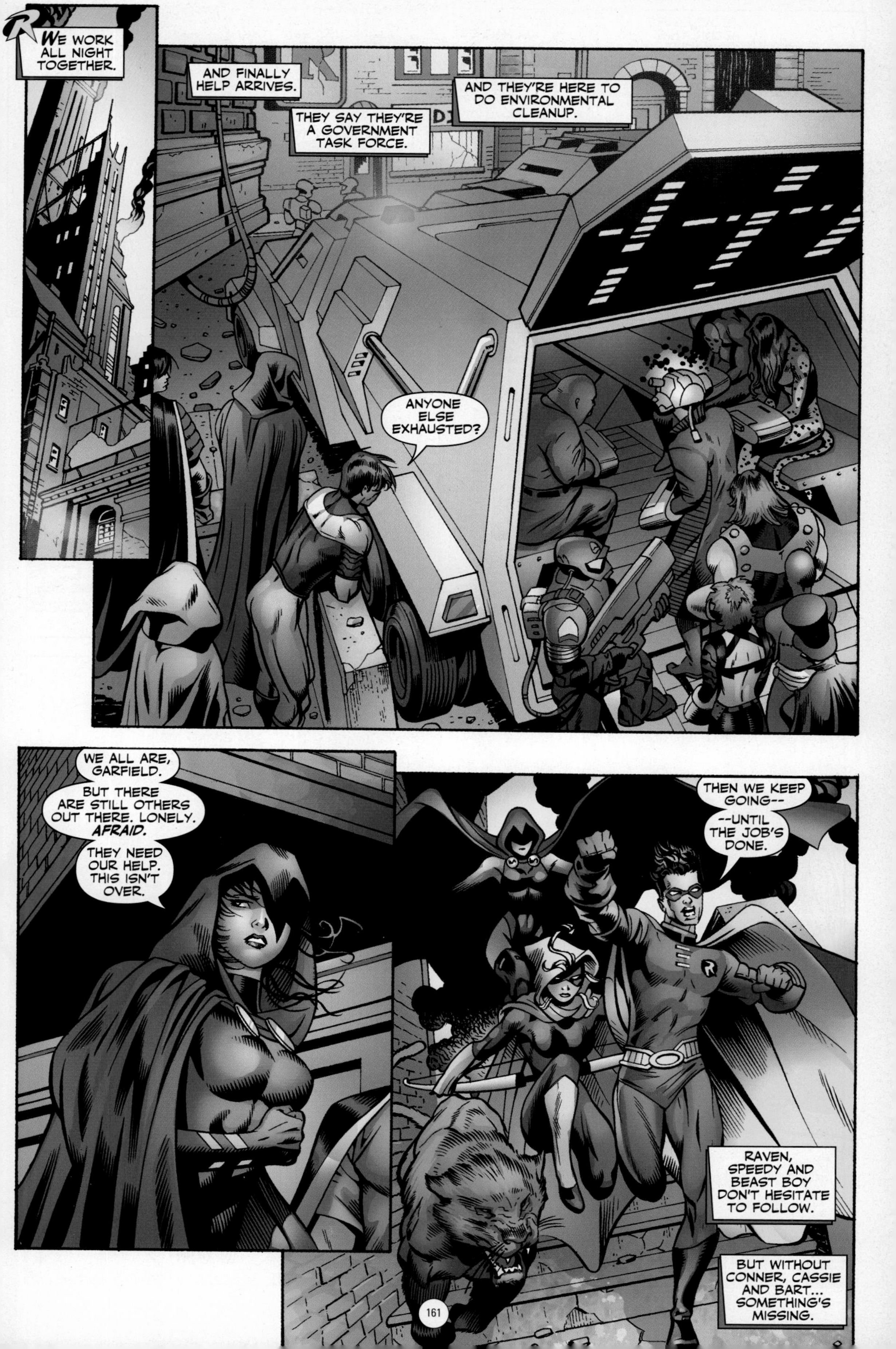

WE WORK ALL NIGHT TOGETHER.
AND FINALLY HELP ARRIVES.
THEY SAY THEY'RE A GOVERNMENT TASK FORCE.
AND THEY'RE HERE TO DO ENVIRONMENTAL CLEANUP.
ANYONE ELSE EXHAUSTED?
WE ALL ARE, GARFIELD.
BUT THERE ARE STILL OTHERS OUT THERE. LONELY. AFRAID.
THEY NEED OUR HELP. THIS ISN'T OVER.
THEN WE KEEP GOING--
--UNTIL THE JOB'S DONE.
RAVEN, SPEEDY AND BEAST BOY DON'T HESITATE TO FOLLOW.
BUT WITHOUT CONNER, CASSIE AND BART... SOMETHING'S MISSING.

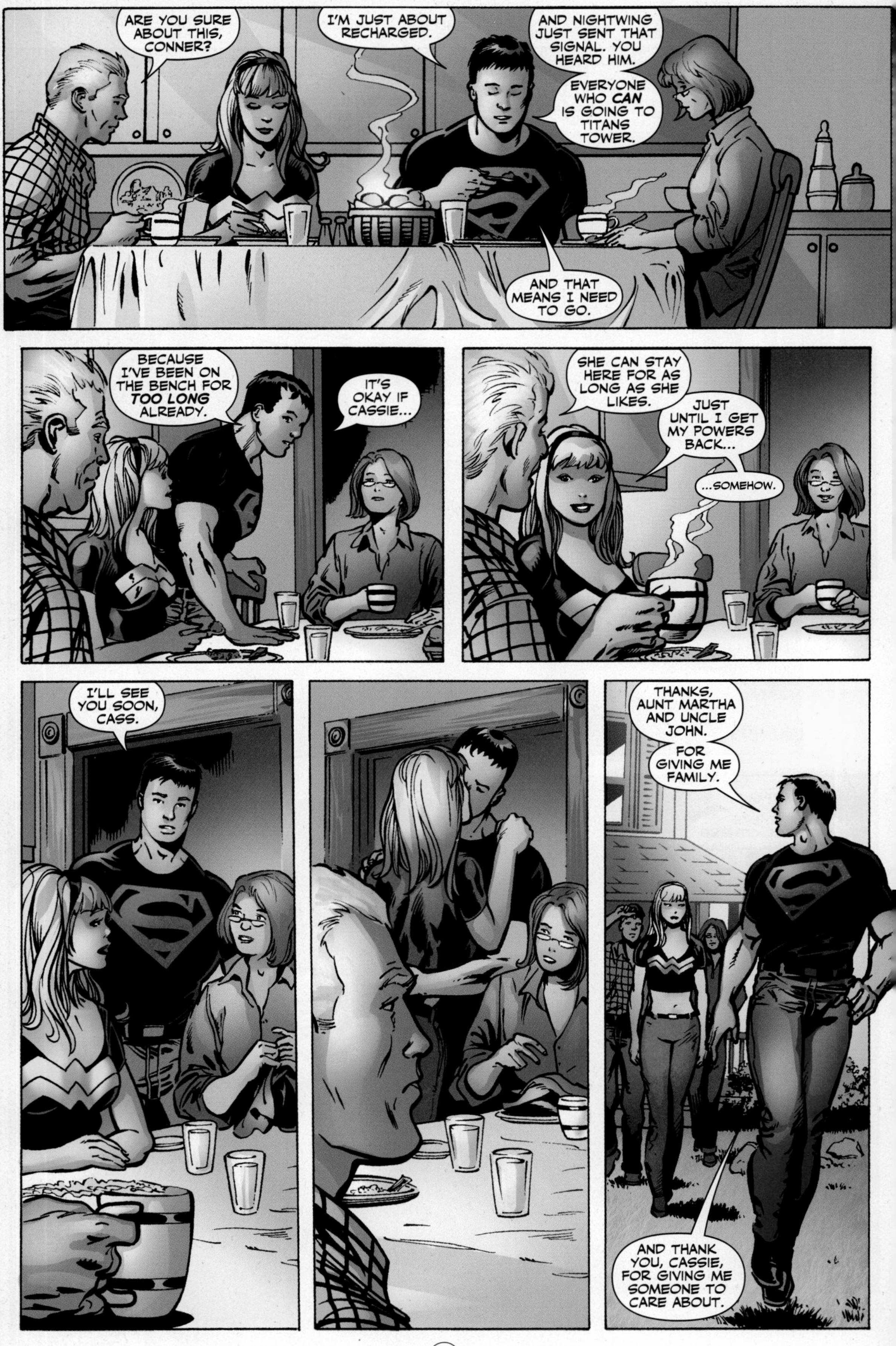
ARE YOU SURE ABOUT THIS, CONNER?
I'M JUST ABOUT RECHARGED.
AND NIGHTWING JUST SENT THAT SIGNAL. YOU HEARD HIM.
EVERYONE WHO **CAN** IS GOING TO TITANS TOWER.
AND THAT MEANS I NEED TO GO.
BECAUSE I'VE BEEN ON THE BENCH FOR ***TOO LONG*** ALREADY.
IT'S OKAY IF CASSIE...
SHE CAN STAY HERE FOR AS LONG AS SHE LIKES.
JUST UNTIL I GET MY POWERS BACK...
...SOMEHOW.
I'LL SEE YOU SOON, CASS.
THANKS, AUNT MARTHA AND UNCLE JOHN.
FOR GIVING ME FAMILY.
AND THANK YOU, CASSIE, FOR GIVING ME SOMEONE TO CARE ABOUT.

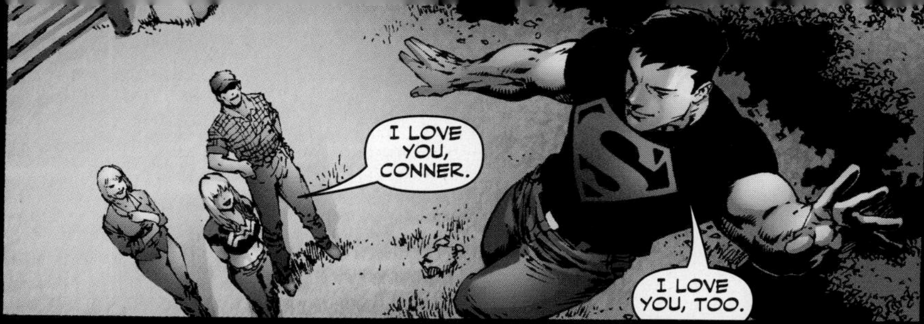
I LOVE YOU, CONNER.
I LOVE YOU, TOO.

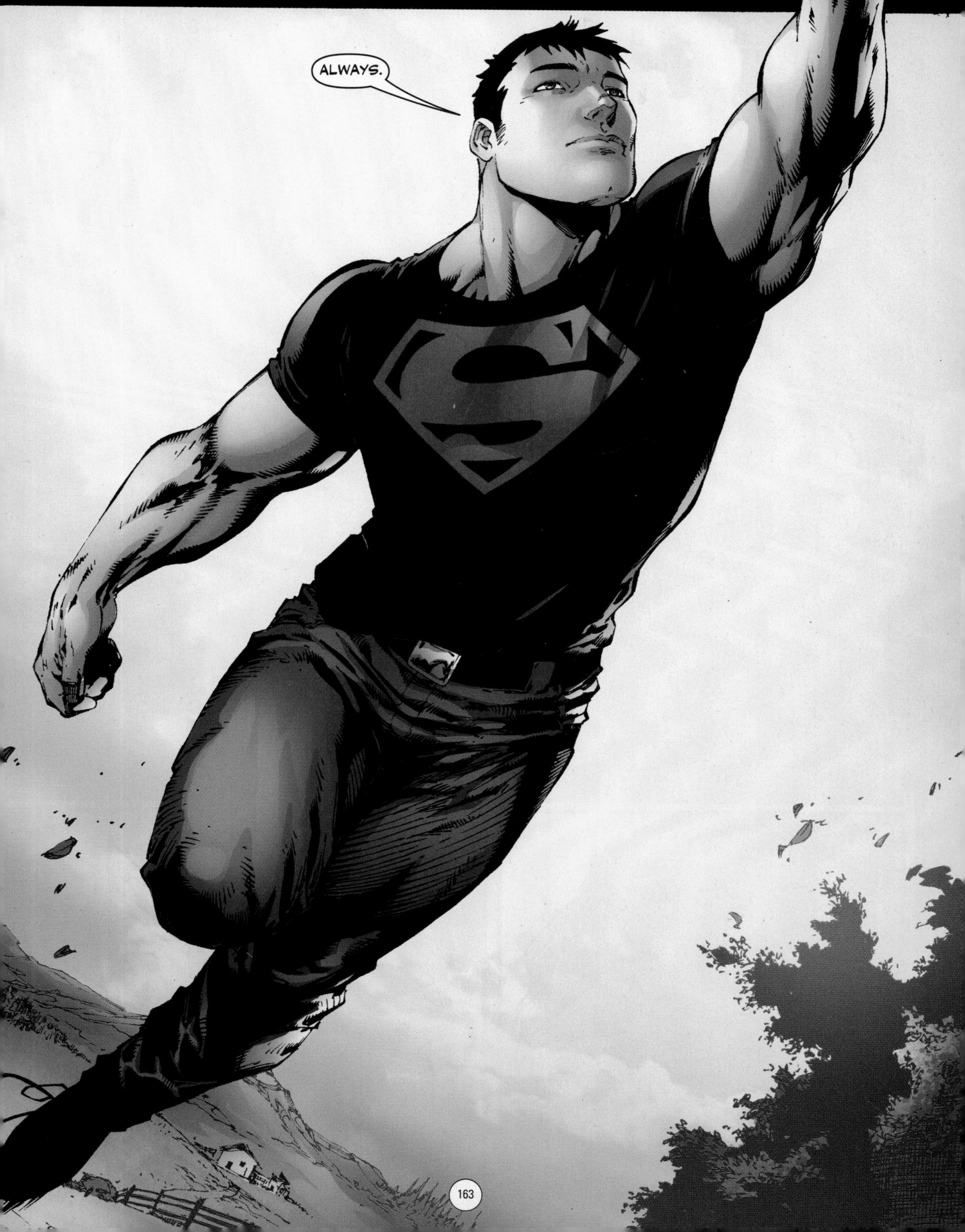
ALWAYS.

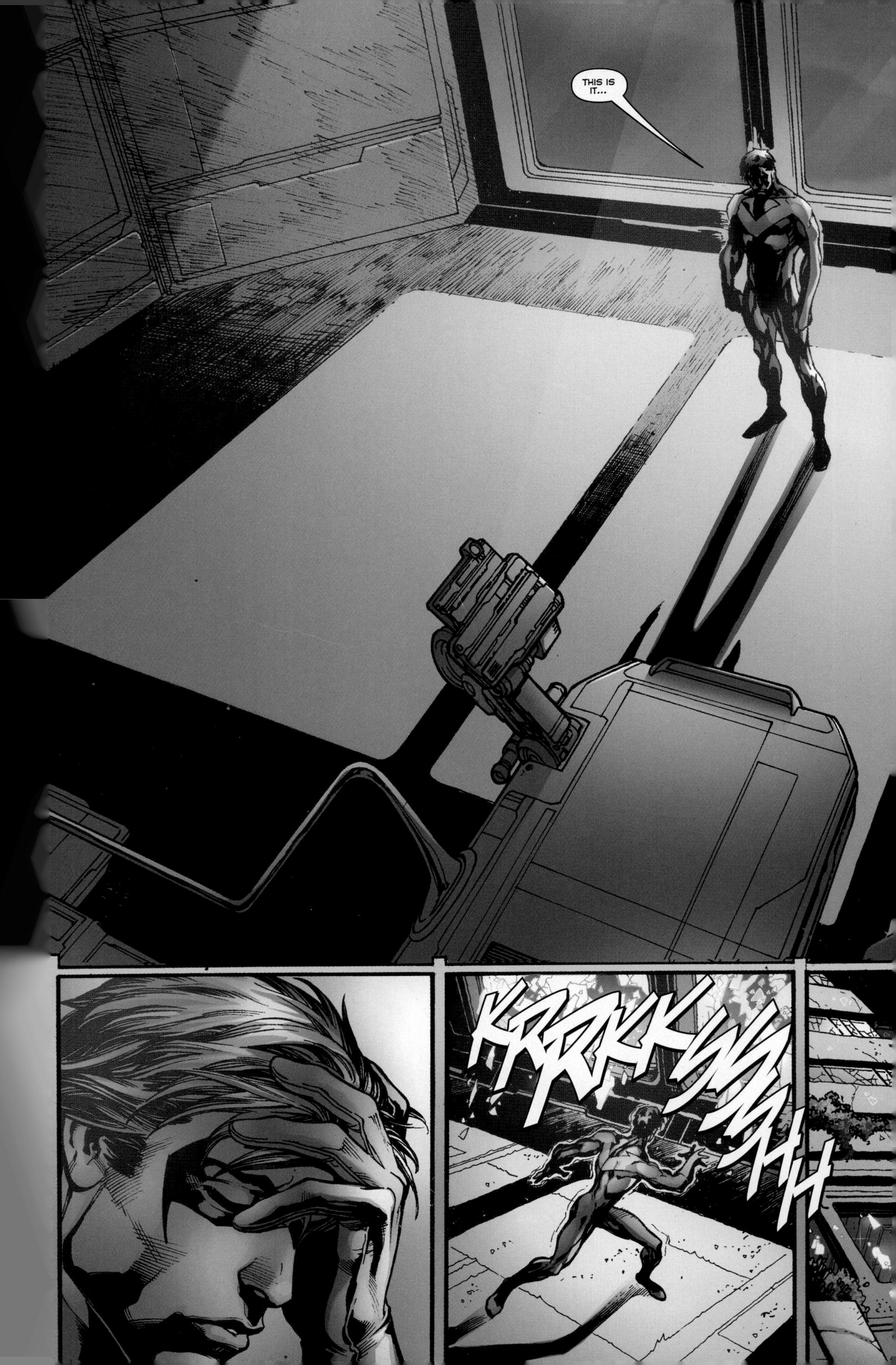
THIS IS IT...
KRRKKSSMMHH

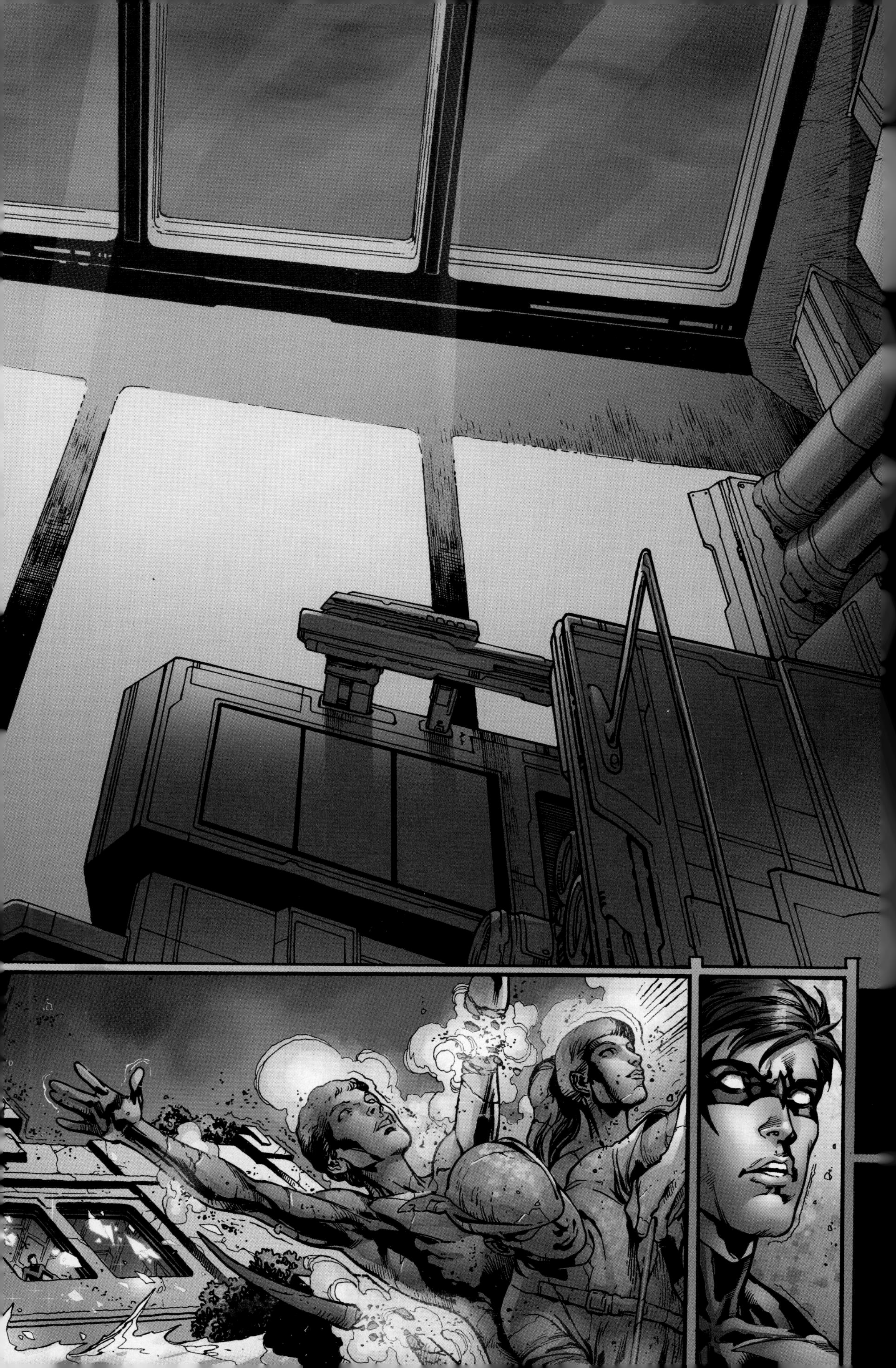

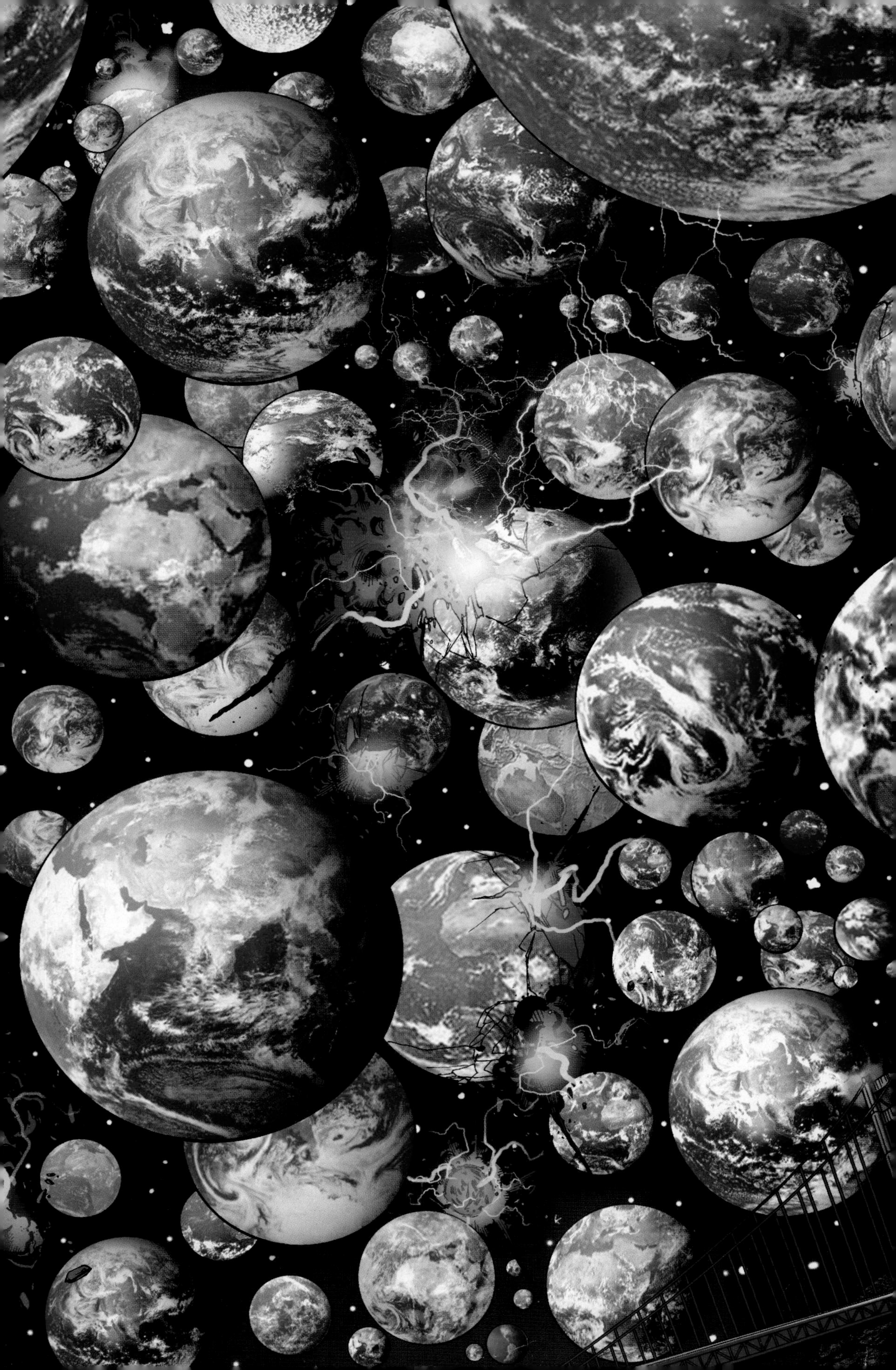

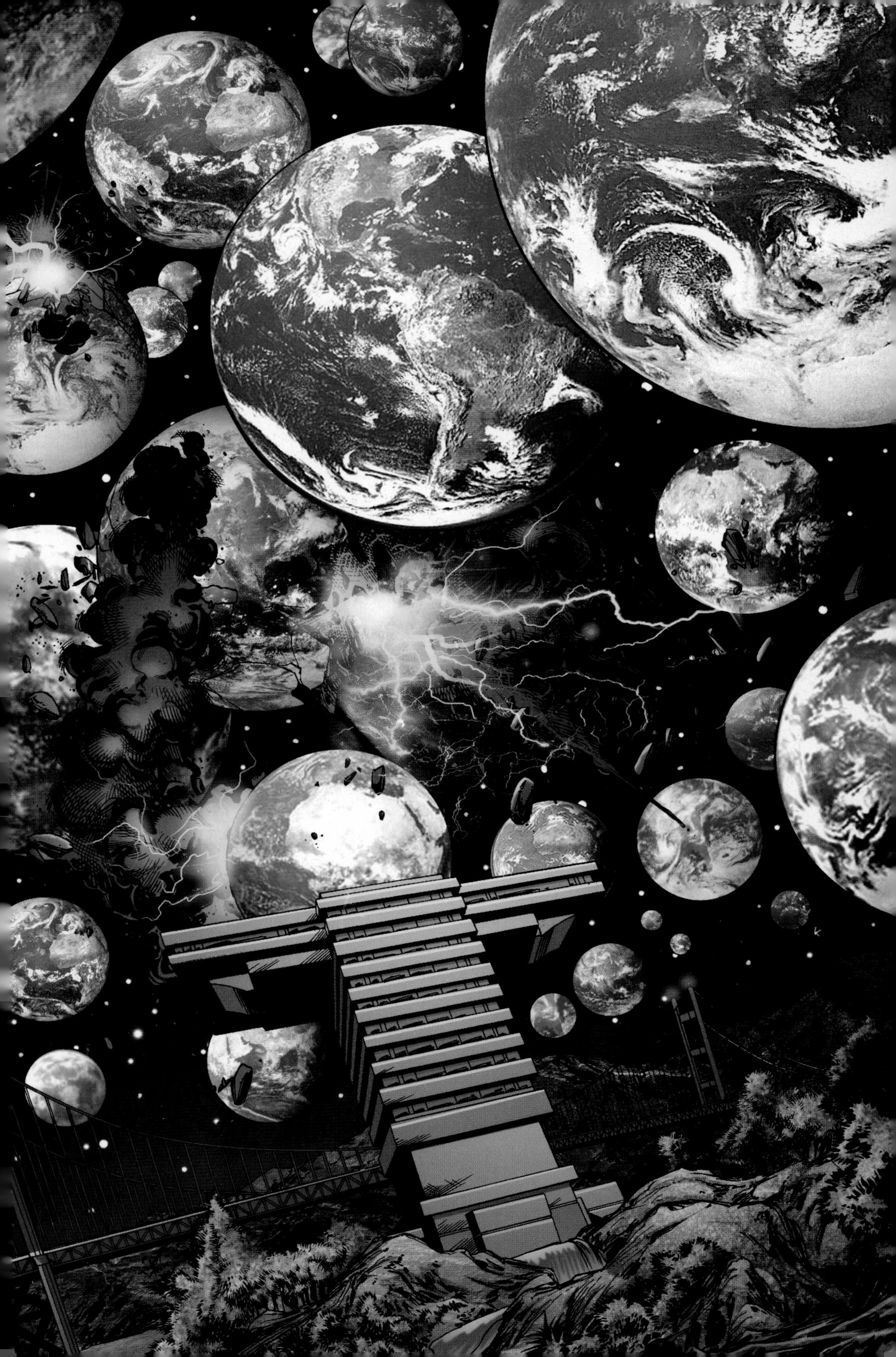

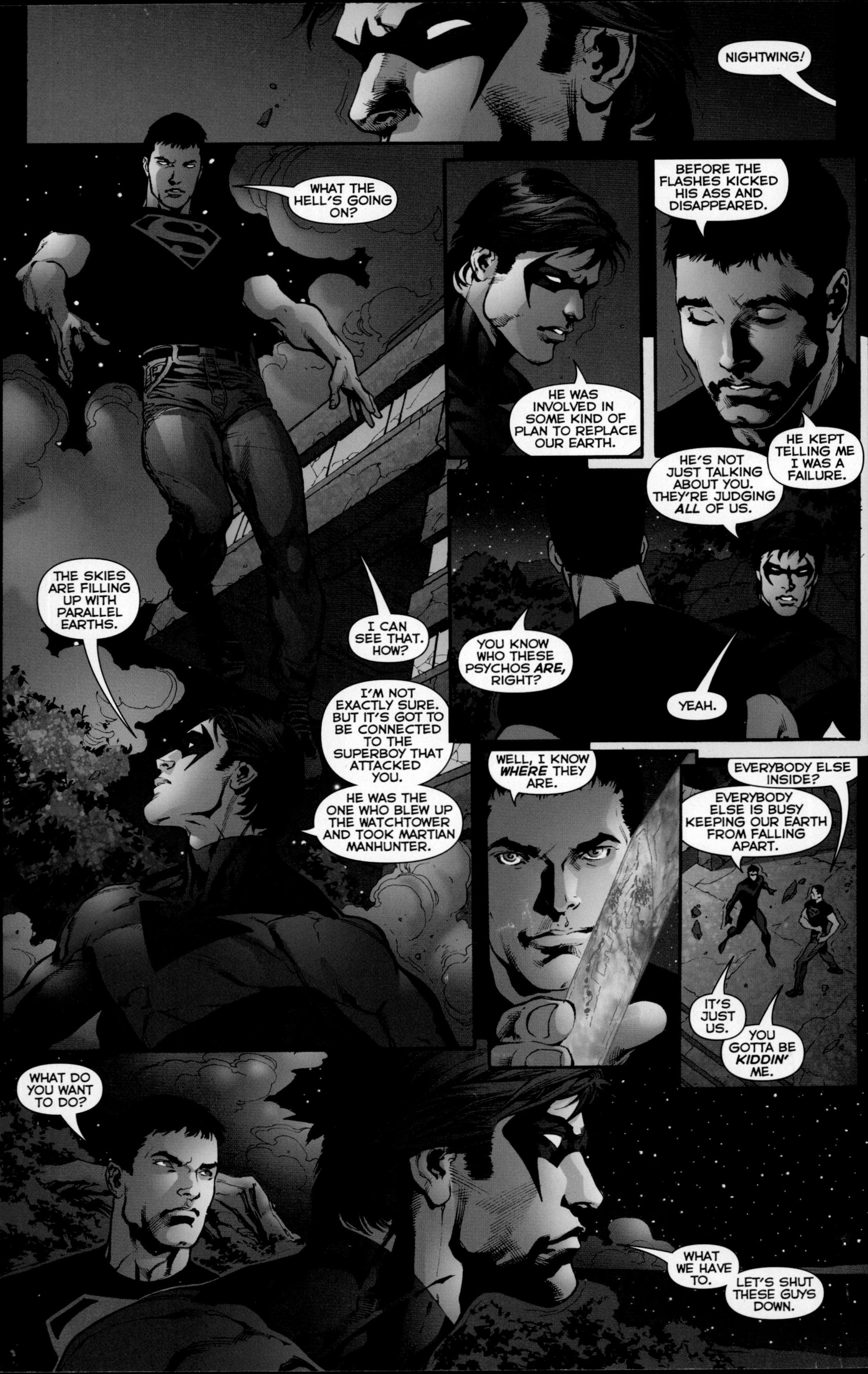
NIGHTWING!
WHAT THE HELL'S GOING ON?
THE SKIES ARE FILLING UP WITH PARALLEL EARTHS.
I CAN SEE THAT. HOW?
I'M NOT EXACTLY SURE. BUT IT'S GOT TO BE CONNECTED TO THE SUPERBOY THAT ATTACKED YOU.
HE WAS THE ONE WHO BLEW UP THE WATCHTOWER AND TOOK MARTIAN MANHUNTER.
HE WAS INVOLVED IN SOME KIND OF PLAN TO REPLACE OUR EARTH.
BEFORE THE FLASHES KICKED HIS ASS AND DISAPPEARED.
HE KEPT TELLING ME I WAS A FAILURE.
HE'S NOT JUST TALKING ABOUT YOU. THEY'RE JUDGING ALL OF US.
YOU KNOW WHO THESE PSYCHOS ARE, RIGHT?
YEAH.
WELL, I KNOW WHERE THEY ARE.
EVERYBODY ELSE INSIDE?
EVERYBODY ELSE IS BUSY KEEPING OUR EARTH FROM FALLING APART.
IT'S JUST US.
YOU GOTTA BE KIDDIN' ME.
WHAT DO YOU WANT TO DO?
WHAT WE HAVE TO.
LET'S SHUT THESE GUYS DOWN.

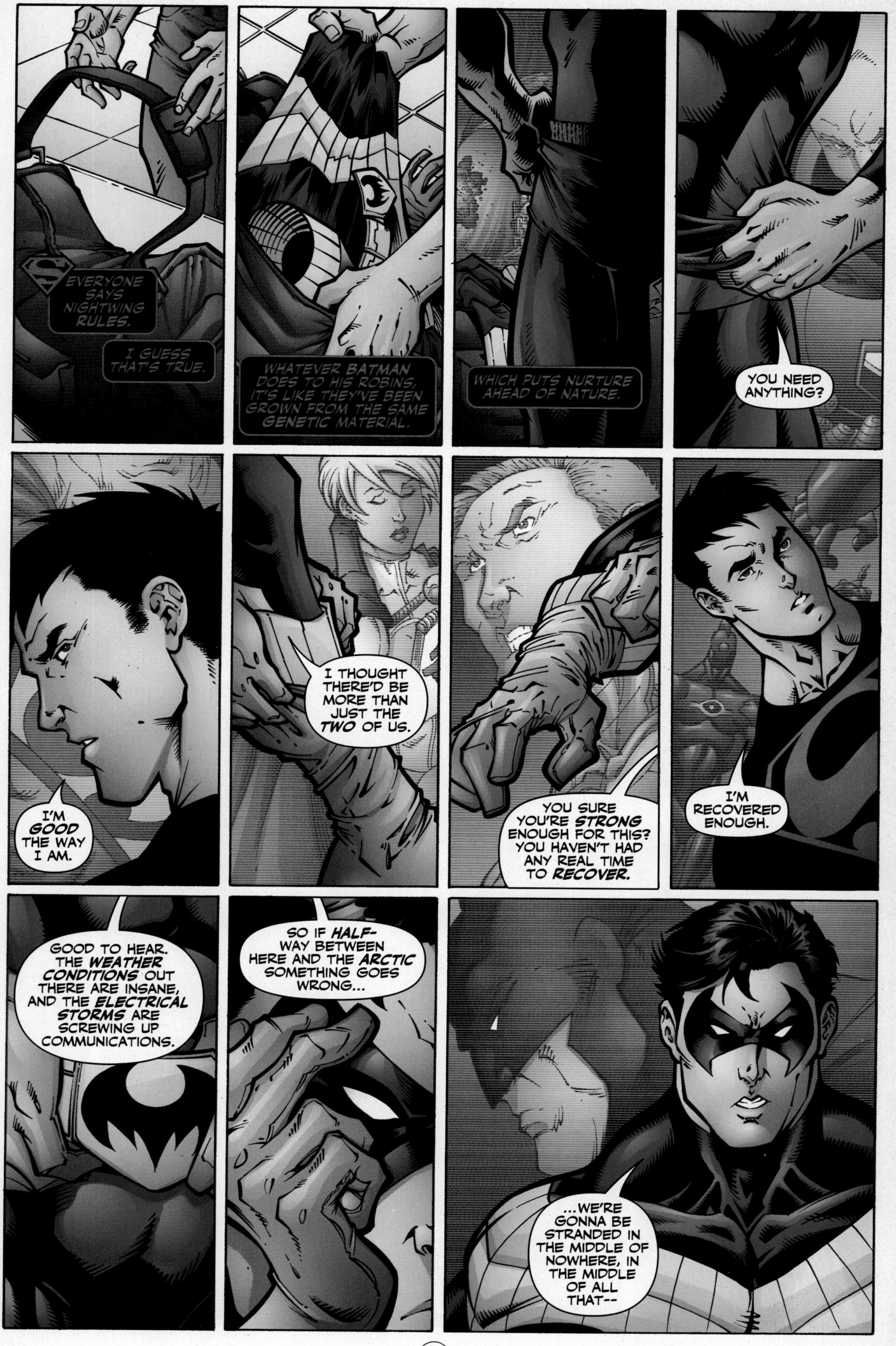
EVERYONE SAYS NIGHTWING RULES.
I GUESS THAT'S TRUE.
WHATEVER BATMAN DOES TO HIS ROBINS, IT'S LIKE THEY'VE BEEN GROWN FROM THE SAME GENETIC MATERIAL.
WHICH PUTS NURTURE AHEAD OF NATURE.
YOU NEED ANYTHING?
I'M GOOD THE WAY I AM.
I THOUGHT THERE'D BE MORE THAN JUST THE TWO OF US.
YOU SURE YOU'RE STRONG ENOUGH FOR THIS? YOU HAVEN'T HAD ANY REAL TIME TO RECOVER.
I'M RECOVERED ENOUGH.
GOOD TO HEAR. THE WEATHER CONDITIONS OUT THERE ARE INSANE, AND THE ELECTRICAL STORMS ARE SCREWING UP COMMUNICATIONS.
SO IF HALF-WAY BETWEEN HERE AND THE ARCTIC SOMETHING GOES WRONG...
...WE'RE GONNA BE STRANDED IN THE MIDDLE OF NOWHERE, IN THE MIDDLE OF ALL THAT--

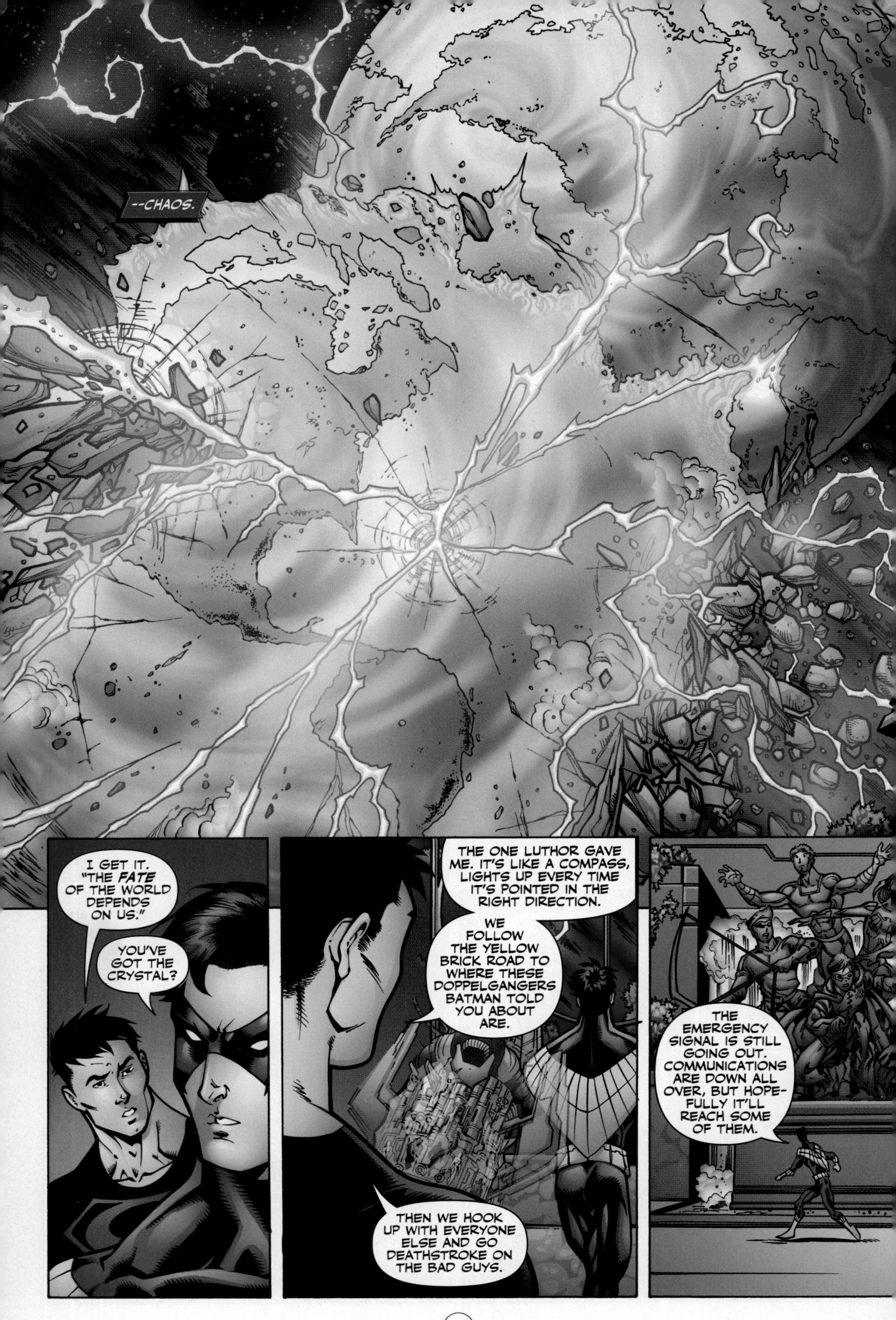
--CHAOS.
I GET IT. "THE *FATE* OF THE WORLD DEPENDS ON US."
YOU'VE GOT THE CRYSTAL?
THE ONE LUTHOR GAVE ME. IT'S LIKE A COMPASS, LIGHTS UP EVERY TIME IT'S POINTED IN THE RIGHT DIRECTION.
WE FOLLOW THE YELLOW BRICK ROAD TO WHERE THESE DOPPELGANGERS BATMAN TOLD YOU ABOUT ARE.
THEN WE HOOK UP WITH EVERYONE ELSE AND GO DEATHSTROKE ON THE BAD GUYS.
THE EMERGENCY SIGNAL IS STILL GOING OUT. COMMUNICATIONS ARE DOWN ALL OVER, BUT HOPE-FULLY IT'LL REACH SOME OF THEM.

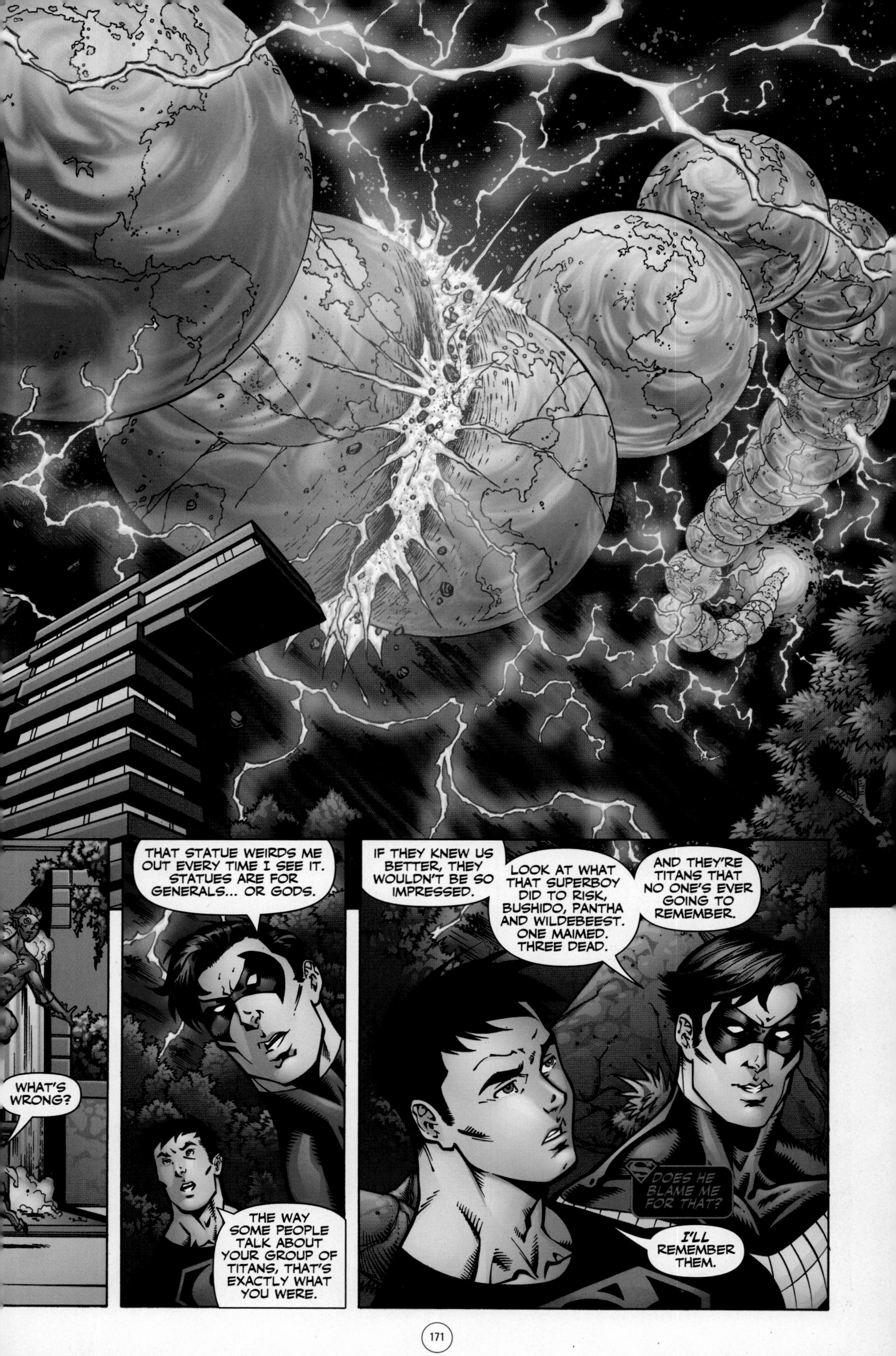
WHAT'S WRONG?
THAT STATUE WEIRDS ME OUT EVERY TIME I SEE IT. STATUES ARE FOR GENERALS... OR GODS.
THE WAY SOME PEOPLE TALK ABOUT YOUR GROUP OF TITANS, THAT'S EXACTLY WHAT YOU WERE.
IF THEY KNEW US BETTER, THEY WOULDN'T BE SO IMPRESSED.
LOOK AT WHAT THAT SUPERBOY DID TO RISK, BUSHIDO, PANTHA AND WILDEBEEST. ONE MAIMED. THREE DEAD.
AND THEY'RE TITANS THAT NO ONE'S EVER GOING TO REMEMBER.
DOES HE BLAME ME FOR THAT?
I'LL REMEMBER THEM.

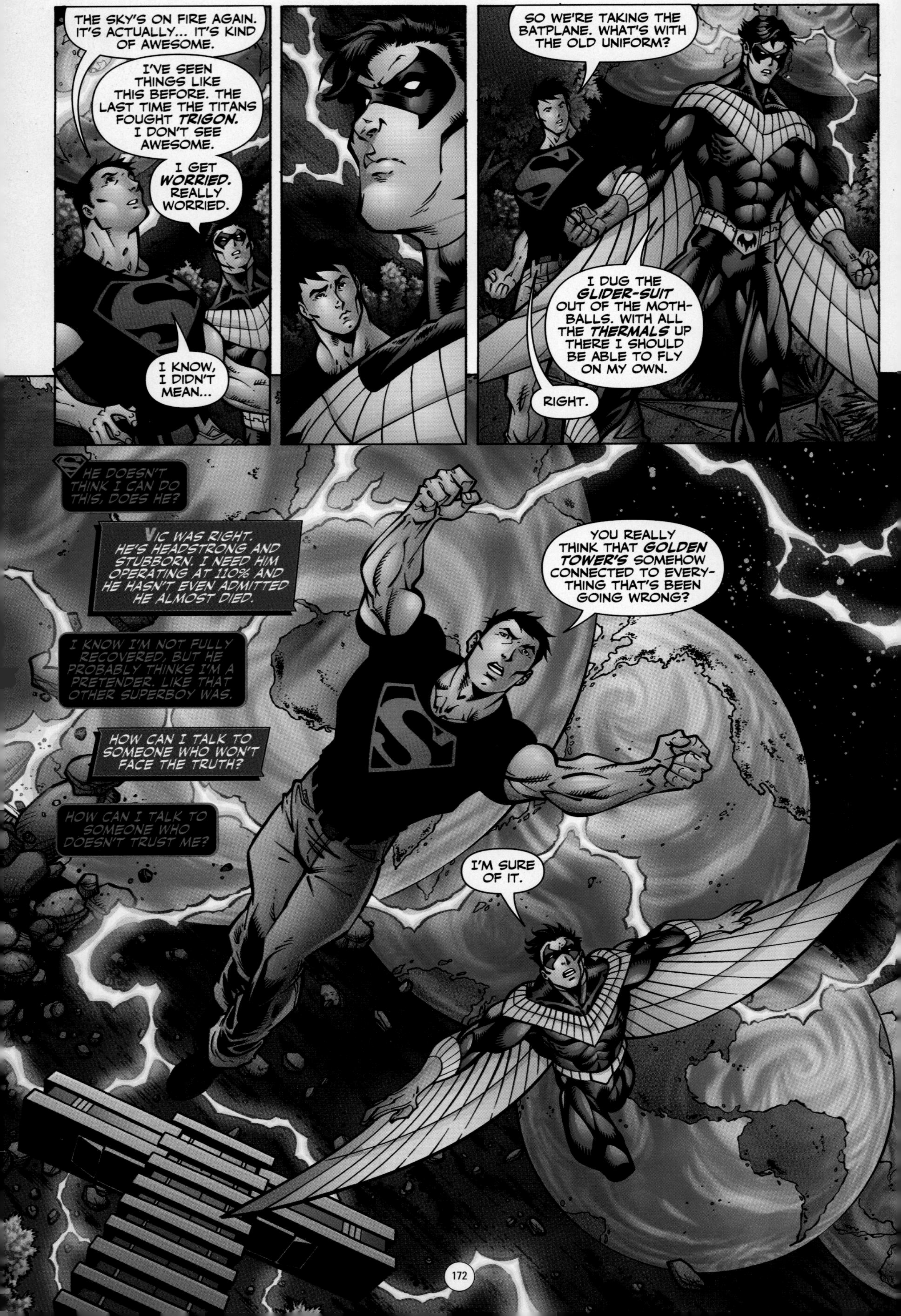
THE SKY'S ON FIRE AGAIN. IT'S ACTUALLY... IT'S KIND OF AWESOME.
I'VE SEEN THINGS LIKE THIS BEFORE. THE LAST TIME THE TITANS FOUGHT TRIGON. I DON'T SEE AWESOME.
I GET WORRIED. REALLY WORRIED.
I KNOW, I DIDN'T MEAN...
SO WE'RE TAKING THE BATPLANE. WHAT'S WITH THE OLD UNIFORM?
I DUG THE GLIDER-SUIT OUT OF THE MOTH-BALLS. WITH ALL THE THERMALS UP THERE I SHOULD BE ABLE TO FLY ON MY OWN.
RIGHT.
HE DOESN'T THINK I CAN DO THIS, DOES HE?
VIC WAS RIGHT. HE'S HEADSTRONG AND STUBBORN. I NEED HIM OPERATING AT 110% AND HE HASN'T EVEN ADMITTED HE ALMOST DIED.
I KNOW I'M NOT FULLY RECOVERED, BUT HE PROBABLY THINKS I'M A PRETENDER. LIKE THAT OTHER SUPERBOY WAS.
YOU REALLY THINK THAT GOLDEN TOWER'S SOMEHOW CONNECTED TO EVERY-THING THAT'S BEEN GOING WRONG?
HOW CAN I TALK TO SOMEONE WHO WON'T FACE THE TRUTH?
HOW CAN I TALK TO SOMEONE WHO DOESN'T TRUST ME?
I'M SURE OF IT.

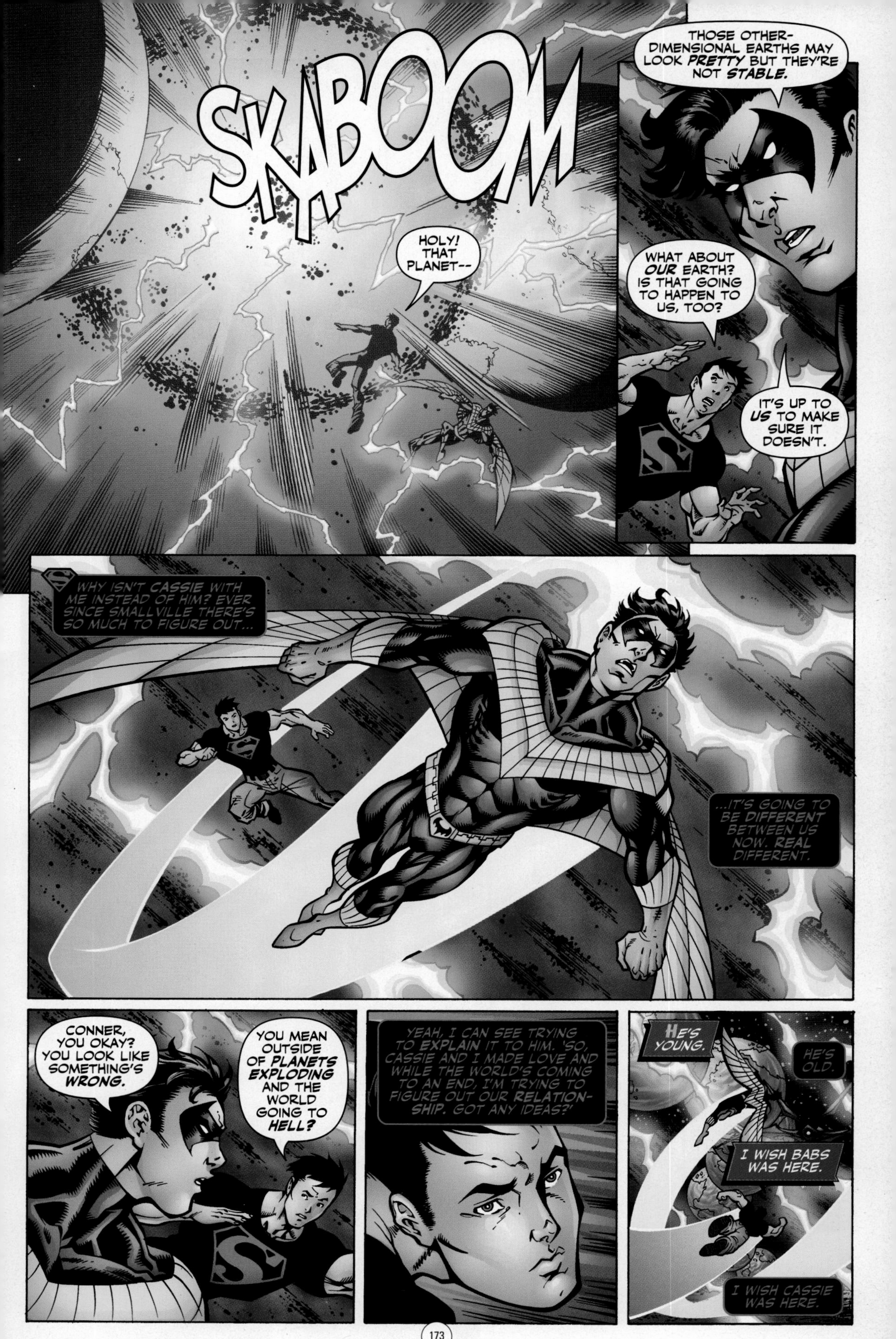
SKABOOM
HOLY! THAT PLANET--
THOSE OTHER-DIMENSIONAL EARTHS MAY LOOK PRETTY BUT THEY'RE NOT STABLE.
WHAT ABOUT OUR EARTH? IS THAT GOING TO HAPPEN TO US, TOO?
IT'S UP TO US TO MAKE SURE IT DOESN'T.
WHY ISN'T CASSIE WITH ME INSTEAD OF HIM? EVER SINCE SMALLVILLE THERE'S SO MUCH TO FIGURE OUT...
...IT'S GOING TO BE DIFFERENT BETWEEN US NOW. REAL DIFFERENT.
CONNER, YOU OKAY? YOU LOOK LIKE SOMETHING'S WRONG.
YOU MEAN OUTSIDE OF PLANETS EXPLODING AND THE WORLD GOING TO HELL?
YEAH, I CAN SEE TRYING TO EXPLAIN IT TO HIM. 'SO, CASSIE AND I MADE LOVE AND WHILE THE WORLD'S COMING TO AN END, I'M TRYING TO FIGURE OUT OUR RELATIONSHIP. GOT ANY IDEAS?'
HE'S YOUNG.
HE'S OLD.
I WISH BABS WAS HERE.
I WISH CASSIE WAS HERE.

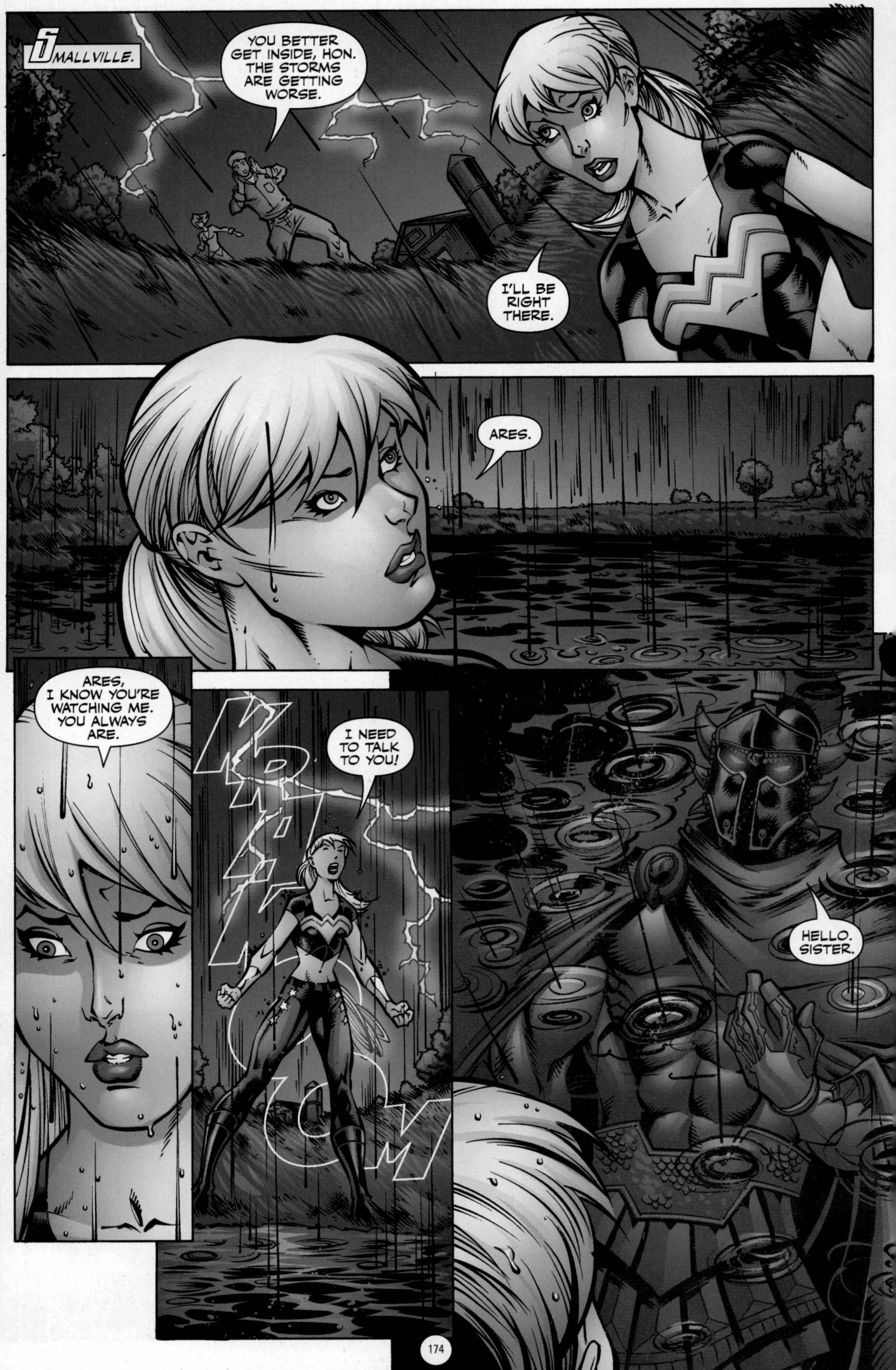
SMALLVILLE.
YOU BETTER GET INSIDE, HON. THE STORMS ARE GETTING WORSE.
I'LL BE RIGHT THERE.
ARES.
ARES, I KNOW YOU'RE WATCHING ME. YOU ALWAYS ARE.
I NEED TO TALK TO YOU!
HELLO. SISTER.

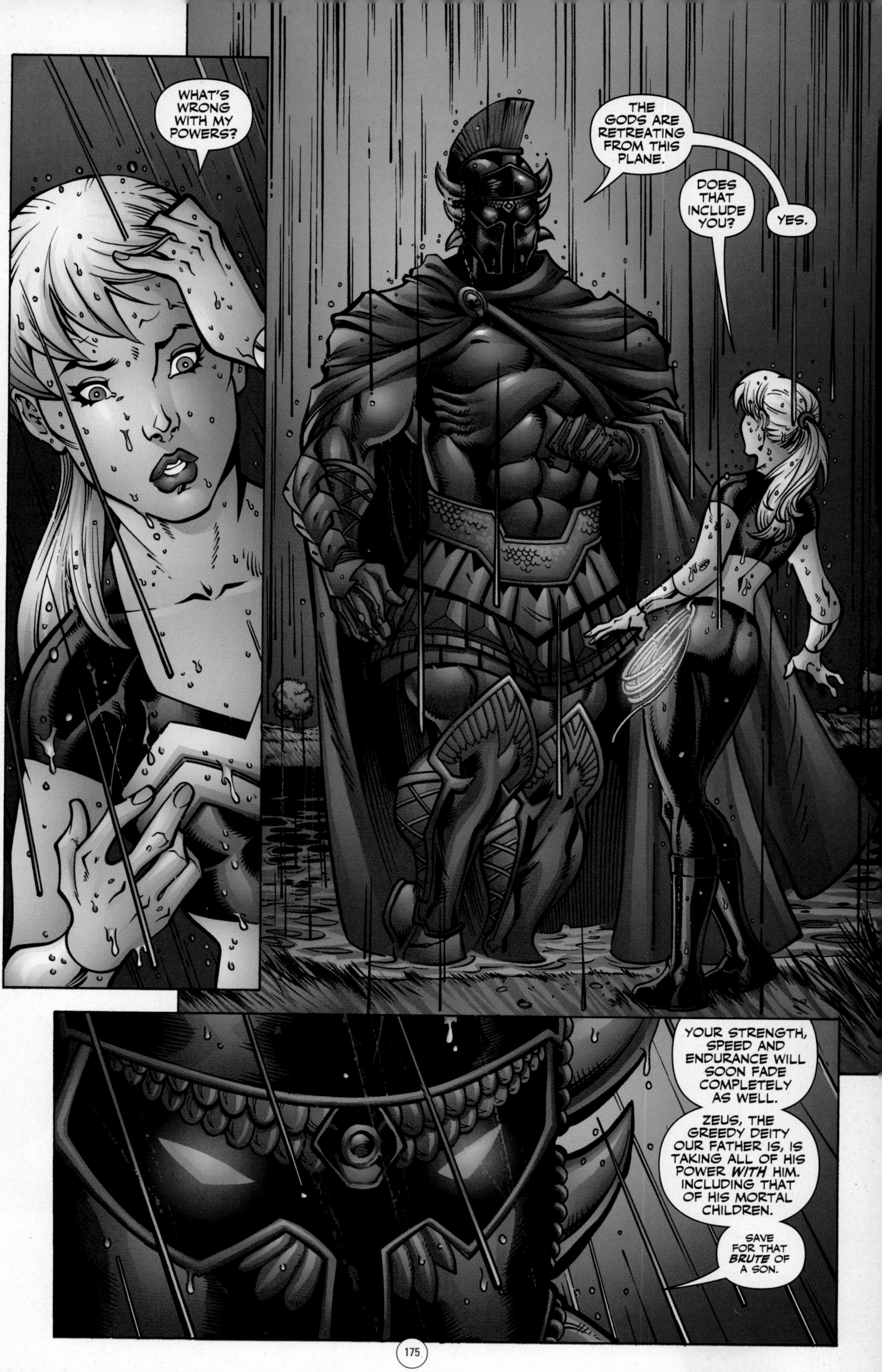

WHAT'S WRONG WITH MY POWERS?
THE GODS ARE RETREATING FROM THIS PLANE.
DOES THAT INCLUDE YOU?
YES.
YOUR STRENGTH, SPEED AND ENDURANCE WILL SOON FADE COMPLETELY AS WELL.
ZEUS, THE GREEDY DEITY OUR FATHER IS, IS TAKING ALL OF HIS POWER *WITH* HIM. INCLUDING THAT OF HIS MORTAL CHILDREN.
SAVE FOR THAT *BRUTE* OF A SON.

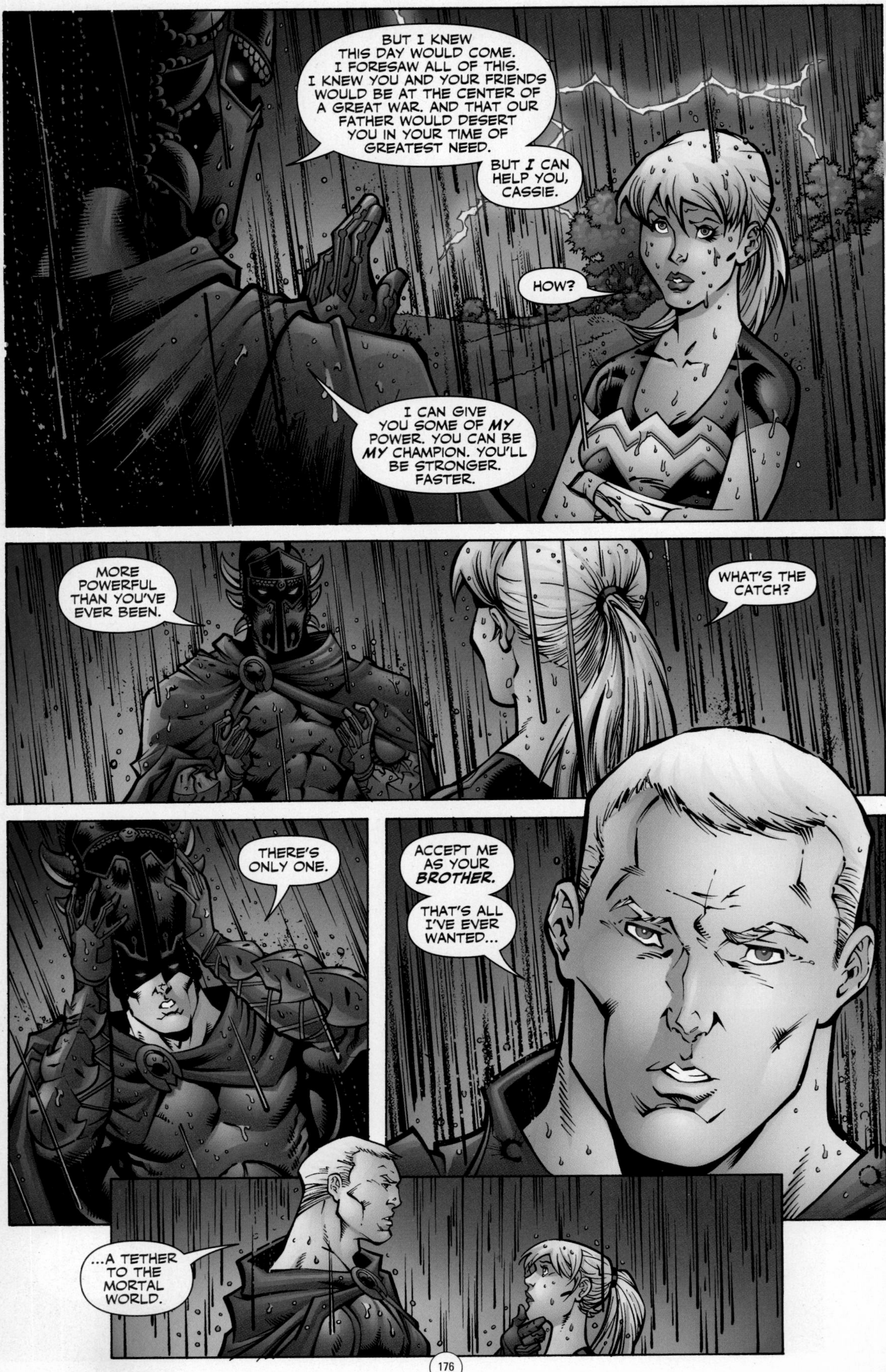

BUT I KNEW THIS DAY WOULD COME. I FORESAW ALL OF THIS. I KNEW YOU AND YOUR FRIENDS WOULD BE AT THE CENTER OF A GREAT WAR. AND THAT OUR FATHER WOULD DESERT YOU IN YOUR TIME OF GREATEST NEED.
BUT *I* CAN HELP YOU, CASSIE.
HOW?
I CAN GIVE YOU SOME OF *MY* POWER. YOU CAN BE *MY* CHAMPION. YOU'LL BE STRONGER. FASTER.
MORE POWERFUL THAN YOU'VE EVER BEEN.
WHAT'S THE CATCH?
THERE'S ONLY ONE.
ACCEPT ME AS YOUR ***BROTHER.***
THAT'S ALL I'VE EVER WANTED...
...A TETHER TO THE MORTAL WORLD.

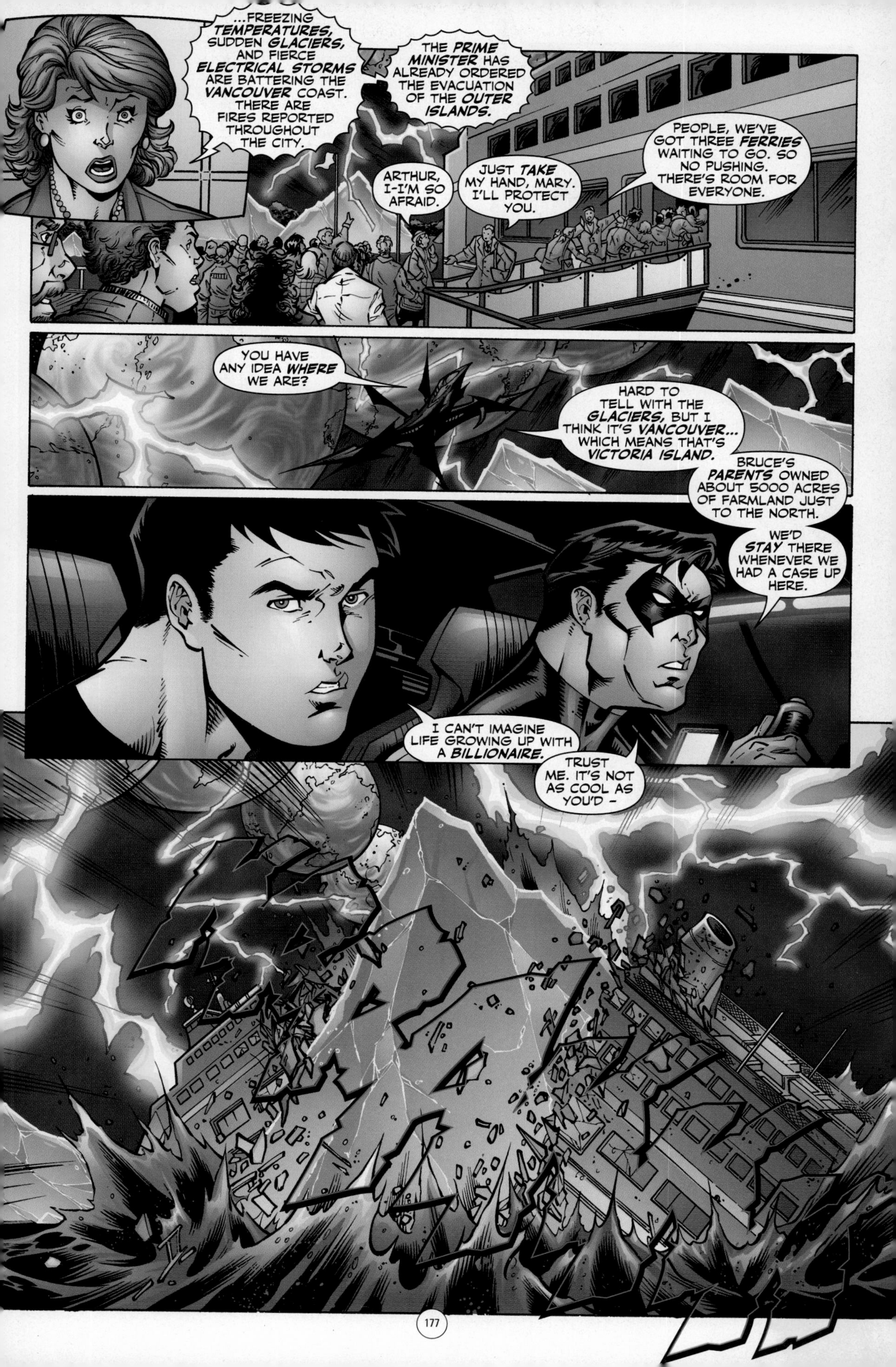
...FREEZING TEMPERATURES, SUDDEN GLACIERS, AND FIERCE ELECTRICAL STORMS ARE BATTERING THE VANCOUVER COAST. THERE ARE FIRES REPORTED THROUGHOUT THE CITY.
THE PRIME MINISTER HAS ALREADY ORDERED THE EVACUATION OF THE OUTER ISLANDS.
ARTHUR, I-I'M SO AFRAID.
JUST TAKE MY HAND, MARY. I'LL PROTECT YOU.
PEOPLE, WE'VE GOT THREE FERRIES WAITING TO GO. SO NO PUSHING. THERE'S ROOM FOR EVERYONE.
YOU HAVE ANY IDEA WHERE WE ARE?
HARD TO TELL WITH THE GLACIERS, BUT I THINK IT'S VANCOUVER... WHICH MEANS THAT'S VICTORIA ISLAND.
BRUCE'S PARENTS OWNED ABOUT 5000 ACRES OF FARMLAND JUST TO THE NORTH.
WE'D STAY THERE WHENEVER WE HAD A CASE UP HERE.
I CAN'T IMAGINE LIFE GROWING UP WITH A BILLIONAIRE.
TRUST ME. IT'S NOT AS COOL AS YOU'D -

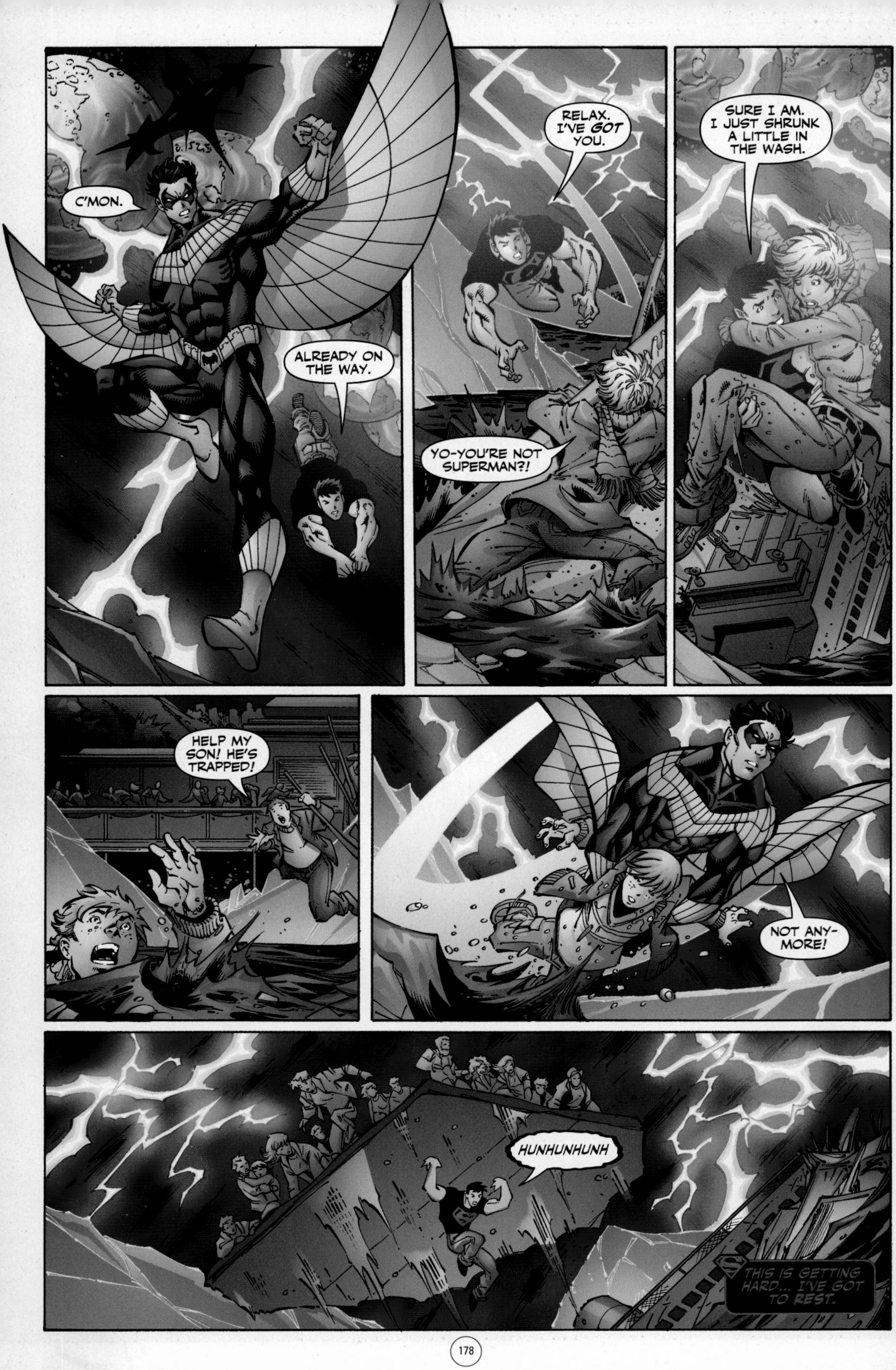
C'MON.
ALREADY ON THE WAY.
RELAX. I'VE GOT YOU.
YO-YOU'RE NOT SUPERMAN?!
SURE I AM. I JUST SHRUNK A LITTLE IN THE WASH.
HELP MY SON! HE'S TRAPPED!
NOT ANY-MORE!
HUNHUNHUNH
THIS IS GETTING HARD... I'VE GOT TO REST.

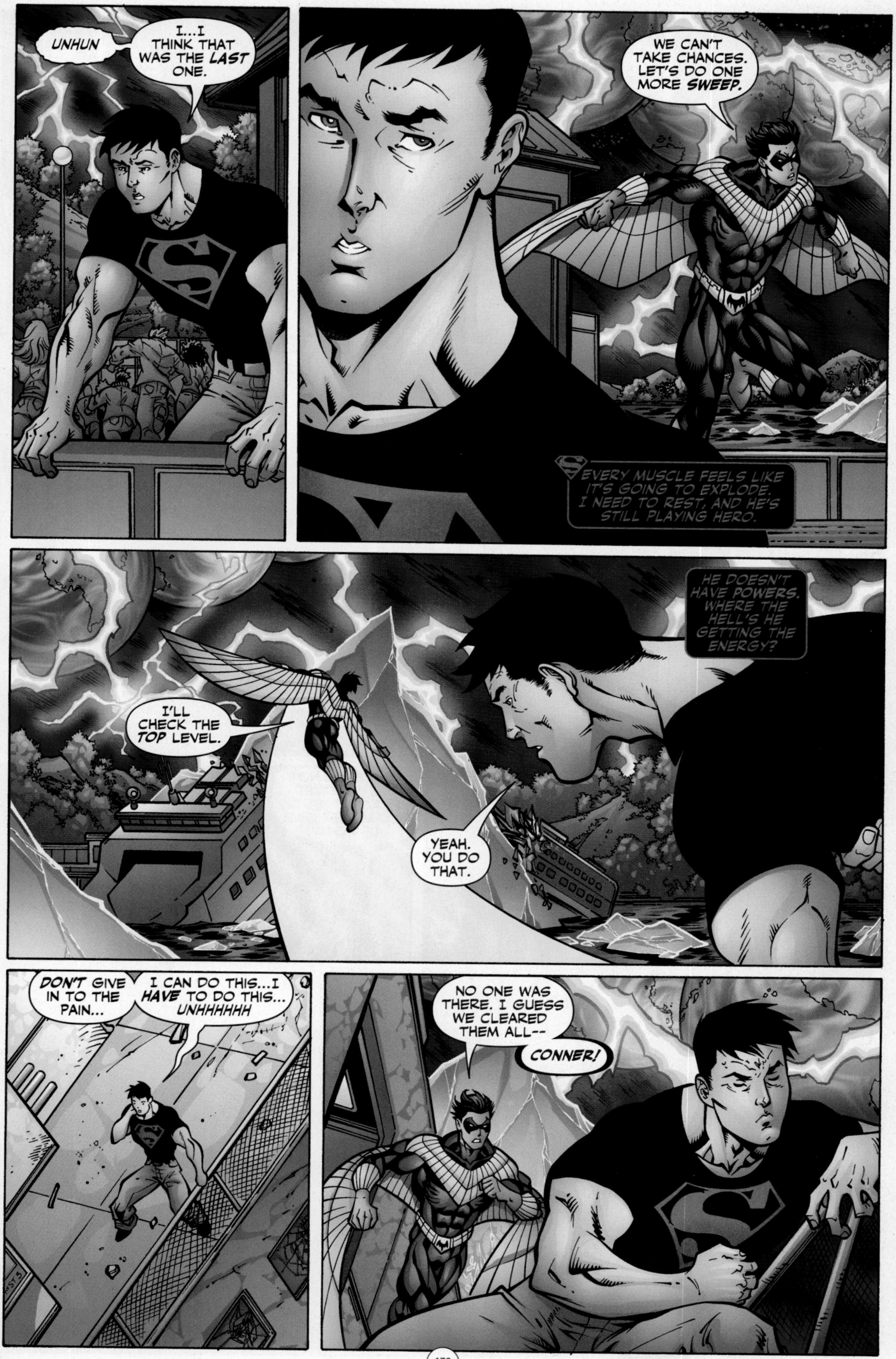
UNHUN
I...I THINK THAT WAS THE LAST ONE.
WE CAN'T TAKE CHANCES. LET'S DO ONE MORE SWEEP.
EVERY MUSCLE FEELS LIKE IT'S GOING TO EXPLODE. I NEED TO REST, AND HE'S STILL PLAYING HERO.
HE DOESN'T HAVE POWERS. WHERE THE HELL'S HE GETTING THE ENERGY?
I'LL CHECK THE TOP LEVEL.
YEAH. YOU DO THAT.
DON'T GIVE IN TO THE PAIN...
I CAN DO THIS...I HAVE TO DO THIS... UNHHHHHH
NO ONE WAS THERE. I GUESS WE CLEARED THEM ALL--
CONNER!

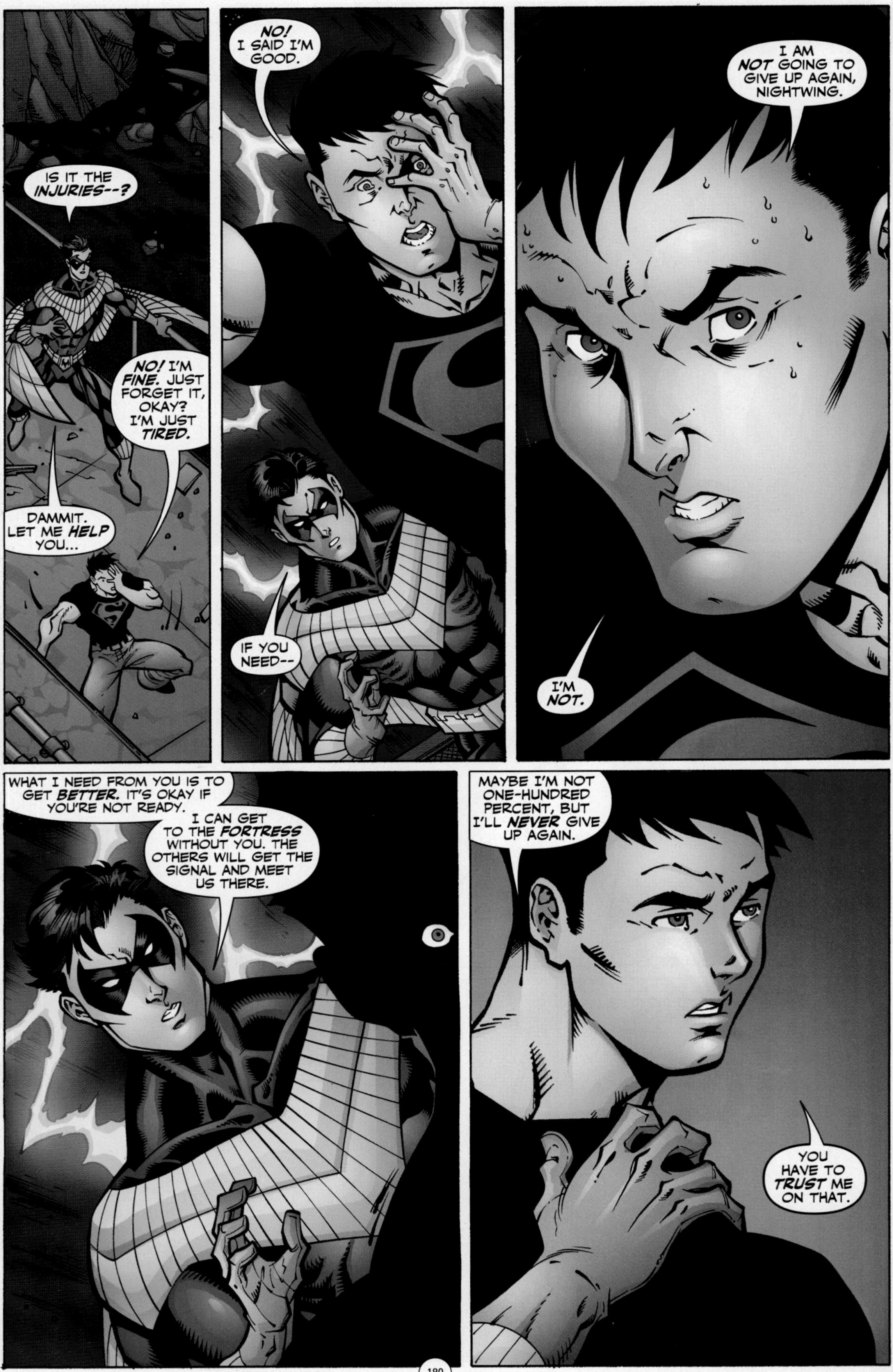
IS IT THE INJURIES--?
NO! I'M FINE. JUST FORGET IT, OKAY? I'M JUST TIRED.
DAMMIT. LET ME HELP YOU...
NO! I SAID I'M GOOD.
IF YOU NEED--
I AM NOT GOING TO GIVE UP AGAIN, NIGHTWING.
I'M NOT.
WHAT I NEED FROM YOU IS TO GET BETTER. IT'S OKAY IF YOU'RE NOT READY.
I CAN GET TO THE FORTRESS WITHOUT YOU. THE OTHERS WILL GET THE SIGNAL AND MEET US THERE.
MAYBE I'M NOT ONE-HUNDRED PERCENT, BUT I'LL NEVER GIVE UP AGAIN.
YOU HAVE TO TRUST ME ON THAT.

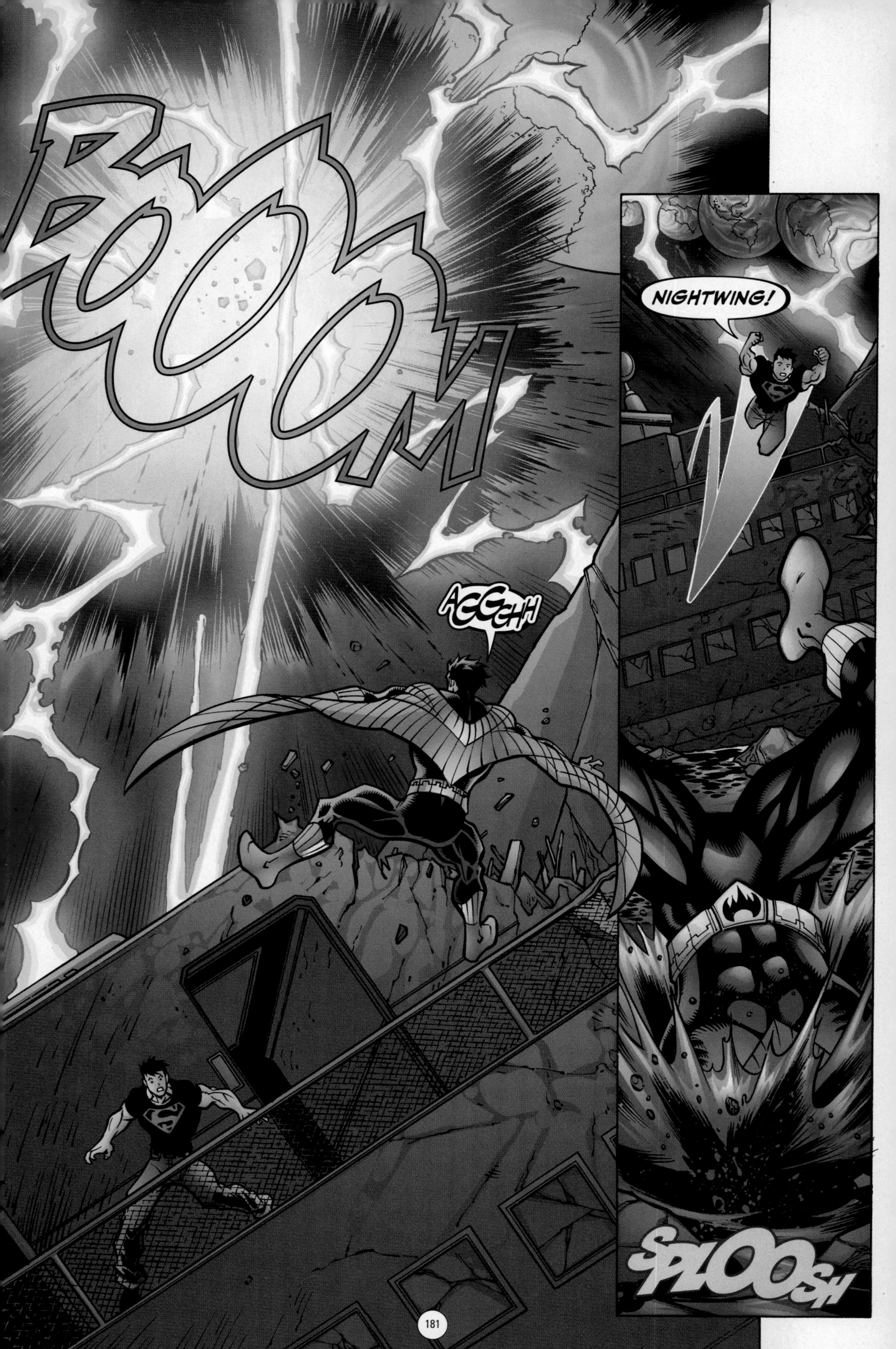
BOOOM
AGGGHH
NIGHTWING!
SPLOOSH

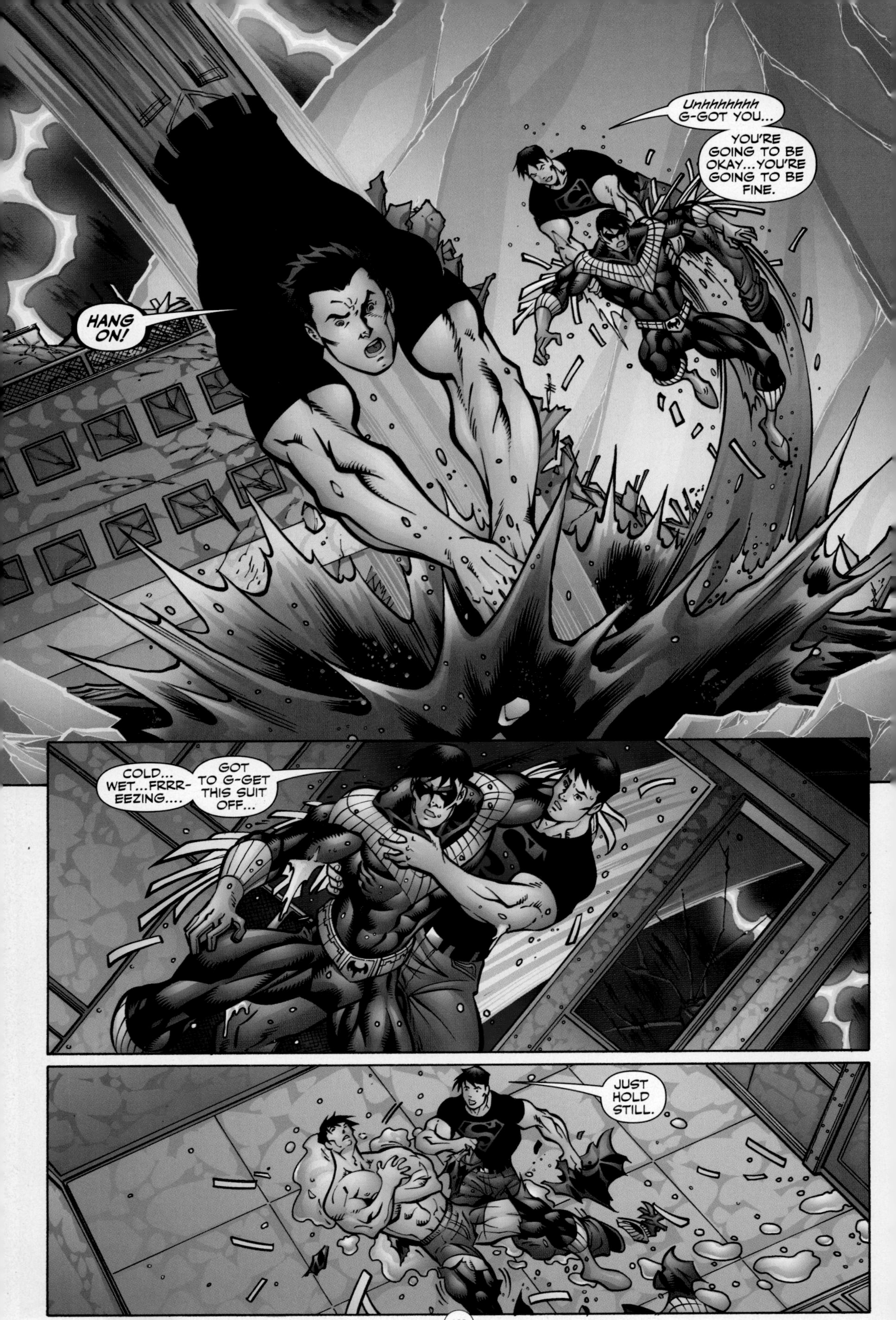
Unhhhhhhh G-GOT YOU...
YOU'RE GOING TO BE OKAY...YOU'RE GOING TO BE FINE.
HANG ON!
COLD... WET...FRRR-EEZING....
GOT TO G-GET THIS SUIT OFF...
JUST HOLD STILL.

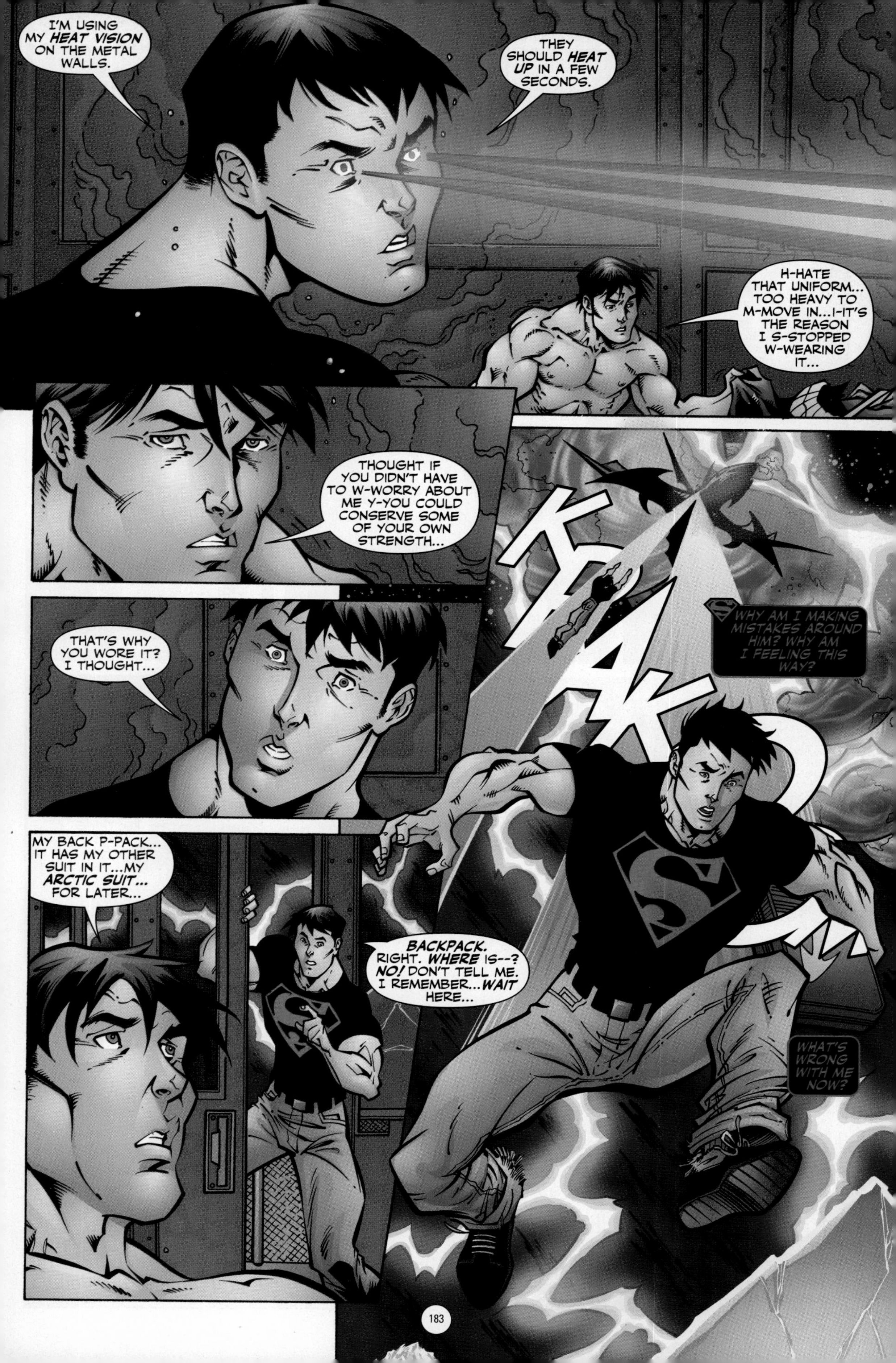
I'M USING MY HEAT VISION ON THE METAL WALLS.
THEY SHOULD HEAT UP IN A FEW SECONDS.
H-HATE THAT UNIFORM... TOO HEAVY TO M-MOVE IN...I-IT'S THE REASON I S-STOPPED W-WEARING IT...
THOUGHT IF YOU DIDN'T HAVE TO W-WORRY ABOUT ME Y-YOU COULD CONSERVE SOME OF YOUR OWN STRENGTH...
THAT'S WHY YOU WORE IT? I THOUGHT...
MY BACK P-PACK... IT HAS MY OTHER SUIT IN IT...MY ARCTIC SUIT... FOR LATER...
BACKPACK. RIGHT. WHERE IS--? NO! DON'T TELL ME. I REMEMBER...WAIT HERE...
KRAKOOM
WHY AM I MAKING MISTAKES AROUND HIM? WHY AM I FEELING THIS WAY?
WHAT'S WRONG WITH ME NOW?

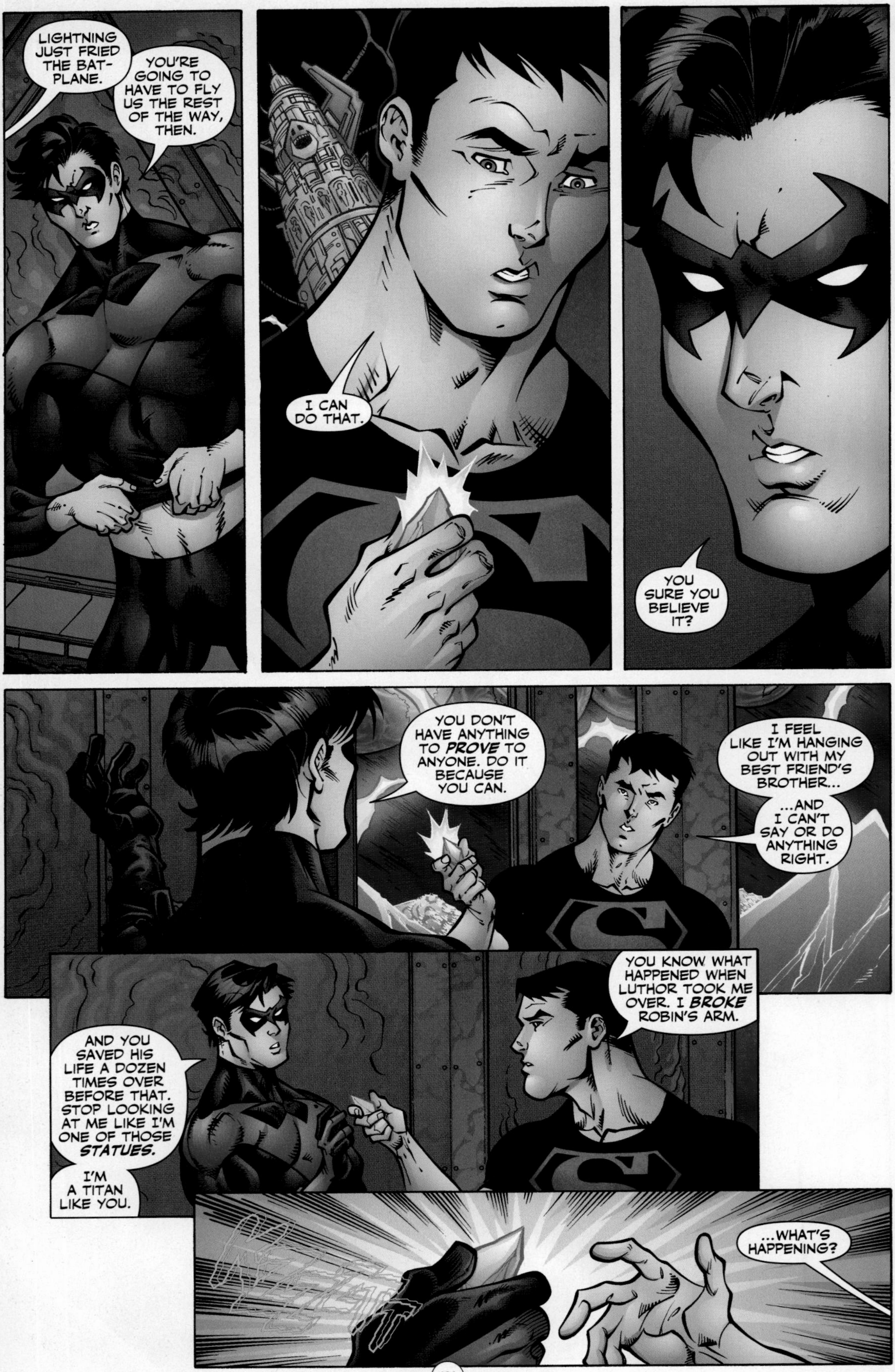
LIGHTNING JUST FRIED THE BAT-PLANE.
YOU'RE GOING TO HAVE TO FLY US THE REST OF THE WAY, THEN.
I CAN DO THAT.
YOU SURE YOU BELIEVE IT?
YOU DON'T HAVE ANYTHING TO *PROVE* TO ANYONE. DO IT BECAUSE YOU CAN.
I FEEL LIKE I'M HANGING OUT WITH MY BEST FRIEND'S BROTHER...
...AND I CAN'T SAY OR DO ANYTHING RIGHT.
YOU KNOW WHAT HAPPENED WHEN LUTHOR TOOK ME OVER. I *BROKE* ROBIN'S ARM.
AND YOU SAVED HIS LIFE A DOZEN TIMES OVER BEFORE THAT. STOP LOOKING AT ME LIKE I'M ONE OF THOSE *STATUES.*
I'M A TITAN LIKE YOU.
...WHAT'S HAPPENING?

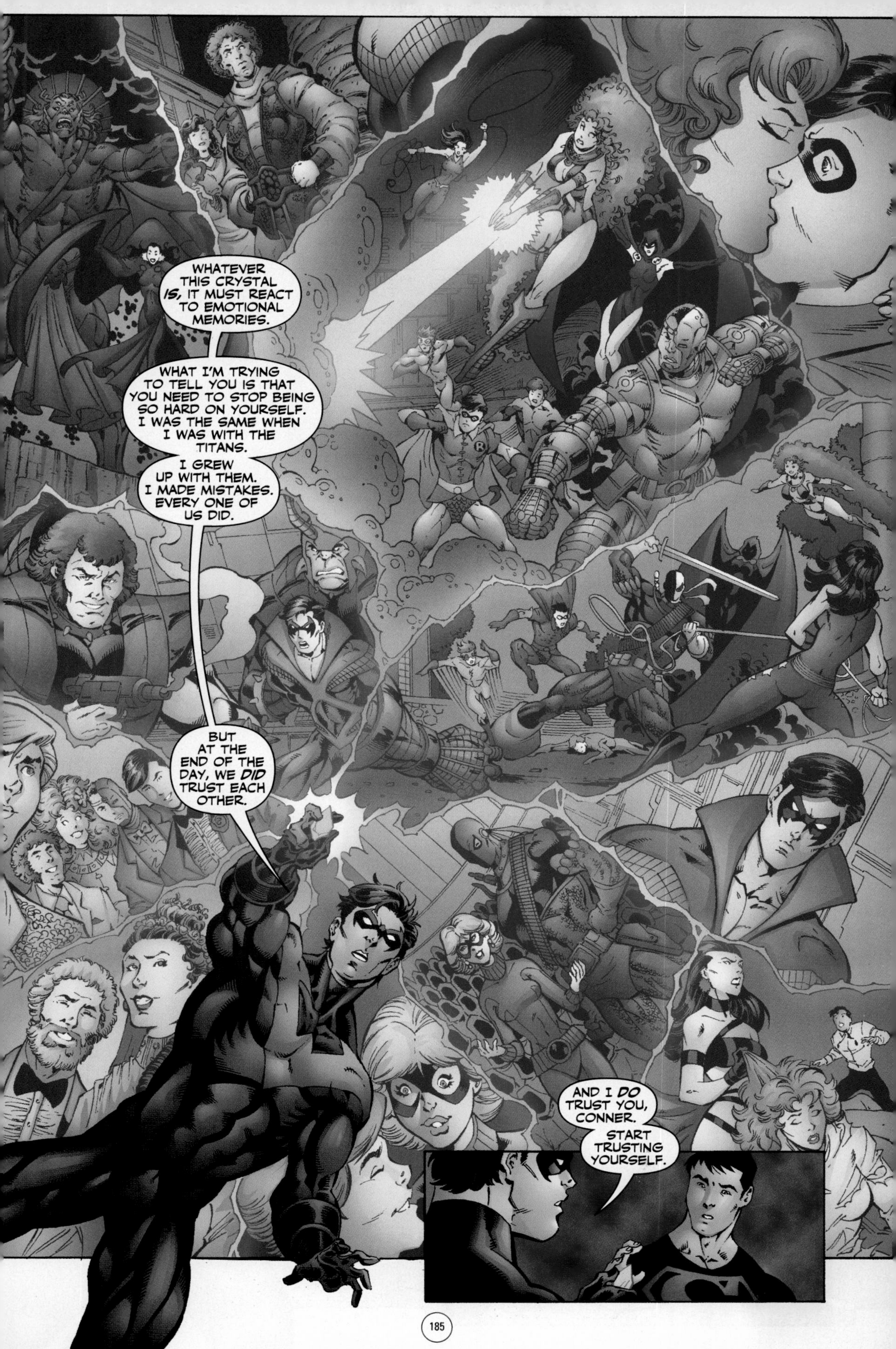
WHATEVER THIS CRYSTAL *IS,* IT MUST REACT TO EMOTIONAL MEMORIES.
WHAT I'M TRYING TO TELL YOU IS THAT YOU NEED TO STOP BEING SO HARD ON YOURSELF. I WAS THE SAME WHEN I WAS WITH THE TITANS.
I GREW UP WITH THEM. I MADE MISTAKES. EVERY ONE OF US DID.
BUT AT THE END OF THE DAY, WE *DID* TRUST EACH OTHER.
AND I *DO* TRUST YOU, CONNER.
START TRUSTING YOURSELF.

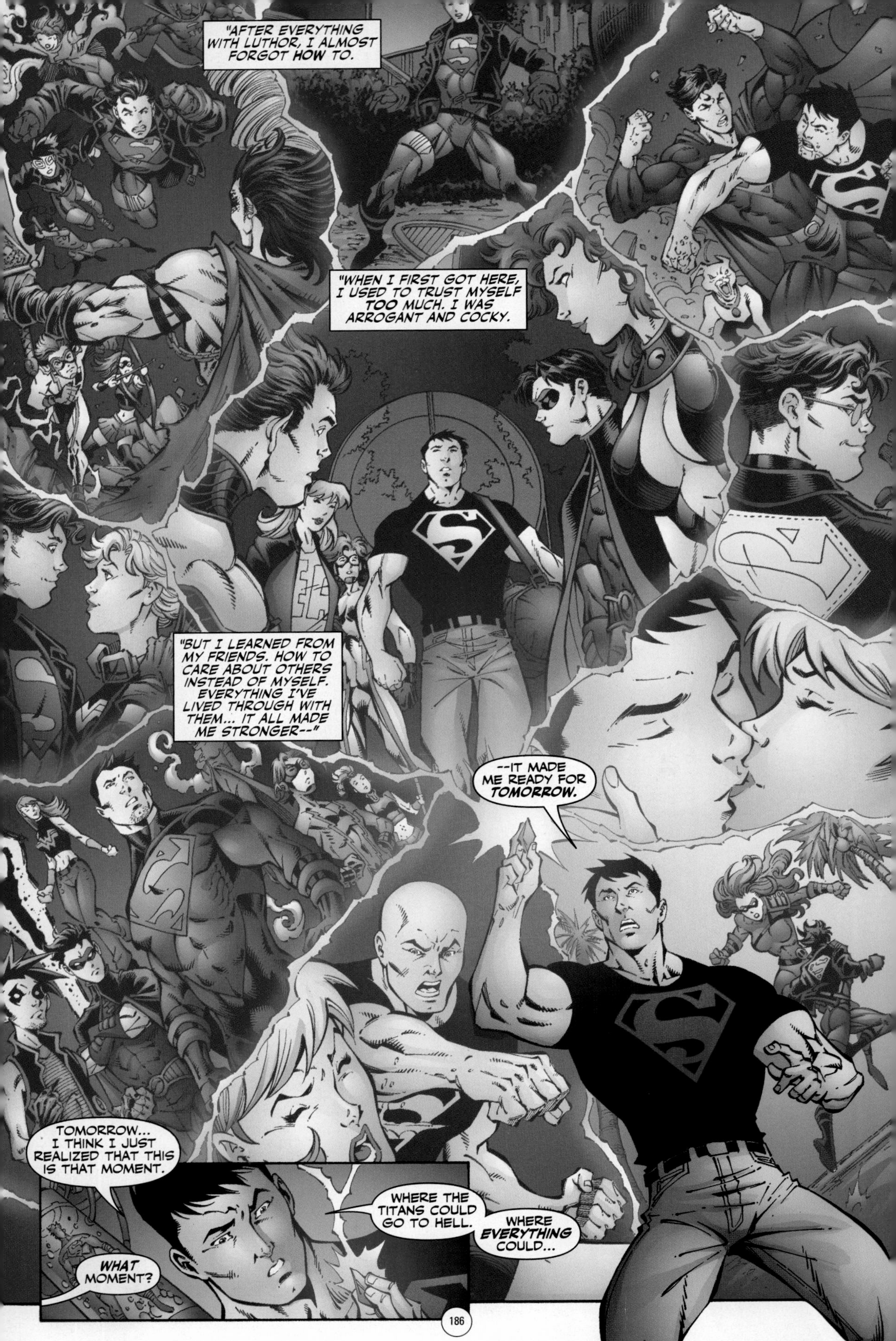
"AFTER EVERYTHING WITH LUTHOR, I ALMOST FORGOT HOW TO.
"WHEN I FIRST GOT HERE, I USED TO TRUST MYSELF TOO MUCH. I WAS ARROGANT AND COCKY.
"BUT I LEARNED FROM MY FRIENDS. HOW TO CARE ABOUT OTHERS INSTEAD OF MYSELF. EVERYTHING I'VE LIVED THROUGH WITH THEM... IT ALL MADE ME STRONGER--"
--IT MADE ME READY FOR TOMORROW.
TOMORROW... I THINK I JUST REALIZED THAT THIS IS THAT MOMENT.
WHAT MOMENT?
WHERE THE TITANS COULD GO TO HELL.
WHERE EVERYTHING COULD...

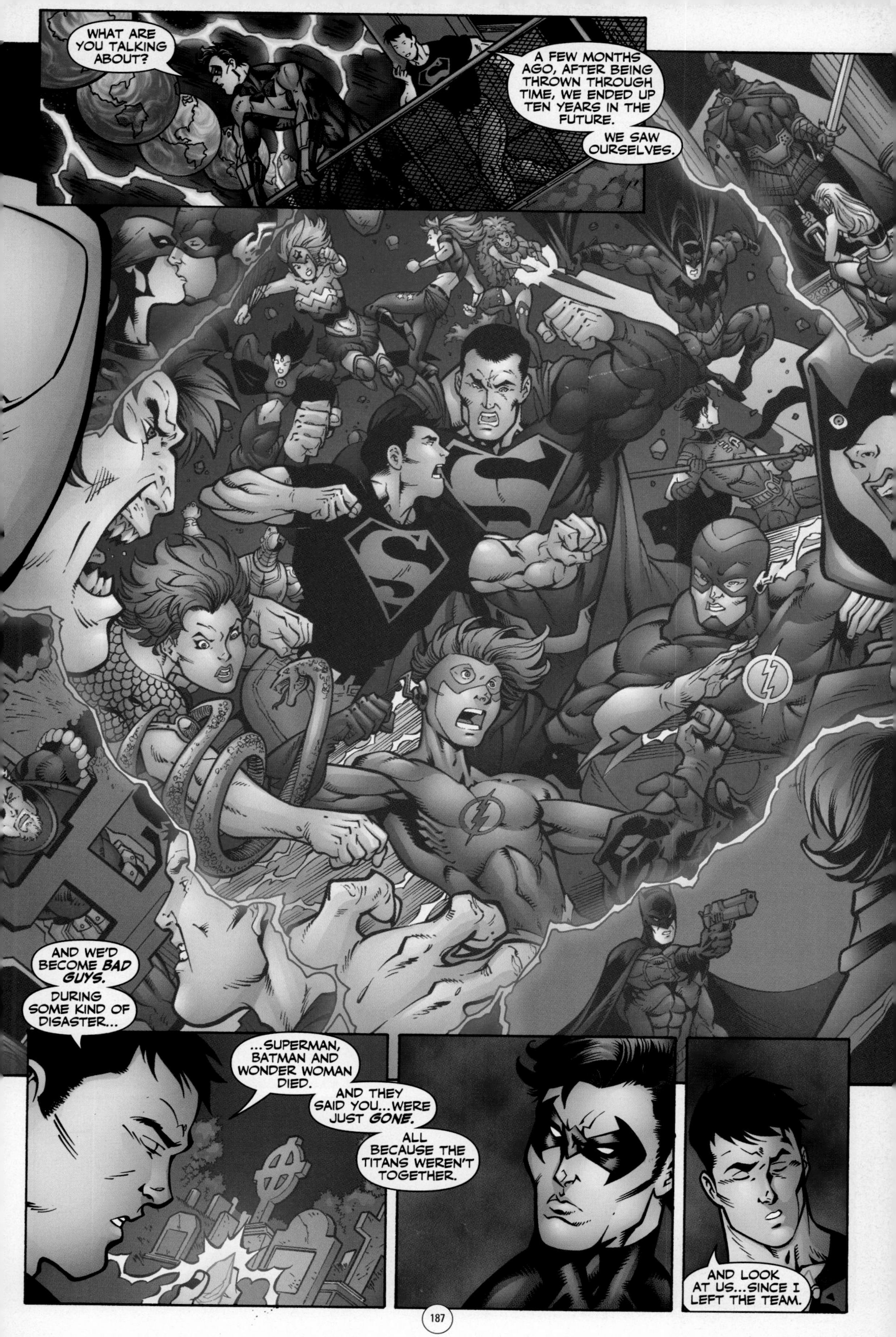

WHAT ARE YOU TALKING ABOUT?
A FEW MONTHS AGO, AFTER BEING THROWN THROUGH TIME, WE ENDED UP TEN YEARS IN THE FUTURE.
WE SAW OURSELVES.
AND WE'D BECOME *BAD GUYS.*
DURING SOME KIND OF DISASTER...
...SUPERMAN, BATMAN AND WONDER WOMAN DIED.
AND THEY SAID YOU...WERE JUST *GONE.*
ALL BECAUSE THE TITANS WEREN'T TOGETHER.
AND LOOK AT US...SINCE I LEFT THE TEAM.

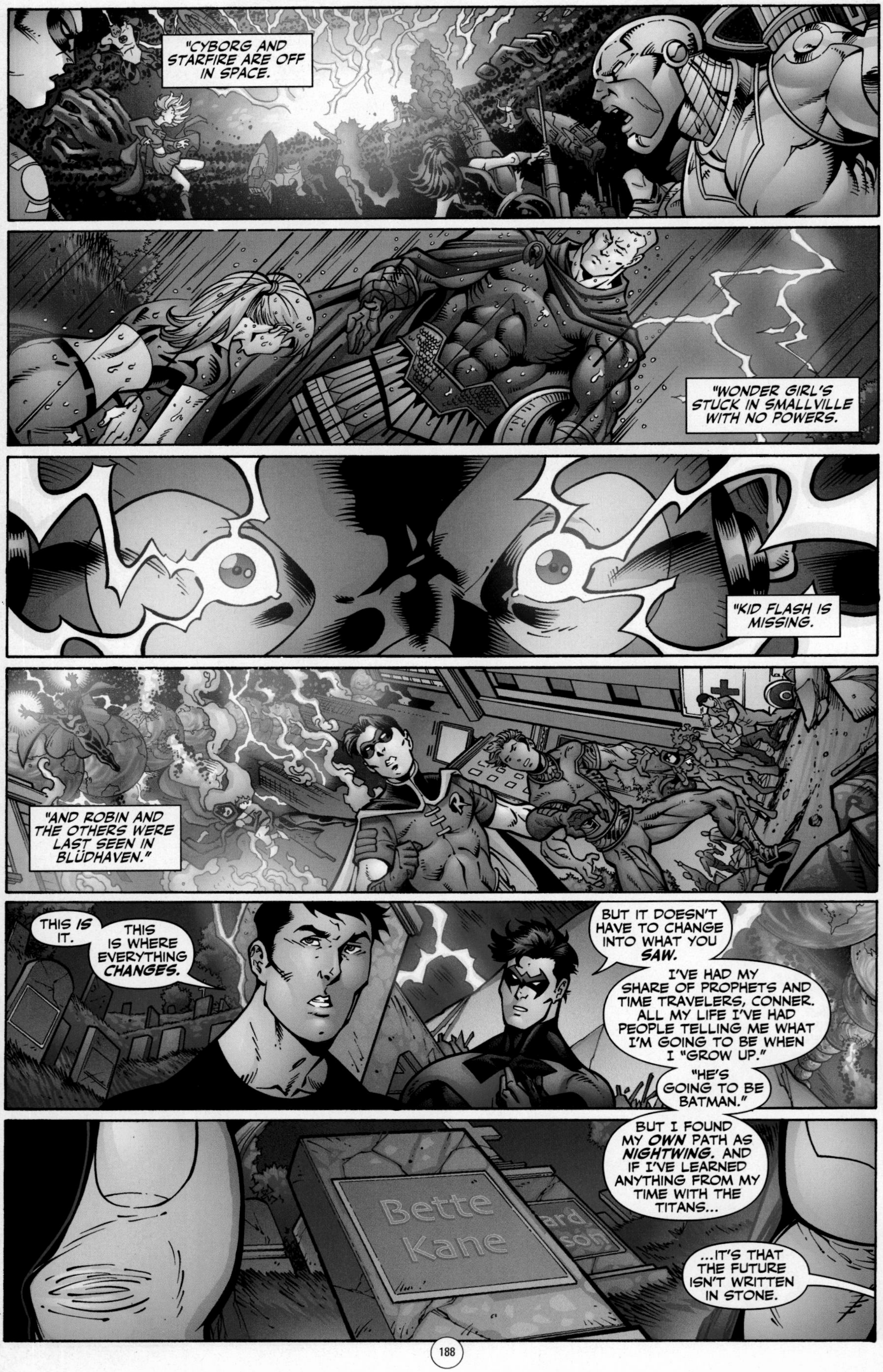
"CYBORG AND STARFIRE ARE OFF IN SPACE.
"WONDER GIRL'S STUCK IN SMALLVILLE WITH NO POWERS.
"KID FLASH IS MISSING.
"AND ROBIN AND THE OTHERS WERE LAST SEEN IN BLÜDHAVEN."
THIS *IS* IT.
THIS IS WHERE EVERYTHING *CHANGES.*
BUT IT DOESN'T HAVE TO CHANGE INTO WHAT YOU *SAW.*
I'VE HAD MY SHARE OF PROPHETS AND TIME TRAVELERS, CONNER. ALL MY LIFE I'VE HAD PEOPLE TELLING ME WHAT I'M GOING TO BE WHEN I "GROW UP."
"HE'S GOING TO BE BATMAN."
BUT I FOUND MY *OWN* PATH AS *NIGHTWING.* AND IF I'VE LEARNED ANYTHING FROM MY TIME WITH THE TITANS...
Bette Kane
...IT'S THAT THE FUTURE ISN'T WRITTEN IN STONE.

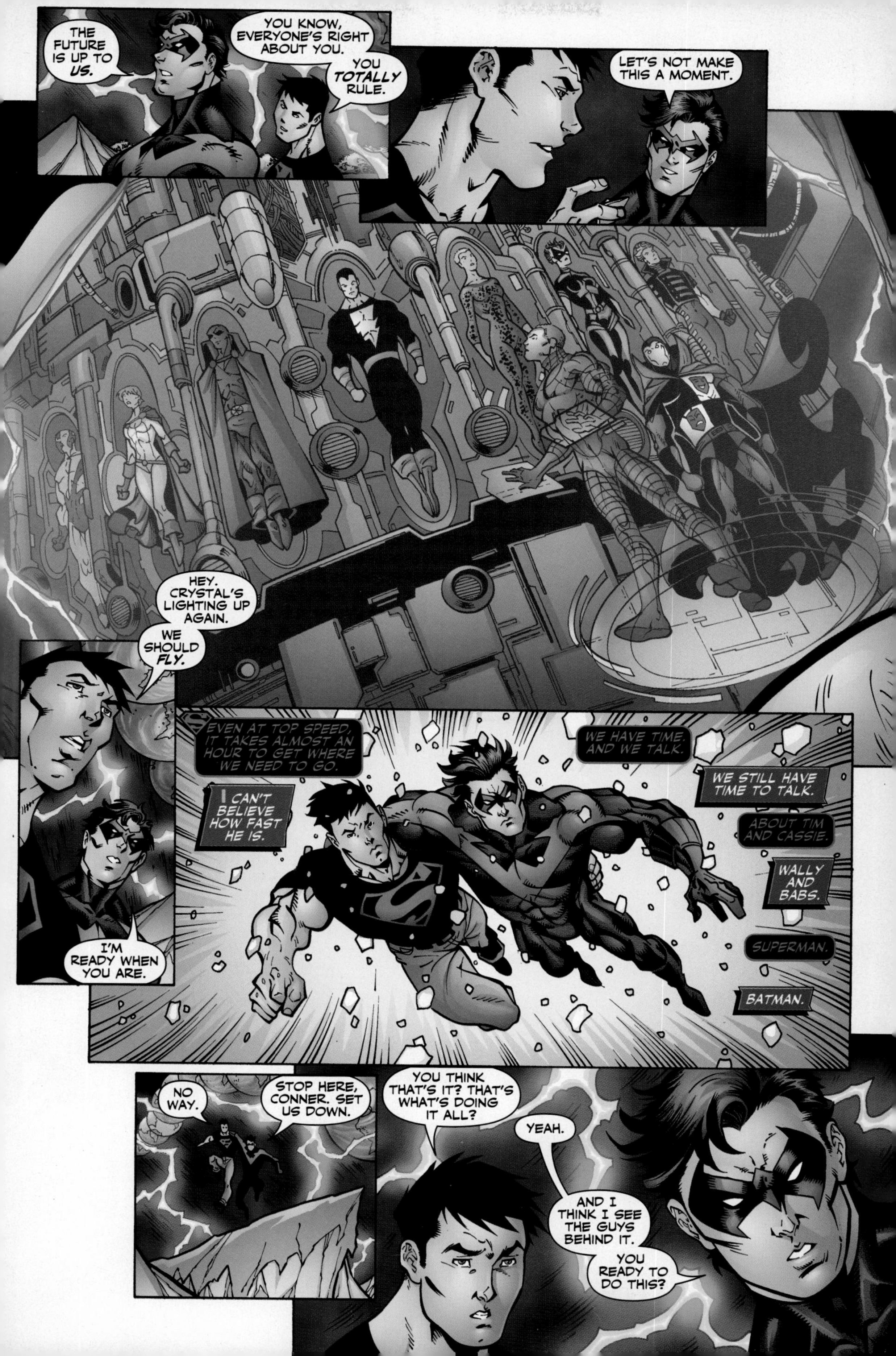
THE FUTURE IS UP TO *US*.
YOU KNOW, EVERYONE'S RIGHT ABOUT YOU.
YOU *TOTALLY* RULE.
LET'S NOT MAKE THIS A MOMENT.
HEY. CRYSTAL'S LIGHTING UP AGAIN.
WE SHOULD *FLY*.
I'M READY WHEN YOU ARE.
EVEN AT TOP SPEED, IT TAKES ALMOST AN HOUR TO GET WHERE WE NEED TO GO.
I CAN'T BELIEVE HOW FAST HE IS.
WE HAVE TIME. AND WE TALK.
WE STILL HAVE TIME TO TALK.
ABOUT TIM AND CASSIE.
WALLY AND BABS.
SUPERMAN.
BATMAN.
NO WAY.
STOP HERE, CONNER. SET US DOWN.
YOU THINK THAT'S IT? THAT'S WHAT'S DOING IT ALL?
YEAH.
AND I THINK I SEE THE GUYS BEHIND IT.
YOU READY TO DO THIS?

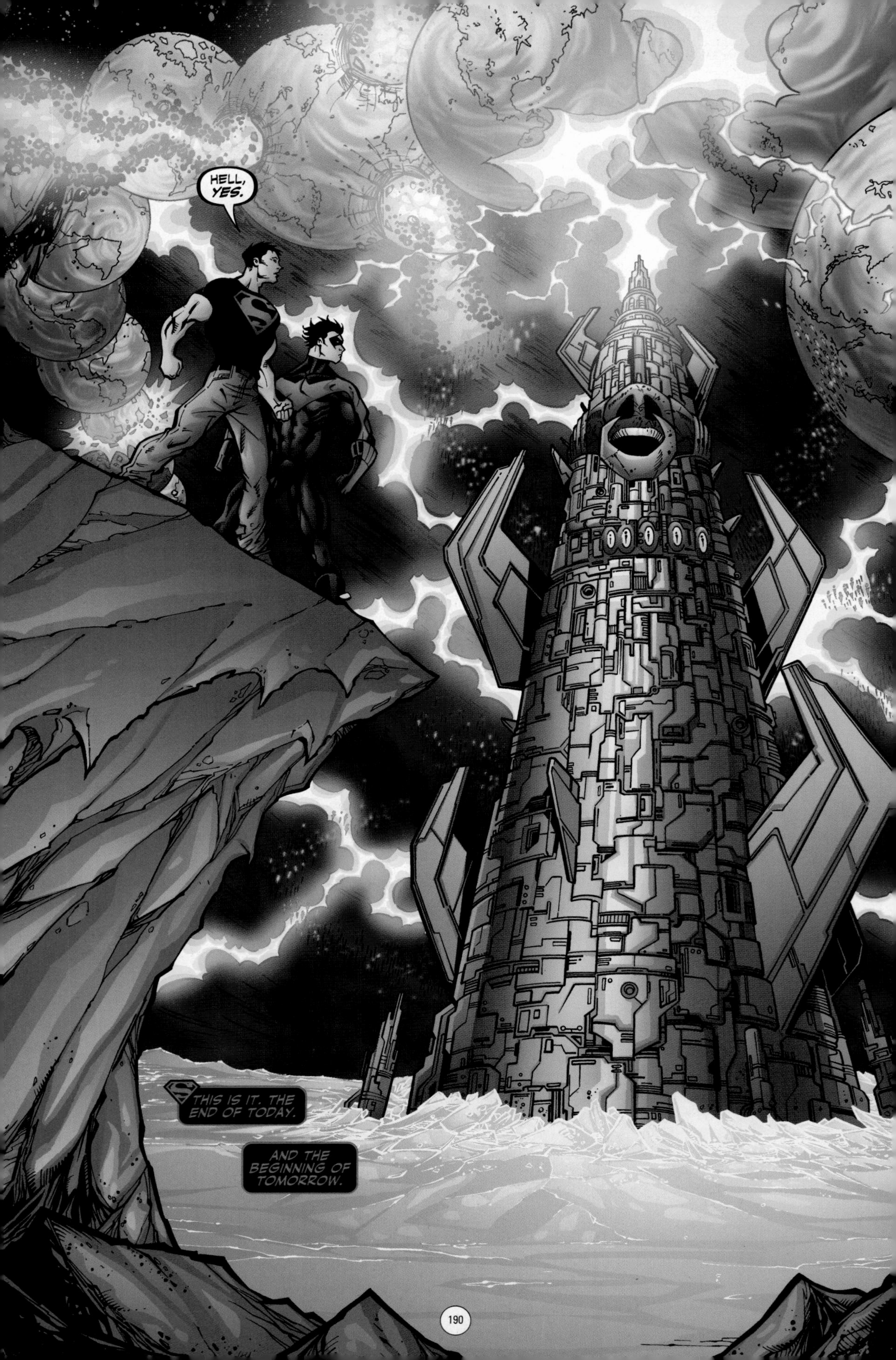
HELL, YES.
THIS IS IT. THE END OF TODAY.
AND THE BEGINNING OF TOMORROW.

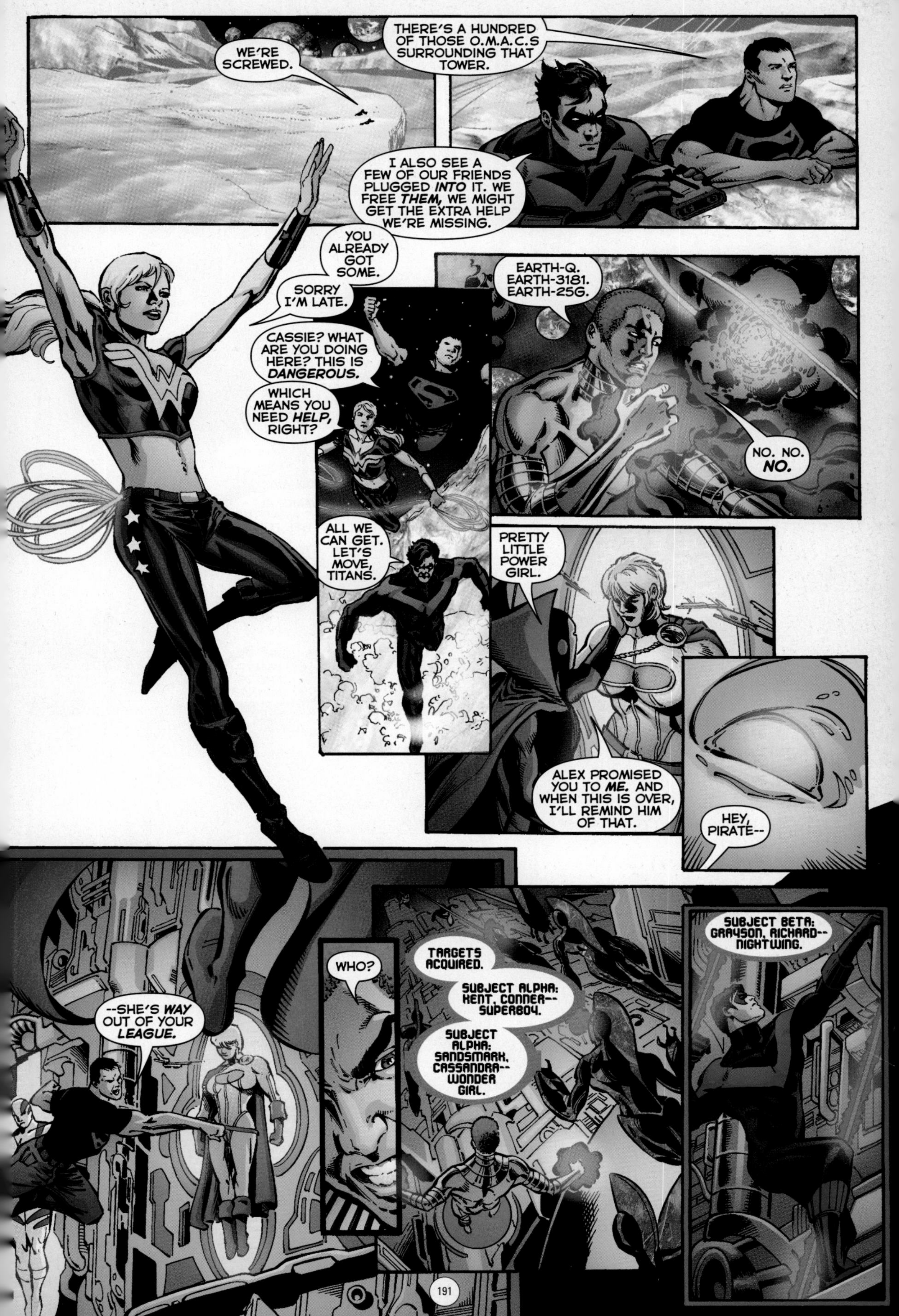
WE'RE SCREWED.
THERE'S A HUNDRED OF THOSE O.M.A.C.S SURROUNDING THAT TOWER.
I ALSO SEE A FEW OF OUR FRIENDS PLUGGED INTO IT. WE FREE THEM, WE MIGHT GET THE EXTRA HELP WE'RE MISSING.
YOU ALREADY GOT SOME.
SORRY I'M LATE.
CASSIE? WHAT ARE YOU DOING HERE? THIS IS DANGEROUS.
WHICH MEANS YOU NEED HELP, RIGHT?
ALL WE CAN GET. LET'S MOVE, TITANS.
EARTH-Q. EARTH-3181. EARTH-25G.
NO. NO. NO.
PRETTY LITTLE POWER GIRL.
ALEX PROMISED YOU TO ME. AND WHEN THIS IS OVER, I'LL REMIND HIM OF THAT.
HEY, PIRATE--
--SHE'S WAY OUT OF YOUR LEAGUE.
WHO?
TARGETS ACQUIRED.
SUBJECT ALPHA: KENT, CONNER-- SUPERBOY.
SUBJECT ALPHA: SANDSMARK, CASSANDRA-- WONDER GIRL.
SUBJECT BETA: GRAYSON, RICHARD-- NIGHTWING.

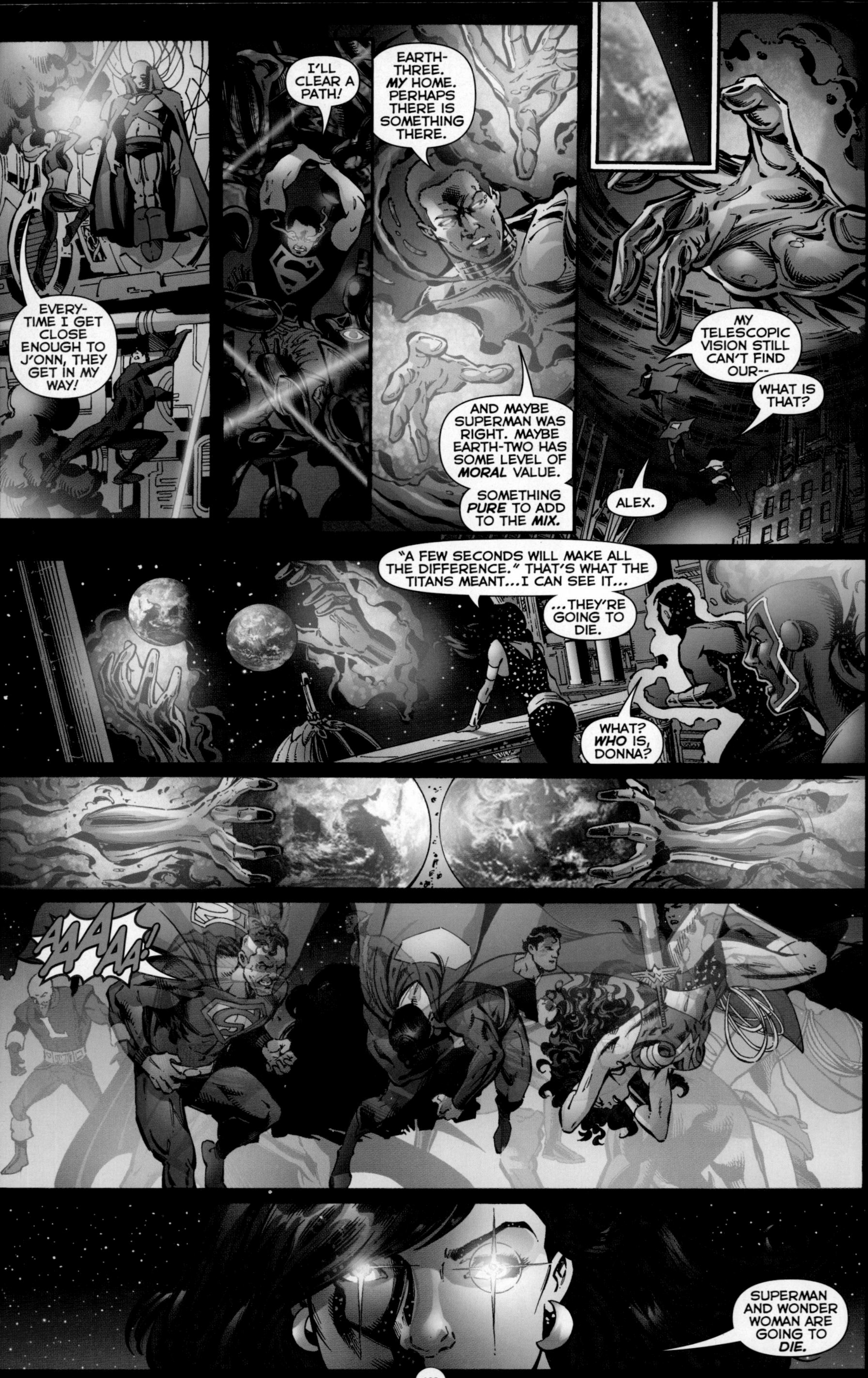
EVERY-TIME I GET CLOSE ENOUGH TO J'ONN, THEY GET IN MY WAY!
I'LL CLEAR A PATH!
EARTH-THREE. MY HOME. PERHAPS THERE IS SOMETHING THERE.
AND MAYBE SUPERMAN WAS RIGHT. MAYBE EARTH-TWO HAS SOME LEVEL OF MORAL VALUE.
SOMETHING PURE TO ADD TO THE MIX.
MY TELESCOPIC VISION STILL CAN'T FIND OUR--
WHAT IS THAT?
ALEX.
"A FEW SECONDS WILL MAKE ALL THE DIFFERENCE." THAT'S WHAT THE TITANS MEANT... I CAN SEE IT...
...THEY'RE GOING TO DIE.
WHAT? WHO IS, DONNA?
AAAAAA!
SUPERMAN AND WONDER WOMAN ARE GOING TO DIE.

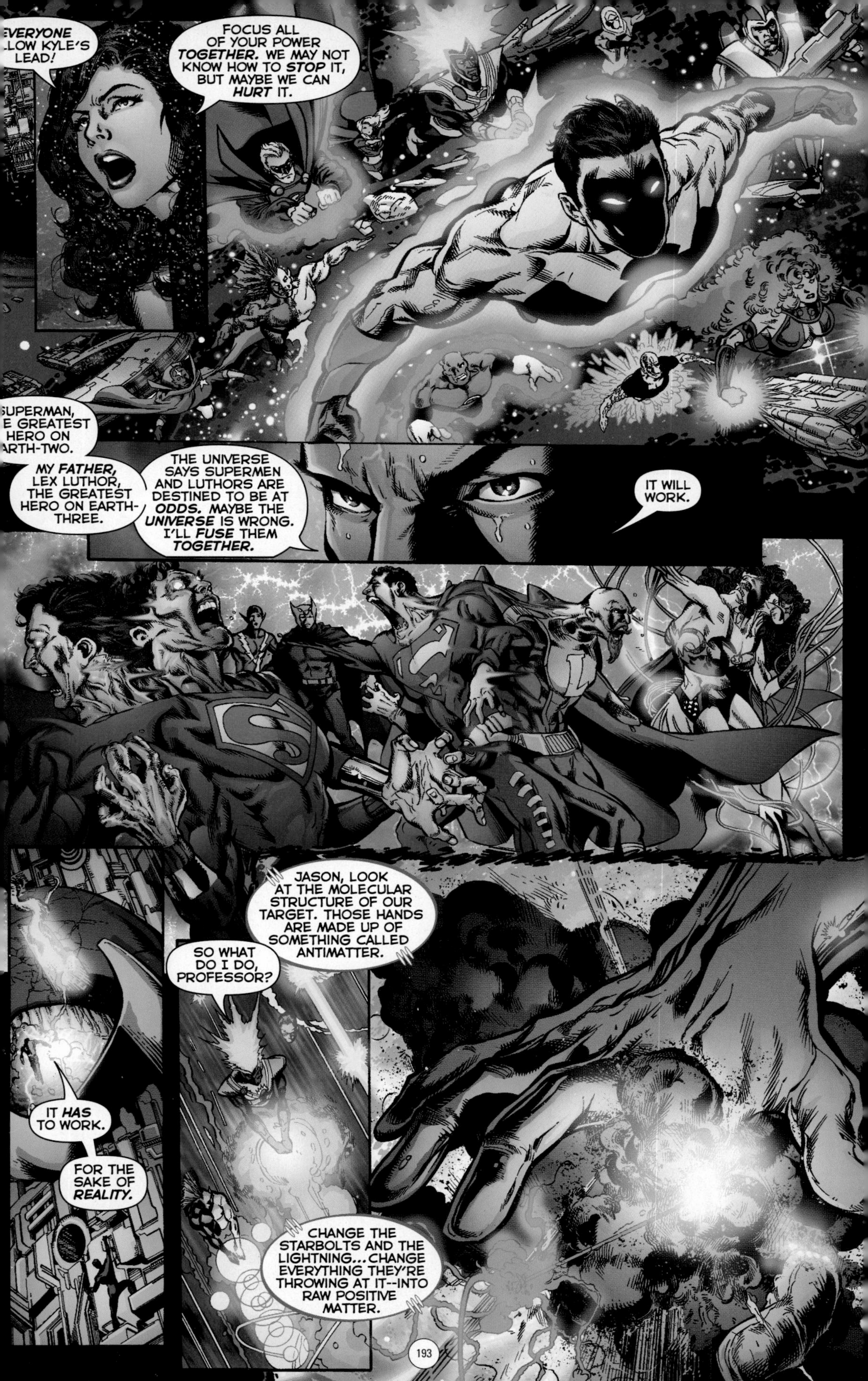

EVERYONE LLOW KYLE'S LEAD!
FOCUS ALL OF YOUR POWER TOGETHER. WE MAY NOT KNOW HOW TO STOP IT, BUT MAYBE WE CAN HURT IT.
SUPERMAN, E GREATEST HERO ON ARTH-TWO.
MY FATHER, LEX LUTHOR, THE GREATEST HERO ON EARTH-THREE.
THE UNIVERSE SAYS SUPERMEN AND LUTHORS ARE DESTINED TO BE AT ODDS. MAYBE THE UNIVERSE IS WRONG. I'LL FUSE THEM TOGETHER.
IT WILL WORK.
JASON, LOOK AT THE MOLECULAR STRUCTURE OF OUR TARGET. THOSE HANDS ARE MADE UP OF SOMETHING CALLED ANTIMATTER.
SO WHAT DO I DO, PROFESSOR?
IT HAS TO WORK.
FOR THE SAKE OF REALITY.
CHANGE THE STARBOLTS AND THE LIGHTNING... CHANGE EVERYTHING THEY'RE THROWING AT IT--INTO RAW POSITIVE MATTER.

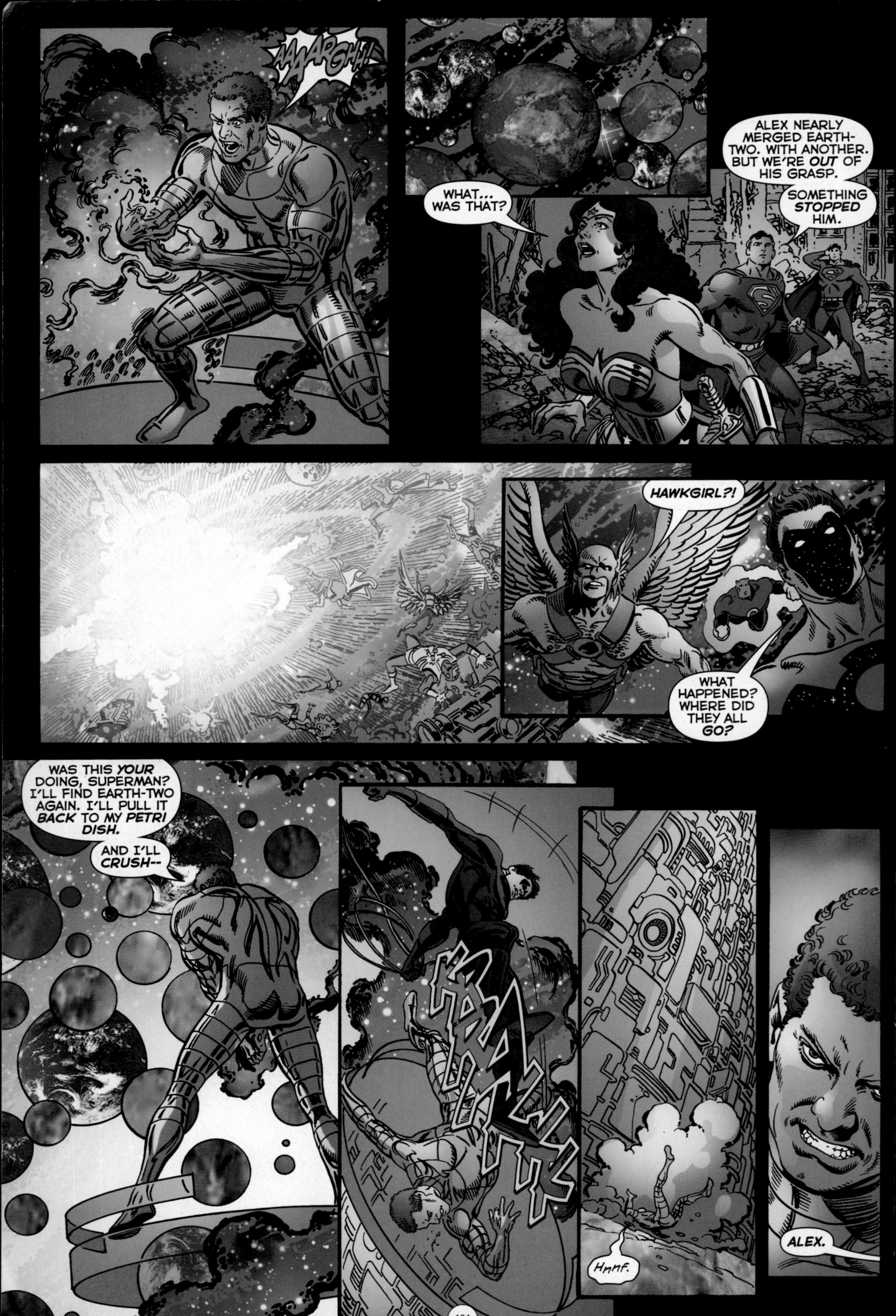
AAAARGH!
WHAT... WAS THAT?
ALEX NEARLY MERGED EARTH-TWO. WITH ANOTHER. BUT WE'RE OUT OF HIS GRASP.
SOMETHING STOPPED HIM.
HAWKGIRL?!
WHAT HAPPENED? WHERE DID THEY ALL GO?
WAS THIS YOUR DOING, SUPERMAN? I'LL FIND EARTH-TWO AGAIN. I'LL PULL IT BACK TO MY PETRI DISH.
AND I'LL CRUSH--
Hnnf.
ALEX.

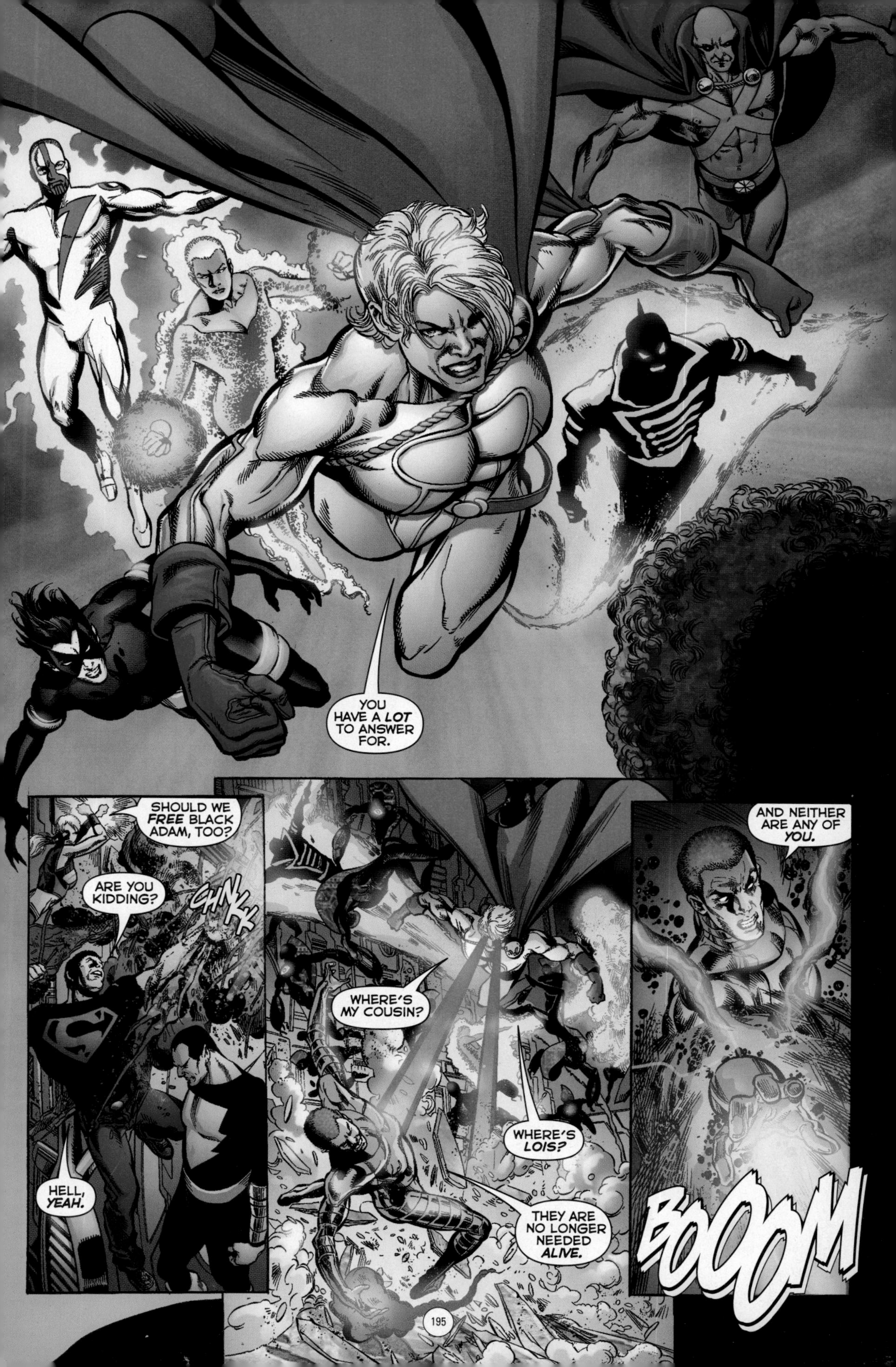
YOU HAVE A LOT TO ANSWER FOR.
SHOULD WE FREE BLACK ADAM, TOO?
ARE YOU KIDDING?
CHNKK
HELL, YEAH.
WHERE'S MY COUSIN?
WHERE'S LOIS?
THEY ARE NO LONGER NEEDED ALIVE.
AND NEITHER ARE ANY OF YOU.
BOOOOM

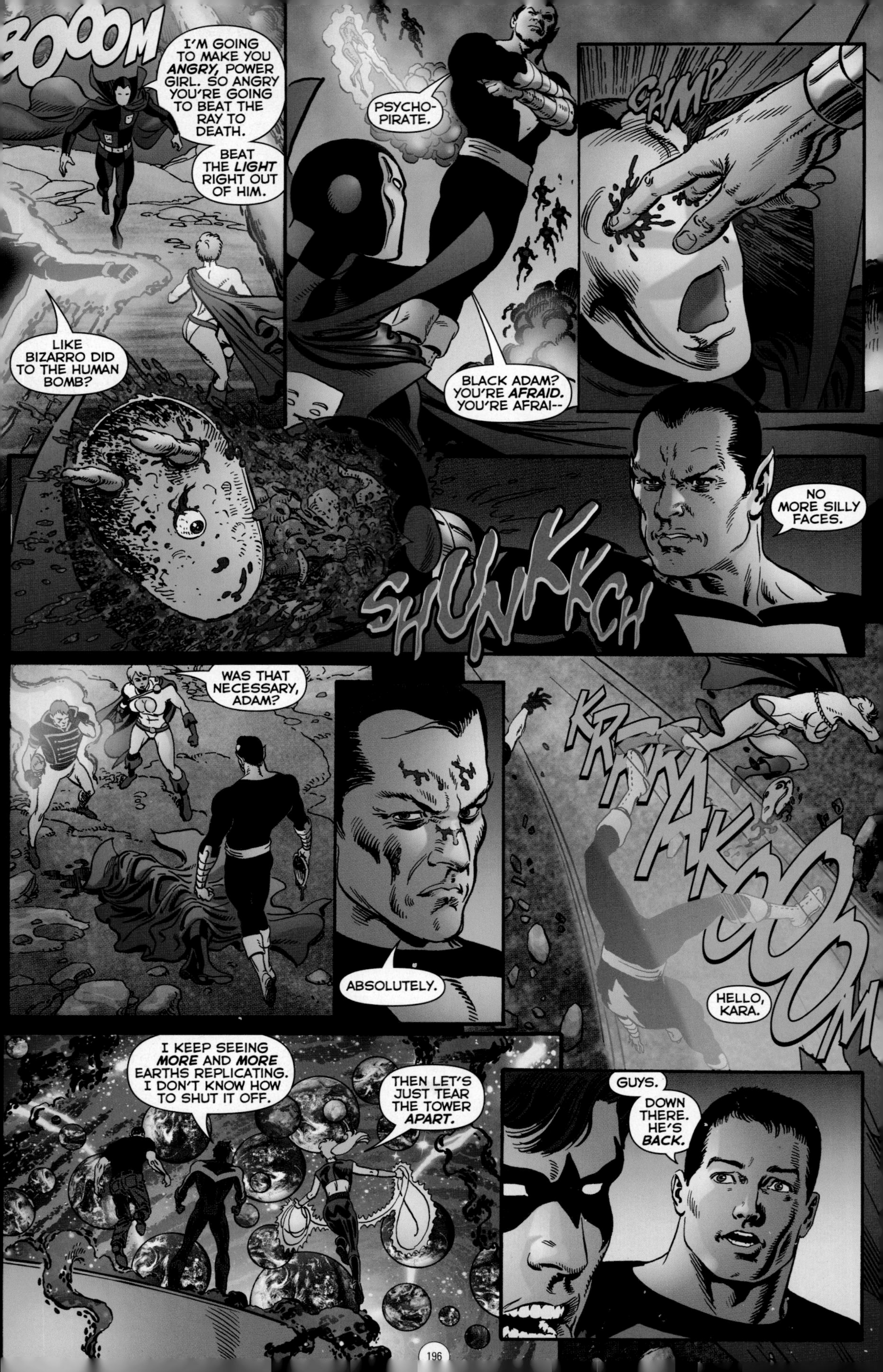
BOOOM
I'M GOING TO MAKE YOU ANGRY, POWER GIRL. SO ANGRY YOU'RE GOING TO BEAT THE RAY TO DEATH.
BEAT THE LIGHT RIGHT OUT OF HIM.
LIKE BIZARRO DID TO THE HUMAN BOMB?
PSYCHO-PIRATE.
BLACK ADAM? YOU'RE AFRAID. YOU'RE AFRAI--
CHMP
NO MORE SILLY FACES.
SHUNKKCH
WAS THAT NECESSARY, ADAM?
ABSOLUTELY.
HELLO, KARA.
I KEEP SEEING MORE AND MORE EARTHS REPLICATING. I DON'T KNOW HOW TO SHUT IT OFF.
THEN LET'S JUST TEAR THE TOWER APART.
GUYS.
DOWN THERE. HE'S BACK.

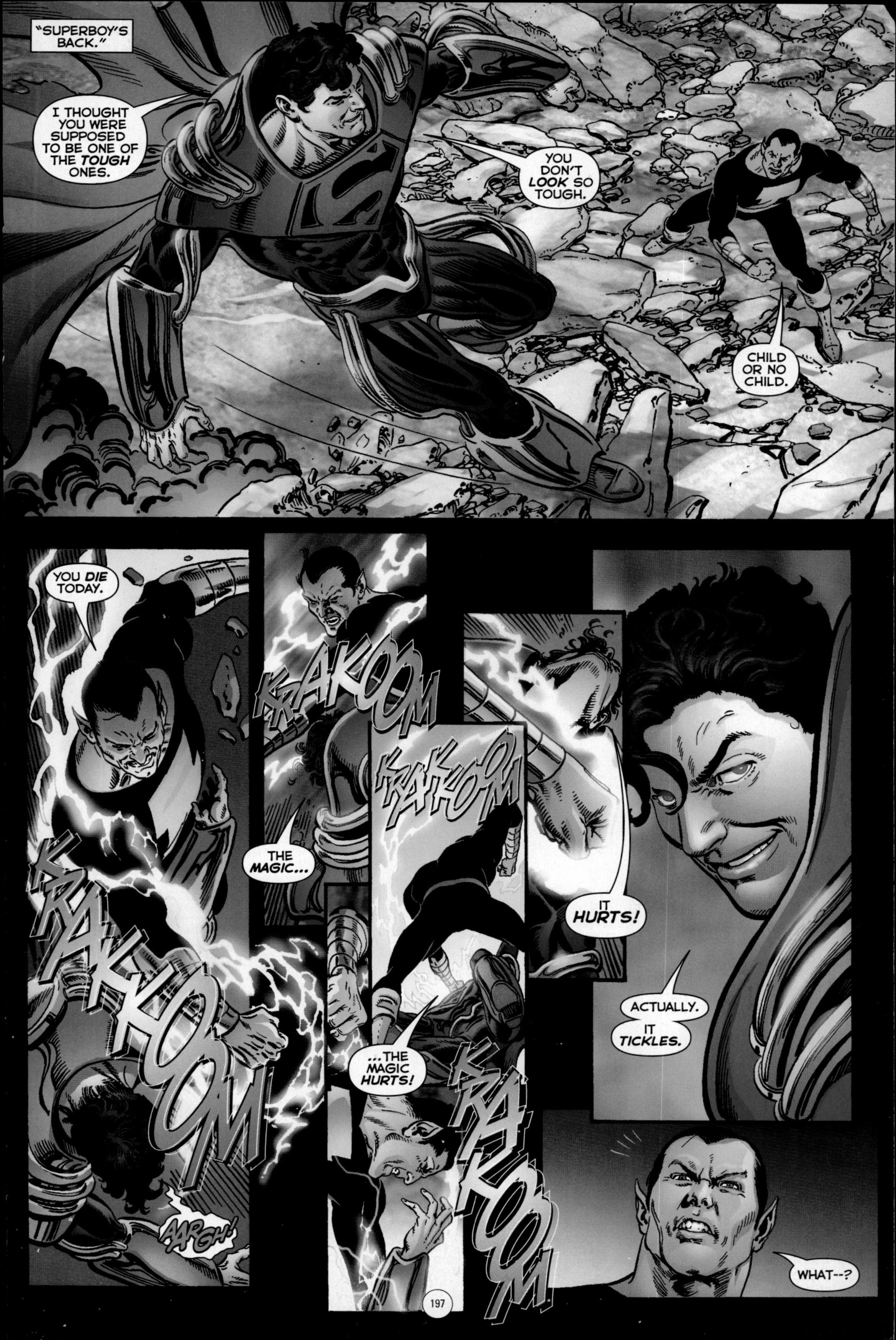
"SUPERBOY'S BACK."
I THOUGHT YOU WERE SUPPOSED TO BE ONE OF THE *TOUGH* ONES.
YOU DON'T *LOOK* SO TOUGH.
CHILD OR NO CHILD.
YOU *DIE* TODAY.
KRAKOOM
AARGH!
THE *MAGIC*...
KRAKOOM
KRAKOOM
...THE MAGIC *HURTS*!
KRAKOOM
IT *HURTS*!
ACTUALLY. IT *TICKLES*.
WHAT--?

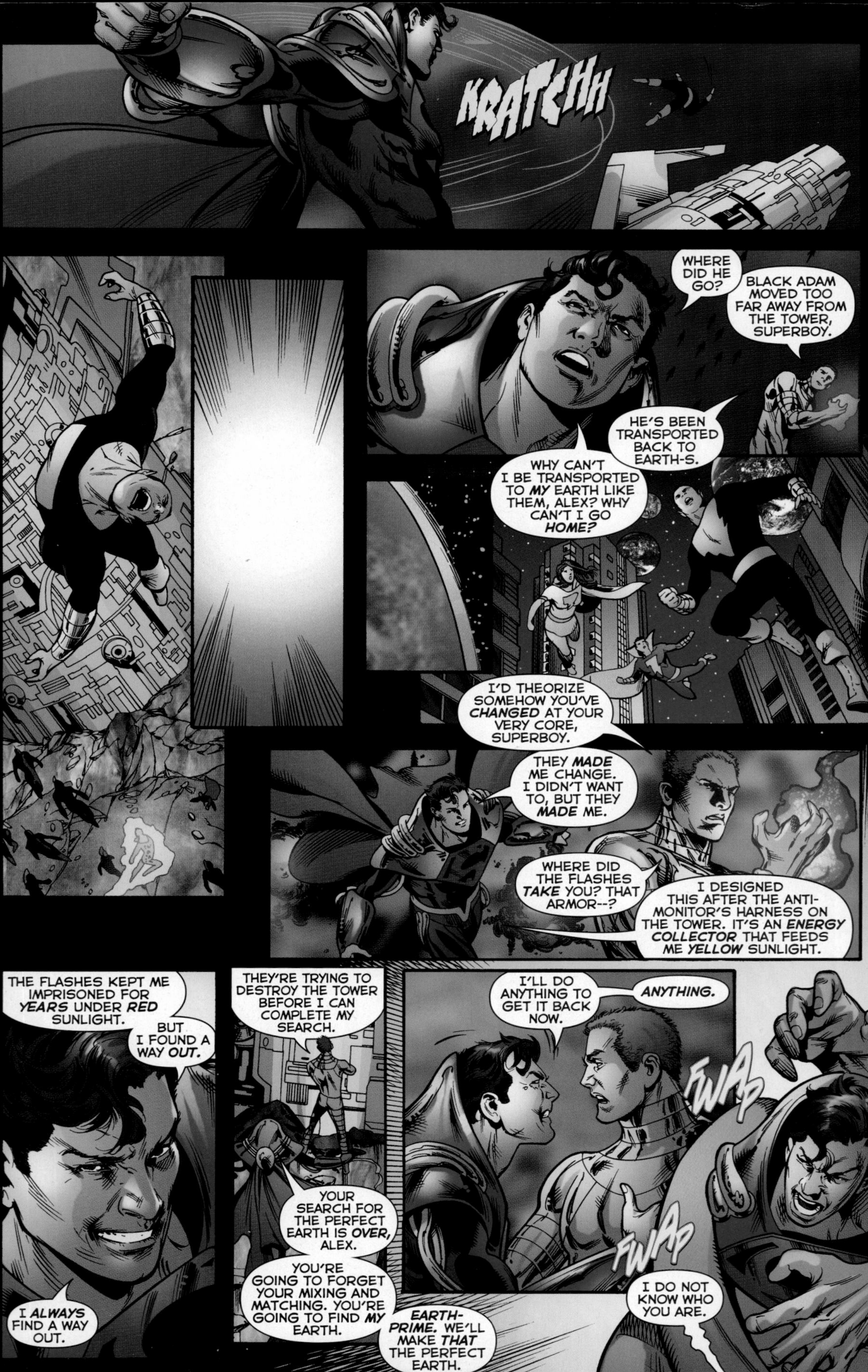

KRATCHH
WHERE DID HE GO?
BLACK ADAM MOVED TOO FAR AWAY FROM THE TOWER, SUPERBOY.
HE'S BEEN TRANSPORTED BACK TO EARTH-S.
WHY CAN'T I BE TRANSPORTED TO *MY* EARTH LIKE THEM, ALEX? WHY CAN'T I GO *HOME?*
I'D THEORIZE SOMEHOW YOU'VE *CHANGED* AT YOUR VERY CORE, SUPERBOY.
THEY *MADE* ME CHANGE. I DIDN'T WANT TO, BUT THEY *MADE* ME.
WHERE DID THE FLASHES *TAKE* YOU? THAT ARMOR--?
I DESIGNED THIS AFTER THE ANTI-MONITOR'S HARNESS ON THE TOWER. IT'S AN *ENERGY COLLECTOR* THAT FEEDS ME *YELLOW* SUNLIGHT.
THE FLASHES KEPT ME IMPRISONED FOR *YEARS* UNDER *RED* SUNLIGHT.
BUT I FOUND A WAY *OUT*.
I *ALWAYS* FIND A WAY OUT.
THEY'RE TRYING TO DESTROY THE TOWER BEFORE I CAN COMPLETE MY SEARCH.
YOUR SEARCH FOR THE PERFECT EARTH IS *OVER*, ALEX.
YOU'RE GOING TO FORGET YOUR MIXING AND MATCHING. YOU'RE GOING TO FIND *MY* EARTH.
EARTH-PRIME. WE'LL MAKE *THAT* THE PERFECT EARTH.
I'LL DO ANYTHING TO GET IT BACK NOW.
ANYTHING.
FWAP
FWAP
I DO NOT KNOW WHO YOU ARE.

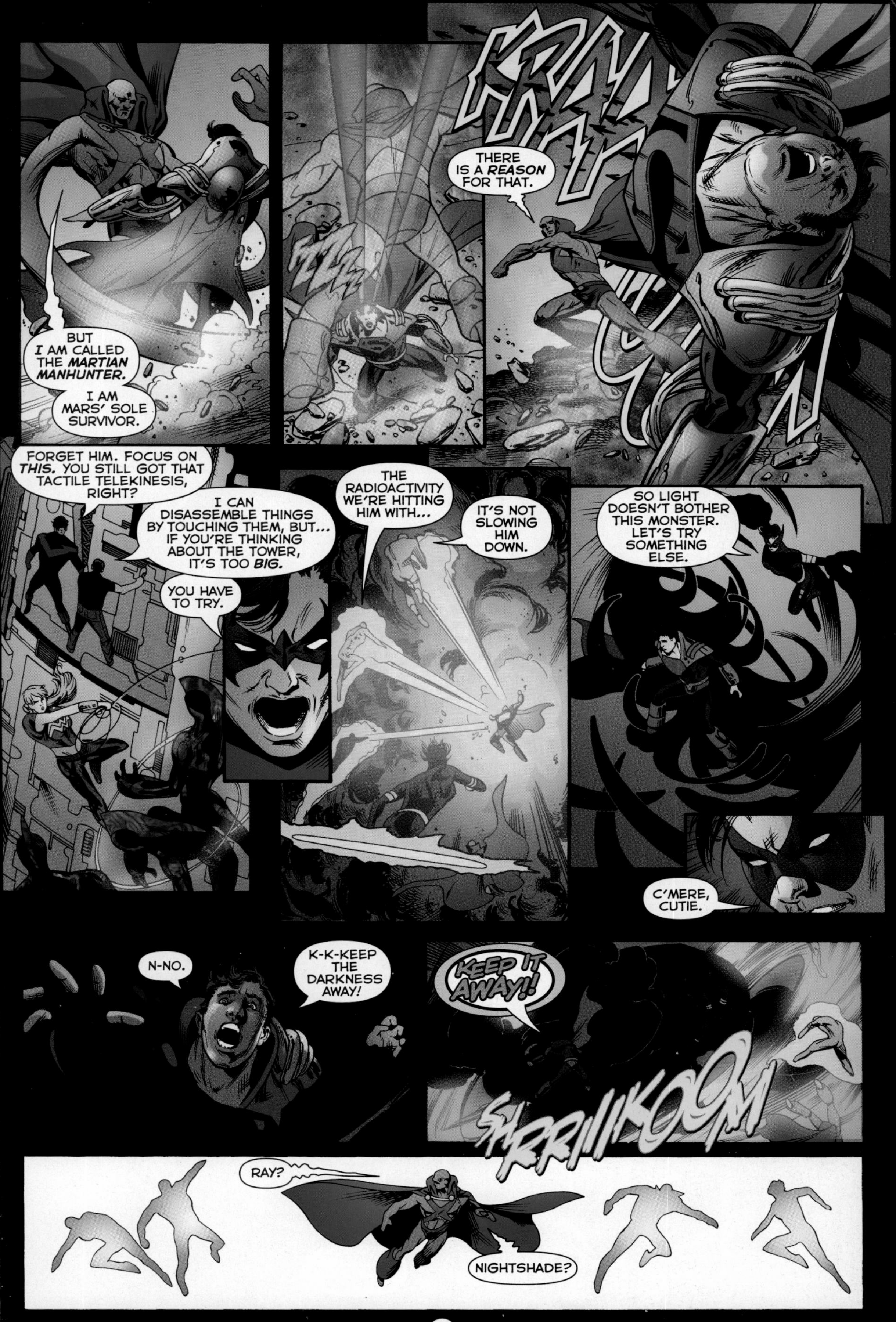
BUT I AM CALLED THE MARTIAN MANHUNTER.
I AM MARS' SOLE SURVIVOR.
FZZZ
THERE IS A REASON FOR THAT.
FORGET HIM. FOCUS ON THIS. YOU STILL GOT THAT TACTILE TELEKINESIS, RIGHT?
I CAN DISASSEMBLE THINGS BY TOUCHING THEM, BUT... IF YOU'RE THINKING ABOUT THE TOWER, IT'S TOO BIG.
YOU HAVE TO TRY.
THE RADIOACTIVITY WE'RE HITTING HIM WITH...
IT'S NOT SLOWING HIM DOWN.
SO LIGHT DOESN'T BOTHER THIS MONSTER. LET'S TRY SOMETHING ELSE.
C'MERE, CUTIE.
N-NO.
K-K-KEEP THE DARKNESS AWAY!
KEEP IT AWAY!!
SHRRIIIKOOOM
RAY?
NIGHTSHADE?

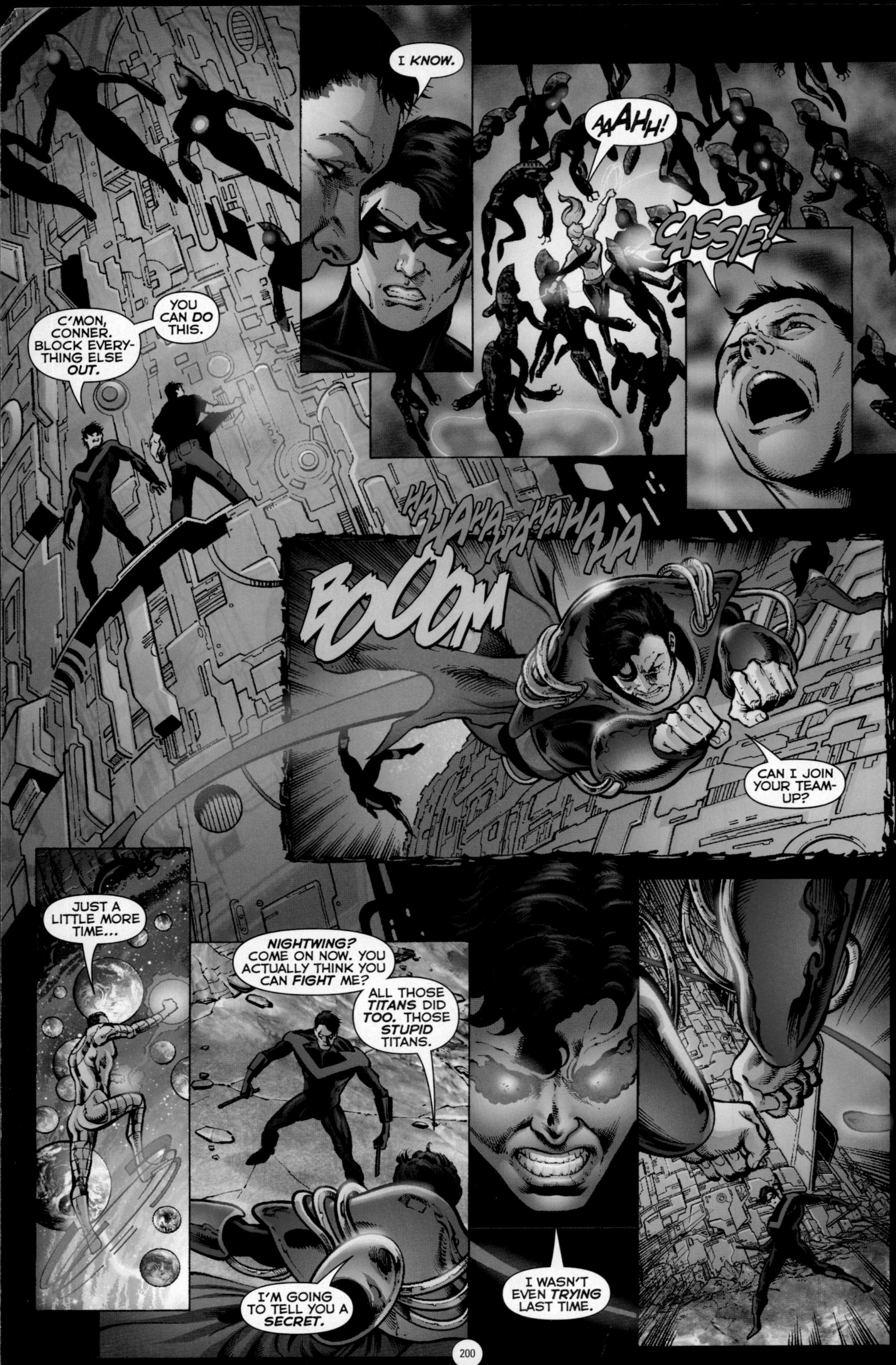
I KNOW.
AAAHH!
CASSIE!
C'MON, CONNER. BLOCK EVERYTHING ELSE OUT.
YOU CAN DO THIS.
HAHAHAHAHAHAHAHA
BOOOM
CAN I JOIN YOUR TEAM-UP?
JUST A LITTLE MORE TIME...
NIGHTWING? COME ON NOW. YOU ACTUALLY THINK YOU CAN FIGHT ME?
ALL THOSE TITANS DID TOO. THOSE STUPID TITANS.
I'M GOING TO TELL YOU A SECRET.
I WASN'T EVEN TRYING LAST TIME.

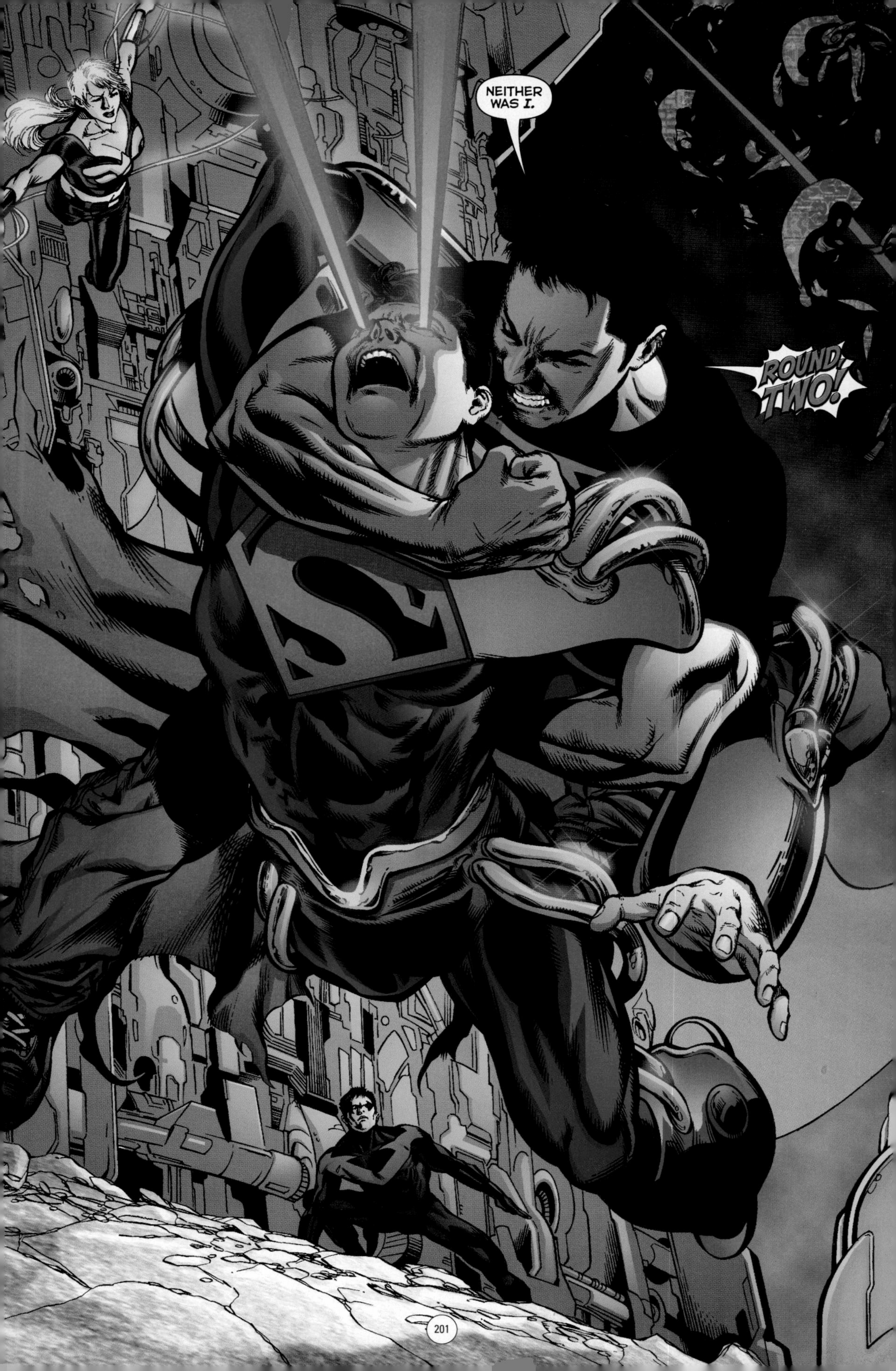
NEITHER WAS I.
ROUND TWO!

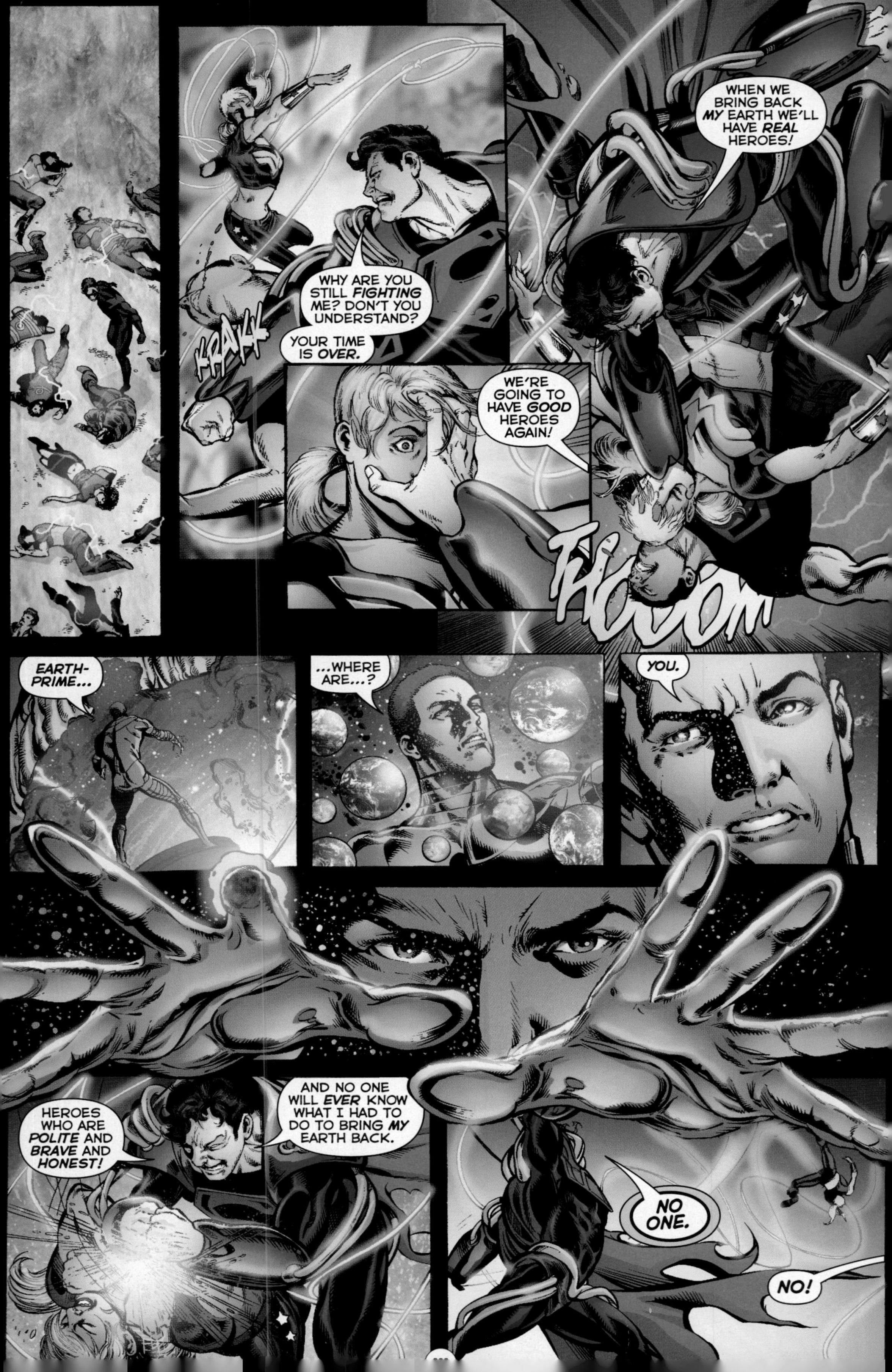

WHY ARE YOU STILL FIGHTING ME? DON'T YOU UNDERSTAND?
YOUR TIME IS OVER.
KRAKK
WHEN WE BRING BACK MY EARTH WE'LL HAVE REAL HEROES!
WE'RE GOING TO HAVE GOOD HEROES AGAIN!
FWOOM
EARTH-PRIME...
...WHERE ARE...?
YOU.
HEROES WHO ARE POLITE AND BRAVE AND HONEST!
AND NO ONE WILL EVER KNOW WHAT I HAD TO DO TO BRING MY EARTH BACK.
NO ONE.
NO!

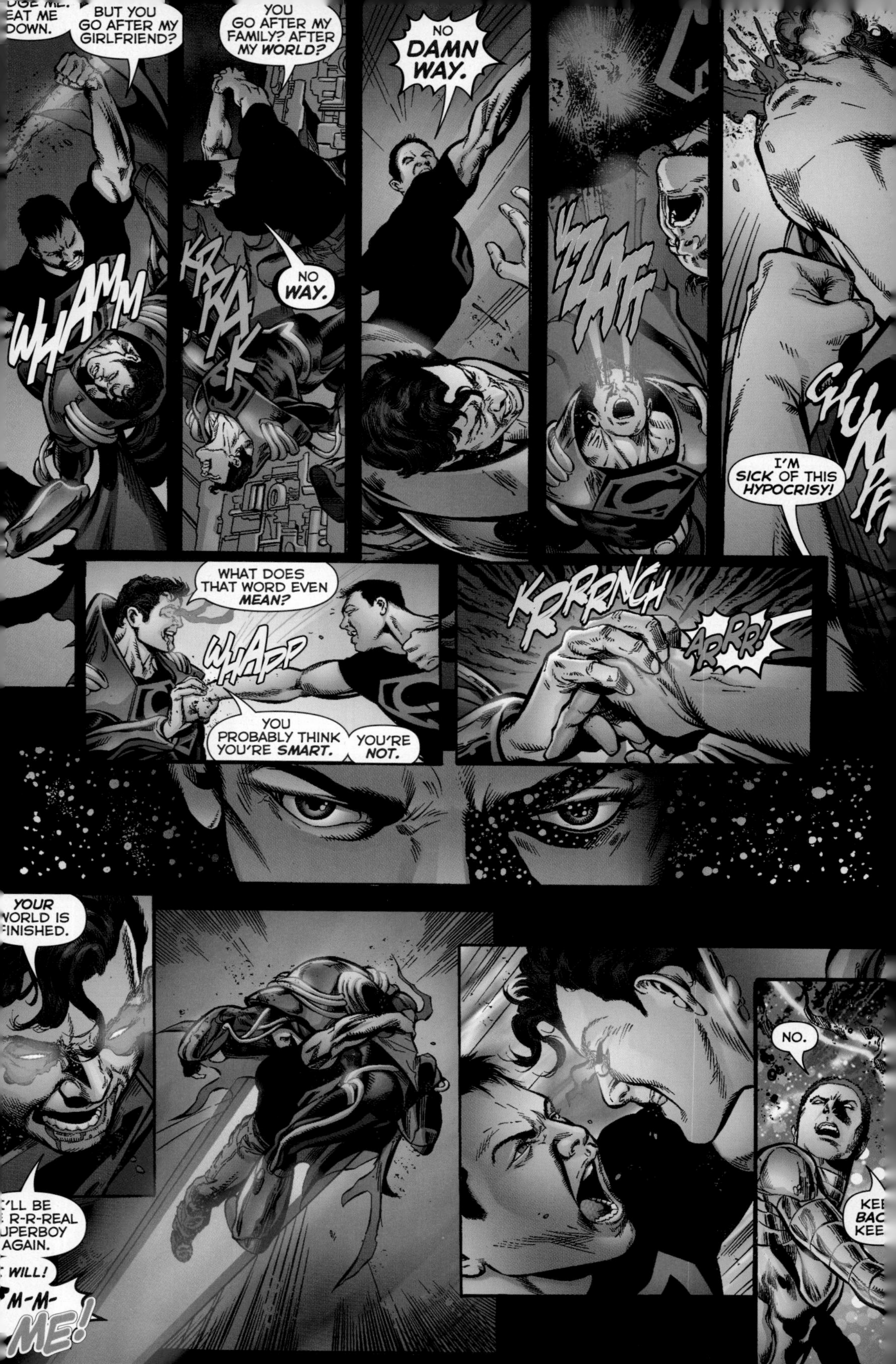

UDGE ME. EAT ME DOWN.
BUT YOU GO AFTER MY GIRLFRIEND?
WHAMM
YOU GO AFTER MY FAMILY? AFTER MY WORLD?
KRAKAK
NO WAY.
NO DAMN WAY.
ZZAT
I'M SICK OF THIS HYPOCRISY!
WHAT DOES THAT WORD EVEN MEAN?
WHAPP
YOU PROBABLY THINK YOU'RE SMART.
YOU'RE NOT.
KRRRNCH
ARRR!
YOUR WORLD IS FINISHED.
I'LL BE THE R-R-REAL SUPERBOY AGAIN.
I WILL!
M-M-ME!
NO.

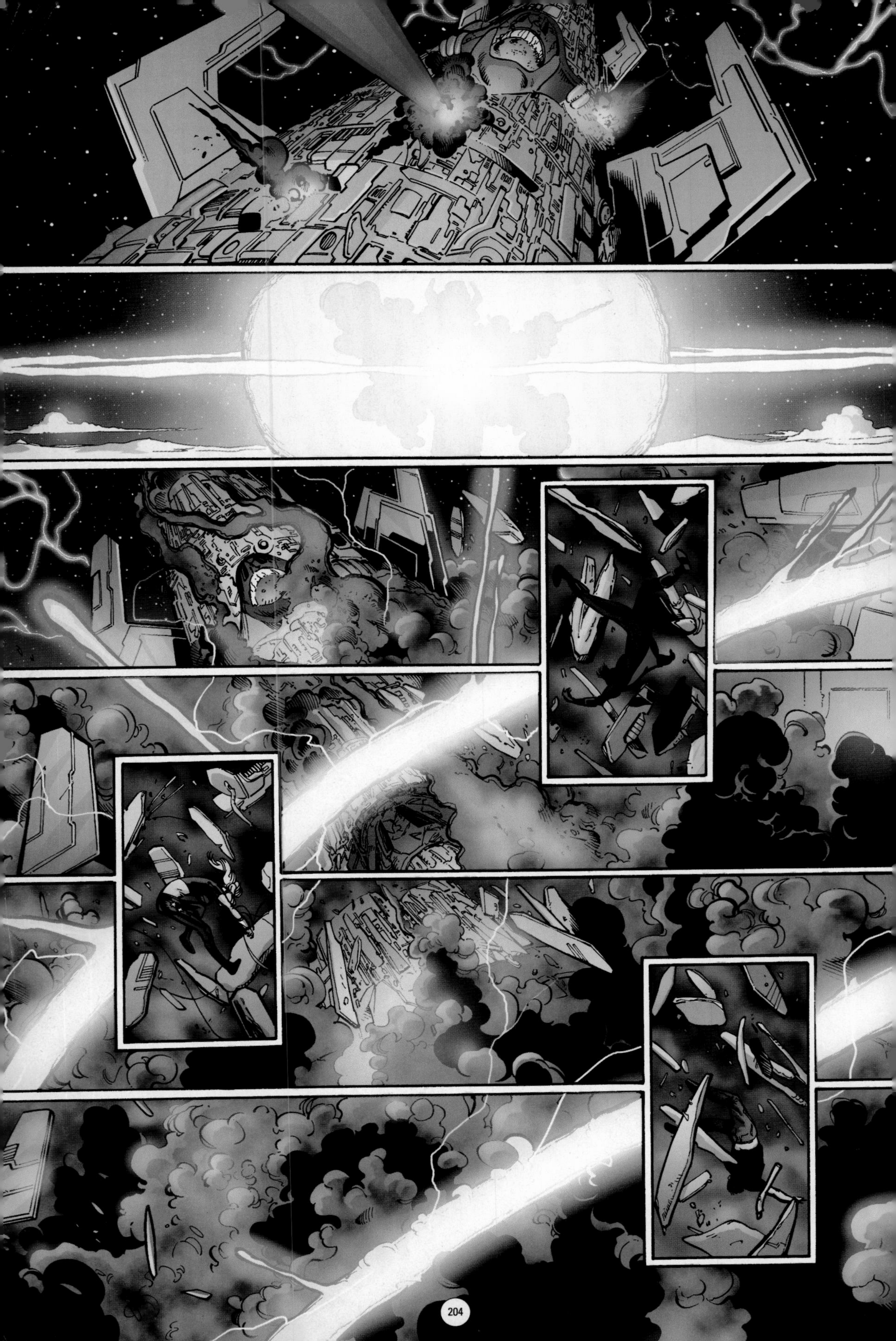

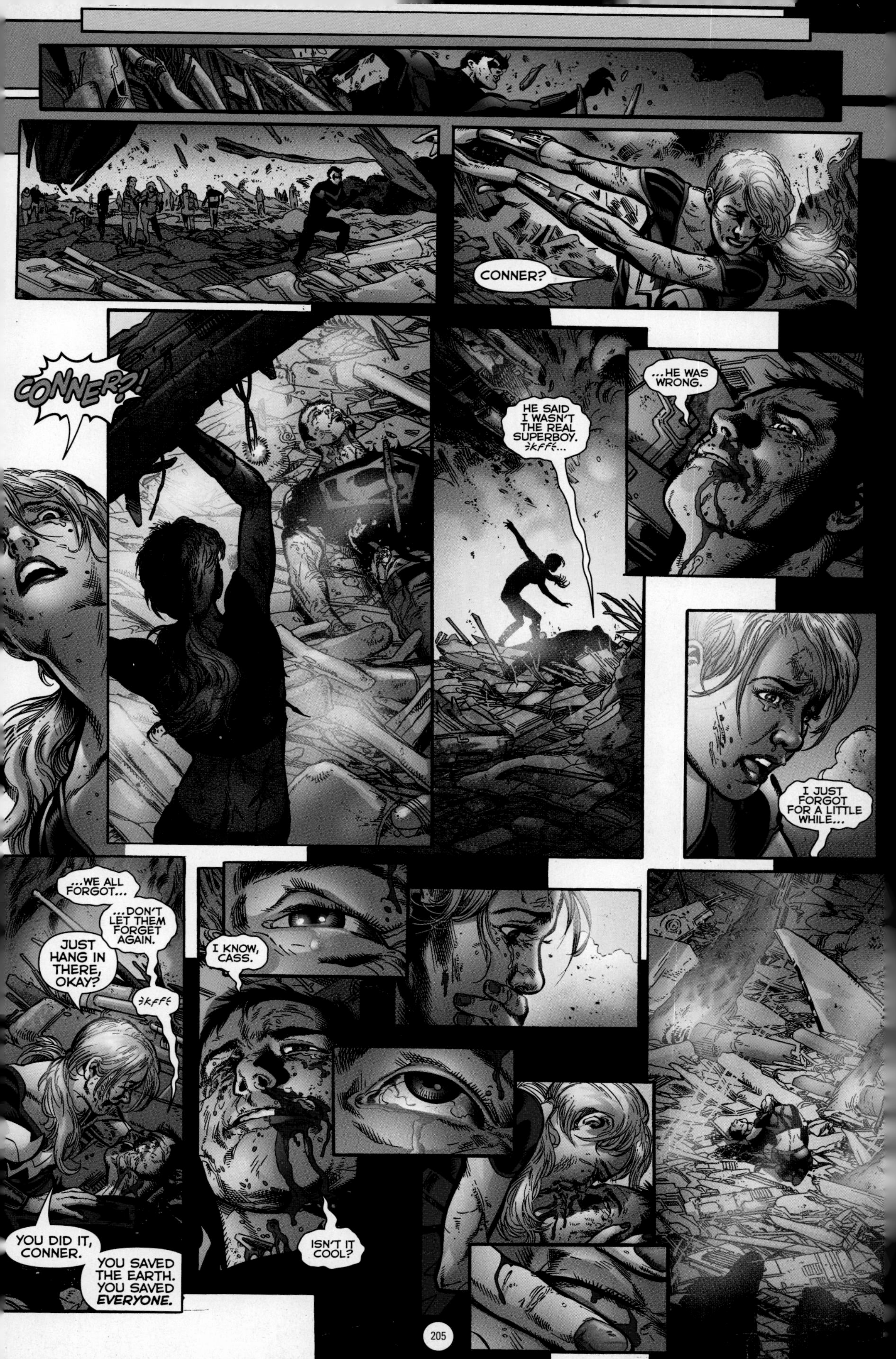
CONNER?
CONNER?!
HE SAID I WASN'T THE REAL SUPERBOY. *KFF*...
...HE WAS WRONG.
I JUST FORGOT FOR A LITTLE WHILE...
...WE ALL FORGOT...
...DON'T LET THEM FORGET AGAIN.
JUST HANG IN THERE, OKAY?
KFF
I KNOW, CASS.
YOU DID IT, CONNER.
YOU SAVED THE EARTH. YOU SAVED EVERYONE.
ISN'T IT COOL?

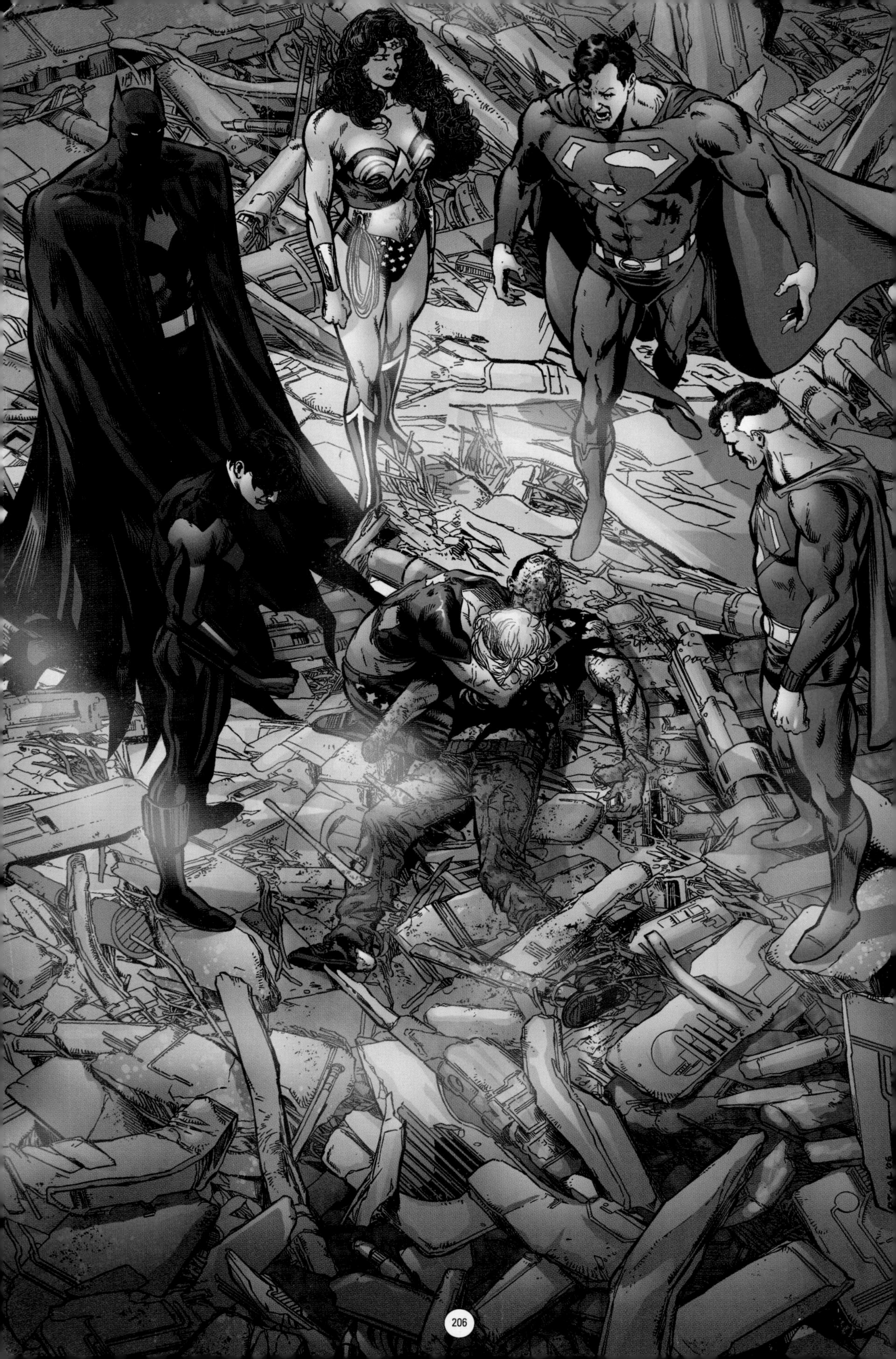

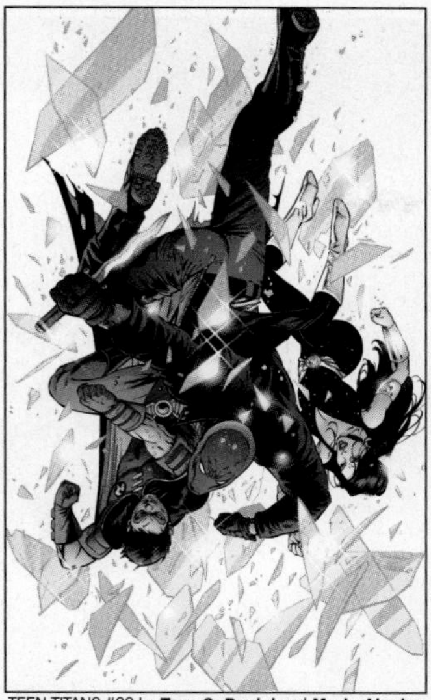

TEEN TITANS #29 by **Tony S. Daniel** and **Marlo Alquiza.**
Color by **Jeromy Cox**

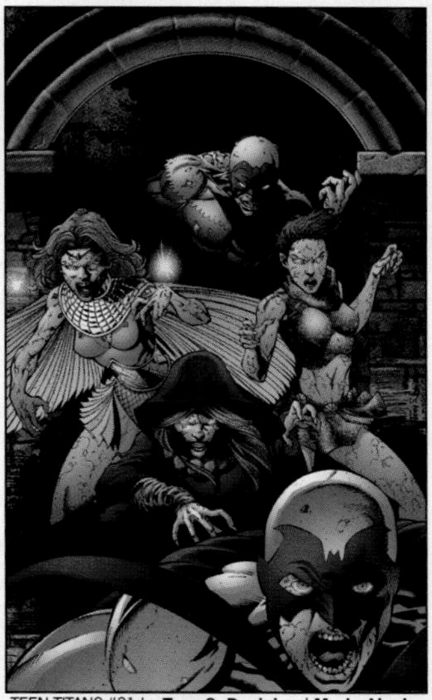

TEEN TITANS #31 by **Tony S. Daniel** and **Marlo Alquiza.**
Color by **Jeromy Cox**

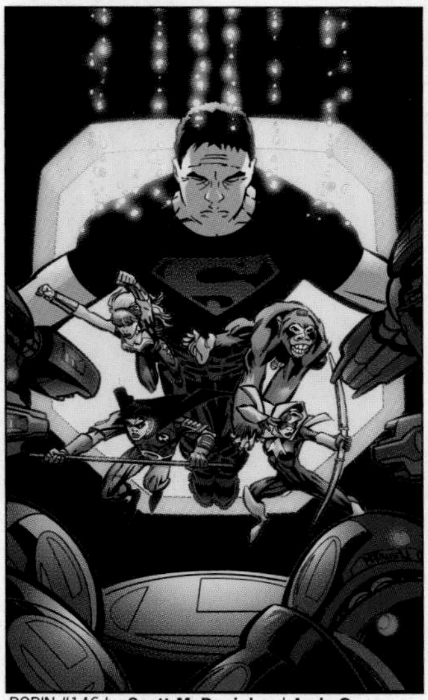

ROBIN #146 by **Scott McDaniel** and **Andy Owens.**
Color by **Guy Major.**

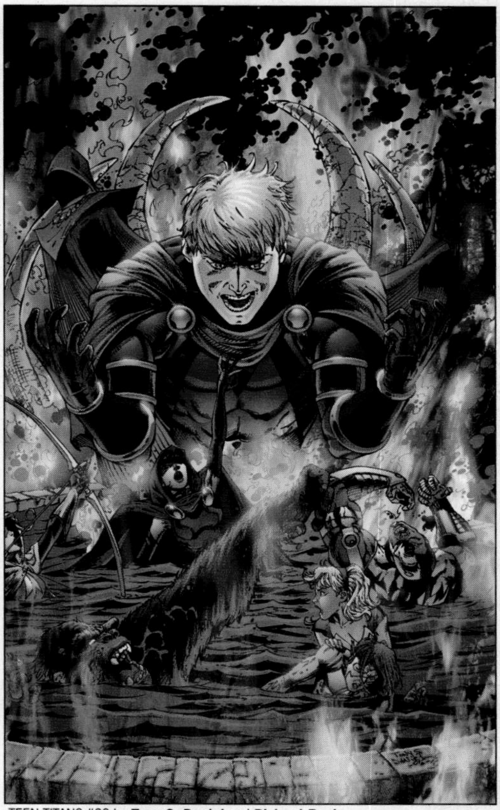

TEEN TITANS #30 by **Tony S. Daniel** and **Richard Bonk.**
Color by **Jeromy Cox**

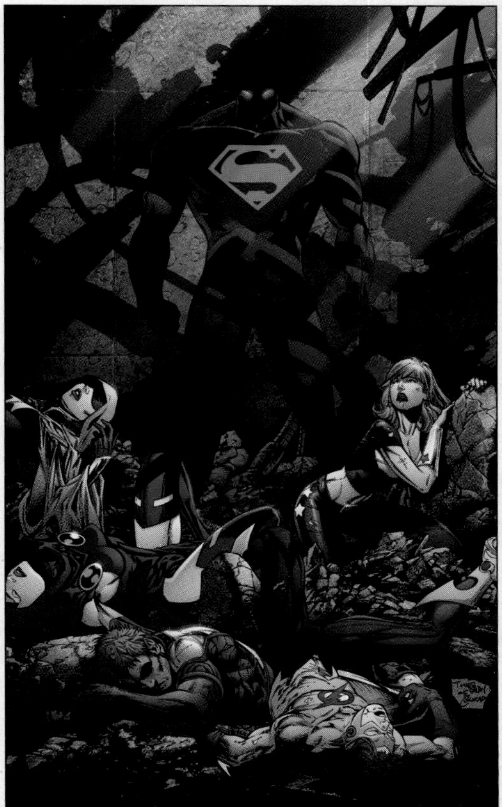

TEEN TITANS #32 by **Tony S. Daniel** and **Kevin Conrad.**
Color by **Jeromy Cox**

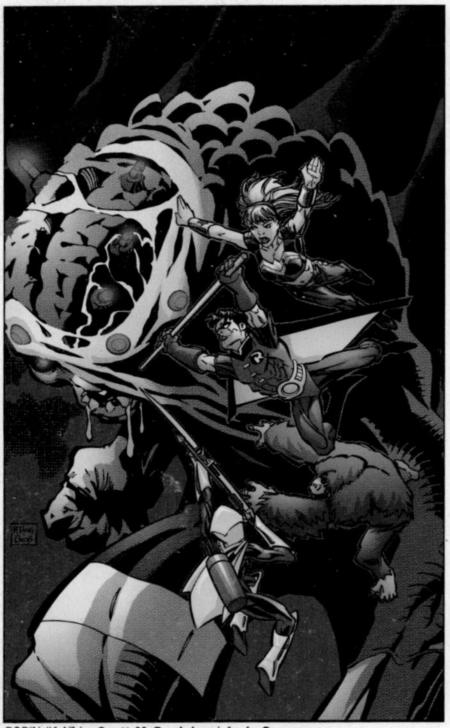

ROBIN #147 by **Scott McDaniel** and **Andy Owens.**
Color by **Guy Major.**

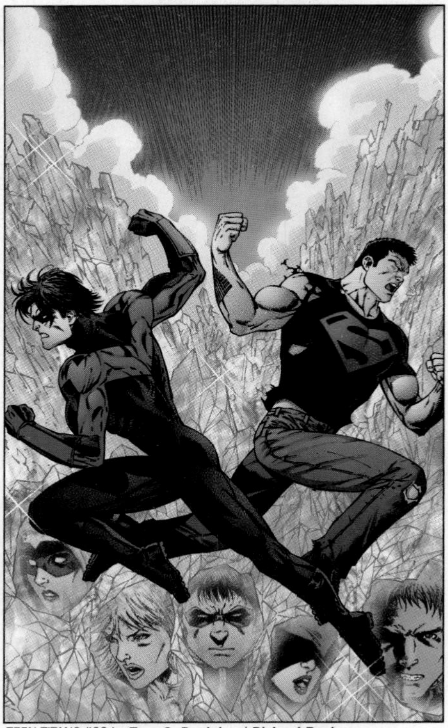

TEEN TITANS #33 by **Tony S. Daniel** and **Richard Bonk.**
Color by **Jeromy Cox**

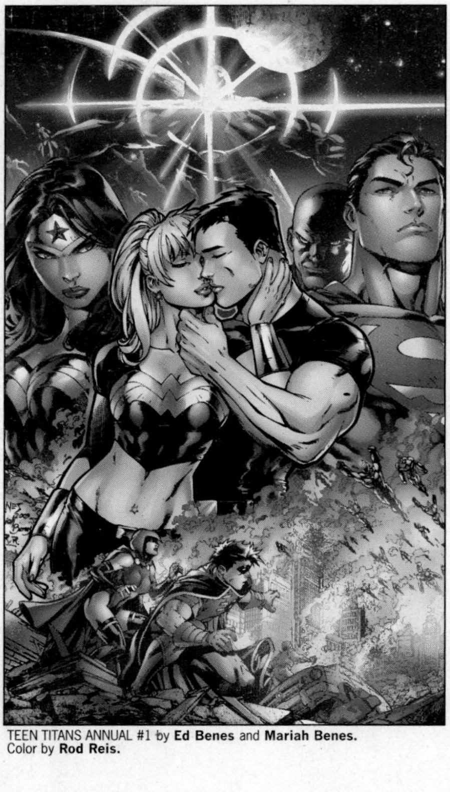

TEEN TITANS ANNUAL #1 by **Ed Benes** and **Mariah Benes.**
Color by **Rod Reis.**

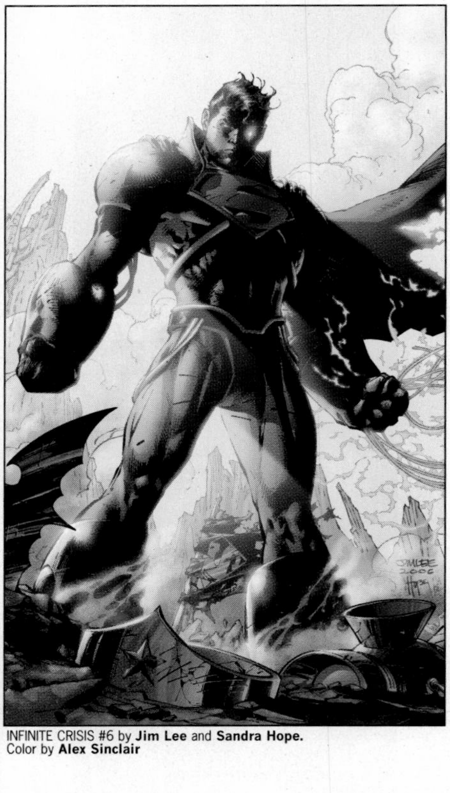

INFINITE CRISIS #6 by **Jim Lee** and **Sandra Hope.**
Color by **Alex Sinclair**